EARTH
HORIZON

EARTH HORIZON

Facsimile of Original 1932 Edition

by

Mary Austin

New Foreword
by
Marcia Muth

SOUTHWEST HERITAGE SERIES

SUNSTONE
PRESS

SANTA FE

Sunstone books may be purchased for educational, business, or sales promotional use. For information please write: Special Markets Department, Sunstone Press, P.O. Box 2321, Santa Fe, New Mexico 87504-2321.

Library of Congress Cataloging-in-Publication Data

Austin, Mary Hunter, 1868-1934.
    Earth horizon : facsimile of original 1932 edition / by Mary Austin ; new foreword by Marcia Muth.
        p. cm. -- (Southwest heritage series)
    Originally published: Boston: Houghton Mifflin, 1932.
    Includes bibliographical references and index.
    ISBN 0-86534-539-2 (softcover : alk.paper)
        1. Austin, Mary Hunter, 1868-1934. 2. Authors, American--20th century--Biography. 3. West (U.S.)--Biography. I. Title.

PS3501.U8Z465 2007
818'.5209--dc22
[B]
                                                        2006052309

Published in Santa Fe

WWW.SUNSTONEPRESS.COM
SUNSTONE PRESS / POST OFFICE BOX 2321 / SANTA FE, NM 87504-2321 /USA
(505) 988-4418 / ORDERS ONLY (800) 243-5644 / FAX (505) 988-1025

I

THE SOUTHWEST HERITAGE SERIES

The history of the United States is written in hundreds of regional histories and literary works. Those letters, essays, memoirs, biographies and even collections of fiction are often first-hand accounts by people who wanted to memorialize an event, a person or simply record for posterity the concerns and issues of the times. Many of these accounts have been lost, destroyed or overlooked. Some are in private or public collections but deemed to be in too fragile condition to permit handling by contemporary readers and researchers.

However, now with the application of twenty-first century technology, nineteenth and twentieth century material can be reprinted and made accessible to the general public. These early writings are the DNA of our history and culture and are essential to understanding the present in terms of the past.

The Southwest Heritage Series is a form of literary preservation. Heritage by definition implies legacy and these early works are our legacy from those who have gone before us. To properly present and preserve that legacy, no changes in style or contents have been made. The material reprinted stands on its own as it first appeared. The point of view is that of the author and the era in which he or she lived. We would not expect photographs of people from the past to be re-imaged with modern clothes, hair styles and backgrounds. We should not, therefore, expect their ideas and personal philosophies to reflect our modern concepts.

Remember, reading their words and sharing their thoughts is a passport back into understanding how the past was shaped and how it influenced today's world.

Our hope is that new access to these older books will provide readers with a challenging and exciting experience.

the port of New Orleans from the ark of a traveling circus, a monstrous creature with the necessary blood-sucking equipment, had cried, 'Holy Jaysus, and is *that* a muskaytoe!' Mary, the middle one of three listeners, was quite certain that the first time of telling the elephant-mosquito story, Father had said 'Holy Jaysus.' But the next time it was 'Holy Moses'; and it is well known that a story once told by parents must on no account be altered by so much as a jot or tittle. Something — the down-drawing of Mother's lip, the sudden flicker of warning in her father's eye — caught Mary on the verge of correction and became the point of attachment for cobweb-fine distinctions in the *nuances* of grown-up behavior. Things that weren't to be said in front of Mothers! Things that passed in a twinkle between Father and you, which must not even be admitted to have passed! Things that were unqualifiedly right and apt between you and Father, and yet subject to that singular obligation of adulthood, of refraining, in the presence of certain people, from what was in your mind!

You were always sure of Father after that, sure that he wouldn't say the interdicted word in the forbidden conjunction; and yet utterly intrigued by the skill with which — if he caught you watching him — he prolonged the delicious possibility that he might, if only from forgetfulness; until, by that nearly imperceptible veering of his glance which took you in at the same time that it left you completely out, Mother, or whoever for the occasion con-stituted authority, was allowed to win the decision. Things which mustn't be said in company — oh, absolutely, mustn't be said! — to all the implications of which Mary might be admitted. Years afterward, when she was to see him clumping clumsily about on crutches, one leg drawn up under him in a cramp of agony which escaped by sweating gasps... *My God!... oh, my God!...* other incredible words... if Mother came into the room he would change them. It was worth — because there was so little else of intimacy and understanding to recall — it was worth remembering even with tears that Father never minded saying '*My God*' before Mary.

There were other anecdotes and narratives. After a few days at

St. Louis, Father and Uncle William went on by train to Alton, set eagle-wise on the cliffs between the river and the woods that came down darkly all along the watercourses. There were cousins settled there, particularly a cousin Tom Perrin, a printer and finally, in a small but not unimportant way, a publisher, to whom Father was attached, and whom afterward the children slightly knew. But all that they ever certainly heard about their father's family was that the Hunters of Yorkshire were originally of good yeoman stock; that Grandfather Hunter had been for a part of his life a tailor; that Grandmother had been Jane Todd, a Scotch woman; and that the family had spent several years of George's youth in Rochester. The Cathedral there had made a profound impression upon him, for which the little prairie town lacked any figure of comparison.

All that country in the crotch of the Ohio and the Mississippi was known as Egypt; a black-soil country, subject to flood and fever, hot, and opulent with corn. Men of the Upper River, who had elected their homes on the not less fertile but more stubborn prairies, would go down in the summer season to work in the corn, leaving their families to subsist largely on milk and wild berries; or with long strings of canoes filled with wild honey and skins to trade, coming back with their profits in cotton and corn; reason enough for the by-name of the modern Illiniwek — 'Suckers' — going and coming, up river, down river, as fish to spawn.

North of Alton the woods stretched thickly along the muddy and obscure creeks, giving place intermittently to those inexplicable flat and treeless spaces, which in summer became one billowing, trackless sea of grass and flowers, that smelled sweet and in the spring was rosy with wild phlox and alive with the stir of insect hosts and the glint of light given back from the wind-stirred blades. Up from the dark lines of lush and woody growth that mapped the watercourses, thin vapors rose and spread, indistinguishable from their own shadows, over the grassy sea that, with its seasonal changes, green, gold, and flowery pied and winey red after frost, afforded the perpetual incitement of space and motion.

Because of its plenitude of wild game, all this country roundabout was known as the Black Hawk Hunting-Ground. The Illiniwek[2] had claimed it — but before that there had been Mound Builders — who, after the French had broken their power, had been driven out by the Sauks and Fox, pressing westward before white encroachment. The Potawatomies, on that same tragic regression of the native tribes, had lingered in the neighborhood, as also the fierce, intelligent Kickapoos; and as late as the eighteen-seventies there were still to be discovered groups of degenerate tribesmen, whose blood had been mixed with that of French trappers and *coureurs de bois*, gypsying about the tangling creeks and wooded mounds, exchanging splint baskets and deer meat for powder and ball.

Hereabouts, early in its territorial history, a settlement over which hung the faint shadow of history had been effected on the banks of the principal creek, called Macoupin, for *macoupina*, the foodful white artichoke that grew plentifully along its banks. While the county had been still claimed by the French, Ninian Edwards,[3] with a battalion of three hundred and fifty mounted men, had passed by here on his way in 1812 to the taking of Fort Peoria, crossing the ridge of mounds later to be known, in that curious poverty of the naming faculty which was the earliest true note of Middlewesternness, as Bunker Hill, Honey Point, Shaw's Point. In the spring of 1815, a German, David Coup, appropriated the mound which ever after bore his name, rising to the extraordinary height of forty feet above the general level of the prairie. In the succeeding year two English families settled on the present town site, afterwards organized as the county seat and called Carlinville.[4] In 1852 it was reported that good land was still to be had there for the taking.

In that year the railroad, inching along from St. Louis to Chicago, completed the span from Alton to Carlinville, and on the first train arrived George Hunter, sharp with the English hunger of land, already determined upon the intellectual life for himself, and a place not without credit in the Republic, which, once he had espoused, he supported with all that he had of intelligence and devotion. He found the town laid out four square, pierced with four roads to the horizon, named, in the prevailing Middle-western fashion, North and South Broad, East and West Main Streets. In the middle of that square rose the two-story frame courthouse, supplanting an earlier one of logs. And on the present site of the grade school, the only other two-story building, known as the seminary, because of the school for young ladies conducted in its lower story; the upper floor being given over to the meetings of the various lodges and secret societies that no frontier town which thought proud of itself would willingly have been without. About where the modern high school stands, rose the Methodist Church, the most important in the community, and across from it the only free school, larger but not very different from an earlier log structure which had been built to accommodate Stith Otwell, the first Methodist preacher, whose wife refused to live there because the puncheons of the floor which had been laid down green had so warped and shrunken that at night, alone in the house, she could hear the wolves shouldering underneath and sniffing at her young brood.

Provided with a fireplace extending across the whole of one end, and a window at the other made by taking out a log and covering the space with white paper oiled with bear's grease, the building served for three decades of young 'Suckers' as the fount of learning. Many young men who afterward served notably in their State were proud to have got their start there, even though it was told to George Hunter that it was the custom, when the student had pro-gressed just so far in his books, to turn him back where he could be more comfortably handled by the teachers.

The population of Carlinville was then about seven hundred; less than the census of 1850 showed, having been decimated the previous year by a plague of Asiatic cholera. There was — proud distinction among prairie towns — a library started in 1834 by Don Cameron, whom Mary recalls as a figure of somewhat faded culture and impractical habits, father of Ann, one of the most intelligent and most cherished of her own teachers. There was, at the time George Hunter gave his allegiance to its future, one doctor in the town, John Logan, tall, saturnine, of the Lincoln mould,

high-cheeked and dark enough to warrant the tradition of Chero-
kee blood which was categorically denied by a younger relative of
his who afterward became a candidate for the Vice-Presidency.
But Doctor John never denied it. There was one notable lawyer,
John M. Palmer, who later became Governor and a presidential
possibility, and was already a figure of legend — the barefoot-boy,
self-made-man legend so dear to the Middlewestern heart;
a sturdy, sanguine man, with whose family the Hunters became
through two generations singularly intimate. Two other itinerant
attorneys appeared frequently at the Macoupin County Court, one
Abe Lincoln from Springfield, and a shorter, sleek, blond man
called Douglas.

Young George did not at first make a continuous residence at
Carlinville, but returned twice, as his means afforded, to Alton to
study at Shurtliff College, and in 1855 visited his father in England, bringing away with him on that occasion his sister Mary, for
which — Grandfather Hunter being strictly of the opinion that
a daughter should remain a handmaiden in her father's house until
she went to a house of her own — he was not forgiven until, by
espousing the Northern cause in the Civil War, young George won
back the parental approval. His sister Mary remained in Alton,
in the dressmaking trade; William went farther west and was not
heard of for years; while George, having read law in the office of
John Rinaker, of the 122d Illinois Regiment, was admitted to the
bar in 1858.

He must have been at that time about twenty-three or four
years of age — he was never sure of his date, though he gave
twenty-eight on his enlistment — marked with ambition and
promise, gifted with a natural taste for literature and public life.
Among those who knew him then, his well-stored memory, his
ready gift of words, his flexible and argumentative turn of mind
are favorably remembered. For the whole of his life thereafter his
name appears in the local papers as connected with every forward
community interest.

It is quite probable that one of the inducements which George
found for settling in Carlinville was the number of English families

already established there; the McMillans, the Mayfields, the Palmers, young Dr. Mathews who came in 1854 and afterward married Betty Palmer, and Richard Rowett. 'Dick,' as he was universally called, was a year or two younger than George, Cornish born, and probably the dominating member of a lifelong friendship. He was taller, broader-shouldered, witty, emphatic, dark, and indubitably possessed, for what was always referred to as the 'fair sex,' of a roving eye. They were, the pair of them, a social asset; handsome, well-whiskered, carefully dressed, eminently correct in deportment, both of them excellent conversationalists; and that in the eighteen-fifties was a greater social desideratum even than to be lavish of hirsute adornment. George was short rather than tall, gracefully made, his hair, which he wore, after a fashion of the time, long and brushed straight back, of an auburn tinge, his eyes blue, his whole appearance — I have this from young ladies who knew him — characterized by that much-admired quality of sensibility. Taken together, they were the sort of young men who seriously discussed Robert Ingersoll and this new theory of Evolution in private, but could be seen, as a matter of deportment, attending church in each other's company, or 'rising to make a few remarks' on all suitable occasions; invariably parliamentary, and yet with just the right amount of 'begging to disagree' with one another as they played discreetly about the edges of the inadmissible. They were, of course, meticulously strict as to what could, and could not, be said to and before the ladies.

Intellectual life in the Middlewest, in the decade of the Civil War, and perhaps for a decade before and after, was more forthright and wide-angled than it has ever been since. That was the day of the Debating Society, of the 'Literary' Circle, of the Lyceum which actively circulated, through its lecture bureau, the best available intelligences. The Temperance Movement had begun; Woman Suffrage had somewhat formlessly come to life in the general assurance, offered to young women by press and pulpit, that they had no rights at all, which they were disposed to take as a challenge to demonstrate that they had all the rights in the world. The Mormons had lately been expelled from the State in a fine confusion of moral sentiment, and, steadily intensifying in the South, brooded the irrepressible conflict.

From early in its history, there had been a station of the Underground Railway at Carlinville, in which, though there is no explicit mention of his name, all George Hunter's friends were more or less involved. It seems likely, therefore, that this might have been the interest, quite as much as their common Englishness, which drew young Hunter and Rowett into an intimacy with a family of Shepherds living at Sauls's Prairie, out Palmyra way. Their place was a notable hide-out for runaway slaves, and several times narrowly missed getting the family into serious trouble with a neighborhood strongly touched with Southern sympathies. That the young men were — considering the distance and the state of the country roads — frequent and welcome visitors at Sauls's Prairie we know from the son of the house, not too young to make good use of that acutely objective type of memory which is the hall-mark of the literary temperament. This Francis, who afterward, under his mother's name of Grierson,[5] was let in for an unbelievably romantic career, became a friend of Mary Austin and the purveyor of valuable personal mention.

There were odder things to happen than the way in which, fifty years after the event, Francis Grierson was to be drawn back into the story begun on the banks of the Macoupin, to strengthen the links of understanding, not only for the people who played in it, but of the strange and subtle influences of the place. But these must wait upon the unwinding of the events set in motion when in 1861 George Hunter resigned his newly set up law practice and, in the week's interval between the close of his three months' volunteer service and his enlistment as Captain of Company K, Seventh Illinois, married Susanna Savilla Graham.

II

Susanna Savilla was the daughter of Milo Graham,[6] who had come into Illinois from Ohio in 1839. Milo's father had apprenticed him, lame from his early youth, to a tailor, much against the choice of his soul which had been for the study of medicine. Making the best compromise possible between inclination and necessity,"the young man had worked at his trade until he could teach himself pharmacy, traveled alone on horseback to Carlinville, and in the course of a few years established himself in a drugstore which he built and owned.

The young woman whom Milo married was Hannah, third daughter of Jarrot and Mary McAdams Dugger; and to be one of the Duggers meant something rather explicit in the first half-century of Macoupin.

According to the family tradition in which Mary was brought up, the original founder of the family had been one Pierre Daguerre, who accompanied the Marquis de Lafayette from France and on the conclusion of the war had settled in Virginia, marrying there a Miss Tucker, of whom were begotten four sons and perhaps daughters of unrecorded names. The sons recalled that their father had been known as Colonel, an office to which he was supposed to have been promoted, but of which no record can be found. Considering that these things happened in Virginia where honor accrues by mere residence, the title probably means what it might be expected to mean.

As for the Tuckers, it ill becomes a Middlewesterner to lay profane hands upon their history. They came into the country in the first half of the sixteen hundreds, and occupied it extensively. Colonel Dugger, at any rate, justified his adoption into the first families of Virginia by getting himself killed in a duel on account of an aspersive remark 'passed' upon a visiting Northerner, a guest of his wife. Shortly after, the three older sons emigrated to Tennessee, and are next heard of enlisting in the War of 1812 from

Sumner County in that State, and were present at the battle of New Orleans. There was also the traditional assurance that the American Daguerres[7] were collaterals of the distinguished French chemist, Louis Jacques Mandé Daguerre,[8] inventor of the daguerreotype. The relationship, though without any authentication, is borne out by a marked family resemblance. There was also a traditional connection with the family of James K. Polk. A letter from Cousin Bill — Captain William Dugger, son of Joseph Castlebury, second son of Jarrot — the white-headed boy of the tribe at the time — relates: 'Just a few days before the battle of Nashville, I was one of several officers who paid their respects to Mrs. James K. Polk.[9] As I was presented to her she said, "That is the name of my earliest young friend." She asked me whose son I was. I told her I was the grandson of Jarrot Dugger and Polly McAdams. She held my hand and said, "Are you the grandson of Polly McAdams! I loved her dearly!" '

Of Jarrot, eldest son of Pierre, who by the time he comes into the story was spelling his name Dugger, there is, apart from the history of the family, not much to say. He married Polly McAdams in Sumner County in 1811, and shortly afterward enlisted for the War of 1812.

In 1818, on the admission of Illinois to statehood, the two brothers, John and Wesley, with their families, moved to Madison County, and in the eighteen-twenties Jarrot and Polly followed, settling in Carlinville in 1833. Jarrot planted the first orchard and organized the first Sunday School. The frame house which he built on the site of the earlier log cabin still stands, the fields that he cleared and fenced still produce. In 1844 he was the proprietor of one of the four or five stores about the square, and served acceptably for several terms as County Commissioner. There were Duggers in the Black Hawk War,[10] which was not properly a war, but merely a concentrated incident of pioneer life in communities in which a youth was counted a man as soon as he could shoot straight and grow a beard. The roster of the third generation of Duggers serving in the Civil War reads like the record in a family

Bible. In 1852, Jarrot's son, Samuel, established the first newspaper in the town, known as the 'Macoupin Statesman.' There was a Dugger who helped to carry Abraham Lincoln to his grave and one who served on the commission for his monument.

There was never any doubt as to where the Duggers stood in the community which they helped to build and populate. They were plain people, neither rich nor poor, devoid of airs, loving the soil, good bargainers, the women rather outmatching the men in that quality indispensable to pioneer society, known as mother-wit. While they lived they were respected, and wherever they went — they tended to scatter westward in the fourth generation — or whenever died, the local papers carried long notices of their decease and lists of their achievements. It was not until Mary's generation that they left off having their dead sent home to the acre reserved for Jarrot's estate to be a family burying-ground.

Strangely, their name has almost passed away from the place that knew them, but their blood still persists there. It persists also in direct descent from Polly, through Hannah her daughter, through Susanna Savilla and *her* daughter, and its emergence in Mary, great-grand-daughter of Polly McAdams, wife of Jarrot Dugger, son of Pierre Daguerre, is the sole excuse for this mention — if excuse were needed. For of all that the Duggers accomplished or became, so much was of the soil, of the solidly middle class, Middlewest, that considering the odd, the unconformable gesture she has made, except for Polly, you might suppose that Mary was hatched from a cuckoo's egg.

Except for Polly!

Whatever in Mary makes her worth so much writing about has its roots in the saga of Polly and Hannah and Susanna Savilla, in the nurture of which she grew up. For the Middlewest is not to be known nor measured nor understood by one who does not know that saga and realize how completely it was true, not only for the Duggers, but for the Hendrickses, the McAdamses, the Bartons, the Penns, the Padens, the Womacs, the Woodses, the McClures, the Turnbulls, and Hoekers with whom they intermarried. There is something in Mary which comes out of the land; something in its rhythms, its living compulsions, which dominates over her French, Scotch, Irish, Dutch, English, even the far-off traditional aboriginal strain, governing her own progressions, coloring her most intimate expression. It is the source of that roving mind's eye that includes for her, in its implications, the whole American continent, and at the same time, in its rejection of the male ritual of rationalization in favor of a more direct intuitional attack, providing the key to her approach.

It is to the things that the Polly McAdamses discovered in their westward trek that Mary's generation owed the success of their revolt against the traditional estimate of women at the rating of an effect produced, and reëstablished for them the criterion of a result achieved. Chief of the discoveries of the Polly McAdamses, as it was told to Mary, was the predominance of happenings of the hearth, as against what happens on the battlefield and in the market-place, as the determinant of events. What they found out was that the hope of American democracy and the justification of the Declaration of Independence depended precisely on the capacity of the Polly McAdamses to coördinate society, to establish a civilization, to cause a culture to eventuate out of their own wit and the work of their hands, out of what they could carry with them into the wilderness. It depended upon their capacity for picking up their hearths and carrying them, along with all their cultural and spiritual implications, with no more labored equipment than a wooden pestle and a mortar of Indian make, a tin grater for corn meal, a deep pot and a frying-pan, and *their own intention.*

That was how Polly, wife of Jarrot, came into the country of the 'Eellanoy' sitting on a bundle of pieced quilts and blankets of her own spinning, on the tail of an ox cart, and with an unrelinquished claim on all the sanctions of civilization and the preciousness of womanhood in her heart. She knew how she would have to do what she had in mind, lacking the inventions with which 'Yankee ingenuity' was already beginning to mitigate the labors of women on the far-off Atlantic coast, without the help, relinquished consciously now for the first time in history, of a recognized serving class.

That is the first thing to remember about Middlewestern women: that they were not Middlewesterners when they came; that they had not yet lost, but only voluntarily and temporarily surrendered, a life more gracious and abounding than they came to meet. Whether they came from East or South, from England or Germany, they had to some extent taken the measure of what they were to do. What they threw up on the screen of their future was the pattern of eighteenth-century elegances, of a social life still touched with the tradition of distinction, of the separateness of social caste where now, since 1776, no caste was to be tolerated. Up to the Civil War, and perhaps a little after, there were families in Carlinville having liveried servants, and in family Bibles, on the page set aside for births, old entries of slaves born on the paternal plantation, before the family set out for the Northwest Territory where no slaves were to be held.

There is not much to determine the social background on which Polly McAdams turned her back, but that little is explicit. When the President's Lady, who acknowledged herself Polly's dearest friend, was asked how she adjusted herself to the White House after her residence in remote Tennessee, she answered with surprise that she had always known a life of social precision and a certain amount of elegance; always worn silk and been accustomed to service — a background her dearest friend must to some extent have shared, before she set out to bake Johnny-cake and wear linsey-woolsey of her own weaving in the wilds of Illinois.

Polly was the daughter of William McAdams, born in Pennsylvania, but serving through the Revolutionary War with the North Carolina Continentals.[11] At the close of his service he married Mary Hendricks, of whom, in 1792, his daughter Polly was born. About that time the McAdamses seem to have been swept West in the rush of Revolutionary veterans to avail themselves of public grants of land, and are next heard of in Tennessee. That was while the Black Hawk Hunting-Ground was still infested by Indians incited by the French. Nevertheless, a settlement involving William McAdams and some of his Tennessee neighbors had been effected about 1802 or '03 in what was afterward Madison County, north of St. Louis, where the women under guard planted cotton and corn, while the men cut timber and hunted game. On a day when the guard was for some reason off duty, the Indians raided in great numbers, driving off the women and children to be held at Spring Cove for ransom. At dawn, while they lay waiting, the signal agreed upon for just this contingency came, a single rifle crack, at which the women threw themselves flat, covering with their bodies their young children; while the Indians springing up in alarm received the full volley.

Although the settlers brought off their families uninjured, this adventure into the far country of Eellanoy must have disappointed them, since we hear of the McAdamses again in Tennessee, where Polly married the son of Pierre Daguerre in 1811, and the next year saw him off to the war. And in the early eighteen-thirties, the whole tribe of Hendrickses, McAdamses, and Duggers emigrated to Illinois. It must have been in the years between that the friendship with Sarah Childress — she who afterward became the First Lady in the Land — was begun and cemented. And this was how American women were trained to win the land from savage hordes and to walk discreetly beside their husbands in the highest offices to which they could be called, women and ladies both.

One heard, when one was young and had a listening ear, how it was accomplished; how Polly persuaded Jarrot, her husband, to build a water-wheel to which the spinning-wheels of the neighbor women could be attached, so that their hands the while could go on with the piecing and quilting; how when he had raised the first seedling apples, Polly invented a way to preserve the fruit in the wide-mouthed crocks which were the precursors of the screw-topped glass jars, which gave place to the world-encompassing canned food business. Polly's 'spiced apples' went notably with the venison pot-pie, which was the local company dish, or with tom-turkey stuffed with pecan meats and roasted before the fire.

The little Hunters knew them as the perfect 'snack,' when they came home ravenous from school and it was still an hour and a half to supper time; and it was only the other day that Mary, who never forgets a recipe, taught the method of making them to Mary Hunter the third — fifth from Polly — and Betty Applegate, out of the firm, flattish little seedling apples planted by the Spanish pioneers of New Mexico on the Rancho Peña Antigua two hundred years ago.

There was not only good eating but good talk at Polly's. All her stout sons and good-looking daughters; William McAdams, and the other Revolutionary soldiers he drew to her fireside; Major Winchester, who, besides having enlisted in 1812, had captained the rescue party when Polly, aged nine, lay on the ground and with her young body helping her mother to cover the younger children; Peter Cartwright, the circuit rider and hard-fisted evangelist who defeated 'that second-rate lawyer,' Abe Lincoln, for the Legislature; the young Palmers, one of whom was later to be Governor and Democratic Gold-Standard candidate for President, were also of that company. Abe Lincoln, too — there is in the possession of the Duggers a letter of Lincoln's that the historiographers know nothing about, which has the sanctity of a holy relic.

And that was how Mary happened to hear not only the saga of Polly, but of most of Macoupin County, handed down through Cousin Bill; through Aunt Sally, who married Wesley, a notable woman of the skaldic temperament, and a great practical joker; and Aunt Lindy Paden, who, though no Dugger, being tied twice through marriage into the family, deserved the name; through these and those other women who wore moccasins or went barefoot as the case was, wove and spun, exchanged quilt piecings and nursings of their children at need, who became midwives for one another, watchers of the sick and washers of the dead, and, when the wilderness was won, wore silk and sat in the parlor and were ladies in every title to the name. Polly's last notable exploit was to teach the women to make of arrow-root and native herbs a sort of pap, which was immensely remedial in the cholera plague in 1851, when there were not enough well left to nurse the sick and bury the dead. Mary recalls her great-grandmother slightly, when her parlor-sitting days were come, as a sibylline and rather fearsome old lady, who overflowed her chair completely when she sat — it was from Polly's side of the house that the Duggers took the disposition toward portliness that characterized them all in middle age — so that at her funeral, which Mary clearly recalls, the body had to be brought out of doors to the casket, which could not be conveniently carried in.[12]

Hannah, the fourth daughter, married Milo Graham, and sustained the good looks, the excellent good sense, and the courage of Polly. Though, indeed, all the daughters were valiant; it was only because she was her very own grandmother that Hannah figured more interestingly on Mary's horizon. There were two stories about her that the child always heard with that special sort of interest that becomes prophetic. One was about the tailor-made dress, which was the first time that anybody in Carlinville had heard of such a thing — forty years before it became the fashionable wear. It was on their wedding journey to St. Louis, where Milo replenished his stock, that he bought for his handsome bride a fine length of broadcloth, which, as probably the last piece of tailoring he ever did, he made up for her at home; an act so unprecedented that it narrowly escaped being scandalous. Disapprobation was further augmented when, shortly afterward, there came along one of those traveling vans offering the new French invention of the daguerreotype. The Duggers all felt themselves elected to patronage of daguerreotypy, and Milo had his young wife pictured in the very dress he had made for her, for which she was promptly 'Disciplined.' To be 'Disciplined' in the Methodist Church meant that, due notice being given all around, the offending members were called to the front seat on the following Sunday and had the Church Discipline, so far as it respected their offense — in this case Vanity — read out to them, after which a sermon was preached on the subject. One must suppose that the church was well filled on that occasion, and that it was at the properly dramatic moment — I am sure that Hannah would have seen to that — the young matron walked down the aisle with her limping and totally unperturbed Scotchman beside her, *wearing that particular dress!* It was so exactly the thing Mary would have done!

The other story was even more precisely in the family tradition. Unaccountably, Milo's store caught fire in the night — this was some years later — and when discovered was too far gone to be saved. Hannah came down to have a look at the fire. All the town was out, for the drug-fed flame threatened all that side of the square; and the next that was seen of Hannah was at daylight, selling hot gingerbread to the bystanders, and all that day, as the countryside came in to the rare spectacle of smoking ruins, she sold them bread and gingercakes, and kept on selling until the store could be rebuilt and business restored.

Hannah inherited Polly's aptitude for cookery: 'Aunt Hannah's gingerbread,' 'Aunt Hannah's smokehouse' — there is a rumor of them yet among the Dugger kin; also there was a particular conserve of mixed quince and pear and sweet apple — huge greenish apples of crisp translucent flesh, does anybody grow them still? — which required to be set in the sun after being sealed in glass until all the ingredients had combined into a luscious honey-red delight. Susanna Savilla used to keep a special jar of it for company occasions, a wide-mouthed jar that had served in the 'old' store to hold those lucent crimson, green, and golden waters which were in those days as much the recognized hall-marks of pharmacies as ever striped poles were of barber shops. Mary treasures to this day an imitation Wedgwood vase with a Shakespeare medallion, which was one of the decorations of the 'new' store that was built in part by the sale of Hannah's gingerbread. Grandfather Graham gave it to her when, to retire, he sold out to his son William in 1880.

There were three children of Hannah's bearing that survived her, Susanna, William, and Mary, besides the three that died — six in eleven years — and the seventh which she died trying to deliver. That was the hazard of early American women, and husbands were supposed to accept it as the inscrutable will of God. Sixteen months later, Milo was married again to Eliza Ann Boring, a widow with one child.

Susanna Savilla, the eldest of Hannah's daughters, was ten when her mother died, not thought too young to assume the responsibilities of elder sister until the advent of Eliza Ann. All of her recollections centered around the household. She recalled the death of her grandfather Jarrot in 1850. She lived through the cholera epidemic, but remembered it only because her sister Clara Elizabeth died. The only other event before the death of her mother which she clearly recalled was the celebration on the occasion, in 1852, of the arrival of the first railroad train, at which she might have seen, but did not note, the red-headed English lad she was afterward to marry. The stepbrother, Alexander Boring, was accepted brotherly by the little Grahams, and Susanna Savilla always spoke well of her stepmother. There is no doubt that Eliza Ann took the greatest pains with her stepdaughters, according to her lights. Susanna, who became 'Susie' in the unassailable democracy of school, used to tell how she encouraged them in the use of Cucumber and Elder-Flower Cream, steeped in buttermilk, which she taught them to make, and how before they sat down to their sewing at two o'clock in the afternoon, as did all well-brought-up young ladies, their stepmother carefully laced them into their hourglass corsets for the preservation of their figures.

The sisters grew up in a bevy of cousins and step-cousins — somehow one can't help imagining that, when children came by the dozen and kin by marriage counted almost as close as kin by blood, family life was more interesting than it has ever been since. Life in the Middlewest in the decade before the Civil War was a very pleasant affair. For the Dugger young, who were so largely rural in their affiliations, it included fishing parties, wild-berryings and hazel-nutting, apple-parings, associated with the making, on a considerable scale, of apple butter; as Mary recalls it, especially at Aunt Sally's, where the orchards were notable — a general gathering of the clans, young people, in pairs, stirring the bubbling butter in huge iron pots under the apple boughs in the crisp October air. In the winter, there were spelling-bees, molasses-candy pulls, straw rides and sleighing to the accompaniment of bells, sheet-and-pillow-case parties and singing parties, which in those days were undertaken with an approach to seriousness. They sang 'Ro-oll o-on, Silver Mo-oo-on,' 'Darling Nellie Gray,' and masterpieces of humor like 'Not for Joseph,' and for a touch of spiciness, 'Walking Down Broadway.' There were also duets, such as 'Larboard Watch' and 'Call Me Pet Names.' For the young people not committed by their parents to the Methodist Discipline, there were dancing parties; but even Methodism afforded certain measures of relief from monotony; camp meetings on Pentecost Hill, where, if one did not come entirely under the sway of the rip-roaring evangelist, one was touched with an emotional seriousness which led often to the condition of becoming engaged; there were Baptist 'immersions' on the bank of the Macoupin; there were Watch Nights at the Methodist Church, and the subdued entertainment of 'sitting up' with the dead. There was also the annual Hunt Supper, carried on, with the others, into Mary's time.

Susie learned all the household arts that were proper to young ladies, which included several varieties of needlework, the making of toilet waters and sachets, and, in particular, cordials. There were recipes for cordials which ran in families. I remember one which began with a quart of brandy, an equal measure of crushed sugar — the kind of hard white sugar which came in paper cones — to which was added, beginning with May cherries, a quart of every fruit in season until — but why go on! Susie never became very expert in making cordials because by that time Susie had 'turned Temperance,' which meant total abstinence. Besides, the making of cordials rather went out of use when you could buy in Uncle Joe Dugger's store, where they were classed as groceries, brandies such as peach, lavender blackberry, cognac; along with Jamaica rum, Irish and Scotch whiskey, Madeira, sherry, claret, and Malaga wines; Holland gin and schnapps. Ale, porter, cider, and such small-beer were classed as confectioneries. Spinning and

weaving had gone out by that time, though still to be found occasionally in remote country places. Why, indeed, should a young
lady spin or weave when at Uncle Joe's there was so liberal a
supply of cassimeres, jackonets, challis, 'durable hats,' and
'French traveling goods' — whatever that might mean. There
were also skirts, which meant hoops — of from five to forty springs
—and the same sort of boots for which President Lincoln was
publicly scored for paying twenty-five dollars for three pairs.

For all of which reasons Susie turned to reading: 'Godey's
Lady's Book,' which provided a great deal of serious if somewhat
condescending advice on what 'pure young womanhood' ought to
know, for 'nothing having the slightest appearance of indelicacy'
was ever published for Godey Brothers' 'fair readers.' She read
her stepmother's favorite, the 'Philadelphia Ledger,' a mildly
William Hearst type of 'escape' literature of the time. She read
Lydia Maria Childs, Harriet Beecher Stowe, Augusta Evans, and
Maria Cummins, as they came along, and the over-saccharine
Jennie June. Susie was ambitious to be a school teacher, which
was the only liberal profession open to young women, and even
aspired to a writing career, of which, except as she observed it
through the women contributors of 'Godey's Lady's Book,' she had
not the faintest idea. At school, which she attended along with
Betty Palmer and a whole bevy of Mayo girls, her compositions
were faithfully reported in the local papers as educational events.
For the rest, Susie helped her stepmother with the other children,
taught in the Methodist Sunday School, sang in the church choir
— she had a sweet, pretty alto — and in due course of time
became engaged to George Hunter, who, in 1860, opened an
office on the second floor of Milo's drugstore building.

III

IT WOULD have been Susanna Savilla whose account of the Civil War and what led up to it intrigued Mary into believing that she herself had lived through it. She knew better, but she believed it. How else could she express the intensely personal quality of reports of that war, except as a thing seen? She saw Susie and Mary Ann Graham going about their young lady affairs; Susie, 'ably assisted by ten young ladies,' presenting what was called a colloquy on her graduation from Miss Richmond's High School; Susie having three months at Monticello, the select Academy for young ladies, reading papers that, according to the local papers, exhibited a 'maturity of thought and elegance of diction that abundantly testify to the intellectual capacity of the female mind'; and sister Mary Ann of the snapping black eyes and the ruddy color, that the last time her niece and namesake saw her, after the birth of thirteen children, had not yet washed away; Mary Ann with plenty of 'bounce' and a deft hand with the voluminous skirts that, after hoops had been widened to the last possible inch of convenience, were being looped and flounced and panniered to give the tiny-waisted, swimming effect, requisite to the prevailing concept of feminine fragility.

They were all at it in those days, trying to confirm the ladyhood of American women as against their womanhood, too obviously triumphant over the servantless house and the annual confinement. Mary Ann always managed to be 'dressy,' even when her Scotch father kept her down, in the matter of garniture, to fringes and plain rows and rows of narrow velvet ribbon. There is a story of how she once outdid herself; after being taken in her turn by her father on one of his semi-annual stock replenishing trips to St. Louis she came back with the roomiest possible hoopskirt, inside which she swam elegantly down the church aisle the next Sunday, only to discover that no amount of tilting it this way and that would get it in between the benches, so that she had finally to sail out again amid the discreet smiles of the congregation. But what was that to a young woman with the courage to begin, at nineteen, her garland of thirteen children, in an age in which those that died in infancy were not counted?

Susie, if less handsome than her sister, had the flushed pink complexion, the Scotch harebell eyes and the mouth delicately curled which deserved the popular encomium for her type, 'sweetly pretty.' Her hair, extraordinarily thick and long, was dark brown, parted and plain combed. But no Methodist dictum ever quite kept out of it the suspicion of a wave on either side the serene, full forehead, confirming the tiny cleft in her chin and the dimple in her left cheek.

Not that Mary saw her mother and her mother's sister so. What she believed was that she saw *with* them the plangent time, beating up the war storm in the South. She saw, as they saw, the vast curved sweep of Donati's comet, waking the ancient sense of portent. Not that the Middlewest did not know all that everybody else knew about comets, with their visibility to all the world. What they felt was that the portent was to *them*. Out of the appreciation of destiny which great open spaces excite in their human habitants crept the ancient human dread by which the comet was made to serve for oracle. War could not have been a stranger visitor. All that summer, between more immediate concerns, such as the proper hang of a polonaise or this new game out of the modish East, called croquet, there were sudden flurries of political interest. Susie did not go to Alton for the Lincoln-Douglas debate, but she heard direct reports of it from young George Hunter and a half-score of Dugger kin, and she heard both candidates separately in her own town, out of which she gathered for Mary a likeness of immortal Abe unlimbering himself to speak, like a tall ungainly bird, under whose wingspread arms his sleek, duck-built adversary could have walked. Other Carlinvillians, who went down to St. Louis for the horse-racing entertainment proffered to a fattish, pop-eyed, deeply bored Prince of Wales, came back with an alarmed sense of tension. Lincoln's election meant ruin to business interests centered there and quickened economic apprehension all through the Upper River. All the latter part of October was a continual furor of torchlight processions, bands, transparencies, young ladies as allegorical figures on floats, and a great waving of flags.

The delayed ratification of Lincoln's election, which took place at Springfield, Susie had occasion to remember because of the holes burnt by firecrackers in her new percale sunbonnet which went so nicely with her pink sprigged calico, all flounced and piped with pink. In April, when the redbuds were out along the Macoupin and the maples dripped sweet sap, there was a brief and unsuccessful attempt to raise the Confederate flag over St. Louis.

The event raised a sudden ardor of opposition in the young naturalized English, in the grandsons of Revolutionary soldiers who chiefly populated the Upper River country. Within twenty-four hours of the call for volunteers, George Hunter, Dick Rowett, and Manning Mayfield went arm and arm, as the fashion of young men friends was in those days, to enlist. The grandsons of Polly McAdams were not far behind. Within three days the Seventh Illinois Volunteers was in full swing.

Company K was formed at Carlinville and went into camp on the County Fair Grounds, part of the old Jarrot Dugger homestead, and christened itself the 'Macoupin Invincibles.' Its first concern was to prevent itself from foundering on the basket-loads of dainties which came pouring in from the neighboring farmhouses.

It must be understood that to Mary this was a wholly romantic war. It was fought chiefly by Father, General Grant, and Cousin Bill Dugger, although of course there were other Carlinvillians who helped along. Within ten days after the fifteenth of April, ten thousand Suckers had volunteered; which had nothing to do with the fact that the total State armament in arsenal consisted of three hundred and sixty-two altered United States muskets, one hundred and five Harper's Ferry and Deninger rifles; two hundred and ninety-nine horse pistols and one hundred and thirty-three musketoons. Father's regiment bought their own guns, paying each fifty dollars out of their thirteen dollars a month pay. There was a good deal of complaint of the time wasted on military training, when everybody knew that all that was needed was a good gun and a man behind it to put the Rebels in their place. Did not Company K already have Dick Rowett for Captain and Hunter and Mayfield as lieutenants! Their earliest military exploit was the accepting of a silk flag made by the Carlinville ladies, bearing an eagle and thirty-four stars, inscribed on one side, 'Macoupin Invincibles,' and on the other, 'The Union Must Be Preserved.' Lieutenant Hunter made the speech of the occasion.

That summer the women put in the corn, and in July, Lieutenant Hunter came back for reënforcements, of which he secured forty in his own district, for by that time it was understood that the war would be for longer than three months. On this occasion, he arranged to come back for Susie in August. Early in that month, the fifer of Company K wrote home, 'We have a noble set of officers, kind and accommodating... every man in Company K is pleased with them.' And the next news was that Captain Rowett had been promoted to General and George Hunter made Captain in his place.

Susanna Savilla, aged eighteen years and four months, sedately closed her school term with a 'Convention for Arranging a Course of Study for a Seminary,' with the help of Betty Palmer, of which the papers spoke highly, and set about her modest trousseau. She looked for her young Captain on the first of August, but the summer floods were up, the wires down, and nobody knew when there might be reprisals to Grierson's raid, which had swept southward in April carrying alarm and devastation in its path. All that night Susie walked the floor; a performance totally unguessed by her Sunday-School class of young girls whom she met next morning, dressed as one to whom the bridegroom might at any moment appear. Jane Conley — she that was Jennie Mayo — described Susie's dress as changeable rose and lilac silk, with silk mitts and a bonnet to match, rosebuds under the bonnet brim and a white lace mantle. She said it was a relief to everybody when, Sunday School being over and Church about to begin, Susie took her place in the choir. Nobody could have borne it another minute not knowing how the first of the army brides was dressed. She said there wasn't a girl in the church that wasn't more excited than Susie, and how satisfyingly dramatic it was at the end, when people began to walk out, and there in the church porch was the attractive young soldier in his Captain's uniform, waiting to take her away on his arm. They were married that afternoon at Milo Graham's house, and Milo kissed her, which, Susie always said, was as much of a novelty as getting married.

That being Sunday there was little merry-making — Susie's girl friends in white over wide hoops, with hair dressed low, with flowers; home-made ice-cream and cake, and a prayer from the minister that brought tears to all eyes, after which Nettie Constance sang:

> When shall we meet again,
>   Meet ne'er to sever;
> When shall Peace wreath her chain
>   Round us forever:
> Fond hearts can ne'er repose
> Safe from each blast that blows
> In this dark vale of woes —
>   Never, no, never!

To escape the importunities of the townspeople, nearly everyone of whom had a son or husband or brother at the front, the young people had to slip away to Plainview, and the next morning workmen crossing the town square saw three chairs tied together and hoisted to the top of the flagpole, for the gallant Captain and his bride. (Three *cheers*, or course, and I'll wager anything there were plenty who didn't know they were pronounced any other way. I've even letters from Cousin Bill which advise me that I come by my poor spelling honestly.)

It was a romantic war. They called Captains gallant, and plain soldiers 'Boys in Blue.' They talked of Glory, claimed God exclusively for the Union side, and damned the Rebels heartily. They wrote home in Byronic terms. I recall talk of a 'bloody and pandering plague of lying partisans,' and language even more explicit. Every regiment had its poet; Sergeant Flint of the Seventh Illinois celebrated every event with appropriate verse, which, as verse went at that time, was rather better than you would have expected. It came back to Mary in so many ways, at her mother's knee, in the houses of her kin, and soldiers' reunions, at Burgdorff's cooper shop, as a thing already familiar by experience.

Captain Hunter took his bride to Cairo, where his regiment was now stationed. Later they steamed down to Fort Henry (February, 1862), and at Fort Donelson came into touch with Unconditional Surrender Grant. Gallant Captain Hunter's company was reported to have 'sustained half the loss of the regiment,' a matter of twenty casualties. Rowett behaved with great gallantry in the action of April 6. Grant's last line was formed. Grant comes riding down it shouting, 'They come, they come! Army of the Tennessee, stand firm!' The host grows desperate; the Seventh engages; the earth trembles; the sun is hot behind the wrathful smoke. I quote now from memory. It was a period of magnificent phrase-making. Captains died telling their men to 'keep the old flag in the wind.'

In December of '62, Captain Hunter took his young wife back to Carlinville, and early in '63 she joined him at Corinth with their infant daughter, who had been christened Hannah for her grandmother. But the swamps of Corinth were no place for constitutions not enured to Mississippi fevers. In a few months, while a battle was being fought, the Captain was called from the field to his tent in time to see his daughter turn her head and die.... 'Look away... look away yonder... your eye never beheld a grander sight than this, the Northwest's battle pride! They move firmly. There is harmony in their steps. Ten thousand bayonets flash in the blazing sunlight. They are moving in columns on the bloody plain. Their drums sound like a death-knell.' So the local historian.

Years afterward, Mary found a neglected book of battle pictures of the Civil War, which she suspects was the source of her earlier conviction that she had seen the war in person. What pageantry, what pomp, what attitudes! Since then she has lived through the aftermath of another war, in which she discovered little romance. Did that go with the short-range weapon, with the loss of the sense of men in armies, moving rhythmically, the sense of direct, dramatic conjunction? Did the great war phrases rise directly out of the personal conflict, word in the mouth and sword in the hand? There was never a war so rich in phrases. Everybody knew now that they were fighting to 'free a suffering people from the yoke of unendurable oppression.'

In '63, Captain Hunter had surrendered at Corinth to repeated attacks of the little understood malarial fevers which plagued the district. Unfit for field service, he was, on account of his legal qualifications, kept on court-martial duty until, at the end of his three years' enlistment, he resigned, and in 1864 returned to civilian life. Unwounded, he was yet never again to enjoy the finely strung good health and spirits which he had taken into the war.

Of all that is written of Captain Hunter's war service, there is nothing that does not become him as an officer and a gentleman. His adjutant reports him an excellent organizer, knowing how to keep up the morale of his men. He was immensely popular with them and their families at home. To the day of his death there was the reminiscence of gallantry in the way they touched their hats to him.

Mary recalls at the last, a fair, stoutish man with a wooden leg stumping to his funeral, weeping... Captain, my captain!

In field reports written by him, or in his hand under Rowett's name and in letters published in the local paper, there is a quality of forthrightness such as by no means appears in war documents generally. His expression is virile, direct, cool, and somehow graceful, lacking the Byronic note which characterizes too many contemporary writings. It is English rather than American, but without any touch of self-consciousness.

On his return from service, Captain Hunter reopened his law office over Milo Graham's drugstore, and built a little house in

First South Street; that little house which is now the inconspicuous ell to William Burgdorff's residence. There was ground enough about it to afford him the necessary outdoor life demanded by his want of health, in amateur experiments with small-fruit growing. There in 1866 a son was born, named James Milo for his English and American grandfathers. There had been another son born during the war, who breathed and died subject to the shocks of Susie's war experience. In the two years following, a score of small upsettings, such as follow in the wake of wars, settled about him.

First, there was the affair of his sister Mary, the one who had come out of England with him in '53 and settled in Alton, developing a knack for millinery and dressmaking at which she maintained herself. All during the war, Rebel prisoners had been interned at Alton on comparatively easy terms. Among these there had been a young Colonel Charles E. Lane, whom Mary met, and at the close of the war, when Colonel Lane was given his freedom, George discovered for the first time that his sister had engaged herself to him. The engagement led, with all its implied betrayal of the cause for which Captain Hunter had endured so much, to a quarrel between the brother and sister. There was, however, a quasi-reconciliation, when Colonel Lane, ruined by the failure of the Confederacy, disappeared into the then unknown West and was not heard of for a year or more. Mary, apparently resigned to the loss of her lover, came to Carlinville and decided to establish herself there in the millinery business. Somehow or other, George scraped the money together for her, and with it she set out for St. Louis to make the necessary purchases of stock. The next that her brother heard from her was that she had bought a marriage 'set-out' with the money and a ticket to Omaha, where Colonel Lane, who had contrived to establish himself on the Pacific Coast as a mining engineer, met and married her. Besides the natural resentment, there was the loss of the money, which was needed by the young couple in Carlinville, and though Mrs. Lane returned it finally, and there were fairly affectionate exchanges later — especially after sister Mary named her second son George — the brother and sister never saw each other again.

It was also about this time that there began to be a great uneasiness on account of Susie's son James, then little more than a year old, who showed incipient symptoms of lameness, traceable, as was believed, to the state of his father's health. One should say here that all the Hunter children carried — as did so many of their generation — the mark of that inheritance. Susie was frightened and her young husband harried and oppressed. It was no sort of time to hear what had to be heard in the spring of 1868, that another child was to be expected. A strange new note had come into the thinking of the granddaughters of the women who had borne their dozen or so cheerfully and with the conviction of the will of God strong in them, a note ominous to young husbands not yet habituated to self-realizing attitudes on the part of the fair sex. It was plain to the wife of the half-invalided and not yet established attorney, with one seriously ailing child on her hands, that another was not desired, was not, in fact, welcome.

IV

THE one relieving item in that summer of 1868, in which Captain Hunter's second daughter was born, was that Mrs. Mary Snyder, she that had been Mary Patchen, called on the Hunters at the little house on First South Street. This would have been between two and three months before Mary Hunter was born.

In the Rain Song of the Sia, Earth Horizon is the incalculable blue ring of sky meeting earth, which is the source of experience. It is pictured as felt, rays of earth energy running together from the horizon to the middle place where the heart of man, the recipient of experience, is established, and there treasured. By whatever road it reaches him, by the four-flowing ways of the earth, by the zenith or the nadir, experience is always significant and mysterious; never so significant as when most mysterious, most potent when least understood, exciting in the heart that subtle sense of relationship to the earth horizon which is the nurture of the spiritual life.

In this fashion experience may be carried about as an amulet, a fetish; neglected and dropped; dispossessed by death, it may be picked up and carried by the finder without loss of its potency, its inherent capacity as of a seed to come alive from within and burgeon. This is a true report. At the Middle Place, where all influences of the Earth Horizon come to equilibrium, experience explains itself, flowers and fruits to the holder.

It is not likely that the people in this book have known any more about their experience than do most people. No more did Mary when it happened to her, but having a feeling for experience such as other people might have for old porcelain or Spanish Primitives, for its potencies and mysteriousness, she often knew when she fingered it, as you might know of a strange coin or an ornament picked up in a dusty shop, that value inhered in it. Even when you have no notion *what* value, you put it in your purse for a lucky piece.

Mary's particular amulet of experience happened first to George Hunter, the hard and bitter kernel of it, of which he was never heard to speak, a year or two previous to his marriage. 'Of its value to him nothing whatever was known except the opinion obstinately entertained by his closest man friend, to whom, if to anybody, he might have made intimate admissions. It had implications upon which his friend's insistence brought on a quarrel between them that became a sore issue to both of them for the rest of their lives. It was the only experience of his life which served, as it did oddly enough, to tie Mary into a train of activities outside the range of her tribe.

The Duggers, into whose clan George Hunter married, were never bookish. They had, as all early Americans seemed to have had, a conventional attitude toward English classicism; they could all quote Shakespeare a little, they knew their Scott and Byron, they had heard something of Mr. Dickens even if no more than they had read in the papers which in the forties had demonstrated the American disposition to celebrate the literary great, even though the celebrants might not have read them or liked what they read if they did. But like other Middlewesterners, the Duggers were generally unaware of what was going on in their own country in their own time, or of what was coming to it out of the most prolific literary and æsthetic period of Europe.

Nevertheless, there were a few of the English-born for whom the umbilical cord of their native culture had not yet been severed, had not, until after the birth, amid war, of an intenser, more local Americanism, ceased to beat.

Until the interest of war overlaid every other, George Hunter continued to buy first American editions of Keats and Shelley, Mrs. Browning and Ruskin, and to keep pace with the writers of genuine distinction in the United States; with Herman Melville, Hawthorne, Poe, and Longfellow, particularly with Emerson. For the years that he was still reading law and discussing politics with Manning Mayfield and Dick Rowett, about the time that the Grierson-Shepherds had moved from Sauls's Prairie to St. Louis, the nexus of his connection with current literary thought was the

Patchen family. At their home, a notable farm a few miles from the town, still known as the Patchen Place, he met not only the head of the family, Charles Patchen, but his young sister Mary, then teaching the public school at the county seat, an exalted intellectual position for a young woman in the eighteen-fifties.

What was still more exceptional for women in such positions, Mary Patchen was beautiful, with a beauty of the essential inner structure of the mind which, when Mary first knew her nearly forty years afterwards, was still evident. She had a figure called in her day 'statuesque,' and that clear, white, and rosy skin which goes with the bluest of blue eyes and pale gold hair. She was taller than George and perhaps a year or two older, but it was said to be delightful to those who knew them to hear the young couple discuss, as they often did at her brother's house, the literature and æsthetics of the day. They attended Lyceums, and when the new 'Atlantic Monthly' was established, read it together and aloud for groups of Middlewesterners, then as now willing-minded, even avid toward what was called culture, and unfitted for getting it except through the medium of more easily habituated minds. Gradually the association between the young law student and Mary Patchen grew to be one of those relationships which become, through their recognized fitness, a community possession. They were not publicly known to be 'engaged'; that was not the fashion of the time; they 'kept company,' which was equally binding, and in its perfection of suspended romanticism probably just as enjoyable.

Among the opportunities afforded by the Lyceum for extending education beyond the period of youth, curtailed as it was by the exigencies of pioneering, was the 'lecture course' on popular sciences, consisting of from four to six lectures delivered week by week for the term of which the lecturer remained a resident of the community or perhaps divided himself between two or more adjacent towns. One of the most popular of these, a course in astronomy, was then being carried on by a man of reputed learning, an intelligent and entertaining talker. His name was Hutchinson, and he had not been in the town very long before, on his own evidence, he discovered himself somehow kin to the Patchens and was invited to take up with them his bed and board.

It was not very long after this that George Hunter received a peremptory note from Miss Patchen notifying him that their friendship was at an end. This was followed in short order by the return of the books and letters that had passed between them and the forbidding to him of the Patchen home. No explanation was directly forthcoming and nothing came back in response to young Hunter's plea for an explanation, a hearing. But in the course of a week or two it leaked out through the Patchens that, on an occasion when he had been to town after the mail, Mr. Hutchinson had returned in a condition of evident distress, the cause of which he permitted to be drawn from him at the evening board. He had overheard, he said, at the post-office, a young man speaking of Miss Patchen in a manner totally wanting in that respectful reserve which good usage demanded from young men. He had denied that there was 'anything between them' but an 'intellectual friendship' which he meant to break off when it seemed advisable. No, Mr. Hutchinson did not know the young man's name, but he described him with such meticulous and unmistakable detail that Miss Patchen fainted and had to be carried from the room. This was what was expected in those days of young ladies offended in their deepest sensibilities.

Good manners of the period did not permit discussion of so delicate a situation. So far as can be discovered, after being refused a hearing by both Miss Patchen and her brother, George Hunter remained commendably silent. Their not having been officially engaged rendered it improper for the partisans of the young lady to call the young man to account. Miss Patchen, however, carried a high head; such private humiliations as she suffered were kept so closely within the family circle that the only friend who found himself in a position to offer her the subtle consolations of appreciation was Mr. Hutchinson. He was so far skillful in that direction that, before the community had time properly to divide itself into partisans of one or the other of the young people involved, it had to adjust itself to the marriage of Miss Patchen and the lecturer and their departure on a wedding journey. Before they had returned from it, two or three weeks later, the shock was deepened to indignation by the arrival from Mr. Hutchinson's home of a warrant for his arrest on a charge of bigamy. He had, it appeared, a wife and two children in New England.

It is impossible now, with our casual and rationalistic method of dealing with such matters, to reconstruct the white heat of community reaction on the arrival of the sheriff and his prisoner. We are far, too far, from that realization of woman as precious in herself to the pioneer group, with a kind of preciousness intrinsically damaged by whatever depreciated her potential motherhood. Perhaps they were just as far in the Middlewest fifties from the still earlier tribal practice of surrounding that preciousness with dignity and emotional security; but they were not stranger to the realization that women must be protected in the public giving of themselves to their social function. Inasmuch as Hutchinson had taken advantage of the hurt susceptibilities of Mary Patchen to press his own advantage, he was that much more open to summary retaliation for the indignity of a false marriage. The community gathered itself into a posse.

There was a new building going up at the end of West Main Street, to a convenient beam of which a rope was made fast, with the intention of attaching the other end of it to the admitted bigamist. Except for the prompt and whole-hearted intervention of Mary Patchen's brother — who as one of the offended might be listened to — the lynching would undoubtedly have been accomplished. By community consent Mr. Hutchinson was returned to the sheriff who returned him to his lawful wife, on whose account he was, in due course, subjected to the legal penalty.

Miss Patchen went into the seclusion which the refined sensibility of the period demanded. Public opinion completely exonerated George Hunter; he was so far regarded as the victim of Hutchinson's machinations that no demand of his for restoration of his standing with Miss Patchen could have been disregarded.

That he made no such demand was credited to his sense of his
own undeserved indignity. So far as is known, neither of the young
people made a gesture of reconciliation. It was too much to have
been expected. Miss Patchen saw nobody except the young Mr.
Snyder who had been fetched from the State College at Urbana
on an emergency call to supply her post at the public school.
It was necessary for him to confer with her frequently; in the
course of which her beauty and charm, public report of which
all events confirm, working together with the appeal of her
undeserved situation, resulted in a few months in a second
marriage. At the end of the school term the Snyders returned
to Urbana.

And here at the end of ten years they were, calling on the
Hunters at the little house. It was a way of saying that Mary
Patchen understood now that George had been entirely blameless
in that ten-year-old tragedy of their youth, and as an amend was
entirely in keeping with the good manners of the period, which
took all infringements of the gentlemanly code with a devastating
seriousness, and was no doubt salving to the young attorney's
pride. Susie was, on the whole, pleased with the attention, for
though all she had heard was a young-girl version of the affair
at the time it had occurred, and she had never believed anything
about it derogatory to her young husband's credit, it was agreeable
to have what passed in the code of the time for a public retraction.
It remained for Mary Patchen herself, many years after, to take
up the experience and hang it about young Mary's neck, as an
amulet against loneliness of heart.

In the following September, the ninth to be exact, on the stroke
of midnight, between a Wednesday and a Thursday, Susie's
second daughter was born. Uncle Alex — who was waiting about
the house to carry word of her safe arrival back to Grandpa's,
and perhaps because for the reason that he was the first of the
family to welcome her, had always a special affection for the
child — used to say that after the first protesting squawk, she had
looked solemnly on the world as the 'noticingest' baby he had
ever seen. Later she was named Mary, and when asked for which

of the Mary-kin — there were at least six, including her great-great-grandmother Mary Hendricks, who might have been entitled to it — her father had twinkled for the first time since the young lady's arrival. Said he, 'Let them fight it out among them.'

V

OF THE little house on First South Street, where she was born and spent two and a half years, Mary recalls but two or three unrelated flashes, significant only as the index of a dominant interest. The earliest must have been when Mary herself was two years old: a family gathering, of a Sunday afternoon, probably to inspect Susie's newest baby, Jennie. The house was full of people, unidentified, but having a sense of kin, with Mary trotting along a boardwalk between the house and the corner of the front yard to the gate in the picket fence. She recalls, besides that, the thick green of the maples overhead and the grass coming up between the boards of the walk. If you say that it is incredible that a child of two, or a month or six weeks less, should have remembered, you know nothing of what it means to grow up in the midst of a Middlewestern clan. At five years of age Mary was able to name forty-three of her mother's kin, to say nothing of those whose pictures she recognized in the family album. That no more were recalled for this occasion is proof of its early occurrence.

The second recollection, even more definitely attested as to date, occurred later in the same year. It was also a Sunday, and the family had been to call at Uncle Jim Valentine's — *Uncle* because he was brother to your step-grandmother — at a house from which they moved shortly after. It had been a long call because there had been the projected move to discuss, and the possibility of the Hunters' following them to the neighborhood south of town where both families lived for years afterward. On the way home, the road went down a little slope and up what seemed to Mary a vast weary hill. Father was carrying the baby; perambulators hadn't come into use yet. That was how Mary remembers so accurately. Jennie was wearing the christening robe. There was always one such in the poorest family, worn for the event, and for two or three company occasions, before it was laid away in lavender to await the inevitable next. All infants of that time wore absurdly long clothes, but *the* robe was always long enough to fall modishly over the father's arm almost to the floor, as the child was carried up the church aisle. Christening robes were all one pattern, a spreading front of alternate ladder-like arrangements of insertion and tiny 'French' tucks, with ruffling at the bottom and down the sides. Distinction was in the design and the fineness of the material and needlework, which people craned their necks over the pew ends to observe. Every member of the congregation grew tolerably familiar with the christening robes of respective families; it was only when the family was very rich that each robe was laid aside to be added to the future trousseau. Several of Mary's friends made wedding petticoats of theirs. On this occasion, she remembers perfectly how beautifully Jennie's robe flowed over Father's arm. The day was warm; the hill loomed enormously. Mary wilted down in the middle of the boardwalk. Father made a gesture of passing the baby to Mother, to pick up his older daughter.

'Let her alone,' said Mother. 'She'll come when she finds she has to.' And to Mary, 'Look at Jim, he's not complaining,' which was too familiar an admonition for Mary to realize that it was also unfair, since Jim was already well on the road to five. Feeling very small and faint, she sat on the hot boardwalk and saw the rest of the family disappear over the top of the hill. Mary never doubted that she was abandoned. She lay under the weight of that certainty without motion or sound, an event not to be coped with. Finally over the hill a figure appeared, it drew near... Papa! The recollection snaps off like a broken stick. What I suspect is that the instant relief appeared, Mary laid her head on the boardwalk and went to sleep. I've known her to do things like that.

One other instance has no date, but since it undoubtedly occurred on First South Street, was either in her second spring or late the same autumn. She was out-of-doors, blue and a flicker of color overhead. Jennie was in the cradle — a low hooded cradle with solid rockers easy to move about, as distinguished from the crib-cradle to which you were promoted as soon as you ceased to be *the* baby. Outside, beyond the cradle's rim, pale round flowers in the grass. Bindweed! Mary knew that was what you called it...

pale films of color fluttering, and a feeling that went with it... it was a long time before you got a name for the feeling, but bindweed you never forgot. Only — this was very odd — when the recollection came back to you, there was sometimes a singular confusion, the bindweed was always there, but it was Mary in the cradle, and Jennie did not come into the picture at all. So it is just possible that Mary was less than two years old when it occurred — bindweed has a long season of blooming and proves nothing.

The only thing worth noting in all these is that they occurred out-of-doors. Not, as it was afterward proved, that there weren't other things remembered out of the first two and a half years, but these were the only things that spontaneously recurred to mind.

One incident of the hegira from First South Street, marked for Mary the beginning of a series of occurrences which was to become the source of a good deal of bewilderment and blame from which she was never able to extricate herself. Brother Jim, in virtue of his status of 'going-on-six,' had been permitted to ride to the new home on the last load of goods, which he fell off of going down Mayo's Hill, and without making any outcry had managed to scramble back on the way up the next; an exploit which lacked something of the fine flavor of success which he imagined for it when Mother discovered how much of the spring mud had scrambled back with him. Nevertheless, it was an exploit which deserved re-telling, but the mistake Mary made was in telling it as something she had seen. Mother set her right. To say that you'd seen things when you hadn't was storying, and storying was wicked. But you did see it; you shut your eyes and there it was as plain as plain, Jim sitting on the mattress on the back of the wagon, down Mayo's Hill between the huge white house on one side and the rail fence with the wild-plum thicket on the other.

'You just imagined it,' said Mother.

'What is 'magine, Mama?'

'Thinking you see things when you don't.'

But how could you? And how did you know the difference between seeing and thinking you had seen? It seemed to be always happening; grown-ups thought it funny, but Jim, who was a stern moralist, after the way of brothers where their sisters are concerned, told on you, and Mother said she supposed she'd have to punish you or you would grow up a story-teller. Well, you *did* see them. If you got punished for it, you'd simply have to stand it.

The new home was about a mile from the square, at the end of Plum Street, on the town's southern limit. Forced by his army heritage of ill health to spend a large part of his time out-of-doors, Captain Hunter hoped to turn it to account by further adventures in horticulture and stock-breeding. He had an Englishman's feeling for the land and what could be done with it. Perhaps he had really never cared for the practice of law; he was never notable at it. The only echo of his practice which reached his children was the pains he took to see that members of his company and their families — troubled and inarticulate individuals — the man with the wooden leg — touching their hats and calling him Captain as they came and went — got everything that was legally coming to them in the way of back pay and pensions. And Mother saying that he ought to insist on their calling at his office because of a prepossession they seemed to have that advice offered at his home or theirs did not require to be paid for.

About the time the Hunters had settled into their new home, the city passed an ordinance taking in as much of the Plum Street place as would ensure the election of Captain Hunter as City Magistrate. The line, as I recall it, passed between the barn and the house. The Judge, as it thrilled his children to hear him called, was genuinely popular in the minor offices of town and county, such as called for detachment and unself-interested judgments.

It was in these years before events began to happen one after the other, while Mary was between three and a half and five and a half, that the roots of trouble showed themselves, had to be reckoned with, and to her small capacity overcome. It began as I have described with her not always knowing whether she had seen things, in the sense that other people saw them, or hadn't. It had something to do with the quality of experience. Whether it happened in a picture, in a book, or in a story she was told, either it flashed instantly into a picture, or it didn't. And the picture stayed. According to the degree of her interest in it, it stayed to the minutest detail! — the form and especially the color and feeling that went with it. It was perhaps the intensity of feeling evoked which accounted for the conviction that the event in question took place in her presence — Great-Grandmother Polly being carried off by the Indians, the wolves snuffling under the puncheon floor at the minister's children, the slain on battlefields crawling in heaps — they *happened* to her. After Mary learned how wicked it was, as well as annoying to your parents, to talk about things as though you had been there when you hadn't, she made for herself a criterion of distinction which served in most cases. If you saw things the way other people meant seeing, you saw all around them, matching up with houses, people, earth, and sky, you saw them as *belonging*. But if the picture failed to match, if around the edges of the event you found ragged fringes of grayness, the chances were that you had *imagined* something you had only heard about. In general this worked, but not always. To this day there are a few of these recalled images which she is not sure about.

And then there were dreams. Until you found yourself laughed at, you supposed they really must have happened; and then you discovered that dreams had a way of fading out, murky and yellow at the edges. Still, there were a lot of things — like the Great Snow. When Mary was a child, there were still people in Carlinville who dated things from the Great Snow in '36, when the flakes fell fifteen feet deep on the level, and men driving their hogs to market in Alton had to dump out their wagon-loads of corn and fodder and abandon the hogs to make the best of it; only to find them, after the thaw, piled on one another for warmth, frozen stiff where they stood. Or Annie Pritchard who married and set out barefoot on her wedding journey to Ohio — you looked at old Annie Pritchard and wondered how she could ever have been young enough to have a wedding. By dint of attaching these things to the teller of them, Aunt Sally, or Grandma Berry, you arrived at notions of reality distributed in time.

There was another dreadful difficulty which Mary was always getting into, which she was never able to correct because there was never any way of knowing in advance when it was going to happen. Mary said things; unaccountable, inexcusable things that annoyed visitors. She would be sitting in her little chair, being a good child according to prescription, which determined that good children, when there was company, should be seen and not heard, and suddenly in a lull in the conversation out they would come, the things that simply should not have been said; things about people, the way they felt; the reasons, generally inadmissible, for doing this or that; the things going on in people's minds, of what they carefully weren't talking about. No particular instance occurs; not knowing she was going to say it, Mary didn't always know, until she was confronted with the general consternation, that she *had*. Nor had she any notion why it should prove so annoying. She was scolded about it; she was punished; Mother sometimes shed tears of pure vexation; sometimes she said, 'I think the child is possessed.' She said people would think she had been gossiping and Mary had repeated what she had heard, though the truth was that nothing was further from Susie's habit of mind than gossip. Not one of her children ever heard her say an unkind or misrepresentative thing about anybody.

Pressed to explain her transgression, Mary said it was like a little bird that hopped out of her mind, onto her tongue, before she could stop it. When she was older she began to realize that it was as if a hidden spring in her mind had been freed by something noted, a look, a tone, something so slight that before it could be named the spring was off, and out had hopped the little bird. Subjected to parental disapprobation, Mary wept, promised not to do it again; and did it. To this day, let her come into a room where there is a situation being saved, a secret antagonism guarded, and unless she is warned by expecting something of the kind, Mary in the first half-minute can quite innocently explode the whole works. Sometimes if she feels, without being able to put her finger on it, guile working underground, she can release the hidden spring herself, and with the flick of the little bird's tail, all the card houses come toppling to the table, for anyone to pick out the winning one as he is able.

How much of this came before, or after the arrival of I-Mary there is no recalling. She came so suddenly and always so inevitably that I doubt if anybody ever knew about her, or could have been made to understand. This would have been a few months after Mary had passed her fourth birthday. Jim had turned six in July and in September was invested with a primer and started to the public school. He started to school with Pa, going to his office in the morning, and home in the late afternoon, but on blustery days such as this, he was kept in the house. Mother was kneading the bread and Jim was studiously reciting his A B C's. At the other corner of the bread board, Mary was busy with a bit of pinched off dough and looking over his shoulder. 'A,' said Jim, and 'O.' 'O,' said Mary, making her mouth the shape of the mark. Presently Jim pointed out 'I.' 'Eye?' said Mary, plumping one floury finger on her own. 'No,' said Mother, 'I, myself, *I* want a drink, I-Mary.'

'I-Mary.'

Something turned over inside her; the picture happened. There was the familiar room, the flurry of snow outside; Mama kneading bread; Jim with his molasses-colored hair 'roached' on top, so that the end of the curl fell over in the middle of his forehead; Mary in her flannel frock and blue chambray pinafore, on her stool at the corner of the board... how small her hand looked beside Mama's ... the grimy bit of dough rolled out like a worm... And inside her, I-Mary, looking on. I-Mary, I-Mary, *I-Mary!*

Always until she was quite grown up, I-Mary was associated with the pages of books. The mere sight of the printed page would often summon her, and since her coming was comfortably felt — there was a reason for that which comes next — it was sought in the contemplation of print. Mary insisted on being shown everything in Jim's primer. Jim liked showing it, even when he had to resort to authority for the exact meaning of what he showed.

Thereafter, if Mary found a picture in a book with printing under it, she demanded to be told what it said. When stories were read her, she was never happy until she had got the page in hand and stared hard at it. I-Mary didn't always come out of it; still, you couldn't tell, it was always worth trying.

You wanted her to come because with I-Mary there was always a sense of something assured and comforting that you had expected and never found elsewhere... when you lay in the crib forlorn with that dreadful feeling which went by the name of 'fevernague,' and you thought you would feel better if only Mama would take you up, as she did, and nothing happened! — when she sat down at twilight to rock the baby, and Jim leaned against her shoulder while she told stories about the war and old times, and you forgot and leaned against her knee until you felt it subtly withdrawing... 'hadn't you better get your stool, Mary?'... So Mary sat on her little stool, Jim leaned against Mother's shoulder, and Jennie sat in her lap. But I-Mary suffered no need of being taken up and comforted; to be I-Mary was more solid and satisfying than to be Mary-by-herself.

VI

ALL these things come back with the shattered brilliance of light through stained glass. I remember the orchard with great clumps of frail spring-beauties coming up through the sod; the smell of budding sassafras on the winds of March, and the sheets of blue violets about rotting tree-trunks in the woodlot. I remember the tree toads musically trilling, the katydids in the hickory tree by the pump, and a raw Yorkshire lad who had come to work for Father, not able to sleep because of them. I more than recall the hot honey-scent of red clover, and the heavy, low flying bumble-bees; long walks in winter over the snow with Father, and the discovery of green fronds of fern and leafy wild blackberry vines under the edge of February thaws. I remember mocking-birds — there was one whose nest was in the hedge nearest the house — and the butcher bird that used to catch the young chipmunks first out of their mounded homes, and hang them on the thorns of the osage orange, from which Mary and Jennie would perilously retrieve them for proper burial.

Clearly, and yet with the effect of vast lapses of time, as though they had occurred as long ago as the Great Snow that Grandma Berry talked about, I recall the host of winged or crawling insect pests that came out of the unredeemed edges of the prairie to devastate the fields; army worms; tobacco worms; potato bugs... early every summer morning the children had to get out with tin cans and collect the spotted potato bugs from the young vines. Down in the bottom lands, crayfish would raise little tumuli between the hills of young corn, which they would strip in a single night. But the tobacco worms were the worst; green, inching crawlers, that if neglected for twenty-four hours could cut down the most promising young crop to the bare ground. Epic struggle of man with the creeping, flying things for the fruits of the earth! I don't know why poets and historians have so neglected it. Along the back of my mind marches a stream of anecdotes, humorous, tragic... Old Man Sauls... Sauls was the original settler for whom Sauls's Prairie was named, he was what was known as a 'character.' Mary's father used to collect, and relate with relish, instances of his salty and occasionally acrid wit. Sauls himself was a tobacco-eater; great gobs of it moving ruminantly between his jaws... I haven't seen one for forty years. Good tobacco could be raised in that neighborhood, when the worms permitted, by getting up betimes and working late. A few 'leaf-growers' managed it when other farmers surrendered before the massed assault, but there came an occasion when even old man Sauls had been obliged for a neighborhood occasion — a funeral, perhaps, or a barn raising — to take his eyes off his crops for certain hours, after which he returned to what had been a promising field of leaf, reduced to earth as bare as the back of your hand. And while he leaned on the fence taking stock of his loss, 'fit to be tied,' as the saying was, with vexation, he heard himself accosted by a thin, small voice, 'Mr. Sauls! Mr. Sauls!' Off to one side he discovered, inching along the topmost rail a green straggler of the devastating host. 'Mr. Sauls,' it said, 'will you lend me a chaw o' terbacker?' That was how defeat went down in the annals of the Middlewest, incident as fine as cobweb to bind us to heroic-comedy of the past.

Then there were the songs that Susie sang to her children; one feels them tighten still about the heart. Summer twilights she would sit by the open door, rocking the baby, while Jim and Mary sat on the step, until Jennie came to sit between them, and little Susie was rocked until Susie died, and Georgie came — that was one of the ways in which events began to be remembered in order, recalling who was 'the baby' when they occurred. Susie sang war song — 'Nicodemus the Slave,' 'Tenting Tonight'; at which prickles lifted along the back of your neck; camp-meeting songs... 'Where, oh, where are the Hebrew children?' It was the fashion among sophisticates a year or two ago to congratulate themselves on the discovery of the Negro spiritual, fifty or sixty years after they were sung beside the dark forests and the rolling rivers by impassioned farmers on Pentecost Hill. Susie knew half a dozen of them. She could go back of that and sing songs of her own youth that must have come down to her from the gatherings around the open hearth of Polly McAdams:

> Weep not for me, the veteran said,
> I bow to Heaven's high will;
> But quickly from yon antlers bring
> The sword of Bunker Hill!

How it rang out and haunts still the aching chambers of memory in Polly's great-granddaughter! There was a version of 'Yankee Doodle,' I recall, which had more verses than I have ever been able to discover since, a song about angels pouring 'lasses down on this nigger's head — shoo-fly! and that sprightly ditty of Billy Boy and the charming Young Thing who could make a cherry pie quick as a cat can wink its eye, which Mary, who prided herself very early on being able to make a cherry pie, considered a gross exaggeration.

It was on evenings like this that Mose Drakeford sang himself across the scene. Mose, in the pre-war period, was the town's sole 'colored man.' Where he came from I never knew, but with his family he lived in a sort of feudal relation to the Burke family, and probably came out of Virginia with them. During the summer it was his custom to cut wood in the Bottoms, which he peddled about. One heard him coming up out of the shadowy region, with its vague menace of the unknown, heralded by his voice, deep and mellow like a French horn, which, it was said, could be heard a mile and a half away — 'Co'd wood, co'd wood!' Between these professional announcements of his passing, he sang for his own entertainment long crooning notes that rang out now and then to trumpet phrases... 'Swing low, sweet chariot'... 'Play on yo' harp, little David'... 'Oh, Lord, how long!' — A voice as black and rich and mysterious as the Black Bottoms themselves.

Mose was an unforgettable item of the town's life. Mose and his wagon miraculously constituted an entity with bits of wire and string, and Mose's mule, his head garnished with a straw hat out of which his ears stuck jauntily, and his front legs protected by a pair of Mose's discarded trousers. Mose was of the opinion that the 'muel' could keep the flies off his 'hind laigs hisself.'... But to

Mary he was a voice in the dark, inextricably bound up with the mucky smell of the Bottoms and the malarial vapors that rose out of them after the sun went down.

Somewhere in these night memories there is a thin sliver of memory charged with aching portent... cool wind, black void, and fiery whiteness of the stars; two children taken out on an upper balcony to see the constellation of the drinking-gourd go by... the gourd dipper that hung by the old oaken bucket at the well-sweep repeated in stars against the northern sky — and a high piercing plaint

> Foller de drinkin'-gou'd!
> Foller de drinkin'-gou'd!

Two or three years ago I found the other end of that tag of memory in a volume of Texas folklore. The song itself was a cipher by very simplicity concealed, of the long trail taken by runaway slaves, bearing north by the star pointer of the drinking-gourd, picking up the way marks of creeks and rivers toward the stations of the Underground. Susie would tell the children about that; later there was a house in town where they used to play among closets and passages dedicated to that illegal use. Once Mary had pointed out to her, in the town square of a Saturday afternoon, a limping man who was said to have got his game leg in an effort to stop the transportation of a group of such runaways, but though she often looked for him, she never again succeeded in identifying him. The significance of the drinking-gourd song was probably explained at the time it was heard, but only the feeling of it lingered — the *beau geste* of the Middlewest, the high romance of succor.

Looking back I can see that all the really important things had happened, or began to happen — all this song and story and the I-Mary episode, and the discovery that Mother did not like to be leaned on by her, and that the little bird hopped in her mind more freely when Pa was in the room — by the time Mary was five, or at the most 'going-on' six.

And then God happened to Mary under the walnut tree.

When I first wrote of how Mary went down to the walnut tree at
the bottom of the orchard,[13] as she did in Experiences Facing
Death, Mary-by-herself, and felt herself in the bee and the bee in
the flower and the flower in God, I put her years at seven, but I
know now it couldn't have been. At seven, Mary was in the fourth
grade at school, and the winter after she had a ticket to the circulating library, and was walking a mile each way every day to
school. But at the time of the adventure of what was afterward
called 'The Practice of the Presence of God,' she went timidly for
the first time alone to the bottom of the orchard; it was the first
clear recollection of the way the land lay between her house and
Rinaker's Hill, which was farther away than it ever seemed again.
Another marker for the date is the experience about to be related,
wherein the God-of-the-Bible, who, in that early time, was not yet
identified with the God the little bird sang about, had not yet issued as a tribal bugaboo, who might be, and frequently in your
own interest was, circumvented, as I shall describe. That couldn't
have happened until after the practice of spending Sunday at
Grandpa's — which, in a good Scotch-Presbyterian way familiar
to his youth, began Saturday night — had been established. And
that didn't happen until after Mary had begun to go regularly to
school at six. So that the very latest that Mary's religious experience could have dated would, by the evidence of the wild foxglove,
be late June of the summer of half-past five.

All the years that they lived at the end of Plum Street, after the
fall of '74, whenever the weather permitted, the two older Hunter
children were sent to Grandpa's Saturday night as a preparation
for early morning Sunday School. The rest of the family came in
to the sermon at eleven, and after midday dinner at Grandpa's,
there would be 'visiting' — all the Duggers were great visitors —
and, in the afternoon, hymn-singing in the parlor with Aunt Effie
at the piano and Grandpa playing the flute. The children were
expected to stay to the morning sermon, and I recall a game of 'I
saw it first' invented by Mary and Jennie to get them through its
intolerable boredom. The rules of the game were that you began
with the choir and worked down the congregation, choosing what

you saw in the way of personal adornment, feather, or ribbon or brooch, which for the rest of the week became the prototype of 'dressing-up' plays, and of those truly enchanting structures of hickory leaves pinned together with thorns and adorned with what you had, which occupied long summer afternoons to build. The choosing had to be done noiselessly, but I think always honestly, and of course you had the privilege of bestowing choice selection on Ellen and Suze Cogan, by whom they were gratefully received. Not that the young Cogans had not a church of their own to go to, but the Cogans were Cath'lics, and it is well known that *they* always have to keep standing up and sitting down and kneeling and reciting, so that there is practically no time for making up games about the congregation. Besides, the priest wouldn't like it. But for little Methodists there was simply nothing provided by way of getting through church without making a disturbance.

The item of Sunday observance which made the sharpest impression on Mary was Sunday morning prayers at Grandpa's. They were always held in the parlor, and Grandpa invariably read a chapter out of the Book of Revelation, while you sat on the haircloth sofa with your feet hanging over, sliding, sliding, and hitching back, which if you happened to be wearing your thin summer clothing was an unpleasant experience. Mary, who was always under the compulsion, through the magic of words, to listen to any kind of reading no matter what it was about, hated the Heaven of the Book of Revelation. It had streets of gold, which you know in reason must be hard to walk about on barefoot, as angels are always shown doing; there was only one tree there; and there was a huge beast on the throne, with seven heads, which couldn't be gratifying to look at. To cap all, you spent your time there playing on harps, and since the only harps Mary knew anything about were called 'juice-harps' (Jews' harps), which she couldn't play on, anyway, Heaven sounded more boring than church. Above everything, Mary wanted to avoid going to Heaven f'reveranever; but how to manage it when you were already committed by your parents through baptism!

In the course of time, the fear of Heaven became an articulate worry in which the Cogans were invited to participate. The Cogans knew that there were other places to go to, like Fairyland and Purgatory — but how to get there? Suze was of the opinion that Heaven could be easily escaped by doing something wicked, the wickedest thing you could think of — Well, what? Suze was convinced that it was saying the Mass backward; but how could a Methodist child, who did not even know it frontward, say Mass the other way about? For wild moments Mary even contemplated becoming a Cath'lic herself, but beside the fact that Cath'lics also went to Heaven, she suspected that she wouldn't be let. After a good deal of serious confabulation, the Lord's Prayer was settled upon in lieu of the Mass, but saying it backward without a mistake proved beyond anybody's utmost endeavor. You got around that at last by saying it straight while walking backward around the tree fetish down by the pond. After which you clinched matters by reciting in concert three times as the wickedest word you knew, The Devil, The Devil, The Devil.... After that peace descended on Mary's soul; she positively would not be allowed in the Heaven of Revelation.

In order, however, that you may not suppose that a life lived in a religious mode too instinctive for exposition is in any way associated with priggishness, it remains to set down the one obdurate naughtiness of Mary's youth. She *would* listen to reading, whether it was intended she should or not. The sound of words flowing in patterns of suggested significance drew her as clover scent draws bees. To this day nothing rests her so completely from the professional struggle to force English words to render up the last translucent drop of meaning as hearing Greek drama even tolerably pronounced, and no aphrodisiac stirs like the smooth sound of the 'Divina Commedia' in Dante's original. So, when Mary heard her mother reading Father to sleep evenings after his asthma had been bad or the pain in his leg insistent, nothing would keep her from creeping out of her bed across the hall, and crouching at the crack of Mother's door — always left ajar lest the children should need her — listening. Too many times she was spanked awake when Mother made a last round before the lights were out and found her asleep there. But nothing, no remonstrance, no penalties, would prevent her for more than a night or two from returning to the siren sound.

It was absurd, because she seldom understood what she heard. It was disobedient; it was charged with mysterious possibilities of 'catching her death' on the bare floor in her thin nightie, but listen she would, and only her cleverness in getting back to bed before sleep quite overcame her put an end to the parental quarrel. After George became 'the baby' and the responsibilities of elder sister were forced on Mary by the alarming increase of her Father's ill health, the forbidden vigils ceased along with the night readings which gave rise to them. There came a time when Mary was glad to cover her head with the bedclothes and plunge drowningly into oblivion of the sound of her father's crutch clumping back and forth in the room across the hall, to the strangled gasps of excruciating pain.

What makes Mary's delinquencies stand out against the general sum of family misbehavior was the, on the whole, exemplary conduct of the other members. If Jennie ever did anything that the most captious parent could take exception to, I can't recall it. When George, Jr., came along, Mary herself, in elder-sisterly fashion so protected and excused him that other people seldom got to hear of his naughtiness. And as for Jim, who got himself into trouble quite as frequently as other boys of his age, he had a way of extricating himself that was so much in the mode of parental preferences that he seemed somehow always the gainer by it. Jim could never bear to be at odds with anyone. He confessed at the drop of a hat, took his punishment, wept copiously and made up. After these emotional reconciliations with his mother — Mother always wept too when Jim had been severely naughty — the air of chastened virtue in which he went about afterward was simply unendurable.

Mary admitted things, without confessing; that is, she admitted wrongdoing on the basis of having thought it out and taken her chances, which probably wasn't always the case; and she seldom repented. There is scarcely any accounting for these things, but

the truth about Mary is that she seemed to have been born with a
bias against the emotional treatment of what might be called
moral problems. Yes, she had taken off her shoes and stockings
and gone wading in the Branch, when Mother said not, but Mother
had simply said the water was too cold, and when Mary felt of it,
it was as warm as it ever was when the children were allowed to go
wading; if she was to be punished for it, she 'sposed she'd have to
stand it. As a matter of fact, she wasn't punished for it as often as
she deserved. That was where I-Mary came in. If punishment did
not follow sharply on the act, if Mary went upstairs to meditate on
her misdeeds, it allowed time for that swift interior turning, like the
way you do when the wind blows your skirts about and you have to
whirl right about to bring them to place again, and there was
I-Mary, against whose complete detachment from the event
Susie, who never punished her children because she wanted to, but
from a sense of duty, was generally helpless.

What neither Mary nor her mother realized was that the detachment was hardily secured, not to avoid punishment, but to
evade the felt falsity of the forced emotional situation. There was
an identical attitude in the little squabbles between the brothers
and sisters, of which the young Hunters had the normal number.
Mary would never 'kiss and make up,' not even or especially when
Brother Jim had been worked up to the magnanimous admission of
its being his fault, as in fact it frequently was. 'I don't see,' said
Mary, 'why I have to kiss him just because you know we've had a
fight. We have lots of them that you don't know about.'

'Well, then,' Susie, in extremity would have to retort, 'we'll see
what your father has to say about it.'

Father always let you know that he was displeased when you
made Mother unhappy. 'And besides,' he would say, 'if you don't
take your punishment, how are you ever going to learn to behave?'

'Well, then,' said Mary, 'you punish me' — which, as a matter of
fact, he almost never did.

Looking back I can see now that the distinction of moral attitudes between brother and sister, which widened with the years,
was that Jim had been early taken with the emotional acceptance

of a current psychological pattern on which Christian ethics of the
time were based. Commandment and prohibition were valid for
him as given; if he had been forbidden to go into the water; that
the water turned out to be fine had nothing to do with it. He was
'tempted,' yielded, and later, convicted of sin, repented and was
reconciled. But Mary was a born pragmatist. 'Grace,' for her,
was an inward condition, *bestowed*, not achieved. Grown up, Jim,
more or less, abandoned the pattern for his private conduct, but it
remained for him, as still largely in middle-class America, the criterion of judgment for other people's behaviors. He never got over
feeling that his sister's rejection of the emotional basis of moral
judgments was, in some obscure way, reprehensible.

VII

MARY was started to school at five and a half, six months before she was legally entitled to it, a difficulty easily got around by a City Magistrate. Jim had duly entered at six, and the only reason I have ever heard offered for putting Mary ahead so was that, after a winter rendered companionless in this fashion, her mother did not know, when the spring opened, what on earth to do with her.

I have often wondered why it never occurs to those bright young men who write books about what is the matter with American Education, and American Intellectual Life generally, to describe what has happened in terms of the Great American Renunciation of the nursery governess and nursery help of every description. In Mary's time, families were beginning to be not so large as in Polly McAdams's and Grandmother Hannah's, and the recession of pioneer exigencies which made it practicable to keep an eye on all the brood at once by making them partners in household enterprises, and the introduction of longer-time schooling for elder sisters, had left the youngsters in evil case. There was, as one frequently heard said, 'nothing else to do with them' but crowd them into the schoolroom as early as possible, to begin these incredible sessions of desk-sitting and the stultification of young intelligence by hours of mock business, occasionally punctuated by boring recitations. Even as late as the eighteen-nineties, when Mary taught school herself, mothers devoid of all resources of 'help' remonstrated at having the first and second grades turned out of school as early as three in the afternoon. On being told that the extra hour of fresh air and sunlight was necessary to growth and health, they sighed and said, 'Well, at least when they were in school, I knew where they were.'

It was probably some such argument that led to Mary's being set out in April of 1874 with her little tin bucket of cold and not very digestible lunch, to be enrolled, after a daily mile-long walk, in the first grade of the public school under Miss Becky Snow. Miss

Becky was a teacher of reputation; she had seen half the young people of the town through their letters and managed somehow not to have them hate her. Years afterward, when Miss Becky had retired to a little white house in a little yard full of flowers, she and Mary became greatly interested in each other, in spite of what I have yet to relate.

Mary was entered for the chart class, which means that she was not expected yet to have a book, no educational paraphernalia other than a diminutive slate and pencil, with which, by the aid of a minimum of marching and singing, and 'recess' and nooning, you were to get blamelessly through with seven hours of unanticipated dullness. Twice a day the chart class was called up and confronted with a pasteboard sheet on which appeared an assorted lot of syllables, words with meanings being judged beyond the mentality of first-year scholars. Mary stood up with her class and said *A-b, Ab, B-o, Bo,* and so on; the only other relief being to go to the blackboard and print the day's lesson, which in Mary's case was generally done backward.

The sole alleviation to boredom was that she sat with Minnie Farrell, and that was curious, because although she had no recollection of Minnie, Mary knew at once that there was an old friendship between them. Minnie had been in the first grade long enough to have learned the permissible alleviations of boredom. You could, for instance, if you did not show yourself too negligent of lessons, which you were supposed to con from the chart with moving lips between recitations, look at pictures. Minnie was well furnished with books of the sort that might be condoned by Miss Becky as of educative value, though just how she managed that with a book of 'Three Bears' and 'Snow White,' I have forgotten. What neither Minnie nor Mary herself, nor any member of her family realized was that Mary could read easy words, words of one syllable, that interested her. No doubt she had milked Brother Jim dry of information as to the meaning of print; probably the quality of high visualization for the symbols of sounds which was always hers had something to do with it — she could always use sounds as figures of speech even though she had not sufficient tone discrimination to carry a tune. So she absorbed the stories of 'Snow White' and 'Three Bears' without in the least realizing that to be able to do just that was chiefly what she had come to school to learn. And one day she was caught at it. She had forgotten to go to chart class to say *A-b*, *Ab*, and before she knew it, there was Teacher standing over her.

'What are you doing, Mary?' Miss Becky demanded.

'Reading,' whispered Mary from a dry throat.

'Oh, no, Mary, you can't read; you are only in the chart class; to say you can read when you can't is a story.' There it was again! But to have it said in the presence of thirty or forty of your contemporaries, who would tell everybody else at recess, called for defending.

'I can, too, Miss Snow, I can ——'

'No, Mary.'

'I *can!*'

'Little girls who tell fibs in school must wear the dunce cap.'

For those whose memories do not go back so far, the dunce cap was a tall paper cone, to be worn in the presence of the whole school, at which it is the privilege of the whole school to laugh. There were two or three ways of wearing the dunce cap: with stoicism; miserably with shamed tears; or by the help of 'funny faces,' when the teacher's back was turned, as a huge joke. Mary had not been in school long enough to know the acceptable behavior. Standing there, book in hand as the symbol of her particular venality, not knowing what else to do, she finished her story. And while she was about it, who should come in with that swift, light-stepping manner of principals, but Xerxes Xenophon Crum. He was a pleasant gentleman with a handsome whisker, and he made a point of inquiring what the little dunce had done.

'Telling a fib. Pretending she can read...'

Right in front of Principal! But it is unwise to push a sensitive child beyond the limit of submission.

'I can.' Mary announced; 'I'm reading now.'

Miss Becky began to get very red in the face.

'That's easily proved,' said the principal. 'Read.'

Miss Becky got redder. 'She probably knows it by heart.'

Xerxes Xenophon called for a first reader. Everybody knows that even over in the back of the book, McGuffey's First contains nothing more erudite than such literary gems as

> I love to see a little dog
> And pat him on the head,
> How beaut-i-fully he wags his tail
> When-ev-er he is fed.

Mary simply sailed through it. With the result that Principal Crum gathered her up, with her lunch-pail, her diminutive slate, and her straw hat, and deposited her in Room Two. For this term she remained until the end, and was automatically shifted at the beginning of next year, when Mary was properly of school age, to Room Three, where she met Ann Cameron, and was involved in the necessity of studying 'gogafy.'

Mary's more than ordinary verbal memory was the source of more than a little educational misadventure. She was always being promoted beyond her years, on the basis of her reading achievement, so that her penmanship was a subject for ridicule, and arithmetic a hopeless muddle for years, thus confirming the popular opinion that people who are particularly 'smart' in one direction are subject to a compensating stupidity in others. The circumstance of her having taught herself reading by the word method undoubtedly had something to do with her being what is called a poor speller. Heywood Broun, who should know, if anybody, what is requisite for literary success, went so far as to name her among the half-dozen worst spellers of his acquaintance, which he generously extenuated as being a trait common to geniuses. What Mr. Broun didn't know is, that if Mary were given a chance to stand up with her arms folded, with the toe of one foot hooked about the other ankle, eyes half-shut, with a swaying motion, she could probably spell down a whole row of columnists. For Mary knows very well how to spell spelling; she learned it out of Saunders's blue spelling book. What nobody ever taught her was how to spell writing.

It was while she was in Room Four, between seven and half-past, that one of the other girls brought to school, and carried away again before Mary had had time to read more than a chapter or two, a book that sent her home breathless with excitement. A book about a girl named Alice and a White Rabbit. 'An' Alice went down the rabbit hole... an' ate something... an' the girl had a round comb like mine, an' please, Pa, couldn't I have it? (Most Middlewestern children stopped saying Papa and Mama when they started to school and began saying Pa and Ma). 'Oh, *couldn't* I?'

'By Jove, Susie' — Pa's eyes were shining — 'she really has been reading it. Alice, you know... Lewis Carroll. We'll have to get it for her.' Ma had a look you perfectly understood, a can't-afford-it look. So many things made her look that way. 'When she is older, perhaps. I can't think it good for children to read so many fairy stories.' You'd heard that before, but this time you thought something would give way inside you. 'I've got a dime in my bank, and Grandpa always gives me a nickel when I know the Golden Text...' but you realized it was no use. You might have cried except that the very idea that you might never be able to go down that rabbit hole after Alice was beyond the use of tears. Pa took you on his knee after supper and read you 'Pilgrim's Progress' in words of one syllable, which was a way of saying, without contradicting anybody, that he didn't think you read too many fairy stories. And the next evening or two after, he came home twinkling in a way that was ordinarily a prelude to surprises in his pockets, which, when searched on this occasion, revealed a small gray book of Alice, the veritable child. Pa opened the back of the book and showed Mary her own name and the stamp of the circulating library... a ticket of her own, good for two books a week!

'But books that Jim can read too; not just fairy stories,' Mother interpolated. She came back to that for years, when it was necessary to account for the queerness of the ideas that came into Mary's head. 'I always *did* think,' said Mother, 'that you were allowed to read too many fairy stories.'

The stipulation about Jim's sharing the ticket proved no curtailment of entertainment. Mother usually selected his share for him, and read it aloud to the other children, which was so much to the good. The only one I recall was 'My Apingi Kingdom,' on account of the gorillas. Besides, it was not more than two or three years later that Mary secured a blackmailing hold over her brother's choice, by discovering his private cache of literature between the cleats of a trunk in his room, large enough to conceal two or three at a time of the thin volumes Jim Valentine lent him. They were called Beadle's Dime Novels, all about Old Grizzly the Bear-Tamer, Deadwood Dick, and another redskin biting the dust. I can't recall that these books were absolutely interdicted; I think it unlikely that either of Mary's parents had ever any further acquaintance with them than came of seeing them on display at news-stands, but the general aura of disapprobation was over the entire field of 'Wild' Westernness. It was supposed to have a bad effect on boys, influencing them to leave home, to chew tobacco, and to be unduly interested in firearms. But Jim needn't have submitted to blackmail, since besides having a rooted objection to 'telling on' other people, Mary enjoyed dime novels too much herself to have imperiled the source of supply.

Another incident of Mary's fourth year at school deserves to be set down if only for the benefit of those whose business it is to realize the choice of the soul of childhood, most of whom could do with more knowledge of it than they now possess. In Mary's school, the excellent old fashion of Friday afternoon 'exercises' was kept up, by means of recitations, dialogues, and singing; all of social grace and critical endeavor provided by the educational system of the times. Mary, by reason of her omnivorous memory, always shone on these occasions, and it was on a day when her own selection had been 'The Lady of Shalott,' that the memorable incident occurred. There was a new Principal for the school, and for that day he had elected to visit Room Four, where everybody, including Teacher, was showing off.

'And now, Mary,' said Teacher, 'suppose you tell us what your piece means.' There she had you. You hadn't supposed up to that time that poetry had been expected to mean anything in particular. 'The Lady of Shalott' you had chosen for its glittering figures, its smoothly swinging movement of rhyme and meter. You got red about the ears because, although you felt sure that none of the others knew any more about the meaning of poetry than you did, and knew quite as well as you did that Teacher was showing off before the new Principal, if they found you caught at a disadvantage, they would titter. 'Don't you think,' said Teacher, in that tone of the Stooping Lady, which children so loathe, 'that when you recite a piece, you ought to know what it means?' Mary swallowed several large marbles in her throat, but she was not ever easily daunted.

'I learned it because I liked it,' she said. The rest of the room did begin to titter. Until the voice of the Principal stopped it. 'I like it too,' he said; 'Tennyson is my favorite author.' It was Teacher's turn to be embarrassed, but Mary wasn't thinking of that; she was busily conning the saving phrase that it might not be forgotten. My favorite author! It was her first time of hearing it, but she knew what it meant. She knew precisely on what compensating occasions she would be able to use it.

VIII

THE business of going to school appreciably widened the known world. There were three ways of getting there and home again; straight up Plum to Second South, which you usually took in company with Pa, on his way to the office, between the brickyard and the Catholic Cemetery, past a gullied thicket where in the spring there were blossoming haws and wild crab-apples, with bluebells under them — there is no wonder in the world like a wild crab tree coming rosily out between tiny bracts of green — and blazing crimson sumach in the fall.

Beyond Cemetery Hill there was a deep clayey gully, across from which the Lancasters still live, and another hill at the top of which stood a general store kept by a German — Roseman — was that the name? There were Indian baskets for sale there in Mary's time, bundles of wild herbs and roots, and huddled in among unfamiliar German sausages and cheeses, quaint wooden implements — looms and cards for wool — not purchasable at that time anywhere else, and now gone even from memory. A block or two farther on there was a log house that stood, for as long as the Hunter children went that way, deep in an acre or so of bluebells. For Mary the rest of the street was beautified by charming little brick houses, bright red with white trimming, as clean and tidy as German thrift could make them, and across the intersecting streets a view of the German Catholic Church, which might have been carved out of wood with a broad knife to accompany a Noah's ark town, the absolute example of its architectural style. That church was Mary's first association with the appreciations inherent in the word, and one of the first things she went to see, returning to the home town after forty years.

Another way which you oftenest took going home from school was down South Broad, past a block or two of the 'best residences,' past the Lutheran Church and more red brick, and by a less built-up section of broken hills and gullies. There you had, inaccessibly across a tangle of gardens, a glimpse of the City Cemetery, so far from its gate, facing another street, that it was years before you actually came upon the cluster of graves visible from South Broad, to find there, unaccountably, reminders of your own widely named clan. Curiously, though you know what it was, perhaps because the hour of going home often brought athwart white headstones on the slope a lovely late gleam, it was never a grave-yard, but a city of romance, seen afar by a wandering knight, whose story Mary used to spin to the other children sitting there to rest midway of the road home.

The Morans, who lived in Irish Row, deserve a passing mention, as providing one of the way stations on that road to the land of books for which Mary as a child was always setting out and, for lack either of knowledge or direction, seldom arriving. There were two Moran sisters, Sally and Grace, of whom Sally went into a convent and thrilled Mary tremendously by writing her several letters during her novitiate. Their father, 'Jack' Moran, was a type of red-headed Irish gentry, more often found in those days than now, an omnivorous reader, a congenital orator, and, when well lit with corn whiskey, a fiery blasphemer who used up the energies of his wife and his wife's sister, praying him out of the condemnation he so incurred. On a large table in the Moran parlor, covered with a Paisley shawl, there were more and hand-somer books than Mary ever saw elsewhere; they were the only really well-bound books she ever saw, and not at all readable — she tried all of them — except in a single instance which you shall presently hear.

Going to Grandpa's, as you did when the weather was too bad for the walk home, was of itself something of an adventure. You were allowed to sleep in Aunt Effie's room and assist at the mys-teries of a young lady's toilet. And there was always the possibil-ity that, besides being allowed to stand at Grandpa's elbow, he might put out his hand and cover yours, while Aunt Effie sang at the piano:

Soon beyond the harbor bar
Shall my bark be sailing far.
Where art thou my guiding star,
Sweet Belle Mahone!

It was rather interesting to be a little afraid of anybody you loved as much as Mary did Grandpa. She worked him endless perforated cardboard book-markers, and learned whole chapters of the Bible by heart, to recite to him, happy if, when everybody was talking so that nobody noticed, she could lean against his shoulder, which did not shift subtly away from her. Sometimes, grinning shyly, he slipped peppermints to her or licorice root or cinnamon drops. That was because he was Scotch. After Mary read 'Scottish Chiefs,' she thought it romantic to have a Scotch grandfather. In one of her excursions to the fields she found what Father said was a Scotch harebell, which she dug up and planted in a pot. Mary had a way of taking it for granted that other people felt about things as she did. When Grandpa kept the pot in the window until the harebell actually bloomed, it never occurred to her it was simply because he was the gentlest-hearted old darling that ever lived, who wouldn't for anything have hurt the child's feelings. She always thought that it was completely established between them that it was on account of their both being Scotch.

Later, when he offered a prize of five dollars to the one of his grandchildren who would first read the Bible through, Mary bored everybody in the family to death, keeping up with the condition that somebody should be able to vouch for the reading. Susie had to make prohibitive ruling that chance visitors shouldn't be asked if they didn't want to hear Mary read a chapter aloud. In the winter that Mary was between nine and ten, she finished it. I forget what Mother did with the money; it was enough that now Grandpa would be able to say, 'My granddaughter Mary has read the Bible *all through*.'

It was during that summer that Grandpa Graham presented each of his daughters with a Singer sewing machine. Susie's children were enormously impressed to see her sit down courage-

ously, albeit with a slightly apprehensive look, to be taught by the
agent to run it; exactly the same look under which Mary taught
her, twenty years later, to use a telephone. And that is why, first
and last, you will hear a great deal of cooking in this book. That
Mary's gift for it was the only one which her family never quarreled with her about is not the chief reason for its inclusion here;
but because it remained, for the period in which her literary gift
was incubating, the sole art which she could happily practice, as
well as the only tangible souvenir she could afford, of the pioneer
period in the history of which she reveled. It was the one art still
persisting in a social complex whose final triumph over the impossible was signalized by a rapid recession from all that the frontier
implied.

Most of the furniture that Mary saw was genuinely good.
Almost everybody had a few good pieces, a sofa or a table. There
was a Seth Thomas clock which, when the house on Plum Street
passed from their possession, Mother sold for a dollar and a quarter,
and which Mary wept not to be able to retain — 'That old junk!'
said Susie, never guessing that the painted glass in the clock door,
of an early American home with the family out in front, had for
Mary the associative value of a family portrait. Years afterward
in New York, she saw one like it at a price she could as little afford
as she could a dollar and a quarter when she was ten years
old.

But cooking recipes were something anybody could collect.
Besides, when you were learning to do them the mind of the teacher
would turn back and resuscitate old tales that went with the dish —
weddings, christenings, wakes. As late as Mary stayed in Macoupin, which was 1888, there were still country neighborhoods where
pie was served for breakfast, four deep — every housewife prided
herself on her special combination. I recall Mrs. Towse's arrangement as having the groundwork of a philosophy of dietetics. She
would begin with something substantial, like mince, or dried
apples with honey and nutmeg; something tart, like plums or
sliced lemon with currants; something luscious, like strawberry or
raspberry; topped off with pumpkin or lemon cream or cheese

custard. You cut down through all four, your size slice. I recall houses where pumpkin pie was two inches thick and served with a great gob of new comb honey.

This was all that kept the artist's feeling for craft, for the perfection of technique, going in Mary until she happened on Indians who could teach her something of the inner meaning of art.

It was really only in the matter of moral attitudes that Mary came into anything like conflict with her time. Mary was born convinced that there oughtn't to be any such thing as moral attitudes. Morals, yes! things you should or shouldn't do on sufficient reason; but why take up attitudes about it? Having a moral attitude meant being emotional about those things, thinking worse or better of people on their account; getting praised yourself or blaming somebody else.

IX

WHEN people began to ask how early Mary first had a notion that she might write, Mother said carelessly, 'Oh, as soon as she could talk,' which goes to show how unreliable family anecdotes are. The first public announcement of her intention which Mary recalls, as her father used to relate, came much later than that, probably the summer she was seven. She could read a little and she had already learned that live people write books and get paid for them. I am sure that she learned that from 'St. Nicholas,' which Pa began to bring home with the first number, and never missed. And at the same time it was while Mary was still so small that she had to have a chair to climb up to Pa's table-topped desk.

Mary liked sitting on Pa's desk when he worked — he often wrote papers there to read at the Grange or the Horticultural Society — which she had leave to do so long as she didn't interrupt. She sat perfectly and quietly happy, looking at books; even when she couldn't read them, it gave her an interested feeling just to look at books — shelves of them going up higher than she could reach. I know what she was looking at that day, because it was one of her favorites, Ben Jonson's Complete Works. There were a number of Complete Works on Father's shelves, Burns and Shakespeare, but Mary liked Ben Jonson because it was bound in red with a tracery of gold; the print was large, almost like the First Reader, and it was written in talk. This, too, was something she had learned from 'St. Nicholas' — that there is a special way of writing the way people talk; Pa would read one part and you would read the other; you hadn't to read it more than two or three times before you had it by heart. Mary could read a little of Ben Jonson, as when somebody said 'Yes, my Lord,' or 'Go, sirrah,' or 'Odds bodkins,' or whatever it was people said in Ben Jonson. She had been reading a little, and then in an interval, when Pa seemed not to be working, she said out of whole cloth, 'Will you leave me all your books, Pa, when you die?' (It couldn't have been so very

GEORGE STERLING, MARY AUSTIN, JACK LONDON, AND JAMES HOPPER
(See pages 297–301*)*

long before he did die, though nobody suspected it, so perhaps that might have been the little bird hopping.)

'Well, that depends. Why do you want them?'

'I will sell them and live on the money until I write a book my own self.' You can see this couldn't have been the first time she had thought about it.

'Well, of course, for anything so important as that' — Father began to twinkle the way he had — 'What kind of books do you mean to write?'

'All kinds,' said Mary with large impartiality, and she never understood why, when Pa related this conversation, which he did on several occasions in her presence, people always laughed. Mary had not yet heard the popular superstition that you can only do one kind of thing, and that to suppose yourself capable of doing more is to get yourself suspected of conceit.

It couldn't have been much after this that she actually began. She wrote poetry with illustrations.

She was perfectly explicit herself on the point of its being poetry; to the great entertainment of the family, because it neither jingled nor rhymed. On the matter of rhyming the young author was proof against attack, because by that time she knew whole pages of 'Hiawatha' by heart, and not a rhyme in it. But though Mary herself could dance to her poetry, waving her arms about, there was no good pretending that it jingled. Then there were the illustrations. Father had wanted his children to draw, wanted it badly enough to send all the way to London for a book that was supposed to teach young people how to sketch. There was a series of drawings in various stages of incompletion of the church at Stratford-on-Avon, which Mary faithfully copied so many times that she recognized it instantly when May Sinclair, hoping to surprise her, drove her down there for lunch from Stow-on-Wold, more than forty years later. But unfortunately the book omitted to tell how you could make real drawings in Macoupin. Father could not draw landscapes, but he could draw with a pencil pictures that made you want to laugh, of Cogan's dog, Old Man Sauls, Horace Greeley. You could tell who they were, although they were always funnier than the real people. That was the trouble with Mary's illustrations to her poems; they were somehow funny, even when she felt them seriously. Perhaps because the one thing she recognizably did learn to draw, besides Avon Church spire, was Horace Greeley. She copied Father's drawing until, to this day, when she sits down to wait for a telephone call, where other people draw triangles and squares, Mary as often as not draws Horace.

As a matter of fact, two or three years before she was able to write even absurdly, Mary's literary effort was begun in the half-remembered, half-invented tales with which she entertained the other children. These were flagrantly popular in tone, shaped to the demand of her audience, for adventures in which they could recognizably participate, well punctuated with shivers and satisfactions suited to their years. Almost all that she knows about short-story-telling, all except what the Indians taught her, Mary learned sitting in the midst of a haymow, of a hot summer's afternoon, or around the rim of the old rock quarry, with several pairs of feet dangling in the cool shaded water, or while the corn popped over open fires and the snow flew outside with a soft damping swish against the window-panes. Even yet Mary meets fireside groups demanding a story 'such as you used to tell Mother' (or Grandmother!) involving everybody's favorite adventure.

In May, 1877, there appeared in St. Nicholas a short-story version of 'Ivanhoe,' which appealed to Mary as the most entrancing story of her experience. Said Father, 'I hope you will read all of Scott when you are older,' the sort of thing it was never safe to say to Mary unless you expected it to happen. Just how long it was before she discovered a complete set of Scott on the center table at Moran's, I do not know, probably no longer than it took her to learn to note such things; 'The Works of Walter Scott, Bart. Complete with Footnotes and Appendix,' bound in tan cloth with gold tooling, after the fashion of well-printed English books. The paper was thin, the print fine, and the footnotes and appendix ran all around the pages in still finer print, like lace-edged ruffles on a dress. Father, who was consulted on the expediency of asking Mr. Moran to lend you 'Ivanhoe' out of his lot, was of the opinion that it was 'too old' for you. So Mary confessed; 'I've already read "Lady of the Lake." ' This she had turned up on the top shelf of Father's bookcase, and had been afraid to ask permission to read lest it be interdicted, so she had read it anyway to be safe. Besides, it was as easy as anything, words of one syllable almost — 'The stag at eve had drunk his fill' — she could say whole passages of it right off.

On which showing, 'Ivanhoe' was borrowed and brought home. How the child ever got through with it, I can't imagine. Father read much of it aloud, and abridged whole paragraphs with explanation, which Mary faithfully went over alone, making wide guesses at the unpronounceable words. She also read the notes and the appendix. There was the quality of revelation about reading 'Ivanhoe' with-footnotes-and-appendix. What Mary knew after 'Ivanhoe,' completely and absolutely knew, was that she wanted to write books 'with-footnotes-and-appendix.' She wanted to write books that you could walk around in.

By her father's advice, Mary read no more Scott for several years; but from that time she had a criterion: books were either to be walked about in, or 'paper on the wall.' The phrase she probably plucked out of the common speech. Wall-paper had but recently made its way from the genteel East. There was none of it in Mary's house, but Grandpa had it on the parlor, and the year that Mary was born, he began to stock it along with the other oddities of furnishings such as were offered in drugstores of the period. It was the way of people, when they wished to pay a modish compliment, to tell you your clothes fit 'like the paper on the wall'; pasted flat over an artificially firmed outline. It was about this time that 'glove-fitting' corsets came into vogue. What Mary meant by a wall-paper book was one you couldn't walk around in, as you did in 'Alice in Wonderland' or 'Ivanhoe,' with notes.

It is impossible to say, after so many years, to what extent Mary herself associated other experiences — the presence of God under the walnut tree, the Friend in the woods, I-Mary — with the wish and the intention to write. It never occurred to her to speak of these things except occasionally to Sister Jennie. It never occurred to her in those days to wonder if they were experiences peculiar to herself. Later she tried to discover, tried to draw out of her brothers, reminiscence, incident, theory, anything that would have given a clue. That was when they were in their college years and it was then too late. They had both of them acquired emotional and moral biases about all such matters which made of their answers something more or less than the fact. And neither of them really wanted to hear what went on in their sister's mind; perhaps in their college years, brothers never do.

In any case, if Mary had wanted to talk about her intimate experiences, there wouldn't have been any words. Even for religion, which was the one intimate experience Methodists were fond of talking about, the only words they had for them were words of 'feeling.' Certainly she would not have described the I-Mary experience as a feeling. It was a reality, as real as when in dreams you pick up your feet and go floating in the desired direction, as real as when you sat idling at your school desk bright summer mornings and through the upper open third of the window you saw white clouds against the blue, and mysterious trepidation going on in all the upper rooms of the trees, so that presently you lifted and drifted through the window, curved and circled — as you had once — you thought every minute you could recall the trick — you almost had, and suddenly the bell rang or Teacher spoke to you. I-Mary was as real as that. When you were I-Mary, you could see Mary-by-herself as part of the picture, and make her do things that, when you were she, could not be done at all; such as walking a log high over the creek, which gave Mary-by-herself cold prickles even to think about.

It happened to her at that age when there is a necessity upon childhood to invent languages to the significance of which their elders are not privy, such as the much-prized 'dog-latin' of pre-adolescent days, that she found herself in possession of a language which the elders actually did *not* understand. She knew very well where she got it; it was the language spoken by talking animals in dreams, at the age when children do dream of talking animals. It came oftenest to Mary when she would be chased down a dark way of the woods, in terror of pursuing feet and almost devouring jaws, which she would escape by remembering the speech just in time. It seemed a much more sensible speech than the prevailing iggery-uggery jargon of one's schoolmates, and she taught it therefore to Minnie Farrell, who wrote down most of it in the back of her spelling book, in order that, one by one, privileged playmates might be initiated.

Years after, they discovered that the secret speech, though spelled phonetically in English, was recognizably German in structure. I should have said that, at that time in most Middlewestern schools, German was taught. All the Hunter children at about the age of twelve, which was *after* their 'dog-latin' days, when they were nine or ten, had had lessons with Professor Witte, whom nobody who studied with him ever forgets. But when the girls set about uncovering the direct German parentage of their secret language, they could find nothing nearer than the circumstance that, during the first two and a half years of Mary's life, her father had been having a teacher come to the house on First South Street to practice conversational German with him, *and never at any other time.*

In her tenth year suddenly Mary began upon a serious piece of writing, the initial impulse to which has been so completely lost, the plot so blurred, so little related to current reality, that I suspect it of being not so much a creation as a partial recovery of something heard and forgotten, floated up to the surface of a mind beginning faintly to be stirred by pre-adolescent activity. It was written in verse, verse that this time rhymed, and had a progressive rhythm like the movement of slow chimes, and for theme and story was entirely outside the dimension of Mary's experience. The composition, as far as Mary got with it, had no title. She called it 'A Play to be Sung,' and where in her Middle-

western, Methodist small town she could have found out that
there are such things as plays written to be sung, I do not know.
That she could never have heard the word 'opera,' I feel as certain
as that she could never have seen one.

At her age Mary could have had no experience of dramatic
entertainment other than the Friday afternoon 'dialogues' with
which all children were familiar. Young children were not expected to attend evening entertainments, and at the distance the
Hunters lived from town, with a baby always keeping Ma at
home, and with Pa's ill health, the children had only twice been
able to attend the Christmas Eve entertainment at the Methodist
Church, and were once taken to a traveling magician's show at
the Courthouse Hall, rather against Ma's consent than with it.
Two scenes of Mary's play as they might have appeared in the
stage of that time are still vivid, and with this singularity, that,
whereas the remembered pictures from dreams or from made-up
stories have a way of fading out irregularly all around, these scenes
have sharp edges and square corners surrounded with blackness,
as pictures might have, or true stage memories. The setting is a
castle with a conical-topped round tower at one end and a squarish
bulk, such as is known, I believe, as a 'keep,' at the other. In the
first scene the walls rise directly from the level of a garden, and
from the tower window a lady leans and sings several verses about
a garden, which are in reality directions for her lover, who is
stealing through the park below, toward her lighted window.
Every stanza ends with the refrain:

Come softly under my window and I will unbar to thee.

But whether he did or she did, I have now no recollection.

The second scene is the front of the same castle, with a terrace
reaching the length of the house, and a lawn below; not a night
scene, but still dim, as it might have been twilight or early morning. The door from the terrace is open and there is the sound of
voices within. Suddenly a sword flies out of the door and a man,
following rapidly, snatches it up from the turf and turns to fight
another who is pursuing him, sword in hand. The two of them

cross swords, and a lady comes out on the terrace and watches, with something of curiosity and cruelty on her face. The costumes are of perhaps the seventeenth century, certainly only such as Mary could have seen in picture books. There is an old man in the story somewhere and a white-faced, lying woman; the whole thing utterly unaccounted for and every way inexplicable. About the whole business, this is singular; that when Mary looked at what is known as Harry Esmond's house at Cliveden (that was in 1908), she was reminded of the 'Play to be Sung,' and again, at a house with two towers, and a connecting terrace, albeit square towers, which May Sinclair showed her near Stow-on-Wold, the scene repeated itself almost as if on the actual stage.

Mary worked on this composition at intervals for two or three years before discarding it. Some fragments of it which turned up years later between the pages of an old arithmetic, which was the device adopted by her for keeping her work finally from family inspection, are still preserved. The versification is far in advance of anything she was capable of for another seven or eight years. But to this day no clue is afforded of the source. One supposes it might have been a half-memory, visualized in a dream, of something overheard on those forbidden occasions when Mary crouched outside the parents' door in her bare feet and flannel nightie so long ago, but what? Would a search of the back numbers of the old 'Scribner's,' 'Harper's,' 'The Century' (whose founding Mary recalls perfectly), or the occasional illustrated London journals which reached Father, have anything to reveal? You may be sure that nothing readable ever came into the house on Plum Street that Mary did not take toll of it.

X

Mary lived in the house at the end of Plum Street until the spring of 1879. During the last two or three years the boundaries of the known world extended themselves yearly to include the whole of Rinaker's Hill, where began that long series of adventures of the Wild, which need not be set down here with too great particularity, since they are precisely the same sort of adventure chronicled in 'The Land of Little Rain' and 'The Land of Journey's Ending.' She was bound to have written something of the kind no matter about what country, for to Mary all places were beautiful and interesting so long as they were outdoors.

There were always for Mary two interchangeable approaches to the mysterious complex called Nature. She could pass by way of the little animal's frisking response to bright airs and warm sun, the incentive of color, the contented hum and lively chirruping of other small creatures, so easily into the little human's appetite for handling and possessing, the delightful plunderability of forest and stream and thicket. At any least, unpreëmpted interval of wading the Branch, of luring crayfish out of their holes, of gathering hazel-nuts or black haws or red, there was always the chance of being caught up into an absorbed contemplation of the mere appearance of things for their own sake; the pattern of a leaf or blossom, the way a shadow falls; the arresting complexity of moss or lichen repeating in fantastic miniature the way that the world of fairy lore repeats the incident of the world as it is; the branching forest, the intricacies of the thicket, the fragility of the flower.

Even in company with the Cogans, Jim Valentine, and such odd companionships as the neighborhood afforded, the children seldom went far into the Bottoms without their elders. There was something attractive about the Bottoms in the early mornings, drenched with dew and alive with the flitter and click of insect hordes, across the thick black mire of which sprang tall purple weeds, clumps of tawny-throated prairie lilies, brush heaps over-run with the scarlet and orange of trumpet vine. Toward noon, however, the air lay heavily on the eyelids, there was a mucky, suffocating smell rising along the slow muddied creeks under tunnels of grapevine and overarching boughs, down which kingfishers darted, and shitepokes rose creakingly, trailing their attenuated legs. Out of the blackest shadows cardinal flowers streaked up like slender torches, and over the glassy surfaces of the creek, wicked heads of water moccasins made noiseless rings. At certain seasons there was good cat-fishing in the Macoupin, and fresh-water mussels with thin pearly shells to be prodded out of the oozy mud with your bare toes.

The happiest excursions to the Bottoms were those on which Father's business took him to the scattered small farms, where pumpkins and watermelons throve amazingly and log-cabin gardens were thick set with old-fashioned flowers, touch-me-nots, kiss-me-quicks, balsam apples, love-in-a-mist, and scarlet runners. Log cabins with antlers over the doors — ('Oh, quickly from yon antlers bring') — with coonskins on the outer walls, hand-turned, corded beds, hickory chairs with 'slippery-ellum' plaited seats, and frequently, in dark corners, ancient looms at which it was possible to observe bent figures sending, almost by the sense of touch, the shuttle to and fro, weaving blankets and rugs that would be shown later at county fairs. Many of the Bottomites still cooked at open fires, well furnished with cranes and bake kettles, and oh, delight! round-pointed johnny-cake (journey cake) boards. Once, when Father had pushed their excursion on to a point where there were Indian mounds, mysteriously arising among mazy creeks, the children were taken raspberrying and afterward at supper regaled with that utterly delectable pioneer dainty 'raspberry slump,' cooked in a deep kettle over an open fire and served with thick cream from the 'spring-house.' Another well-remembered refreshment known as a 'piece,' a general Middlewestern term for between-meals sustenance, of which growing children are so universally in need, consisted of a thick round off a fresh-baked crusty loaf, plentifully spread with the thick sugary residue of the family sorghum barrel — did I say that cane grew succulently in the mucky Bottoms and there were sorghum mills to be visited?

All of a continuity with these early excursions to the Bottoms were the yearly community occasions, such as the Old Settlers' Picnic, at which there would be speech-making, 'yarn'-swapping, singing of old songs such as made a net of sentiment binding up the history of the western world. I recall the gusto with which Cousin George Dugger would lead, eyes half-shut, in complete and happy surrender to the long swing of the melody — melody which had much in common with the Negro spirituals and must have grown out of kindred swellings of fear and the sense of dependence on the God of the dark forest and rolling rivers, great rivers flooding down with long sweeping motions.

There were also Old Soldiers' Reunions, deepening the conviction of a special ethical passion behind the events that they commemorated. There were county fairs with their exhibitions of household arts and — always of more than ordinary interest to Mary, although still beyond her knowing why — the quaint, the tragi-comic gestures toward what could be called the fine arts; wax flowers, picture frames of varnished shells and 'specimens,' perforated cardboard mottoes, 'spatterwork.' Does anybody remember the meticulous arrangement of pressed flowers, ferns and autumn leaves, pinned into place on white cardboard, over which a finely stippled background was 'spattered' with India ink by means of a toothbrush and a fine-toothed comb? Silent and intent, Mary would pass from one to another of these curious perversions of the pioneer feeling for craft, from pieced quilts to tufted counterpanes, to infinitely time-consuming 'mosaics' patched together out of every bright colorful scrap of paper, advertisements from nursery catalogues, from calendar headings and fashion plates, Mary uncritical but inquiring, patiently absorbing their meaning into herself. Oh, it has been easy enough for Mary to gather up public credit for a certain preëminence in judgments of American folk art, the field has been so largely uncontested!

But it is also certain that she spared herself nothing of the process of tuition.

Mary would try over the things noted — she took premiums in the children's department two or three times, once for apple jelly, once for a collection of verbenas from her own garden, and again for some childish collection of wild-wood plunder, I forget what, probably pressed wild flowers. With such material as she could summon, she would attempt the prevailing 'fancy work,' dabbling at it broodingly, and, to her mother's vexation, never bringing anything tangible to pass. But Mary was not really interested in making 'air castles' or 'everything jars.' There was merely a sacred rage in her, a kind of hereditary compulsion upon her to feel out with her hands everything that caught her attention. Once the 'feel of it' was acquired, she had a fine creative contempt for the demand that she produce a 'thing,' in most cases neither useful nor beautiful.

There was one set of community adventures that up and down the Mississippi Valley no one escaped: the plague of fever and ague. It came in, as we supposed, on the dank, slightly fetid air of the Bottoms, and it was thought a merciful act of Providence that its real virulence did not begin until the corn was laid by in August and diminished after the first frost. The little Hunters fevered and shivered with the rest, shivered until their teeth shook, and fevered until their bones ached, and had huge boluses of quinine forced down them with bitter doses of dandelion and calomel and anything that could be imagined of a taste so evil and lingering that the demon of malaria gave up before it. In the course of time, most people gained a sort of immunity to seasonal attacks and a train of consequences lasting on into middle life even more to be dreaded than the alternate fever and shake.

The little Hunters were rather better off than most children of their acquaintance, for Grandpa Graham kept an eye on them and applied the universal timely remedies, although my recollection is that he rather tended to estimate the virtue of remedies on the nastiness of their taste. The Hunter children had toothbrushes, which was by no means general, and they did not wear asafetida around their necks to ward off contagion. They had their regular Saturday baths, but it wasn't until they grew up that they lived in a house with a bathtub. There were people in Carlinville who had tubs, painted tin they were, and gave off when you stepped in them, a sound like stage thunder, but there still lingered in the Middlewest a notion that prevailed in the youth of their parents, that much bathing was unhealthful, since no later than the time of their grandparents, in that hub of American culture, Boston, baths had been forbidden by law except on the advice of a physician. Vaccination was practiced on compulsion, and in a manner that did often constitute it a menace. As for this new disease of diphtheria, nobody knew what to make of it, and appendicitis had not separated itself from the long list of intestinal disorders which went by the general name of cholera. Tight lacing was beginning to be damned along with tobacco and the demon drink. Textbook physiology was introduced into Mary's school the year she was thirteen. Babies continued to be brought in the doctor's black satchel, or picked up under the rosebushes.

On the whole, however, the Hunter children grew up in a liberal and enlightened atmosphere, where race prejudice did not exist, where more and better books were read than was usual, and topics of economic and political interest were discussed. They had not yet found out that their parents were poor, nor did Mary, at least, imagine that there was, within the whole circle of the earth horizon, a more desirable location than the house on Plum Street with its adjacent woods and pastures. There were places she meant to go. England, of course, and Out West, and, for no reason that can be discovered, Boston. Certainly it was clear in her mind, by the time she was ten, that Mary would finally live in Boston; she knew nobody that had lived there, and nothing about it besides what she could learn in Longfellow and Hawthorne's 'Wonder-Book' and 'Tanglewood Tales,' but Boston was always securely on her horizon.

There were also books she meant to read. There was Ben Jonson — Father had already read Burns to her — a book called

'Beauties of Ruskin,' and a book which came late into the field of her attention, called 'Progress and Poverty,' which was something like the Bible, only more important, all of which took their significance from obscure connections with her father's interests. And there was a book which she meant by all means to read on her own account, as soon as she could come by it, a book utterly interdicted, a book which must be read for no other reason than that it would imperil her immortal soul, an experience not to be missed. It was called 'bobingersoll.' You heard people like Uncle Peter and Cousin George Dugger talking about it, the man with the wooden leg (the one who cried at Father's funeral) asking Captain Hunter what he thought about it. With prospects like that, the business of growing up loomed enticingly.

XI

THE world of change began to brood over the household the winter of '77. The new baby, named George, had arrived in August the summer before and had become Mary's the moment he was able to be taken about in the new-fashioned perambulator, which was accepted gladly in a nurseryless land, while in England it was still abhorred as 'tempting the woman to roam,' and even prophetic of the horrid spectacle of a male parent pushing his offspring about. The Hunter children welcomed it as extending the distance they could plan their play from the house without abandoning their young charge. They pushed and pulled and lifted it over obstacles, and confidently affirmed the superiority of their baby over all babies of the young clan. But in the winter nights there began to be hurried excursions of Mother to the girls' room with the sleeping child in her arms — 'Take care of the baby, Mary, Pa's sick' — and Mary would hear, through sleep made uneasy by a sense of responsibility, the sounds of pain and restless pacing in the room across the hall.

The children had grown up accustomed to the labored, strangling rhythm of their father's asthma, the odor of burning pastilles, the night alarms, and their own helplessness about it, but this new illness came on so insidiously and intermittently that the only way the nine-year-old daughter had of estimating it was by the increasing pressure of responsibility, the moving of the baby's crib to her bedside, the agony of anxiety when he cried in the night, lest Father should be aroused by it; getting up in the morning thick with sleep, and, before she had anything to eat herself, preparing the baby's soft-boiled egg — her own unaccountably falling asleep in school after uneasy nights, and the hurried flight homeward after school to 'take care of the baby.'

I never knew exactly what was the nature of my father's illness except that he suffered excruciatingly, and that it was agreed by all his physicians that it was the last phase of the trouble that had begun in the swamps of Corinth — I seem to recall a story of his being out posting pickets, running into a detachment of the enemy, and having to stand the better part of the night almost up to his neck in the cold ooze of the swamp. Whatever it was, the trouble proceeded in alternate movements of better and worse for a little more than two years. During the summer of 1877 there was an operation from which much was hoped, and nothing was accomplished. One of the singularities of child psychology I recall. It was that though my brother Jim and I admitted to each other after it happened, that we had known Pa's death might be expected, we never communicated it to each other, and never spoke to each other of our grief. It was to Jennie, old enough to understand though not to anticipate, that all Mary's confidences were made.

The end came in October, the 29th, 1878. But before that, Mary, strained with a vague distress, had twice taken alarm, and taking Jennie with her, without leave asked or given, had left school as the premonition overtook her, and trudged home in a fever of anxiety. So that when a day or two before his death the two sisters set out hand in hand, Mary apprehensive of the worst, nobody sent them back. Mary remembers how she tried to cry, as the most natural way of dealing with the sense of stunned alarm in which their flight had begun, and could not until they came to the place on Broad Street from which the white headstones of the City Cemetery gleamed on the hill, where so often the neighborhood children had sat down to listen to a story, and coming herself suddenly to a more rational feeling about what her father's death might mean, Mary sitting down herself on the boardwalk in tears, and Jennie comforting her as if it were not her father also who was about to be taken. After that, the children were allowed to remain at home until the end — for years it gave the child a pained sense of dereliction that just at the last I-Mary came — there was Mary-by-herself apart and aside, seeing her father so frail and wasted in the bed, his hand straying always toward Mother, alternately moistening his parched lips and wiping her own tears — and the look on Susie's face, worn with grief and watching and luminous with love. Then there was I-Mary, and Uncle Otis with his arm around her, and she hiding her face against him lest somebody should see that she had no tears and think she did not care.

There is much that followed, never forgotten, but not necessary to set down here; all grief is so dreadfully alike. For once Mary had nothing to say; she laid herself dumbly against the sharp edge of sorrow, fearful that she would miss, as she thought she had missed her father's last moments, the least aching instant of loss.

It was indispensable for the family to stay on at the home place, there was livestock to be looked after and settlements to be made. Other members of the numerous kin were always about. Early in December, Mary was taken with a severe sore throat. It was one of those cases in which the doctor was not sent for because nobody knew what the trouble was. At night when her throat ached chokingly, Jennie would put her arms about Mary, stroking her face. So that after Mary recovered from her ailment, Jennie too came down with it. There was a little corner by the fire where she would sit, looking very ill, and trying patiently to respond to inquiry. There came a day when she could neither swallow nor speak. Aunt Effie came down that day and insisted that the doctor should be called, but it was then too late; probably in any case diphtheria was too little understood to have admitted of relief. The next day, in a belated recognition of the virulence of the disease, we buried her. I remember in the bleak little burying-ground looking up at my mother in her weeds and making toward her for the last time in my life the child's instinctive gesture for comfort, and being thrust off in so wild a renewal of Susie's own sense of loss, her rejection of what life had left for her, as leaves me still with no other comparison for the appalling shock and severance of widowhood. From that moment on the hillside under the leafless oaks above my father's grave, and my mother thrusting me away to throw herself upon it, I have no instant of recovered recollection until early the next spring when, as we were about to leave the farm to a tenant, the livestock and farming implements were put up for sale, which marks the end of the life on Plum Street.

In time I recovered from my father's death. For a long time I could recall so minutely how he looked that the sight of a man wearing a shawl — always he wore such a shawl as you may see in early portraits of Lincoln — was a fresh thrust in the wound. As late as 1908, walking London streets, I could pick out the resemblances of type, but doubt if I could recollect them now. Mary Patchen, when I met her, could recall to me little traits and mannerisms which else had gone clean out of my memory. But with Jennie it is not so. She is not changed or gone; nothing is changed, not the bright blue of her eye, the cherry lip, the soft aureole of her hair. Still in the night — such times as when I have written a book and see it for the first time in the cold obscenity of print and know without opening the pages that I have failed, that I have sold myself to the delusion of a task for which I have no endowment, an adventure unrequited — she comes in the first sleep and strokes my cheek with her soft hands. The loss of her is never cold in me, tears start freshly at the mere mention of her name. And I would not have it otherwise. She was the only one who ever unselfishly loved me. She is the only one who stays.

BOOK TWO

'THE THOUGHTS OF YOUTH ARE
LONG, LONG THOUGHTS'

BOOK TWO

'THE THOUGHTS OF YOUTH ARE LONG, LONG THOUGHTS'

I

AGAINST the trauma of grief children are doubly helpless. The appalling thing that had happened to Mary by the loss of her father was that she was also deprived of most of the items that, out of the place where you stay, make home; not alone the house on Plum Street, but the wide circle of activities tangent to it, the community of interest, family ritual, the dramatic climax of Father's daily return, the praise, the blame, the evenings around the lamp. It wasn't only that the little house in town, to which the family moved the following spring, was cramped and unlovely, shorn of woods and pastures, but that the life there was stripped of the familiar social exchanges, of all imaginative excursions.

Young as she was and wholly inarticulate in grown-up affairs, Mary suffered through her mother the strange indignities offered to widowhood by a society which made out of the wife's economic dependence on her husband a kind of sanctity which was violated by his death; dependence that made widowhood, when it happened, little less than improbity. At that time throughout America, the status of Wife and Mother, always spoken of in capitals, was sentimentally precious, a status of being treasured and apart. There was on all hands a general social conspiracy to keep the married woman's sense of her preciousness intact. No matter how poorly, through incompetence, neglect, or misfortune, her husband 'protected' her, she was allowed the airs and graces of the woman apart; she could keep it up in the face of the most flagrant violations of the fact. Then the blow fell and the treasured Wife became the poor Widow, the object of family bounty, not infrequently grudged, the grateful recipient of left-overs, the half-menial helper in the households of women whose husbands had simply not died.

The more precious and delicate her wifehood had been, the less chance there was of her being equipped for earning a livelihood. Susie went out nursing. A woman who has had seven children in fifteen years, and an invalid husband, should know how to do that. Mary, as elder sister, had to manage the best she could when her mother was away from home, with little George to care for and her own schooling to keep up. She would hurry home from school, collect Georgie from the woman who, for a pittance, took care of him during the day, 'clean up,' cook supper, sleep with one ear awake toward the child who became the very apple of her eye, scramble through breakfast, put up lunch for herself and Jim, deliver her young charge, and, if anything went wrong, be held responsible.

That my mother's attitude toward me in those first years of her widowhood was sharpened by reminders of the dearer loss, there is no manner of use to pretend. That she felt toward Mary a personal reluctance, which her love was not always able to overcome, made of their relation a less happy bond than it might have been. Had they not been able later to bridge it by a common deep concern for the meaning and destiny of womanhood, it might have been a warping influence in the child's life.

After the moving to the house on Second South, we spent a lot of time at the Farrells', especially in the evenings. The Farrells were all musical and there was nothing Uncle Billy liked better than a family program. There were three other boys besides Minnie and John, bosom companions of Mary and Jim, and the house was well furnished for entertainment: musical instruments, a magic lantern and all manner of games, such as Authors and Old Maid. It pleased Uncle Billy to have the Hunter children, and Susie, for whom he had the greatest admiration, sitting relaxed and lessened of her grief, glad to have her own young happy without the necessity of exertion on her part. They did theirs; George and Jim joining acceptably in the singing, or accompanying on the triangle or the drum, and Mary reciting old ballads, Longfellow's 'Tales,' and such popular selections as 'Curfew shall not ring to-night' — you should have heard her at that — or 'The Polish Boy'! Then there would be Authors and Old Maid around the long dining-room table; Uncle Billy as noisy as anybody, Susie and Aunt Sophia knitting — they had the art, not uncommon in those days, of going on with their needles without looking at them — and chatting quietly in the background. It was there that Georgie, who could croon a sweet, pretty alto even when he was too young to remember the words, came by a nickname that persisted as long as we lived in the town — Mugs — from his lisped mispronunciation of his favorite song, the immensely popular 'Mulligan Guards.'

It was out of these pleasant evenings that Mary drew the beginning of a more satisfactory relation with her mother, in which they entered upon the thin edge of being women together. Uncle Billy had a way of posing his own behavior before Susie, whose opinion he truly valued, so that Mary, who cared more for listening to the talk of her elders than for card games, came to hear of and to discuss it later. Sometimes Uncle Billy's divagations from orthodox paterfamilias behavior were almost too racy for direct relation, so that he got Aunt Sophy to tell, and then fished for Susie's reaction. That was how Mary learned that on a recent trip to New York — have I said that Uncle Billy was a full partner in Woodward and Farrell, Hardware? — he had actually gone to see a play called 'The Black Crook,' a play in which there was dancing by young women in tights. Although Mary had never seen them, she knew what tights were, long stockings that went all the way up, and disappeared under black velvet shorts; they were black or pink, and it was worse if they were pink; people had a way of saying 'and *pink* tights' as though it were the last word in inadmissibility. Uncle Billy, half-proud of himself and yet prepared to be a little ashamed, waited for Susie's judgment, which was that, since he was indubitably all that the father of a family ought to be, it was not so bad for him to have seen 'The Black Crook' as it was, in view of his young family, for him to have talked about it.

You can see how it was that with momentous moral decisions

like the above going on about her, Mary never told that, occasionally when the two older Farrell boys and Jim were alone, they
taught him to play with real cards, games called Euchre and
Casino. It would have excited in Susie's mind an apprehension
about the one place where, during her forced absences from home,
she felt that her children were really safe. And as for Mary no one
could have told that she had lost what — when she had it nobody
but Jennie had known — all those luminous contacts with beauty
in the brook, in the bird, in the flower, from which Mary's spiritual
life had sprung. No longer were things experienced vizualized as
things seen; the little bird that once hopped on Mary's tongue
chirruped no more. God was not found under the wide elms and
cloudy maples with which the way to school was lined. There
was no sort of emergency in which I-Mary came, nor answered to
if called. It couldn't have been all shock and sorrow; something
must have been owed to the subtle alterations of adolescence, which
took her hard and early. If ever I had any disposition to feel sorry
for Mary — one doesn't, you know, for children to whom God
arrives under walnut trees — it would be for the lonely and over-
anxious fledgling of those orphaned years.

That first summer it was that Mary left off playing with dolls.
She had already been a little weaned from that resource, having
baby George to adore, but at Christmas somebody had given her a
wax beauty with open-and-shut eyes. She did not really play with
it except when younger children visited her, but it was a treasured
fetish of that lost romance of little-girlhood, and she liked, nights
her mother was from home, to think that it kept all night its large
cow-like, cerulean gaze upon her. And then one afternoon under
the Moores' apple tree, one of the children stepped squarely into
its candid waxen countenance. Mary would have liked to have a
good cry over it; she gathered it up and went to look for her
mother, who was entertaining callers, and though Mary carried
Angela Catherine — that was her lovely name — so that nobody
could help seeing what had happened, nobody did. If they had, if
anybody had said so much as a commiserating word, Mary could
have had her cry which would have done her a world of good. In-

stead she sighed and numbly laid the broken fetish away at the back of the bottom bureau drawer — and that was that.

A month later, Grandpa Graham sent her and Mother and George to visit Aunt Mary Peter in Kansas, on their homestead somewhere in the neighborhood of Leavenworth. The baker's dozen of Peter cousins was, I think, almost complete by that time; healthy, hard-headed, self-reliant young Kansans, whose matter-of-fact association was extremely good for her, freckled barefooted youngsters, bred to the open country and the spare life of pioneers. Uncle Peter, in addition to being a homesteader and a cross-roads blacksmith, was now a regularly ordained Free Methodist minister, an alteration of his status which Aunt Mary had taken, as she seemed to take everything else, with a comfortable placidity. If you ask me how Free Methodism differed from Grandpa Graham's kind, I don't know, except that it seemed noisier, and as a typical Kansan variant, I recall that it involved Aunt Mary's stripping herself of the vanities of dress to the point of leaving off her wedding ring, which Susie considered shocking. But Uncle Peter was evidently popular as a preacher. The schoolhouse where he held forth was crowded by other large Kansan families who drove half a day in wagons in order to be there in time, infant children packed about among the baskets filled with ample provision for the noon refreshment. Uncle Peter had a fine presence; tall, well bearded, with the highly denunciatory manner of a curious pioneer type, long since weeded out of close-packed communities, a witch-hunting type that Mary had always meant to trace to its source in American life, and has never yet done so.

I remember everything that happened at Aunt Mary's: the vast roll of the prairies like the suspended breathing of a huge earth creature that might at any moment suspire devastatingly, the rhythmic sweeping movement of the wind-break in the perpetual wind, the strange flowers, our playhouse in the young peach orchard, and the rattlesnake we found sunning there. I remember taking turn and turn riding double with the other children, guarding Uncle Peter's stock grazing on governmental land; watching the dark menacing whirl of a small cyclone that veered off and left us in a dead calm; watching at night the running prairie fires and going next day to see in their black wake the little calcined skeletons of wild things overtaken in mid-flight.

I remember also the only unpleasant episode of the visit, as an occasion when Mary was rude to Uncle Peter. He had said to Mary's mother, 'If you are bringing up your children to think that their father has any other lot in the Hereafter than that of eternal damnation, you are bringing them up to a lie.' Preachers said things like that to people. It made Susie cry; she cried every time she thought of it. Said Mary — Mary who, since she had escaped Heaven, had never taken Hell seriously — 'I guess my father wouldn't want to be anywhere with people who thought that sort of thing, anyway!' Mother made her apologize; it seems it is worse to talk back to Preachers than to other sorts of people. But in every other respect the visit was a great success. You couldn't love your utterly dependable Cousin Annie the way you had loved Sister Jennie; but it was good to think she belonged to you. And when you came away, Aunt Mary gave you a ring which she had worn as a little girl, because you were named for her. (Aunt Mary Lane had already sent me beads for the same reason, and Aunt Mary, Uncle William Hunter's second wife, sent me a silver salt spoon that had belonged to Great-Grandmother Hunter, and Great-Aunt Mary Dugger gave me a book on behavior. The ring is the only one I have yet.)

The temporary contact with outdoors had proved relieving and there was always a tingling feeling of The Plains as a place you might like to be. Going through that part of Kansas, to this day, on the train, the sense of adventure flies like a crest.

And in the second summer came a letter and a check inviting Susie and the children to spend six weeks with Uncle Charlie and Aunt Mary Lane in Boston. Colonel Lane happened to be there on the peak of one of those fortunate strokes which were not too infrequent in his career as a mining man, and had settled his family in a house in Gloucester, which was not then the popular resort it has since become. It was much more like a New England village of Harriet Beecher Stowe or Sarah Orne Jewett, recognizably New England and not wanting to be taken for anything else. The three Lane cousins proved companionable, and Charles, the eldest, had read almost as much as Mary herself, except that he hadn't read about New England. The Lane children had been brought up partly in Western mining towns and partly in British Columbia. What they didn't know about the cradle of American Liberties brought out astonishingly how much the little Middle-westerners did know. What I wonder is, are American children as exclusively brought up today in the literature and lore of New England as they were then. There was, in fact, no other generally accessible literature and lore. Longfellow, Hawthorne, Whittier, Bryant, the author of the 'Biglow Papers': even in 'Uncle Tom's Cabin,' the really telling characters were Yankees. There was nothing of the West but Bret Harte and the interdicted dime novels. Of the Middlewest nothing at all, nor of the South.

What stands out in retrospect, for Mary, is the extraordinary familiarity of everything in Massachusetts; blueberry, bayberry, partridge berry, and ground pine — she knew them from having met them in books. Cousin George used always to be trying to catch her out in them, but never did. She knew pages of Long-fellow and Whittier; she knew what they must see: Boston Com-mon, Bunker Hill, the Old South Church. Her acquaintance with the events that had happened in these places was an amaze-ment to her cousins, likewise her faith in the importance of these things. They began by being skeptical and embarrassed, and ended by being swept into a passion of sight-seeing. All of them, that is, but Jim, who was 'soft' on a girl in Gloucester, his first, much to the dudgeon of the other four, whom, as one going-on-fifteen, he regarded as very small fry. Together the cousins climbed the Monument and the South Church Tower; they went to Faneuil Hall and identified all the contemporaries of Daniel Webster; they went to Longfellow's house and peeked through the gate at somebody walking in the garden who might have been the poet. Nobody but Mary cared very much whether he was or not; but at any rate they saw Boston; all of it that was related to the school histories and Longfellow's poems.

These things had their place in the shuttling to and fro from east to west of the American scene that was to make the background of Mary's life, but the formative, the direction giving item of her adolescence, was what went on in her so inarticulately about what widowhood might mean to a woman like Mary's mother, the earliest social resentment, the first conscious criticism of the organization of the adult life. The same thing must have been going on in the minds of many American women and girls growing up into womanhood, rising into the revolt that was to sweep so many similar items, if not entirely off the social slate, at least to its inconsiderable fringes; but it was years before Mary had, to her thinking on these things, a free intelligent response, and that from a male mind. It was only the second time of my meeting him, and already I had been warned by my American friends in London that, even if I liked him, I might find it socially inexpedient to see very much of him. Yet in the course of an hour or two's conversation, there I was saying freely what I yet hadn't any hope of saying to an American man, and not scamping my social indignation. 'Oh,' said H. G. Wells, 'the way we penalize widows in England!' How many times have I written off against that the causes I have to disagree with him, so far ahead of us all at that time in thinking of woman in terms of her worth to society as against her individual value in terms of her emotional relation to one man!

II

THE mere mention of Longfellow sets in motion the whole train of recollections about what, at the time Mary was spouting pages of him to her British Columbian cousins, began to be called 'culture' in the Middlewest. The word came into common use with him, without intention, but inevitably, as the fruit from the vine, to express what he meant. The Intelligentsia of today are all wrong about Longfellow, holding him as the very nadir of everything that they themselves have not so much sprung from as *away* from; he was in some respects the most important poet we ever had. He was everything that, even in the transplanted wilds of Eellanoy, kept alive in Polly McAdams and her kind the notion of mannerliness, of the gesture they missed and meant, on behalf of their children, to resume, the eighteenth-century gestures of gentility, of elegance, the feeling that went with high white houses with pillared portico fronts, and 'attitudes' of men and women toward each other. He was anticipated in Polly McAdams's time, in the names and patterns of patchwork quilts and woven coverlets; Tulip Tree, Democrat Rose, Ladies' Chain, Swing in the Center, and Washington's Plume. He was the hair wreath in the parlor, and the wax flowers under glass. In books called 'The Ladies' Garland,' 'Affection's Offering,' and the like, one approaches some years in advance of his actual career, the true Longfellow strain; by words of ladylike commendation, genteel, elegant, tony, you climb to Culture as the climax of a series of attitudes which Mr. Longfellow so satisfyingly fulfills that along in the seventies he became the true gesture of National aspiration. Longfellow rather than Lowell, who was suspected of a foreign flourish or two; Longfellow rather than Whittier, whose cool New Englandness fell short of expressing the lush sentimentality of the black-soil country. Never was poet more apt upon his hour, nor one so completely grown out of the heart wood of our native tree of Poesy, so that, however much he may be pruned by the criticism of successive times, there is always the branch on which the children swing, to exercise the pre-adolescent antics of their emotions.

Already, in Mary's time, the didactic old Professor had fallen a little from the peak of his expressiveness for the narrow Atlantic strip which produced him. But he was still, in the Middlewest, indispensable to a 'cultivated' state of mind. That his work was part of the regular curriculum in the grade school was evidence, not of his decline, but of what youngsters of that day were expected to reach up to. Everybody wanted culture in the same way that a few years earlier everybody wanted sewing machines, but culture by this time was something more than it had been a few years earlier, when, as Mary distinctly recalls, a school for young ladies in a neighboring town advertised both 'solid and ornamental cultures,' in the latter classification the making of wax flowers was included. It meant for one thing, more than another, the studious reading of books.

To say that people in Carlinville were, in the late seventies, anxious about the state of their culture, where formerly they had been chiefly concerned about their souls, is to sum up all that had happened to them in the twenty years that succeeded the close of the Civil War. How much the War and its portentous moral implications had to do with it, I don't know, but as I recall the 'best people' of my youth, they seemed to have arrived at being perfectly certain about their souls; secure, whether or not they based their security on membership in any sect, of the rectitude of their moral conclusions. Had they not just accomplished the abolition of slavery! But within the years that Mary could remember, it had dawned on the Middlewest that there was a certain amount of intellectual 'keeping up' that was obligatory. There wasn't, as I recall it, any real doubt of the validity of Everyman's opinion on every practical issue. But there was a general consensus of opinion at the time Mary came to live in the little yellow house that you did have to read to maintain your pretensions to culture.

The status of being cultivated was something like the traditional preciousness of women: nothing that you could cash in upon, but a shame to you to do without. And it was the one item in which, without violating any principle of democracy, you could entertain the pleasant consciousness of being superior to your fellows. Actually its roots were deeper than that. The pioneer stress was over, prosperity had come upon the Middlewest and leisure into the lives of women. The day of large families, families of from a dozen to fifteen, was over.

Although she did not know what she was seeing, Mary was a party to the evolution of the new attitude toward women's immemorial function, notice of which long after it is an accomplished fact, is just reaching the high panjandrums of the Church and State. She still recalls sedate matriarchs who could in the face of social exigencies fall back upon the Delphic utterance, 'Well, I've had eleven, I ought to know.' Or the more dreadful deliverance of unassailable certainty, 'Well, I've lost seven, I ought to know.' She recalls the nods and winks, the ironic 'Some people are so smart!' of the women who hadn't been 'smart' about family limitation, and were proud of it. She can remember and still be moved by the recollection of the anguish of overburdened mothers of eight or ten, for whom the very necessities of life lacked, in the face of the never-to-be-evaded expectation — the time poor little Mrs. Rogers, when she knew there was to be a tenth, climbed up and jumped off the buggy-shed — the whispered trade in nostrums — the strange and fearful menace of the middle years.

All of which brings us around to Mr. Longfellow again.

Into the widening gap which the unadmitted, unnamed practice of family limitation set up between the generations, our burgeoning system of public education was driving a wedge of books. It drove so fast that by the time Mary was twelve, one book, such as was usually kept in Mother's bureau and given to girls to read when they required it, was not enough to close the gap between young girls and young mothers; tradition was not enough; 'Godey's Lady's Book' was too fragile; not even the weekly county paper, which, in the case of the 'Carlinville Democrat,' was, so far as national information went, a fair equivalent of the present-day 'Literary Digest,' answered wholly the need of a democratically constituted society for 'keeping up.' And already, the American disposition to take the needs of women seriously had responded with an answer in the shape of an institution, organized and localized to afford the greatest utility to the greatest number.

All the time I am writing these things, I keep thinking how much faster we could get on with the story of Mary if only I could refer, say, to chapter seven of Lydia Pinkham's 'History of the American Hearth,' instead of having to take time to explain that the institution known as 'Chautauqua,' whatever other claims it made for itself, was, for its time, an extraordinarily effective system of adult education. It was always competently adjusted to the needs of a servantless society, and in its method never unmindful of the lingering tradition of magic, of occult and even fearful influences inherent in what still went by the title of 'book learning.' There was still, in the late seventies, a general notion that book learning wasn't directly applicable to daily life, wasn't expected to contribute to pioneer types of success. It was a spell that worked away from home, the farther away the better, making your achieved local success proof against the counter-magic of the world at large. There were certain books whose sibylline properties were such that, if only occasionally read in, raised the whole threshold of personal defense. I recall that the Dugger men, Uncle Sam and Uncle Wes, Cousin Bill and Cousin Prator, had always a few such, Byron and Shakespeare, Daniel Webster's Orations or Tom Paine, which they never read through, but could mention familiarly and quote from on occasion. Even into Mary's generation this fetishistic use of books prevailed. I remember how Isadora Duncan used to carry about with her and read a few sentences of Marcus Aurelius before dancing; though Isadora didn't realize Marcus as a fetish. Like Cousin Bill, she thought when she read him that she was being intellectual.

It was this inscrutable and possibly explosive property of book learning that made such learning expedient to be attacked in groups; and it was the public school habit which called for the laying-out of such attack in serial formation. Back of that there was the long experience of the word-of-mouth-tradition method of the pioneer, which made it difficult for the Middlewest to realize new knowledge except by talking it over. Still to great numbers of Americans, knowledge is safe and tolerable only in the second person; painters explaining their pictures and poets reading their own works. Chautauqua, through the C.L.S.C., adjudicated all these common intellectual necessities perfectly and still kept them pleasantly within the savors of religious use — where, Heaven knows, I am willing to admit learning ought to be. Whoever on his ancestral bookshelves can discover a stray copy of one of the Pansy books will know more, on reading it, of culture in the American eighties than can otherwise be described.

Where I was, when the things just recorded were the case, was reading Longfellow in the eighth grade of public school. About that time Martin Luther Keplinger, who, besides being a rising young attorney, was Superintendent of the Methodist Sunday School, came to live next door to the little yellow house on Second South, and brought home a young wife, who became an ardent Chautauquan. The Chautauqua Literary and Scientific Circle often met at her house, and it was only the interruptions of her work which kept Mary's mother from being absorbed into its atmosphere of important studiousness, which is, when all is said, the most satisfying social atmosphere in the world. That was how the Chautauqua books came to Mary's house, and she made the exciting discovery that the Literature course for that year included those poems of Longfellow that made up the major English of her own school work. And the Chautauqua book of 'Evangeline' and 'Tales of a Wayside Inn' had a great many more and more informing footnotes than the school edition. It was over those footnotes that Mary's earliest literary friendship began, first with Mrs. Kep, as in neighborly familiarity the young wife was called, and then with Mrs. Rinaker, who was also a Keplinger, and had been, along with Mary's father, an important constructive influence in what was, I am still convinced, the best selected city library in the whole Upper River country.

Longfellow was, however, for Mary, aged twelve, merely an incident. The important contribution of Chautauqua to her education was the course in geology, a science of which, up to that time, Mary had been but faintly aware. There was a textbook not too advanced for her years, and there was a book, but whether it was actually included in the Chautauqua course or only recommended I cannot recall, Hugh Miller's 'Old Red Sandstone,' which Mother glanced at and pronounced 'too old.' It is possible she had other objections. The whole theory of Evolution was still of doubtful admissibility for convinced Methodists. But the title had a calling sound; there was, for the child, a promise in it of reinstatement in that warm reciprocal world of outdoors, for lack of which she was for years, after her father's death, a little sick at heart. I remember the very look of the pages, the easy, illustrative charts, the feel of the author behind the book, the feel of the purposeful earth — I must have been reading it out-of-doors, in my favorite seat in the cherry tree which stood to the left of the door of the yellow house as you came out. I remember how, as I read, the familiar landscape of Rinaker's Hill, the Branch, the old rock quarry, unfolded to the dimensions of a geological map — the earth itself became transparent, molten, glowing.

'Old Red Sandstone' was the first, absolutely the first book Mary ever bought for herself, though it was several years before she could accomplish it out of her scanty pocket money. Immediately she began a 'collection' — Brother Jim had collected birds' eggs somewhat earlier, but this was Mary's first immersion in the mania which overtakes all normal youth. Fossil crinoids were her hobby; in no time at all she had a whole croquet box full, continually being dragged out for other young collectors to gloat over and everybody to stumble upon. The treasure of the collection was a trilobite which she had wangled out of a boy at school, after having reduced it in his own esteem by convincing him that it was not, as he had proudly believed, a 'petrified owl.'

'Old Red Sandstone' disappeared from the family bookshelves about the time Mother gave away Mary's collection to a neighbor's child, after Mary went away to normal school, but the sense of the unfolding earth never left her. There are moments still, when she is alone with the mountains of New Mexico, when the first geological pages of the past begin to open and turn, when they are illuminated by such self-generated light as first shone from the chapters of 'Old Red Sandstone.'

It would have been perhaps the leading of the Wayside Inn Tales that interested Mary in reading, that winter, 'Lalla Rookh' and 'Marmion,' but I do not know what induced her to wade through 'Paradise Lost,' unless it had been the illustrations by Doré, of which Middlewestern Culture was taking notice just then. It was precisely the sort of thing they would have noticed! — Biblical, grandiose, and with no possible reference to reality. Through Milton, the magic of words carried Mary swimmingly much of the way — Lucifer falling from Morn to dewy Eve — and all the dark angelic host — *thick as the leaves that strew the brooks* — as late as when she did reach Vallambrosa she could still quote the more popular passages. But she kept forgetting the sequences of the story, mazed by the magic of the verse — like watching a thunderstorm at sunset. And afterward she had a new category for books, for which there was no word. It was, however, as an index of quality, quite explicit; it was the sort of book that went on in other people's heads. It had never happened at all, the way the Alcott books had happened, it couldn't happen, the way you felt Alice's Adventures in Wonderland might, if you could only get there.

Mother had discontinued 'St. Nicholas' the winter the family left Plum Street. She thought you were too old for it. Mary tried bringing special numbers home from the library, but there were too many reminders; like the broken doll, it was better out of sight. I still think, however, that she was lucky to have been brought up on it — the way she remembers the Trowbridge stories, 'Tinkham Brothers' Tide Mill,' 'Rose in Bloom,' and earlier, 'How Persimmons Minded the Baby.' It was Mrs. Rinaker who tided over the reading of fiction through the adolescent period, with early American novels, 'Queechy,' 'The Wide Wide World,' 'The Lamplighter.' You went along that path to 'Beulah' and 'St. Elmo,' and the first thing you knew you were at 'Jane Eyre' — how you adored Rochester! and then you were at Jane Austen!

But you went in fact much more slowly than that. I am not sure

Mary got any further that winter of '79 than 'The Lamplighter' and Harriet Beecher Stowe. That was the winter that 'Uncle Tom's Cabin' came to town. It was played in the County Court Room, and everybody went, even — or especially — Methodists. Children were brought miles in wagons; you saw them going out later, rolled in bedquilts and tucked under the seats, sound asleep within twenty minutes of the play's ending.

At this date it may be interesting to know that in those earlier performances there were no bloodhounds chasing Eliza across a twelve-foot Ohio River on canvas ice. But there was what was called on the handbills, an 'Apotheosis of Little Eva,' in which she appeared above Uncle Tom's deathbed in a scene-painter's Heaven, in a white nightie which would have been more convincing for having gone oftener to the laundry. Five or six years later, the bloodhounds appeared in leash, for the purpose of drumming up custom, and in this Mammoth Production there were two Uncle Toms and two Little Evas, though what purpose they served besides increasing the cost of the handbills, I never discovered.

Twice after that I saw it, once in a suburb of Boston, degenerated to a farce, with Marks as the stage Jew, and Uncle Tom as a comedy 'black face'; and once more in all its melodramatic glory, the original play, in a French provincial town, with an audience composed chiefly of Senegalese soldiery, fairly pop-eyed over the authentic presentation of the behavior of Whites to Blacks in the great and wealthy *Etats Unis*, and still one of the most absorbing dramas ever written there.

III

AFTER the summer of '82, or thereabouts, events began to present themselves again in an orderly course. We were living on Johnson Street then, in a house my mother built out of the sale of the farm. The pension she had applied for had been allowed, with officer's back pay; other matters had straightened themselves out, so that, though she continued to go out occasionally as general emergency aid, it was chiefly to the houses of her friends, who coveted her warm, consoling interest in their plight. The house was well built, of six rooms arranged in two rows, three bedrooms, parlor, sitting-room, and kitchen; no bath, of course; an outside toilet, and drinking water from the pump, as was the case with all the houses in town except for the very wealthy. There was no central heating such as was beginning to be the fashion for more commodious homes, but there were two fireplaces for burning coal, with imitation black marble mantels, and between the parlor and living-room there were folding doors. The one extravagance my mother had allowed herself was to have the woodwork of the two 'front' rooms 'grained'; which means that it was treated so as to present the natural aspect of an expensive hardwood finish, like no wood on earth, I am sure. Susie was extremely pleased with it, and the work must have been good of its kind, for when I visited the house forty years later, it was still shining and intact.

Outside, ours was such a house as might have been discovered by the score in any Middlewestern town, clapboarded, white-painted with green blinds, its original Colonial lines corrupted by what in the course of the next decade or two broke out irruptively into what is now known as the 'bungalow' type. We lived there about seven years, and Mary was never at home in it at all. At that time nobody ever thought of inquiring what Mary thought of anything, so nobody found out. Several years after our removing to California, when Mother, who was desperately homesick there, was reproaching her for never having shown any trace of such sickness, said Mary unthoughtfully, 'Homesick for what?' and saw that she would have to turn it quickly; 'Isn't it the family that makes the home?' — and Susie managed to be doubtfully content with that. The place was dear to her; she had built it, and except that she would have furnished it more handsomely if she could, it satisfied her expectation. But Mary recalls very well her first going there after the workmen had left and the furniture was partly in place, and being struck with a cold blast of what she was to recognize long after as the wind before the dawn of the dreary discontent with the American scene, which has since been made familiar to us all by the present generation of writers in the Middlewest. But Mary's case was rendered more desolate by her not being able to refuse the conviction that was pressed upon her from every side, that any dissatisfaction she might have felt was inherently of herself, that she was queer and ungrateful and insensitive to the finer aspects of existence. To the extent that she wasn't able to shut it out of consciousness by fixing her attention on something else, Mary was always, in that house, a little below herself, without the relief of despising it, which a kindly dispensation granted to the generation next after her.

To begin with, there wasn't a nook or corner of the house which could be differentiated from any other corner, could be made to take the impress of the resident's spirit, or afford even a momentary relief from the general tone and tempo of the family life. It was all neat and hard and squared up with a purely objective domesticity within which it was not possible even to imagine any other sort of life. There wasn't the alteration of pulse such as might be secured by the coming and going of the head of the house, the relief of readjusting details to the drama of affection; a perpetually widowed house.

My mother was in most respects an efficient housekeeper; everything was invariably clean and tidy; she got through her work with a celerity that was the marvel of the neighborhood. She had an extraordinary knack of stretching money to the utmost, of cleaning and turning and pressing her clothes, so that she always looked trim and well-turned-out. She put all of us, and her house, through the same process, without anybody ever suspecting that it might not be the best process imaginable for everybody.

Outside, things were not much better. Johnson Street was north of the town, between the town and the college; it had been chosen partly because of that, so that the children as they grew up might have that advantage, or that Susie might eke out her income, as it proved desirable, with boarders. This last plan never came to anything. In that small house the intrusion of a 'boarder' proved unbearable, even to the brothers, and Susie discovered that a boarder is a poor substitute for the one thing that binds a woman willingly to the unbroken routine of meals and hours.

The neighborhood itself was new; only a few houses had gone up there, newly married couples and the better-paid sort of work-people. All that part of town was originally prairie, stretching north and north unbrokenly, shorn and treeless, to flat horizons. Up and down the street young maples had been planted, but except for a few trees about the Miller place, which had once been a farmhouse, there was nothing to rest the eye upon. Going to school one went past vacant weed-grown lots, past the foundry, which had once been the woolen mills, and was at the moment, I believe, a tool and hoe works, and so to Grandpa's house on First North, and across the square to school. That was the way you took when hurried, but coming back you spared yourself the time as often as possible to come the longest way around, along East Main, up College Avenue, so as to bring yourself past the more attractive gardens.

I am not, after all these years, going to be blamed, as I was blamed by everybody who knew about it, for my preferences in matters of this kind. Mary was more than ordinarily sensitive to form and proportion. Never so much so as during those years of adolescence when the submerged faculty, that is appeased with the mere appearance of things, came so close to the surface that it was chiefly the want of any possible practical way of accomplishing a painting career that decided her between paint and print as a medium of expression.

I felt the outward scene in those days as other people feel music, its structure, its progressions; felt emotion as color and color as tone. All the family except Mary were to some degree musical, but it scarcely occurred to anybody in those days that not having 'an ear for music' was merely an error in the instrumentation, that all the sensitivities that went with a musical gift were merely transferred to another sensory tract and were active there, capable of ecstasy and pain in a similar, even in a more intensive fashion. To this day Mary can be made sick by living in a room of bad color or wrong proportions, even though, in the stress of other preoccupations, often the first notice she has of inharmony in the objective environment, is physical dis-ease. Susie herself was so sensitive to tone that she never hesitated to say when the piano was badly out of tune that it 'gave her the shivers.'

One of the family jokes was that Mary had a notion that the tool and hoe works was pretty, although what Mary had actually said was not 'pretty' but beautiful, as she had seen it once of a winter twilight, rust-red against a dark blue sky faintly streaked with ruddy cloud, and below the long lines of the brick walls in harmony with the horizon, the pond where youngsters went to skate in winter, blue with the deep-sea blue of thick ice lit with reflected fire of the sky. Well, it *was* beautiful. The mistake was in saying so. And that was why Mary said as little as possible about the house in Johnson Street, which only just escaped being unendurable.

The parlor was the worst. The furniture, except for the piano new and ugly, of a popular type of decoration of cut-in designs picked out in black and gilt. People were then beginning to get rid of their good old pieces and stressing a modern note. The blinds at the undraped windows were dark chocolate, the carpet and upholstery chosen of reds and greens which 'set each other off.' Except for a few family photographs, the walls were bare. Later a lithograph of the martyred Garfield adorned one wall and a cheap papier-maché 'placque' of Lily Langtry another. I do not know what else we would have put on them. There were a few houses in Carlinville where you could see good old engravings, Currier and Ives prints, and a few dark portraits in oil. There were other houses in which you might find bright prints of a slightly later date in black and gilt frames; none of them so bad as they became a decade later; sentimental subjects; Fast Asleep and Wide Awake were the names of the two at Grandpa's, and a black and white Landseer Stag at Bay — some such matter. But there were none of these at our house, perhaps because Susie had never cared to own them. There was not even a Whatnot.

Some day someone will write the history of the Whatnot, with its odd, and for the most part attractive, collection of socio-historical fetishes; the tropic shell carved minutely with the Lord's Prayer; Indian arrow-heads; the glass paper-weight with glass flowers inside, or a picture of the Centennial; the stuffed bird; the wax flowers; the polished buffalo horn; the 'mineral specimens' from California; all those curious keys which unlocked for the ancestors æsthetic emotion and intellectual curiosity. I am sure if I had a proper Whatnot at hand, I could lead you by it through the whole æsthetic history of the Middlewest. I could touch the hidden life, the obscure, the unconfessed root of the art impulse from which I am indubitably sprung. But we had no Whatnot in our house, not even a home-made one of wire-threaded spools and walnut stain.

Looking back, I can realize now that the child with staring eyes and the great mane of tawny curls, who used to creep slowly along the rail that divided the 'art department' of the county fair from the milling crowd, taking in with avid, slow absorption the now obsolete tufted and cut-out and cross-stitched counterpanes, the infinitely fine crocheted antimacassars, the picture frames of shells and acorn cups and prickly seeds, seeing them grow with time more curious and tasteless, and valued for their singularity, was seeing much more than that. She was seeing the passing of that initial impulse toward æstheticism so hardily kept alive for three generations on the contents of Whatnots, and on little else.

Mary herself had accepted the curtailment of her private ex-cursions to the woods, removed in distance by the intervening stretch of town and suburb. Instinct, the ancient fear incident to growing up into a young lady, was at work. At fourteen, Mary felt, without knowing why, that she must be satisfied with being taken on picnics, on fishing and nutting excursions with 'the crowd.' Moreover, Susie had taken pains to impress upon her the childish character of her interest in nature and the inexpedience of talking about it. Especially you must not talk appreciatively about landscapes and flowers and the habits of little animals and birds to boys; they didn't like it. If one of them took you walking, your interest should be in your companion, and not exceed a ladylike appreciation of the surroundings, in so far as the boy, as the author of the walk, might feel himself complimented by your appreciation of it. You must not quote; especially poetry and Thoreau. An occasional light reference to Burroughs was permissible, but not Thoreau. A very little experience demonstrated that Susie was right. You gathered that outdoors as a subject of conversation was boring to most people. Perhaps that is why, with an extravagantly subtle and varied background, the Middlewest has produced no nature writer of note, and the only popularity the Middlewestern scene has had is as a setting for highly sentimentalized human situations. James Lane Allen was the exponent of that in Mary's 'teens. All this restriction was felt annoyingly, especially in reference to the one man Carlinville produced who has made professional standing for himself out of his knowledge of the interrelations of plants and insects. Charles Robertson.[14] Mary began to hear of him after going to live in Johnson Street. She knew little enough in detail except that he was a man of means permitting the leisure for the field excursions which he chose where other men would have been interested in politics or horse-racing. She heard of him chiefly through the commiseration freely afforded to his wife, who was thought of as being, if not humiliated, at least rendered unpleasantly self-conscious by his queerness. People spoke of the hobby of Charles Robertson only a little less disparagingly than they would if it had been a weakness for cards, or a too great conviviality, a little the way they spoke of a man who played the piano for a living. Mary used to see him occasionally setting out with insect net and botany case, or coming home evenings happily mired as to boots, smelling of meadowsweet. He was the one person in Carlinville whom Mary heartily envied, and would have given much to meet. There was no practical reason why she shouldn't except that, where she was genuinely interested, Mary was shy; and Susie was against it. She didn't want Mary 'getting off on that track,' so unsuitable for a woman. Anyway, Mr. Robertson was a married man, and a friendship between a married man and a young girl was held on every ground inadmissible.

I suspect that Mary's mother was more than a little troubled by Mary's interest in men older than herself, since being so much older, they were almost certain to be married, and not subject to friendly advances. The admissible exchanges between men and women, except during courtship, were probably fewer than at any time in the Victorian age. Moreover, Mary had a way of talking to men more directly, even disputatiously, than was usual for young girls. She appeared, as a matter of fact she was, quite innocent of the ritual of ladylike intercourse with gentlemen as set forth in a book that Great-Aunt Mary Dugger had saved out of her own youth, wherein it was described how a Lady was to lead the conversation along genteel bypaths of literary and musical comment, affording ample opportunity for His Whiskers to display for her benefit those gems of wisdom which only gentlemen could produce. The Lady must be sufficiently well read to be able to introduce aptly the most fruitful topics, but she was not to express an opinion on them. According to the book 'the gentleman will tell the lady what to think.'

Not Mary, they wouldn't! They would have to be spry about it or Mary would end by telling them. This was an attitude to make my mother apprehensive, and may have had something to do with her unwillingness to have Mary meet socially the only genuinely scientific man within reach.

I am not meaning to say that Mary hadn't a normal interest in boys of her own age, secrets with other girls and serious discussions as to whether it was proper or not to tell, when you'd guessed who sent your valentines, or if really nice girls would play 'postoffice.' I guessed that it was Jim Lynch who sent me my first valentine; Hugh Minton, whose father was Mathematics Professor at Blackburn, took me to my first college party. Jim Lynch we had known at the Plum Street house; he had a pleasant way of helping girls over mud puddles, never pulled their curls nor put hoptoads in their desks. He was lank, freckled, and red-headed, and I understand that he afterward went to New Jersey and did well for himself, which I hope is true. I am certain that my first interest in another lank, red-headed roughneck, when he was young and Nobel Prizes far from him, was because he reminded me of Jim Lynch.

Mary didn't care for 'post-office'; she thought if she wanted to kiss a boy she'd just kiss him; she didn't see any advantage in working up to it as a game.

Up to this point the writer has done her work badly if you are not prepared to accept the major premise that Mary was more susceptible to ideas fermenting in the social atmosphere than to purely personal intimations of destiny. Items that had to do with social movements and solutions stuck like burrs to her memory, ready instantly to be assimilated to later social perceptions. And to Mary, perceptions of the intricate relationships of men and women in society came much earlier than true intuitions about man and woman. As the determinant of adolescent thinking, the circumstance of being a Methodist and the lack of a Whatnot was much more menacing than anything that at that age could be described as sex experience.

When my publishers, a little in advance of my actually beginning it, began to announce this autobiography, any number of my readers proceeded urgently to hope that 'you are going to tell the truth about everything.'

Said Mary, 'Everything that matters.'

Then the cat was out of the bag. 'It is so important, don't you think, that women should tell the truth about their sex life?'

To satisfy the modern expectation in that direction, Mary would have to tell a great deal more than matters, since to the things Mary cared most about, sex never mattered much. What the interlocutor fails to note is that Mary is just old enough to have realized that, in her youth, women were much too busy fulfilling their sex life to live in the maze of Freudian episodes, complexes and repressions, such as are modernly expected. Opportunities for Freudian shock were singularly lacking to older sisters growing up in families where there is a baby arriving practically every two years. And when, as in Mary's case, your mother goes out nursing, you are likely to be short on amazement at the normal incidents of women's lives. I can't recall being even acutely aware of those phases of the subject which would be the obsession of my grand-daughters if I had any. What I do realize is, on reading 'Elmer Gantry' for the first time, saying to myself, Yes, that was *that*, and wondering faintly how so many vulgarities inherent in the Middle-western environment could have escaped my knowing at the time that they were there. And as for the unimportant lubricities which occupy so much of modern confession, if there were any such lurking under the slurred surfaces of social circles tangent to her own, Mary passed them by wide margins of exemption.

What Mary did suffer from was the general obliquity of female-ness as an index of capacity, particularly intellectual capacity. She suffered from the contempt in which woman's talent was held, from the professional and economic handicaps to a woman's career. But growing up as she did at the western edge of American culture, suffered less than might have been the case farther East from the repressive conventions hedging femininity on every side. Already Mary's set was beginning to spoof at the notion that, though a really nice girl could cross her ankles in company, she must not cross her knees, and at the notion, which Mary found active in some quarters as late as the early nineteen-hundreds, that a hatpin was a lascivious device invented for the purpose of allowing young women to show off their figures by raising their arms in the presence of young men. In Mary's extreme youth, there were still houses in which the limbs of the piano were modestly swathed in ruffles of chintz, and a legend in Carlinville of two maiden ladies of good birth and education, who, having once met and been convinced by Amanda Bloomer, returned to town in the chaste pantalettes elasticked to the ankle below a tunic cut off at least six inches from the ground. By the general consensus of outraged opinion they were reduced, for conscience' sake, to stealing out cautiously at twilight, to trot timorously around the block. I never succeeded in identifying those brave ladies when I grew up, but here salute their memory; brave ladies and brave sally against priggish, sniggering minds! Another gallant lady of my adolescence was the one who stood up in the Methodist pulpit of a Sunday night and called marriage without love 'legalized prostitution' right out loud. He was a brave minister, too, who lent her his pulpit: Brother Wilkins, whom Mary sat under during her most impressionable years, and perhaps owed more to him than either of them thought.

Mary joined the Methodist Church somewhere about the end of her thirteenth year. By that time the clear sense of the Presence which had ceased with her father's death had not come back; only the inner conviction of it ached on, the sense of God standing within the shadow of destiny, that vague homesickness of the spirit which comes upon the majority of youth, which is probably all that many people have of genuine religious experience. I have met few people who do not confess to that sense of lack, the ache of an organ born blind, or, as in Mary's case, made so either by the trauma of grief or those unaccountable shifts of the mechanism of personality which occur at adolescence. Whether the direct perception of what experienced Methodists call Joy of the Lord, would have come back earlier had the child been released sooner to the influences that for her naturally gave rise to spiritual perceptivity, I do not know; nor whether anything better than Methodism could have happened to her in the interim, before it did. Nothing better offered. I recall Mother, Sunday mornings, singing hymns and waiting for me to come and tie her bonnet strings, and Cousin George Dugger, eyes half-closed, face lifted, starting the singing in 'Class' or at 'Protracted Meetings' on Pentecost Hill, and I know that they both got out of it the same thing that Mary ached for, and never did get while she was a Methodist. There is, however, this sole advantage of Protestant sects, that one is more easily rid of them than other religions that take firmer hold on 'belief.' Mary, as a matter of fact, never did give genuine intellectual acceptance to the Methodist doctrine of Salvation. She never felt lost — simply out of touch; and tried as a child tries, to get back by joining the church. For her 'belief' was always so thin a shell to the spiritual urge that it was shed with comparative ease.

There was a revival that winter in our church, which Mary, on account of school work, was not attending. But she felt it. Night after night, left alone in the house, pushing away her books and pressing her face to the window-pane and the dark, she felt it coming to her as afterward she was to feel the call of the tribal drum, and so be drawn to ceremonies strange and moving and unfamiliar to white eyes. Nobody said anything to Mary, nor she to anyone, until at last she mentioned it to Daisy Bird, who mentioned it to Fanny Silsby, so that by mutual agreement the three of them got excused from the classroom at school and went apart in the basement of the old public school and prayed. They didn't, poor dears, know how else to go about it, though Mary, personally, always loathed the mouthy public praying of Methodists. Whatever it meant to Daisy or Fanny, either I never knew or have forgotten. Mary who was, with all her mysticism, as matter of fact as any other Dugger, went the next night to the meeting, went forward at the revivalist's invitation, went through all the motions, and presently announced solemnly that she was Saved — that was the formula — was put on six months' 'probation,' and in due course taken into full church membership. She was a dutiful member; taught the infant class in Sunday School; was, in fact, overconscientious of her duty, to make up for the experience that never came, not at least in that frame and fashion. Brother Jim was also drawn into church membership a year or so earlier or later, I forget which, having made the customary young man's gesture of doubt, and even played a little with atheism.

They are wrong, those modern Victorian commentators, in ascribing hypocrisy to the general behavior-speech of the period. Behavior was the most communicative speech available to a people only two generations removed from practical illiteracy. There were certain intellectual attitudes it was the accepted gesture to take, certain authors to have read; as, for instance, young gentlemen, trembling on the verge of complete commitment to the bourgeois faiths of the day, were expected to have made the gesture of having read and rejected Voltaire and Robert Ingersoll. Most of Mary's young men acquaintances admitted to both of them, at which Mary made the appreciative gesture of shivering at their daring and rejoicing at their escape. It was necessary to their self-respect, and no more hypocritical than that other purely male gesture of growing hair upon the upper lip.

The way Mary knew that they didn't invariably read the wicked Frenchman and 'the Pope of the Infidels,' was that she finally read them herself. She found a volume of Ingersoll in a guest-room, when she was about seventeen, and sat up with him half the night, to her final disappointment. In the years in which the book had been interdicted to religiously brought-up young people, the general American attitude had so widely altered that the Pope of the Infidels appeared a mildly iconoclastic and mildly boring sentimentalist. But, in fact, one knows that in the light of history, he must be reckoned as one of the notable liberators of American thought.

IV

THE really appalling thing about the Methodist morality in which Mary grew up was that its stresses were not upon what the preacher thought, nor what God thought even; the appallingly terrible thing was that you lived your religious life in the judgment of the congregation. Instead of one priest laying up your iniquity before God, you had all the people you had been brought up among, met socially, and did business with, tattling to each other. Measured against a certain freedom of the intellectual life which Protestantism allowed, this was a spiritually crippling condition to be met by youth, and is probably in itself the item which accounts for the general Protestant complaint that the 'Church does not hold its young people.' It creates at the outset tremendous possibilities of conflict between the soul's instinctive choice and the moral prepossessions of the congregation, out of which rise, as out of the cleavages of the earth's crust, mephitic vapors of hypocrisy.

The thing that saved Mary — not without scars — was that there was never with her the slightest hesitation or confusion about the choice of her soul. She was slow sometimes in realizing the extent of her private divagations, and fumbled occasionally at cross-roads, but she always knew, with knife-edged clearness, where she wanted to go. She was finally read out of the Methodist Church for organizing a community theater movement and failing to maintain that Moses wrote the Pentateuch, as you shall hear; but nothing that happened to her in the ten years of Methodism prevented her from making use of salvation where she found it. I suppose, in fact, that morality is, in the absence of true religious intuition, the best personal and social safeguard that a spiritually orphaned society can have. And since Mary did, as the major business of this story is to show, finally shed all the moralities that interfered with her soul, it will be only fair to show, in spite of its ostensible intention to fix and bind, how little Methodism actually interfered with her personal development.

The items that were likeliest to have done so were the earlier Methodist prohibitions against dancing and the theater; neither of which in the local environment meant anything in particular. Dancing, in Mary's youth in the Mississippi Valley, had reduced itself to a merely sexual function. It had grown up there without grace, without any of the means of making it a social ritual, as a measure of social release; one heard of traditions of the early forties when people danced together at barn-raisings and school-house roofings, barefoot, in moccasins or what you had, muscles uncramped from devastating pioneer labors, emotions freed by the whiskey bottle passed over the women's heads, and failing, at the start, of exciting the subtler reactions of rhythmic sensation. Dancing in the United States, as a social art, never quite re-captured that even in the case of that small social group who continued to dance as nearly as possible in the manner of 'genteel' society elsewhere. Brother Jim, before he forswore it in joining the church, danced a little in private houses, but his natural physical clumsiness, the source of which by this time was scarcely suspected, prevented his being captivated by it; while for Mary, whose sex perceptions developed late, dancing as she saw it in the eighteen-eighties revealed nothing of its relation to her own interior problem.

As for the Methodist prohibitions against the theater, Mary had no way of knowing whether or not the commercial theater of her youth was in the least like what the Methodists thought it. All through the Abolition belt, going to 'Uncle Tom's Cabin' was a religious rite in itself, and seeing that other Passion Play of the Middlewest, called the 'Union Spy,' or the 'Confederate Spy,' according as it was performed north or south of Mason and Dixon's Line (at which crossing all the heroes and villains changed sides), was practically obligatory. The curious can still procure copies of the 'Union Spy' at French's, but in the early eighties the 'Union Spy' was usually produced, under the direction of an ex-officer, as a benefit for the local G.A.R. (Grand Army of the

Republic, of course. Imagine living in an age when one has to explain what those initials mean!) In Carlinville it was produced in the 'Op'ry' House, which was the old Methodist Church revamped, the same out of which Susie had walked in August of '61, in her rose-lilac dress to find her young Captain at the door. Brother Wilkins, who had been an Army chaplain, attended the play; Cousin George Dugger drove in from the farm three nights running. All the supers' parts were taken by G.A.R. men, who rebuilt the 'business' from their own experiences.

Another drama of the highest moral implications, for which the prohibitions of Methodism were withdrawn, was 'Ten Nights in a Bar-Room.' I should like to see it again; also 'The Two Orphans.' The point of exemption of such amateur performances was that they were usually undertaken as benefits for one or another public service, the Library, the various local charities, so that one way or another, even after joining the church, Jim and Mary saw or even participated in most of them. They both had quick memories and good deliveries, even without any special acting talent. Mary went further.

Carlinvillians, who prided themselves on keeping up with the larger world, would go down to St. Louis periodically to attend the performances of visiting stock companies. Mary herself, at Uncle Alex's expense and with his connivance — he crossed his heart to die that Susie should never hear of it — saw Joe Jefferson in 'Rip Van Winkle.' I don't know why a commercial performance of 'Rip' should have seemed so much worse for people's morals than an amateur performance of 'The Two Orphans.' But that is how it was. Mary left home early Saturday morning to spend the day among old neighbors in Plum Street — 'spending the day' was the survival of pioneer social practice, still in force — went straight to the station, waited at the depot in St. Louis for Uncle Alex arriving on the later train, had lunch — dinner we called it — at a public restaurant for the first time without her mother, and, after returning to Carlinville, went along Irish Row to Lily Lancaster's to spend the night. Mary, when it came to the things that she recognized as the choice of her soul, hadn't a scruple. Nobody ever found out, for by the time it would no longer have mattered to Mary, Uncle Alex was the father of a family and watched his step; if he hadn't forgotten about it, he wouldn't have wanted it known that he had once connived at parental deception.

What all this came to, in the lives of young people growing up in American small towns, was that the margin of social entertainment reclaimed from crude sensory indulgence was small; so small that a conscientious young Methodist didn't miss much in being inhibited from it. What was lacking to a degree that made the Church itself a victim of the lack was opportunity for æsthetic enjoyment. Music, although partially redeemed by an older folk tradition, was rapidly approaching that phase of vapid sentimentality which attained its highest pitch in the nineties. In the Middlewest, even music failed for the want of professional technique and understanding. Everybody 'took lessons'; the ability to 'play a few pieces' was, for young ladies, the indispensable accomplishment. What mothers of families went through in the way of self-denial to achieve piano lessons for their children was heroic. Even Mary, with not a smitch of talent and with certainly no money to spare from the family income, plodded faithfully, first under the direction of Aunt Effie, and then under 'Cousin' George Valentine, who had been to the Boston Conservatory, and was consequently usually addressed as 'Perfesser' — every little while I run across people of my own age who still suppose that the title of Professor is automatically acquired by teaching virtuosity. Singing was still taught in public singing schools, and religious songs were popular, 'Beulah Land,' 'Rock of Ages,' 'The Sweet By and By,' along with the old favorites which still had power to move. A few years earlier, the Fisk Jubilee Singers had brought those unforgettable Negro spirituals, 'Swing Low, Sweet Chariot,' 'Wrestle, Jacob, Wrestle,' which carried the prevailing religious emotionalism to a higher pitch than it had been able to reach with the then so popular Moody and Sankey 'Gospel Hymns.' Compared with what came after, it wasn't so bad; but the instrumental music that we heard in those days rarely escaped banality. (What one must by no means leave out is the fact that when the Fisk Singers were in town — black as stovepiping they were — Grandpa Graham entertained two of them in his house.) Mary thinks she recalls hearing Blind Tom play when she was four years old, and Ole Bull several years later, but she may only re-member hearing them talked about.

Little as the Middlewest knew of music, there never was a time in Mary's recollection when the people did not aspire to know it. They called the 'Classical' composers by name, and prided them-selves on recognizing the best-known compositions. And oddly enough, the same people not only made no claim to appreciation of the plastic arts, but prided themselves on knowing nothing about them. I suspect Protestantism there. It wasn't alone the implication of Art with every sort of irregularity, including the nude figure, that prejudiced the Middlewestern mind, though that was bad enough. Artists were 'different,' made a point of being so, insisted that in such difference the merit of their artistry inhered. And to be different implied a criticism on what was es-tablished, orthodox, 'normal.' But deeper than that, art, es-pecially pictorial art, had so lent itself to the uses of Roman Catholicism that there was always danger of the taint rubbing off. It was Timothy Cole's reproductions of great masterpieces, in 'The Century' of that time, that first lifted the curse, and even from those, when Mary tried to show them to him, Cousin George averted his face. He did not wish to go against 'The Century,' but the Scarlet Woman was, for him, if not directly in the scene, not far behind the Saints and Madonnas they displayed. Susie wasn't so narrow as that, but then I also suspect Susie of not knowing that a Titian Madonna was Catholic. It was a Christian subject, and if 'The Century' said it was a masterpiece, she ac-cepted it as such.

People hadn't yet begun to say of pictures, 'Well, I know what I like.' Intelligentsia of today, to whom that phrase represents the nadir of æsthetic interest and critical discrimination, do not begin far enough back. Mary is aware of an earlier time when the root of æsthetic interest was purely fetishistic, attention caught and held by secondary considerations of value; strangeness, rarity, historic and social association, mere virtuosity, anything that induced contemplation, enabled you to look at a thing in addition to seeing it. It wasn't until Americans began to look at pictures that they 'knew what they liked.'

It was the World's Fair, as the Whatnot on an unprecedented scale, that initiated the knowing-what-you-like state of mind. It taught Middlewesterners to look at pictures not altogether as curios, but as collective expression, even though for millions it was only their foreignness, their expensiveness, their tricks of skill that engaged. Among so many notable expressions not all Americans remained dumb, they pricked themselves into attention by those flashes of recognition which have nothing to do with art as the ultimate technique of expressiveness, but have to do with the underlying experience, giving rise to the need of expression. It is said that after the World's Fair the chromo, that bright atrocity of color and chiaroscuro, examples of which could in Mary's youth be seen in practically every middle-class American home, sensibly and rapidly declined. The only place you can be sure of getting one now is in repositories of urban resort where immigrants of the first generation hock their household goods during the periodic down curves of American prosperity. The unfortunate item for Mary was that she happened to grow up between the World's Fair and the Centennial — which was the Whatnot at its historical most authentic — when the early American tradition of beauty and suitability in household furnishings and the appurtenances of cultivated living was ebbing fast, and no new æsthetic, native to the time and experience, rising in its place. At this juncture it was the unhappy fate of Methodism to make, and in making lose its chance of leadership in American culture, the mistake of approaching the whole problem of æsthetics on a moralistic transvaluation of the place of the plastic arts in the social and personal life. It wasn't, for Mary's future as a creative artist, so much a menace that her material surroundings through the impressionable years were ugly, but that this was a sort of ugliness which took false emphasis from its moral implications.

I am so little disposed to put blame where it is undeserved that I have taken pains recently to go over the ground of Mary's hope, when she became a Methodist, of finding again the God who came to her first under the walnut tree. There was a mystical life of Methodism, though you hear little enough of it now, which was not missed by Grandpa Graham, nor by my mother and Cousin George. You saw it in their faces; you heard it discussed under terms of Conviction of Sin, Redemption and Sanctification. Other people had favorite Bible phrases; there was a stooped white-haired man who used to come to 'Class,' and now and then would lift a tear-suffused face and cry, 'I've been washed! *Washed in the Blood of the Lamb!*' which to Mary was not a pleasant figure, but she knew what it meant. Great-Aunt Mary Dugger told how she had surely known when she had attained to Sanctification; there was a light around her, and a pleasantness, and the words she was reading in the Bible at the time stood out blackly and higher than she was against the flame. This was not unlike what had happened to Mary at the bottom of the orchard; but nothing that they told her made it happen again. Mary never had a Conviction of Sin, nor was she Sanctified. She went around with a vague homesick feeling for God under the walnut tree, and could not find Him.

At seventeen, Mary did not intellectually know that there are other phases of the Mystic Life than those she heard described, but she sensed the gaps in the accounts she heard. She knew that, as far as Great-Aunt Mary and Cousin George were concerned, there were places where the life of the spirit went on underground. Susie was always quite inarticulate about her own experience, and Grandpa Graham was Scotch. What Mary knows now is, that the underground passages taken by a good Methodist soul were precisely those to which the Mysticism of Romanism had been particularly attached. Mercifully the spirit of man guards him against the frailties of his intelligence; in those cases it made securely to its Methodist goal without openly taking him through the abhorred soul motions of Papists.

The thing that Mary did understand was that her own mystical experience differed from Cousin George's in lacking the positive emotional element. Cousin George went on from peak to peak of religious intensity, dizzy with the joy of it. But Mary felt the Presence of God without feeling anything about it. It was real, as real as anything you saw or felt with your hands, but you couldn't get excited about it. Mary was a pragmatist in religion; she temperamentally demanded that something more should come out of mystical experience than the mere ecstatic notice of its taking place, demanded that she should, so to speak, actually go to the circus and not simply be transported by viewing the procession. All her life it had been necessary for Mary not only to go to the circus, but to bring something back, a count of the zebra's stripes, the clown's jokes, tricks of the bareback rider which she could practice at home on the old mare, without which pragmatic residue you didn't really feel that you had been to the circus.

For Mary, emotion that failed to result in her being or becoming something different, in her knowing or having something that she hadn't known or had before, was a Barmecide feast. Yet for so many of her contemporaries, emotions, particularly the religious and moral emotions, were so patently enough in themselves. It was just one of the ways things are!

When it comes, however, to the felt inadequacy of the moral conclusions that were pressed upon Mary from every side, their shadowy quality was realized through her being made too often the victim of them.

It wasn't until the family had settled well into the house on Johnson Street that Mary began to feel herself harassed by family criticism of her individual divergences on no better ground than that they were divergences. That year Mary had finally overcome the two years' difference in their school grades that divided her from Jim, and, though not yet sharing all his classes, they sat under the same teacher, and Mary began to be the subject of that acute sensitivity of brothers to lapses, on the part of their young sisters, from severest propriety. Well, of course, brothers always did tell on you. It seemed to be part of their official prerogative as arbiters of what could or could not be said to or in front of sisters and the obligation to lick other boys who violated these restrictions. But it seemed to Mary that there was too much relish sometimes in the telling, and, besides, Mary had her own notions of the proprieties.

It was in the business of a spirited self-justification that she first explicitly noticed something of which she had been, ever since that summer in Boston, dimly aware, the extent to which her mother was reshaping the family and her own affectional life around her eldest son, shaping him to that part it was so widely agreed was suitable to be played, and 'sweet' to observe him playing, as the widow's son.

One tries to present a situation, usual enough then, not so usual now, as it occurred, as an incident in the education of Mary. What my mother was proceeding toward, with the sanction of the most treasured of American traditions, was constituting my brother, at fifteen or thereabouts, the Head of the family. According to the tradition, she had a right to expect Mary to contribute a certain acquiescence in a situation which kept the shape if not the content of the best my mother's generation knew of the ritual of sex. It was a way to maintain what the high-minded women of her generation esteemed the crown of a woman's life, the privilege of being the utterly giving and devoted wife of one man who could make it still seem a privilege, although it violated all the other natural motions of the woman's being. Susie was justified, in a compulsion of advice and remonstrance, to persuade Mary into the traditional attitudes. What she missed realizing was that a general social change in those attitudes was imminent, and that both her children were probably unconsciously responding to it according to their natures. Hers was not the only household in which struggles between brothers and sisters were going on, prophetic of the somewhat later conflict between traditionalism and realism which was so to alter the whole status of American marriage. Mary wasn't by any means the only girl of that period insisting on going her own way against the traditions, and refusing to come to a bad end on account of it.

Years after, when the feminist fight, marshaled in the direction of Woman Suffrage, became the occasion of conferences of women from all parts of the world, in the relaxing hour between committee meetings and campaign planning, there would be confidences. 'Well, it was seeing what my mother had to go through that started me'; or, 'It was being sacrificed to the boys in the family that set me going'; or, 'My father was one of the old-fashioned kind...' I remember three English sisters who all together and at once took to window-smashing and hunger fasts because they simply could not endure for another minute the tyranny of having their father spend their dress money every year in a single bolt of cloth of his own choosing, from which they were expected to make up what they wore. Women of high intelligence and education went white and sick telling how, in their own families, the mere whim of the dominant male member, even in fields which should have been exempt from his interference, had been allowed to assume the whole weight of moral significance.

It was a four-minute egg that set Mary going.

I have already related how, scrambling out of sleep rendered uneasy by too early responsibility and not always untouched by the consciousness of her father's recurrent anguish, Mary had acquired a prejudice against the very soft-boiled egg, so that her never very stable appetite revolted at seeing one broken even unsuspectingly before her. I don't know just when her quite justifiable request to have her egg put in the kettle a minute or two before the others began to break down the general disposition to create, out of her brother's status as the Head of the family, a criterion of how eggs should be served. It was only one of many unimportant oddments in which the necessity arose of considering Mary as a separate item in the family ritual which Susie was happily reconstituting around her eldest son. It was to be for Jim as nearly as possible as it had been when the whole affectional and practical interest of the family had centered on Father having what he wanted and being pleased by it. To remember Mary's egg became a constantly annoying snag in the perfect family gesture of subservience to the Head, which all her woman's life had gone to create. And perhaps there was latent in Susie's mind, in spite of her avowed liberality toward the woman movement, something of the deep-seated conviction, on the part of the house-mother, that drove many girls of Mary's generation from the domestic life, that a different sort of boiled egg was more than a female had a right to claim on her own behalf. I can, at any rate, recall very well the completely justified manner with which she would say, on those increasing occasions when it turned out that Mary's egg had not been remembered, 'Well, my dear, if you can't learn to take your food like the *rest* of the family...' But even more it proved a distraction and an annoyance when Mary was left to prepare her own egg. 'Oh, Mary, why do you always have to have something different from the *rest* of the family...' And finally when Jim, consistently playing his part as the complaisant favorite of the house, delivered judgment, 'Somehow you never seem to have any feeling for what a HOME should be'; not in the least realizing that there was growing up in the minds of thousands of young American women at that moment, the notion that it, at least, *shouldn't* be the place of the apotheosis of its male members. In so far as the difficulty about the extra minute and a half proved annoying to Mary, she settled it by deciding that she didn't care for eggs for breakfast. And yet, slight as the incident seems, it served to fix the pattern of family reaction to Mary's divergences.

You are not to suppose, however, that the Hunter brothers and sister didn't get on together as well as other young people. Jim, for instance, always backed Mary up in her demand for control over her own personal expenditures, which was so far in advance of general American practice of the time that ten or a dozen years later the average married man would still get up and leave the room if by chance the talk turned on that burning question, Should a wife have a regular allowance?

Jim was not so tight-bound as that in his version of female morality, partly because, when he was the age to take a tone in these matters, his own mother went about a great deal, participating in this new public business of remodeling the 'liquor situation' for the country at large. Also, Jim was extremely fond of an argument, rather fancied himself in forensic attitudes, and it had to be admitted that none of the girls he knew, and few of the young men, provided him with such satisfying occasions for it as his sister Mary. They argued about everything from Herbert Spencer to why pearls occur in oysters, and it was extremely good for them. There might also have been ameliorations for her moral lapses in the fact that when they were young together, his sister never refused him the first aid and public loyalty which is due to brothers. For the source of the unhappy alienations of later years, one must go further and deeper.

V

In the summer of 1884, Grandfather Graham died. One recalls him sitting, silent and gently minded, under the honeysuckle on the front porch, with his cane in his hand, as though about to set out for the land of no return, or by the evening fire with the Bible across his knees, and his eyes, not on the text, but on that city of Revelation to which Mary had wished so ardently not to go. The day of his death, Mary had been at the house most of the morning helping to prop up the pillows that eased him of his labored breathing, and along toward noon, since he seemed so much easier, she had been sent to look after things at home. An hour later suddenly Mary was seized with heavy sobbing and a cause-less grief, as unfamiliar as unexpected. But when half an hour later, she saw the little lame boy from next door to Grandpa's, coming slowly toward her along the treeless street, she knew at once what the grief had been about.

Strangely, when Father died, he went instantly and completely away, so that those sudden forgettings, the impulse to run and include him in the experience of the hour, had always the double poignancy of making more sure the loss. But my darling old Grandpa was for many years always about, in a shy, faint friend-liness, enclosed in a dimension I could not pass, wisely smiling and close at hand.

At his death the family fell apart. For the old feeling of family solidarity, the young Hunters had to depend on the Graham cousins and Cousin Ellen's three girls. There was no doubt about it, the great Macoupin Clans were breaking up. The Duggers were moving West, into the newly opened lands of California and Oregon. Mary herself went West a few years later, and in her shuttlings to and fro across the continent, the vanished names are always cropping up: outlooks so like, so terribly like the back-ground of Mary's youth, that she has never known how to escape except by completely understanding them; Americanism so absolute that there is no chance at all of its coming to anything by escaping *back* into the womb of European culture. It must, at any risk, strike root and lift a burgeoning top into the native air.

The year after Jim finished with public school, a year of Latin was added to the grammar school course, along with physics and chemistry, immensely exciting. So Mary stayed on and Jim worked his way intermittently through the first year and a half of Blackburn. That winter Mary also took on a new responsibility; she became acutely concerned over the fact that George, then between seven and eight, was not taking properly to reading. George was still an attractive child; thick chestnut curls, china-blue eyes, and cheeks of sunburnt pink, but showing, to a sharp sisterly eye, an undeniable tendency toward pudginess. And decidedly reluctant toward books. Mary was shocked. Susie said, 'Why worry; he'll take to it when the time comes.' She said, 'I should think you would know by this time what comes of trying to be too old for yourself.'

Susie was referring back to something that happened the year before when Mary had come across a book by an author associated in her mind with her father's reading, 'Seven Lamps of Architecture,' copiously illustrated. She read and read, not always understandingly, sick, genuinely sick for someone to talk to about it. And her fairly desperate appeal to her mother hadn't ended happily. Mary had wanted just to turn and savor the work in her mind, make it real for herself that there were buildings in the world like that, strange and lovely whorls and intricate lacings and vinelike twistings of forms in stone; that you could go to them; that she herself might go there sometime; that there were people in the world to whom these things were not strange, but exciting and natural like the beauty of the woods and fields.

Mary wanted more than anything else to read this book with her mother the way Mother and Jim read things and talked them over, as they had read, about that time, Roosevelt's 'Winning of the West.' She wanted something that, since her father's death she had never had, the satisfaction of a child's need of sympathy over an inestimable treasure. Susie thought it all right to read

Ruskin; but not until you were older. And not to make it seem so important. It was all right after you had attended to the real things of life, to have a little of this sort of thing thrown in for sauce; but to read things like 'Seven Lamps,' before you could understand them, was what made you queer, so that people didn't like you. You must be modest in your reading as in everything else. If you talked about reading Ruskin at your age, people would think you were conceited... much more in that key, which seemed to spread like a dull smear over the bright surface of Ruskin, against which all Mary's profounder loyalties were engaged. She simply wasn't going to let her candy be taken away like that.

'I'll bet I could talk to Mr. Burton and Mr. Steward about him,' she insisted, with the note of defiance which is the last one before tears. Mr. Steward was the partner of Mr. Keplinger, living next door, and Mr. Burton was another young lawyer who happened to be the temporary tenant across the street. It was an unfortunate appeal for Mary to have made.

The fact was that Mary found life on Johnson Street dull, so unbearably dull that at times she would break away from it into a kind of secret masquerade, so impossible for her family to imagine that they never really found her out in it. The only kind of misbehavior that advertises itself to people is the kind that they would like to have committed themselves, and Mary's misbehavior was never of the kind that would have appealed to Johnson Street. A few weeks before the affair of the 'Seven Lamps,' Mary had made herself up in the character of a poor widow from Irish Row and begged up and down the street with great success. She got bread and old clothes from the Stewards and others, but Lawyer — afterward Judge — Burton had given her money, and Mary felt that, even at the cost of revealing herself, she had to give it back. Susie referred to that embarrassment now as the sort of thing you got yourself into by reading strange books.

Mary's notion of the proper approach to a book was to put your hand in its and go where it led you. But from the beginning George assumed that the business of a book was to make itself personally agreeable; where it failed to do so, he felt — this is an attitude still making itself evident in American criticism — somewhat miffed.

The phase of college life in which Jim shone was debate and oratory; an enterprise which was peculiarly susceptible of outside aid. My mother put all she had into it; as for Mary, hadn't she always written her schoolmates' compositions? Letters, too; those long effusions which schoolgirls write to themselves under romantic pseudonyms, which parents are so prone to misunderstand, Mary, who never wrote them for herself, but for other girls, was clever at them. She never put anything into one which would give away that they were written by a girl.

It was impossible that Mary should not have been drawn into her brother's forensic undertakings. Her special contribution was in the matter of delivery. Mary had had lessons in elocution from a regular 'Professor' of the art. I have often wondered why Mark Sullivan, or somebody who knows, has not written a proper evaluation of the tribe of 'Perfessers' who circulated through mid-America offering tidbits of cultural technique, elocution, voice-training, conversation, penmanship, character-reading, and the principles of success. They were always handsomely whiskered and wore derby hats; they were the first, the very first emissaries of the practice of manicure; at least I recall that their nails were always carefully pared and polished. Mary had a great many advantages of that sort. As a leading citizen, Grandpa Graham always patronized such gentry to the extent of buying 'scholarships' and Mary was the one of his grandchildren who snapped them up. It happened sometimes that they really did know what they taught. Mary's teacher in elocution must have been genuinely good, since she still, in lecturing, makes use successfully of what he taught her. (I wrote him into 'A Woman of Genius.') That was how it was that when Jim decided to go in for the Oratorical Contest, he put himself into his sister's hands.

The Oratorical Contest was a Middlewestern institution from which such notable culture heroes as William Jennings Bryan admit that they have had much benefit. It would begin with a

LOU HENRY HOOVER
From a photograph taken in London (see pages 311, 312)

competition among the small College Literary Societies, from which the winners would go on to the Inter-Collegiates, and from that to the State and Inter-State contests, so that once a young man's feet were set on that ladder, a long brilliant prospect glittered before him. After Jim won the laurels for his Society, the whole strength of the family was set to get him victoriously through the Inter-Collegiate.

The year of her brother's first success, Mary was at loose ends, and could give herself whole-heartedly to the correction of his disposition to overcome natural awkwardness by a forced violence of delivery and explosive voice production. Mary had started to Blackburn in the fall, but along about the holidays one of those heavy colds to which she was subject had so broken into the term that she was unable to go on with it. There was at that time an Art Department attached to Blackburn, so much better than was usually to be found in small colleges that Mary, who had always a burning wish to paint, was able to occupy herself with it for the remainder of the school year. By that time, in view of the improbability of her being able to command the physical strength for a college course, and because teaching was so patently the only way of earning a living open to girls in the Middlewest, it was decided that she should complete her formal preparation for it at the State Normal School at Bloomington. That was how it happened that when Jim was preparing for the Inter-Collegiate, Mary was out of reach. The first informative news she had of it was that he had taken the lowest place. As all the reports made a point of his forced and awkward delivery, she grieved privately, suspecting that she might have prevented the disaster. When she had to go home herself a month or two later, she confidently expected that something would be said about it, such as, 'If you had been here, Sis...' — anything that would have admitted her to the community of her family interest. But nobody so much as mentioned it.

When I first began on this story of Mary's life, seeking for a criterion of choice among the multitudinous incidents that come crowding on recollection, it seemed to me that it should be of those especial incidents that projected forward into the pattern of achievement, to be set down as they arose, and later absorbed into the texture of social solutions such as it has been Mary's fortune to pursue. From the peak of sixty years such trifling occurrences take their place in the slow progression of woman's mastery over her own talent which it has been the business of Mary's generation to initiate on a scale of social significance. They take their place with the story of Dorothy Wordsworth and Mary Lamb, with what May Sinclair, Beatrice Webb, and any number of American women, who shall be named in their place, went through in the disentangling of their natural endowment from the givingness of women, from their tendency to see in the exactitudes of professional technique only another oddity of the male mind.

Not that Mary was ever in danger of giving away her gift to brother, husband, or lover. She had, for one thing, too much inherent drive; and she had for another the good luck never to meet, until she had trademarked it to herself, with a man clever enough to take the measure of what she had to give.

VI

ALWAYS there will be a doubt in Mary's mind whether she did or did not see the Temperance Crusaders. In the early seventies the papers were full of their performances, and Mary's recollections of two of them, come into the far West of Illinois to explain their crusade, are explicit; a matronly figure in brown merino with trimmings of plaid silk cut bias, and a younger woman in dark blue shot silk with rows and rows of narrow black velvet ribbon around and around it, speaking in somebody's parlor. Mary thinks it might have been Mrs. Mayo's; she was enchanted with the younger one in a pork-pie hat with pink roses under the brim, and the little sacque, cut in square bobs and bound with the same velvet ribbon. It was all too explicit for her not to have seen *something*, though Susie always insisted that Mary was too young for the Crusaders. Anyway, the newspapers of the day were full of their doings; pictures of them praying in front of saloons, or even inside, with astounded and embarrassed barkeepers looking on, and men still keeping their hands on their full glasses, but covering their eyes respectfully while the women knelt on the sawdust amid the spittoons and prayed: women in sealskin sacques; women in plaid dolmans with little flat winged hats; women in voluminous widow's veils that with their suggested ritual always made an immense impression on Mary. A proper widow, one who, having put on that livery of grief in middle life, expected never to take it off again, always wore two veils, a short one with a hem whose depth dignified the duration of her bereavement, worn over the face with just room for a frequent use of the black-bordered handkerchief, and a longer one behind, which took its length and voluminousness from her fortune rather than the depth of her grief, thrown back over the little widow's bonnet with its white ruching, and swathing her to the knees. Just ordinary widows, who hoped to marry again or had their living to make, shortened their veils after the first year, lopping off a foot or two every six months, narrowing at the same time the deep bands of crêpe at wrists and hems. There must have been, for the feeling of them so to have impressed itself on Mary's mind, more than a few widows in those Crusades; but whether she actually saw two of the Crusaders from Ohio where it began, or whether it was some other matter that mixed with the Temperance Crusade in her head, it is impossible now to determine, since there is nobody left of Mary's acquaintance who remembers.

Anyway, there was a Crusade which began in the early seventies and led on to the singular and world-embracing activities of the W.C.T.U. There is no reason at all why Mary shouldn't remember. She remembers the Chicago Fire, the rumor of it, and the gathering of the Plum Street neighbors at her father's house to hear Judge Hunter's report when he came home in the evenings— strange to realize that there were no telephones in those days and even the telegraph was a novelty. She remembers the Keely Motor, so vividly that it always seemed to her that Keely's trial must have taken place in the County Court House. She recalls the rumor of Boss Tweed and Victoria Woodhull, and I am sure she would have recognized Horace Greeley on the street. So whether or not representatives of the Woman's Crusade ever came to Carlinville, the fact of the Crusade and the steady gathering of the forces of Temperance in the Middlewest was never again, so long as she lived there, absent from her mind.

I have a notion that the first organized Temperance movement to reach Mary's home was of English origin. There is evidence that both Mary's father and Cousin Bill Dugger joined the English society of Good Templars, as early as '58, and in '74, Mary herself was wearing the blue ribbon of the Band of Hope, and joining heartily in

> Sparkling and bright in its liquid light
> Is the water in our glasses,

and so on heroically through

> Oh, then resign the ruby wine
> Each smiling son and daughter —

ruby wine figuring in the singer's mind as somehow akin to pink circus lemonade. Also vaguely I recall a public citation of little

Robert Reed, who would not touch tobacco, no, it is a filthy weed!
— in which Mary at the mature age of six and a half was letter-
perfect.

After the Good Templars there were the Temperance Evangel-
ists, Campbell, Gough, and others, the vague but titillating public
confessions of sin and degradation, the testimony of the Old Soaks,
the teary, timorous wives of converted drunkards, the hopeful
interval, the almost inevitable backslidings. Finally, Frances
Willard.

One observes, on the part of the younger generation who know
nothing about it, a disposition to sentimentalize about the saloon
of the last quarter of a century; to reconstruct it as a genial place of
folk resort, the Poor Man's Club, the prosperous merchant's occasion of democratic relaxation. But to the women who prayed
against it, who went on from that to organize against it, who
achieved an unbelievable legislation against the saloon, it was
nothing of the sort. To Mary coming and going on her schoolgirl
errands, it was a place of sour, stale smells, of loud, foolish laughter,
a laughter such as accompanies things not said in the presence of
women, raucous, quarreling voices. It was a place from which
might issue at any moment people you knew, other girls' fathers,
forcible ejections of sodden and bleary men who proceeded to be
violently sick on the sidewalk as a prelude to going to sleep there,
or at best mouthed obscenely their sense of irreparable injury. As
you knew, you hopelessly knew, they had been thrown out, not for
being disgusting, but for not being able to pay for the privilege of
covering up their disgustingness with that other happy state of
being dead drunk. Sooner or later you might meet the mother of
one of your schoolmates, shamefacedly steering her tipsy and abu-
sive lord to the home where your mother wouldn't let you visit, lest
you might see some such spectacle as you actually did meet occasionally on your way to school. Three kinds of drunkards were still
recognized in the Middlewest: chicken drunk, in which a man becomes merely silly; owl drunk, a state of being stupidly clever; and
hog drunk, such as brings a man to the gutter. At the best, there

was always a stench coming out of saloons in the eighties, stale beer, hot whiskey breaths, the smell of vomit, the faint unmistakable odor of maleness on the loose. And on election days, if you had to go out, you realized at once why your mother kept you at home at such times if she could.

Let there be no doubt about it, election day in the Middlewest was the one thing that lent color to the question in the minds of delicate women of their being able to endure the privilege of the ballot. It wasn't supposed in the eighties that you could rid elections of the features that made them dubious occasions for decent women to be about. For Mary, there grew up an implication of disgust about the half-screened doors of saloons in the Middlewest, the odors and suggestiveness, that had no counterpart in her experience until years after she encountered, in the half-screened latrines of the French capital, the same odors and implications of offense.

To realize the intensity of the Middlewestern campaign against the saloon, you must continually subtract from the scene Mary's special capacity for knowing what she sees and being able to state it. Thus you get the substance of what her mother's generation could express only in the quality of shocked sensibility, deal with only under figures of iniquity. For them the 'demon rum' — it was actually raw corn whiskey — menaced the great American motivation, was, in the last quarter of the nineteenth century, the only item that opposed itself markedly to an achieved success. At its simplest that motivation was to possess the land and live on it. Of the time and the town of which I write, practically all of its solid citizenry had sprung from the upper bourgeoisie of Northern Europe, or the landless scions of the least privileged aristocracy. They had come primarily from the British Isles, and latterly from Germany, escaping from oppressive militarism and overripe social privilege. With this prospect of reëstablishing themselves on the new land, they had driven out the wild tribes, subdued the wilderness, and projected into a servantless society their ideals of culture and social continuity. And except for the then faint shadow of special privilege and the saloon, they had achieved a world-singular success. Of the fight against economic privilege there are any number of Happy Warriors now setting down the incidents of a still active campaign. It is, apparently, left to Mary to record neglected aspects of the struggle against the saloon as threatening the elements in American culture which have their common origin in the preciousness of women.

Few people whose social concepts can be sorted under the half-century mark can have any realizing sense of the extent to which the whole American complex in the eighteen-hundreds revolved about that notion of the preciousness of women. To preserve such achieved preciousness, the woman must renounce any effort on her own behalf, she must seem, at least, to rest entirely on her man's capacity for creating around her an atmosphere of exemption, of untouchability. Always she must seem to serve, not her own need of protection, but the quality of protectiveness in her man. She might even have to renounce property, to claim few rights, and to rest her case on the assumed material competence of men in general. If these failed her by death, in a pioneer society there was always another man; if they failed her by incapacity or moral dereliction, she was lost.

And the one nearly invincible moral dereliction of men at that time arose out of the habit of hard drinking. It ate into the family income, and made the thrift and industry of the wife of no account. It reduced the pride of the family to public shame. It added to the perils of child-bearing unmentionable horrors, all the more feared as they were little understood. I realize that there is doubt in high quarters as to the harm an habitual drunkard can do to his unborn offspring; there was less doubt when Mary was young. It was in view of the possibilities that a drunken father was believed to visit on his unborn offspring that the question of divorce and the right of women to choose when and under what conditions they will bear children was first admitted to the Protestant consciousness in the United States. It was only by insistence on that hazard that intelligent women faced out the genuine horror with which otherwise intelligent men met the bare mention of wifely withdrawal and the sanctions of choice. There is no interpretation of the Volstead Act

more in error than the one which assumes it as the transvaluation
of an impulse to persecution. It arose during Mary's growing-up,
in the light of her hard young intelligence, as a measure of protection against an intolerable imposition upon child-bearing women.

Somebody must say these things while there are still living witnesses to the social sequences of the period. What was known as
'hard liquor' begot violence in drinkers, and excited what was, for
the women who made it, a violence of resistance. I remember how
it was for the young Cogans with whom I played. I remember a
pretty German woman who used to bring her three children to our
house to be left until their father recovered from 'one of his spells.'
I recall how she came one night with a great bloody bruise on her
face, and my mother insisting on treating it with some sort of em-
brocation, and the unwiped tears on my mother's face while the
two women kept up between them the pretense of a blameless accident. I remember the first woman who was allowed to speak in
our church on the right of women to refuse to bear children to
habitual drunkards, and my mother putting her arm across my
knees and taking my hand in one of the few natural gestures of a
community of woman interest she ever made toward me. And then
I remember Frances Willard.

She was slight and pretty, full of patience and tact unending and
great charm for women. She had courage, and, within certain
widely accepted limits of Protestantism, great liberality of thought.
She had a statesmanly talent, and political intuition of wider range
and greater spontaneity than any American woman I have ever
known. There is no woman of her time Mary would have regretted
more to miss; notwithstanding that her manner, her method with
her public, her moral sentiments and religious convictions were
cross-gartered to Mary's own.

I do not recall how early my mother united with the Woman's
Christian Temperance Union; probably the first time she heard of
it. At any rate, it was when Mary was still so young that her
mother would not have known what else to do with her while she
was in attendance on its sessions and so took her about to them.
How the women of our town, an important minority of them,

loved that organization! With what sacred pride they wore its inconspicuous white ribbon; with what pure and single-minded ardor they gave themselves to learn to serve it, legal technicalities, statistics, Roberts's Rules of Order, the whole ritual of public procedure. Only women who recall how far back in social evolution the ritual of mass behavior began know how hard it was for them. During those first years there was scarcely a meeting in which they did not more or less come to grief over parliamentary procedure, or one in which somebody was not hurt in her feelings to the point of bursting into tears. And then they would hold hands and sing a hymn and begin all over again. With the result that for precision and directness in the conduct of public meetings, American women finally reduced our Senate and Houses of Representatives to shame.

One recalls, between pity and indignation, the straits they were put to to carry on, how little money they had; women in sealskin sacques and diamond brooches whose husbands looked hurt and sulked at the request for spending money — 'Darling, if there is anything else that I don't *buy* for you!' — the tricks they had to resort to to secure the cash for their Union dues. In all my life I have not seen anything so single-minded, so gallant, so truly Crusading, as those women and their Union. And all the time I was not really liking, not personally approving or agreeing with Frances Willard.

There was already between Mary's outlook and her mother's more than a generation's spacing. For Susie, Miss Willard was prophetic; for Mary she was of period date; since Mary, though she did not know it then, was already as much in advance of her own generation as Frances Willard was in hers.

Miss Willard had had, everybody knew she had had, a perfectly good opportunity to marry, and had put it by as incompatible with the thing she had in her heart to do. But to Mary's generation and the next one after her, it was to appear that marriage should not be a hindrance to the choice of the soul, or, if it proved so, then the item to be remedied was marriage. Marriage should take its chance against the voice within. And, of course, Mary's generation discovered that reshaping marriage, so that the woman shouldn't be torn continually between the man's demand for exclusive attention and the woman's natural social aptitudes, was by no means as easy as it promised. Miss Willard had made, it turned out, if not the most courageous, the most practicable, choice.

And there was her continual expenditure of charm in the pursuit of her social goal; she kept it up and kept it up, precisely as a Religious keeps her holy conventual calm. There was never any break or diminution of the supply. But what Mary's generation was presently to burst out proclaiming was that, given a clear perception of intellectual soundness in her claim, woman should be able to dispense with charm, should rest upon the proved rightness of her cause. One realizes, however, that without her really remarkable psychological divination of approach, Frances Willard would have got nowhere with the American women of her own time. She knew not only what to do for them to help them out of their swathing femininity, as a group; she knew what to do for any particular woman to keep her up to the mark. Without any afterthought of resentment at having to do so, she pitched her appeal, as a song leader does his melody, in the key of her audience.

I do not mean, as you hear modern analysts of the Movement insist, that Miss Willard posed her charm; she produced it; she was the charm itself, the key woman of her time. She had a verse of Scripture for every type of spiritual aspiration and knew when to work it and on what souls, to their complete enchantment. I remember well when my mother's turn came to be shown this mystery... *'Though ye have lain among the pots, yet your wings shall be covered with silver, and your feathers with fine gold...'* None knew better than Mary that Susie had never liked, had genuinely revolted against the routine of housework, the pot-washings and sweepings and potato-parings, the compulsions of meals and hours. It was only for love's sake that she found these things possible. She wasn't alone in that. Housekeeping in the last quarter of the last century was at its dullest. The business of ordering the large pioneer household, with exigencies calling forth all a woman's powers of ingenuity and invention, had dwindled to a petty housemaid's round; important only in their implications, but never in themselves. When I remember with what energy of concentration my mother would work through her daily routine in order that she might free her hands and time for the spiritually releasing labor of her church and her beloved W.C.T.U., I seem to see what was going on in most of her contemporaries. And when Frances Willard, with her marvelous penetration into the precise dimensions of the task that irked, came whispering her magic scriptures at their ears, it was like having the sacred haruspices opened before them for a sign.

There was no manner of doubt that Miss Willard 'sold' her following completely to the program she had in mind. The sore point with Mary was that she should accept as normal and necessitous, that they should be so 'sold.' It was always one of the profoundest items of Mary's appreciation of her own mother that she never did consciously utilize this item of salesmanship over her own audiences. For Susie had power with an audience; sweetness and sincerity shone forth in her, an aura of spiritual integrity and some degree of social divination, so that no matter how unaccustomed the public exigency, how taken unawares, how privately embarrassed she might be, in public Susie was never *gauche*, never anything but simply right and dignified.

But Frances Willard, besides great political talent, had a touch of true statesmanship. It was shown in the way in which she so successfully tied up the Union with other forward movements among women, or unobtrusively included them, or fended them off. A great many of her following were opposed on principle to Woman Suffrage, fought all attempts to ally it with the Woman's Christian Temperance Union. And it was as good as a play to watch the way in which Frances Willard circumvented and overrode them. It may perhaps explain the want of enthusiasm with which millions of American women utilized the ballot once they had secured it, to know how many of them acquiesced in it simply as an aid to the, to them, more urgent matter of doing away with the saloon. Women as a whole are still, as they were in the Stone Age, profoundly unconvinced of the pertinence of the political method, but they accepted finally the utility of the political tool.

Frances accepted it as from on High; in the same way she accepted Prohibition, which had not been included in her original Temperance program. I recall in particular the shock which committed thousands of them to the political method, under the discovery, which passed locally through my mother's hands, of the reports of saloon-keepers' conventions, at which were freely discussed recommendations for the dispensing of free drinks to boys as a measure of trade-building, the creation of appetites, and the general psychology of inducing attendance on the part of adolescent boys at drinking places. How many women by that revelation were swept into suffrage, in advance of their political preparation, will never be known.

One of the items which Mary recalls was the secrecy with which much of the woman's rally was attended. One of the principal sources from which my mother financed her particular activities was the contribution made regularly by the mother of a family with whom the little Hunters had played. The husband was a secret drinker. Three or four times a year he would begin, after longer or shorter periods of abstinence, sipping, sipping, steadily increasing the dose until a state of practically continuous 'souse' was arrived at, ending in a mild attack of tremens, and another period of 'being on the wagon,' and so the round again. All this his wife succeeded in so ritualizing that I do not know to this day how much his children realized of what was implied in their father having 'one of his spells.' Mary came to know it because one of his children began very early to exhibit symptoms of a special type of consequence, believed at that time to be the hazard of hard drinkers' children; and because her sensitivity to color had led her to describing impressions made upon her in those terms; she would say, 'Mr. —— must be going to have one of his bad spells because, whenever he comes near me, he has a dark liverish color.' And so Susie told her. That, too, she said was why he couldn't be humiliated by having his wife publicly join the W.C.T.U. But Mrs. —— used to visit Susie periodically with a greenback folded in her handkerchief — 'So that my prayers may be answered.' Susie would pray, too, over the expenditure of that contribution.

I make these personal notes with intention. That was how the 'Temperance Question' played through the lives of young women brought up as Mary was, and caused them to rise up in an energy of opposition to the saloon and all it implied, an energy unprecedented in American affairs. I write them on behalf of Frances Willard, and the innuendoes which the new psychology makes against the whole spirit and animus of her campaign. Because the influence of Frances Willard in Mary's life was more informing than almost any other of that time. Because there are times when the new psychology seems to Mary no more than another mask for the terror that was in men at any move on the part of women in opposition to the male tendency to magnify their biological importance by reading into the sex relation values that it does not intrinsically have, certainly not for women.

From the beginning of the Temperance Movement there was terror in men and the rage that terror begets. In certain sorts of men the opposition to what was going on, only half-consciously amidst the more explicit activities of the W.C.T.U., was frenetic. It was the undiscussable quality of their opposition that led them to welcome a kind of compromise of indirection in the final clinch of Woman Suffrage, an admissible public fixation upon Suffrage as a symbol of what was really going on, still further masked by the myth of sex antagonism. It was probably because the attention of men was so profoundly engaged with this secret conflict that they missed realizing the speed and explicitness with which the wheels of the Prohibition Movement were going round; kept going by the daily exigencies of women whose fathers, brothers, sons, husbands, whose dearly beloved of every kin, set up in them, through drinking habits, the driving force of anguish.

Past all other possible conclusions, the emphasis from what had begun merely as a Temperance Movement altered to Prohibition primarily because men in numbers insisted on getting drunk. If Prohibition by Constitutional Amendment won't stop it, don't let that deflect your view of the final outcome; some other way will be found. The worst, the incredibly stupid worst, that men do, who are opposed to Prohibition in principle, is to keep on getting drunk. If it should occur to them to band together in a Men's *Temperance* Movement — but men are still too much imbued with a notion of the mystical values of drunken release, too little with the possibilities of mystical release in sex, to take any effective measures against the efforts of women to establish control of both. They are, on the whole, too little intelligent about women.

VII

ALL the time that Mary was in touch with them—from the middle eighties, say, until the latter days of 1900 — circulating in and out of the W.C.T.U.'s, not organically related to them, but using their meetings, drawing their audiences from its following, were small, pointed propagandas against all narcotics; against the double standard of sex morality; for sex education, for penal reform, for the abolition of poverty, for a rationalization of divorce, for family limitation, for almost anything you might mention which has since worked to the surface of our national interest among the liberal-minded. I do not mean to say that these were discussed in the precise terms in which they now come before the public, most of which terms were not then invented. Practically all these matters stemmed from the situation of women married to hard-drinking husbands; the relation of amorousness to alcohol, of degeneracy to drink and venereal disease, and the problems these gave rise to as affecting divorce from the Christian standpoint — they led on to the whole study of eugenics, before we had even a name for it, and to the pathologies of sex, for which, until Havelock Ellis provided them, we had in the United States no popular vocabulary.

As a consequence, the pamphlets dealing with those things that came into my mother's hands and so to Mary, were often obscure to the point of concealing their meaning entirely. When they were too explicit for my mother's delicacy, but not for her liberality, I at least knew that much about them by her putting them on my bureau without comment. The item that fell in most with my thinking at the time was Miss Willard's admitting that, though she had begun by thinking of drink as the cause of poverty, there were times when she wondered if poverty were not one of the causes of drink.

It was Miss Willard's exemption, which she shared with most Middlewesterners, from any understanding whatsoever of the creative life, that, although it did not remove Mary from the circle of her activities, cut sharply off any possibility of her being drawn into the sphere of her personal influence.

Ardently concerned as Miss Willard was to create for women a new scope and medium of expression, she missed so far as could be the faintest realizing sense of the province of the creative Arts.

That this should be true of Frances Willard is singular, since she once had literary ambitions. She possessed a phenomenal vocabulary for communicating what she wanted to say to her chosen audience, along with a total want of literary perception. So that it was one of the outrages of Mary's youth that her mother insisted on dragging Mary's gift before Frances Willard for judgment. For it was the singular, if unnoted, trait of American women of her time — or of Women as such? — that they never doubted their own judgment on matters of which, technically, they knew the least — everything that went by the name of art, culture, taste, fitness, and beauty.

In her teens, Mary had begun to write poetry, quite as bad as at her age was to be expected, and her mother, coming across the least excusable example which Mary herself had thrown into the waste-basket without taking the trouble to destroy, had appealed to Miss Willard to know if it had any value that her mother ought to take into account. Miss Willard either had turned the verses over herself, or advised my mother doing so, to 'The Union Signal,' the organ of her Society, where they were later published without Mary's knowledge or consent. It was quite in the note of the time that neither of them had any notion of the violation of the child's privacy involved. Well-brought-up children were not supposed to require privacy. Fortunately, the horror hadn't to be acknowledged to Mary's friends, since, following an idea rather generally accepted in Susie's generation, it was not published under the author's name. Susie always thought a pseudonym or initials more 'womanly' than the barefaced acknowledgment of your literary wares. But if you ask how Mary realized that Miss Willard's judgment on her gift would be, so far as Mary's literary aspiration was concerned, completely inutile, one could answer it best by saying because Hamilton Wright Mabie was Miss Willard's favorite and completely accepted critic.

And that would be scarcely true at the time, because it was not until the middle nineties that Mr. Mabie began to enjoy that quarter of a century of felicity as the perfect instance of what the American public felt a literary man should be. But he was known to have owed his start on that career to Miss Willard's recommendation, and he was the sort of critic of whom it was later said that 'the only qualities required for his success were a Church membership and an honest face.' He was the sort of critic who liked to be photographed 'among my books'; the sort whose literary labors consisted almost wholly of twanging at the romantic overtones of literature, the tunes, not of experience, but of moralistic sentiments about experience. He was precisely the sort of critic who kept 'The Scarlet Letter' on the reading list of the eighth-grade public school youngster, and made an indelicacy of any mention of the Little Stranger in advance of its appearance. I suspect that it is Frances Willard's identification of her own outlook with minds like those of Hamilton Wright Mabie, Henry van Dyke, and kindred commentators on the contemporary scene, that has led to a rather general neglect of her statesmanly quality.

These were things that came a little later: the whole incident of the bootlegged poem is, because of its continuity, related a little in advance of its occurrence, which was not until Mary was back in college after the interim of normal school, and the nervous breakdown in the middle of the second semester at the State Normal School in 1885.

The breakdown was supposed to have been caused by overwork. There was that item, of course; the curriculum was crowded, the drive cruel and incessant. What did for Mary, however, wasn't the amount of work expected of her, the hours and the mark set, but the unremitting fixation of attention on objective detail, not of true learning, but of pedagogical method. With the exception of Latin, in which she was allowed to continue the work begun in the high school, nothing new or informing was brought upon the scene. At the normal school she was simply redriven over the curricula of public school grades with immense and boring particularity; spelling, punctuation, phonetics, arithmetical devices; history reduced to a precise allocation of names and places, middle initials of unimportant generals, dates of undecisive battles; reading reduced to the rendering of the content of literature in the most explicit rather than the most expressive verbal terms. Along this trail you were nagged and lashed with the utmost efficiency of regimentation, and the least allowance made for individual variation. After five months, combined with cold weather and the stuffy diet of a period in which green vegetables were unattainable at any price, and bad colds not admitted to the category of excuses, Mary was sent home in a condition which old Dr. Hankins looked grave over, and suspected that it might have something to do with the natural incapacity of the female mind for intellectual achievement.

It had something to do, no doubt, with the fact that central heating was not yet reduced to a science, and that the winter diet of the Middlewest in those days was stuffily uninteresting. It had more to do with something Mary was unable to explain, least of all to a physician of those days when small-town practice was still leaning hard on calomel and quinine, and the deep-seated conviction that all illnesses of women were 'female' in their origin, and could best be cured by severe doses of housework and child-bearing. 'The *only* work,' said Dr. Hankins, 'a female should do is beside her own fireside.' But without being able to explain it, Mary was well enough aware that she had broken down under the five months' rasping insistence on a régime that violated all the natural motions of her own mind. Having done little else but go to school since her sixth year, Mary knew that small graduated doses of instruction were an irritation and a hindrance to her. She learned best by subjects, by units of knowledge which had a kind of wholeness in themselves, taking by instinct the center of the field and working out to fringes overlapping the next subject and the next. I understand that the newer educational methods operate somewhat on this known procedure of self-initiating minds; but in the winter of 1885–86 public education was established on the inch-by-inch method, and it was at what was done at the normal school, no matter how impatiently, that minds like Mary's champed upon the bit.

Sometime in her early teens there had begun for Mary a series of experiences which she was far from realizing as singular to her alone. Perhaps they are not singular, except as in her case they became habitual and dominated the whole of her intellectual life. So insensibly they stole into her way of thought that there is no one occasion more than another to measure by; only as they seemed to choose the early hours of summer mornings for their own. As long ago as Mary's tenth summer, the summer before her father died, they had begun at dawn, when it was Mary's business to wake with the first stirring of baby George in his crib beside her bed and steal away downstairs with him, so that Pa, who might be resting after a night of pain, might not be waked by the child's morning prattle. Mary would warm a bowl of bread and milk for them both, or, if the hired man were about, get it warm from the cow, and steal away to the first row of orchard trees, or down between the grapevine trellises, which gave her always a still, ordered feeling, very comforting — the sort of feeling one gets from cloisters — and there George, once he was fed, would play about happily for a while, or, as the warm morning beams fell upon him, drop suddenly into little cat naps, and there the experience would happen. Mary would be watching the dew slip down the clover stems, or the white webby moons of spider webs made thick with diamond drops, and around her would steal a sense of innumerable bright events, of tingling and unattempted possibilities; there would be a sense of swelling, of billows coming and going, lifting and dying away — and then someone would come looking for her from the house to say that the grown-up breakfast was ready. All that had stopped after Pa's death, to begin again at the house in Johnson Street, early mornings when she lay awake or at evening twilight — sometimes after music, or in between the chapters when she read books like 'Seven Lamps of Architecture.'

As she grew older, Mary began to know the billowing sense as the pressure of knowledge, all the knowledge in the world, pulsing just out of reach. It came up *inside* her, she was uplifted with it, rocked upon it — there were times when she could discern within it, dimly, the shapes of specific knowledges — all the knowledge in the world, hers, aching intolerably to escape through her. Every now and then one of the young people who seek Mary's society confess to her, half-shamefacedly, that they have experiences when it seems to them that 'I know everything in the world.' Mary knows exactly how that takes you. By the time she enrolled at the normal school, Mary had had a little experience of coöperating with her experience. She knew that this inward swelling could be contented less achingly if you treated it as an entity, neither feared nor attempted to escape from it, but went along with it. It was, to some extent, self-directive; it had appetites for pictures or music or great poetry, which could be satisfied by being fed. I am not absolutely sure that at that time Mary recognized the Dweller in the Core of her Mind as having had explicit appetites for information; but it did eventually develop a taste for specific subjects, so that inexplicably to everybody else Mary would find herself reading largely on matters that had no objective relation to her life, Egyptology, Oriental literature — ('Oh, Mary, why do you fill up your mind with that truck!') — and all that Mary could say was, 'Well, I just want to.' (Mathematics was one of the things that the Dweller in the Middle Place craved, and Mary never had the intelligence to supply sufficiently.)

It is impossible to describe this experience, so nearly universal that we ought not to be without a proper terminology for it that would not shock the sort of minds that are terrified by the ancestral ascription of it to a Guardian Spirit, or to the dead, or a deific being. Mary never made that mistake. She thought it likely that sometime somebody would come along with the proper word for the Middle Place of the Mind, and in the meantime she called it anything that came conveniently, since at that time the Middle Place of your Mind was no more discussable than your body. There were still maiden ladies when Mary was young who said they had a pain in the chest when they meant stomach-ache.

It was the sort of thing that I have tried to describe that Mary meant when she said that the normal school violated the natural motions of the mind. But it was not then generally admitted that the mind had natural motions, and, if it had been admitted, then it would have been arraigned with pleading the natural motions of your heart to excuse immorality. I have to dwell a little on this, because in a long life of preëminently intellectual interests, Mary hasn't been able to avoid frequent encounters with educational systems, and the unrationalized impression she brought away from the State Normal School of 1885–86 was of the completely cabalistic quality of its method. It was a regimentation of method, of pedagogical sleights, of tricks and devices invented, at enormous expenditure of energy, cunning, and devotion, to accomplish the great American desideratum of getting everybody, no matter of what type or degree of capacity, through the eight grades of the public school system.

There was a reason for Mary's being struck with this aspect of her normal school experience. In the years in which she was being shifted about the Carlinville schools, in an attempt to locate her by her reading capacity, and in complete obliviousness of the frequent 'bad cold' gaps which in progressive studies like arithmetic can work irrecoverable havoc in class standing, Mary had often to resort to Minnie Farrell's older brother, Eddy, four or five years older, who, as an accountant, knew all the school tricks and short cuts, teaching her to get the answer in the back of the book, without bothering her to understand anything. As a matter of fact, though she learned to work it, Mary is not sure yet that she understands long division. She was, at any rate, prepared to recognize a 'teaching device' for what it was when she saw it. All her life long that five months at normal has stood at the back of her mind, a figure for the monstrous inexplicability public school education must have been at that time, and may be still, for minds unfitted to cope with the cabalistic approach. In spite of all the efforts of professional pedagogy, since, to make education educative, Mary is not without a certain horror of the sheer witchcraft which has gone to the fulfillment of the democratic presumption that all that men need to make them equal to each other is uniform school grades. And along with it, she cherishes unending admiration for the energy, the industry, and devotion which have come near to making that the case.

While Mary was at normal school, arc lights were installed in the city of Bloomington, a year or two later at Carlinville. The telephone began to be talked of as practicable; I recall that Hugh Minton and his brother contrived something that actually worked, within the radius of their boy friends. But there was no appreciable relaxation of the idea that obsessed the male mind of that period, that everything that was the matter with women was a direct result of their femaleness.

The term 'normal' to indicate the averageness of human behavior hadn't come into use yet, but the idea was there; there was a human norm, and it was the average man. Whatever in woman differed from this norm was a *female weakness*, of intelligence, of character, of physique. If the difference was in a direction pleasing to men, in charm, in humble-mindedness, in complaisance and provocation, it was counted to her credit; there was a concerted effort in press and pulpit and in social relations to persuade women to vary as widely as possible toward frames of behavior which did not so much come in conflict with man as supplement and complete him. Every sort of temperamental and intellectual divergence was judged a more or less successful attempt at provocation; and every variation from the male rhythm was a sickness. Pregnancy was a sickness, and the two emergences of woman, the first into complete functional responsibility and the second into unspecialized humanness, were times of uncanny peril, stamped with the indubitable evidence of biological reprobation. You may not believe it, but about that time there was a young man writing in first-class magazines, with all the flourish of authentic science, to prove that women were a sub-species, designed primarily for the purpose of propagation and no other.

In the interval of convalescence, Mary not only failed to be properly humbled by her misadventure, she began definitely to realize that the breakdown represented for her the need of a quicker intellectual tempo, a more expansive and varied rhythm. She began privately in her own way to plot and plan to secure it for herself. This was the time when she swallowed her hurt because Jim had failed to realize the contribution she had been willing to make to his oratorical success, and began deliberately to require payment in kind for such exchanges as went on between them. She also, not quite so consciously, set herself in opposition to certain much-admired behaviors of which Jim was the frequently mentioned exemplar. She had long suspected that a slightly posed level of emotional restraint, which was generally described as 'self-control,' was no such thing, but in her brother's case was simply due to his being not so quick in the up-take. The slowness of his reactions always gave him time to interpose the attitude of a superior reasonableness which passed under that term. It was not that he — and other people — had all the instant flashes of enthusiasm, indignation, whimsy, humor, counter-fact and unrationalized rejection, and suppressed them; he simply didn't have them. At least, I suppose it must have been somewhat in that fashion that Mary rationalized to herself a resistance which grew in her with time to the acceptable young-lady behaviors so completely summed up in the lines that Mattie Lumpkin wrote in Ollie Vancil's autograph album in 1887, and so adequately expresses the American woman's ideal for herself and her kind that I cannot do better than quote them:

> Be a woman! On to duty!
> Raise the world from all that's low!
> Place high in the social heaven
> Virtue's fair and radiant bow!
> Lend thy Influence to each effort
> That will raise our nature human!
> Be not Fashion's gilded lady,
> Be a brave, whole-souled, true woman!

Mary was never much taken with the wish of many girls of her acquaintance that they had been boys. She thought there might be a great deal to be got out of being a woman; but she definitely meant neither to chirrup nor twitter. She meant not to remit a single flash of wit, anger, or imagination. She had no idea of what, in her time, such a determination would entail. She was but dimly aware of something within herself, competent, self-directive; she meant to trust it.

VIII

AFTER a month or two Mary began to paint again, so excellent a method, as it proved, of achieving favorable types of objective and subjective coördination that she often recommends it as a corrective to other victims of the great American obsession. She got permission to attend classes at the university in botany and rhetoric. More or less secretly she began to write poetry, which is, though one finds practicing psychiatrists still unaware of it, one of man's earliest instinctive efforts to achieve subjective coördination. She no longer went masquerading, but she satisfied the urge for it by keeping three or four diaries in fictitious characters — she never by any chance kept one in her own; and she fought quite fiercely for her right to a certain sort of interest in various people in whom it did not coincide with her mother's judgment that she should take an interest. It was not, she fully realized, the sort of young-girl interest with which parents are familiar, neither sex interest nor infatuation; it was, though Mary did not know it herself, the born novelist's identification with alien personalities, the scientist's itch to understand by getting inside the material in which he works. But this was quite impossible to explain to anybody but another novelist. For Mary it was a resort of desperation against the things that menaced her undeveloped talent. It was a way of asserting her right to her own states of mind, and securing the instinctively realized need of emotional mobility.

Two or three years later when she was literary editor of her college journal, Mary published extracts from one of the impersonated journals — a man who must have been sired by Edgar Allan Poe upon the author of 'St. Elmo,' with Ralph Waldo Emerson at the baptismal font, and yet showing, here and there, the explicit, uncompromising outlook of Mary-by-herself.

As a final effort toward recovery, Mary spent the summer of '85 in Missouri, visiting Uncle Sam and Aunt Eliza. Mary's summers were always problematical. She somehow failed to develop that immunity to malaria which was normal to all the *Illiniwek*, after ten or twelve years of fever and shakes. Regularly it came on her with the first of the sticky days and the breathless, prickly-heat tormented nights, and she had scarcely recovered from the debilitating effects of its annual bout when she found herself down with the first of the winter's heavy colds. The trip to Uncle Sam's at the edge of the Ozarks is to be numbered as the first successful escape from fever and ague, as it was her last important contact with the family saga.

Uncle Sam, who was that one of the Dugger tribe who helped to carry Lincoln to his grave, kept a general store, a railroad station, and a post-office in a neighborhood reduced by a too prolonged pioneer habit to that chronic state of wantlessness which he struggled not very successfully to remove. This was Mary's first informing contact with constructive poverty; I mean poverty which builds for more poverty, poverty growing out of wantless ease rather than the more dreadful state of accepted economic defeat. Mary had a saddle-horse and rode about all day, looking, looking, with that absorbed attention natural to her, in which all personal response is temporarily suspended, and the onlooker becomes the mere register of experience. Noonings and twilights, there would be long, deliberate conferences with Uncle Sam, a large, slow man with a feeling for the land, the dry native wit of the Duggers, a natural instinct for politics, and the last of the family, as I remember, to eat sugar on his lettuce. He was now come to the time of life when he had pleasure in remembering and re-living the backward-rolling scroll of pioneer life in Illinois.

Much that informs the earlier part of this narrative was learned then, along with items not directly bearing on the subject, provocative to hear; such as that when the railroad first reached Macoupin, people would drive miles to take little trips on it, trying it out as a spider tries the stays of his web, timorously, and then go home subtly altered, somehow, by the certainty that now they were bound at last to the great web of world affairs. He told how, when the news reached them of the discovery of the use of anæsthetics —

that would have been about '44 or '45 — people would burst into
tears, realizing that help was in the world that might have saved a
beloved wife or child, or might be in the world without being
available for *them;* and how men secretly prided themselves on
being born into an era when pain had to be met with what they
had in themselves, which was, oddly, the way Mary was to feel
when she heard about Twilight Sleep, *after* she had been down to
the Valley of Desolation without it and came back with her precious boon. He told her that Uncle Jeff, in his tracing back of the
Dugger lineage, had discovered that there was an Indian strain in
the particular branch of the Virginia family into which the first
Daguerre had married, but said little about it, since in those days,
Indians were still 'varmints.' Uncle Sam himself was of the
opinion that there was more than a little Indian blood in early
American families, and one day they would be proud of it. Also
we talked much of the wantlessness of the people of the Ozarks, and
how it differed from the plain lack of goods which characterized
Uncle Sam's own youth in Illinois. In those days, he said, people
built around their lack, left room for the things they confidently
meant to have, so that these, when achieved, fitted into the habit
of use. But his neighbors on the Pommeltar — it was long before
Mary discovered that this singular locution was Ozark for the old
French *Pomme de la Terre*, Potato, River — having no room in their
thought for new things, when they acquired them, held them
loosely as novelties not netted into their lives by use. That very
summer his own customers had come back to him eager to trade in
for a trifle of cash the cook-stoves he had sold them, so that they
might travel in families to the town a day's journey away where a
circus had been advertised; thus cutting from under him his carefully worked-out expectation of selling them by degrees all the
other items that the possession of a cook-stove implied. He repeated the current witticism of the few Northerners in that region
on the inhabitants, of whom it was said that when they moved
about in wagons on the poor excuse for roads, they accosted each
other, 'Be ye goin' somewhar, or jest a travelin'.' Which Mary has
preserved among her collection of markers... It was Uncle Sam's

conviction that the proper function of business men like himself was to insure that the American customer left off jest a travelin' and went somewhere.

That winter after Mary went home she read 'Progress and Poverty,' by Henry George. She had always meant to, because it was one of the books that was seldom far from her father's hand during those days when he was no longer able to go to his office. I am not sure how much of the doctrine of Single Tax she was able to absorb, how much she could intellectually understand. Taken in connection with what she saw, what passed in review before her in those long sleepy noonings on the shady side of the station beside Uncle Sam, it stirred her, not equally with 'Old Red Sandstone,' but unforgettably. It must be reckoned as one of the formative books; it awakened in her the realization of a new world of phenomena called Economics.

She came back from the Ozarks greatly improved in health, to make a new attempt at college. There seemed nothing else to do. It wasn't yet quite to be taken for granted that parents would invariably tax themselves for the college education of girls as they would for the boys. Susie's consent rested on Mary's being able to make up what was practically the whole of the sophomore year by private study — she had finished Cicero that summer at Uncle Sam's — and on the solemn promise that *if* Susie saw her through, she wouldn't 'throw it all away on some *man.*'

I suppose it wouldn't just naturally present itself to the modern young woman that this meant Mary wasn't to nullify the effort of her schooling by getting married immediately on leaving school. Mary often knew her mother's contemporaries to shake their heads over girls whose mothers had been known to strain their resources to put them through college. 'What a waste,' they said; 'they'll only get married as soon as they're out.' But the implications of emphasis on the word *man* went deeper and revealed what not one of the women who used it would admit, that the secret concern of women of that time was family limitation.

The new knowledge which came into the world with the practical conquest of a servantless society had added anxiety rather than relief to the incorrigible innocence of the period. No mistake that our intelligentsia has made in the interpretation of our immediate American past has contributed so much to their own obfuscation as that of imputing hypocrisy to the sex conventions of the period in which our present revolt from these conventions took its rise. Except, of course, as a certain generally conceded pretense plays its part in all conventions. American women, in the period in which possibilities of marriage dawned on Mary's own horizon, had mastered, in their progressive conquest over the material environment of the family, every implication except that one which involved them in the ever-recurrent expectation of maternity and the demanding, unremitting care of children, unrealizable in the present age of nickel-plated sanitation, prophylactics, and anti-toxins. Medical science served rather to enlarge the borders of apprehension by its discovery of the tragic possibilities involved in the bearing of children to dissolute husbands, or of continuing a defective strain, concealed from the young parents under taboos imposed by the terribly innocent ignorance of the Victorian era. It wasn't without reason that parents imposed restrictions on daughters for whom they took the largely unprecedented pains of putting them through college.

As I recall those latter nineteenth-century decades, all the disabilities of excessive child-bearing were charged to the horrid appetites of husbands. Not only had the current phraseology under which family limitation could be intelligently discussed not yet come into use, but nobody, positively nobody, had ventured to suggest that women are passionately endowed even as men are. Not *good* women! That sexual desire was something to which God in his inscrutable wisdom had sacrificed all women was so much a shibboleth of the period that it was not even successfully camouflaged by teachers and preachers with blague about the sacredness of motherhood. Mary cheerfully gave her promise about not marrying until she had 'made something of her education,' though privately she had made up her mind that about five children would be a nice number. Most of her girl friends rather favored three, and not a few of them had theirs named in advance.

All these things being happily arranged, for the rest Mary knew exactly what she wanted to do. In her reading of George Eliot, Mary had incidentally come across the statement that the novelist had been in her late thirties before she had published anything. This was somewhat later than Mary had expected to defer her own literary career, but served at least as a reminder that there might be years to be filled in with the business of earning a living. Mary's interest in public school teaching had been rather damped by her normal school experience; and Susie's interest in 'Art' as a possible livelihood was completely disappointed by Mary's refusal to utilize it for the only purpose of which Susie could conceive in connection with Art as an education, for the enlivening and adornment of the HOME. The especial type of interior decoration which prevailed at that time was the painting of realistic landscapes and flowers on wooden articles especially manufactured for the purpose; imitations of an earlier utilitarian association, snow-shovels, chopping-bowls, even rolling-pins. 'Snow scenes' were preferred, rendered realistic by liberal sprinklings of powdered glass. These Mary incontinently declined; the most she could be persuaded to was the decoration of sundry strips of bolting silk and other fabrics, which, carefully bunched up in the middle, were tacked to the corners of bookshelves, picture frames, the backs of chairs, and even to the time-honored Whatnot, called 'throws.' Few houses in Carlinville at the time were so poor as not to have two or three of those. I have an idea that they were a Middle-American approach to the bits of tapestry and other draperies by which professional painters contrived an 'artistic' implication of the places where they worked. As it turned out, the sort of Art teaching Mary had access to proved totally inadequate to the only interest that it intrinsically had for her; so she might just as well have made her mother happy. But there was nobody to tell her that.

Of other aids to becoming liberally educated, there was little else, outside of Mary's habit of inordinate reading. She read

everything that other people in the eighties read, and a good deal
more. She could recite whole pages of 'Laus Veneris,' not really
knowing what it was about, but captivated by the swinging
rhythm. She could get off onto 'Childe Harold' almost anywhere,
good for several stanzas... 'The moon is up and yet it is not night'
... 'Oh, Rome, my country, city of my soul!' Of Howells the
only thing that stayed with her was 'Silas Lapham,' and the
Howells style, delicate, undercut, like the illustrations of 'Seven
Lamps.' Oddly, the only writer out of those days who affected her
style was Emerson. I don't know why. The predilection showed
itself early in her college life. Possibly his death in '82 had revived
public attention in his work, and that in turn had recalled associations with her father, among whose books she had found an early
edition of the 'Poems,' and 'Representative Men.'

Betty Mathews, who had been Susie's bosom companion in
their school days, presented Mary with a two-volume set of the
correspondence of Emerson and Carlyle, but what it was that
fixed Mary's literary expression in that key, as it must have been
sometime earlier to elicit Mrs. Mathews's recognition of it, cannot
now be recalled. By this time Mary was eighteen, and Mrs.
Mathews was the only one of her acquaintances who confidently
predicted her literary success, although I know now that Mrs.
Rinaker was not surprised when it actually occurred. Oddly,
that Betty Mathews should have prophesied it appeared to have
been a reason for Susie's setting herself against such a possibility.
There had been, when Mary was still a child, a vaguely motivated
quarrel between the husbands of the one-time bosom friends,
which, after Captain Hunter's death, Betty Mathews had tried to
make up, without any seconding from Susie. It gave to Mrs.
Mathews's encouragement of Mary's literary interest a slightly
clandestine flavor; and curiously enough roused a persistent
though half-suppressed attraction between the two sets of children,
so that of all the young companions of Mary's Middlewestern
days, Lucy Mathews is the only one who has carried on to a degree
deserving mention.

IX

SINGULARLY little deserving of special mention stands out of the crowded two years of college. Blackburn was a small school, which made it possible for Mary to walk about in it, making fruitful contacts with her instructors, as she couldn't have done in the larger universities. She recalls them all with respect, and two or three with affection: Minton, because he was Mathematics, to Mary a science always tipped with a flame she was never able to touch, and because there was a sort of hereditary interest in him. Geometries handed down through families had notations on the margins... 'Prof. Minton tells the story of the spotted pig with this proposition'... or the story of the flying machine, the point of which was that Professor Minton had no faith whatever in aeronautics. 'When a man can lift himself over the fence by pulling on his boot-straps,' he would say, '*then* we will talk about flying.' Professor Conley everyone liked because he was a gentle soul who treated all of his young people as though they were already grown up, and because, being married to one of the Mayo girls, he belonged to the town's social tradition. 'Prof.' William Andrews you admired because it seemed likely he would achieve literary success for himself; he was the only one who could talk intelligently about the professional literary procedure. Also he introduced the modern method of science teaching; science by direct observation and experiment, which of all the things she learned at college has been most contributive to the continued education of Mary. Also he brought Charles Robertson in to lecture to the science department on his specialty, the Adaptations of Flowers and Insects.

As I recall it, Mary was the only one genuinely interested. There came a day when, spring being well on and the orchards blossoming, nobody else came, and Mary had the whole hour with him and his subject. It was a thin little trail Charles Robertson showed her, broadening as it went, so that even yet her happiest relaxation from the world of human reality is to leave everything else and walk in it. I have never written a book of the nature world without regretting the tight little social inhibitions in which I was brought up, which have kept me even at this distance from inscribing one of my own books to him, or at least sending him a copy.

Astonishingly to everybody who knew her, Mary rejected the English majors and elected science in their stead. 'English,' she explained, 'I can study by myself; for science I have to have laboratories and a teacher.' Susie, who couldn't see the connection between science and writing, thought the choice argued instability of purpose, and Mary, to whom the relation of science to what she wished to do was a thing felt rather than rationalized, couldn't explain it. It wouldn't have been modest to give her reason for avoiding a great deal of college English. Always the pragmatist, she had said to herself, but how do they know, these professors? — they've never written any books! As for 'Composition,' she was doing that for herself, poetry, and something unrhymed, the first tentative cast toward what she later did in the 'Land of Little Rain.' The notices of her public occasions in 'The Blackburnian' seldom fail to do justice to her literary reputation, and she was elected Class Poet. I spare you mercifully all quotations.

The one mistake she made which called for remedying was to reject two years in Greek for the sake of four in Latin. Just at that time there was more than a little being said in the thoughtful journals about the inexpediency of the dead languages as a training for modern Americans. Since in any case you could scarcely hope to acquire more than a smattering of each, said the protagonists, where did that get you? Mary despised 'smatterings'; the Latin she had begun in public school she had kept up at the normal. And since nobody had told her that the service of both Greek and Latin was not to be able to translate them badly, but to enlarge your knowledge of English, she went in for being competent in at least one of them. Years later she discovered that a good smattering of each was all she needed, but it was a long time before she was able to get, along with a year of Old English, enough Greek to make good the gap in her understanding.

Another discovery she made was that, profoundly as she was stirred by the higher mathematics in a strange aching way, she had no talent for it. If she got credit toward her degree as having completed differential calculus, I am sure that it was more by the liberal concessions of her teachers than by deserving. Mathematics, together with botany, zoölogy, and other natural sciences, did not deteriorate on your hands the way physics and chemistry have done, so that all she really got out of the last two was the laboratory method. Of them all, it was mathematics which most profoundly affected the deep-self out of which, after years of' struggle, she learned that her work was to proceed. Even those propositions which she could only master sufficiently to make a passable recitation set up in her a spiritual goingness, an awareness of space as one of the dimensions of reality, the dance of time throughout its varying dimensions... in the midst of problems but half-apprehended she would be seized with a sudden dazzle of the spirit... a sensibility for which there is no intelligible speech.

At Blackburn they also taught you something called political economy, like nothing that goes under the name today, and psychology, which was all about the emotions and the will. Then there was the flying trapeze of logic, and something called natural theology, proving that, since there can be no watch without a watchmaker, so there can be no Universe without a Creator. These, with various dabs of history and all the science she could cram, made up Mary's schooling.

Oddly, there was not a word in all this of the one scholarly subject in which Mary can claim a creditable proficiency, not even the word 'folklore.' There was a book of classic myths, which was a handbook to Latinity, and in ancient history, subsidiary to battle notes, small-print paragraphs about lost religions, but the word 'folklore' did not come into general use where Mary could hear it until near the close of 1900. Because there were Indian mounds in Macoupin, and the Piasa Bird and Cahokia Mound not far away, we all of us knew something of what they signified, and Mary in particular followed the growing popular interest in Egyptology in the writings of Flinders Petrie; but without conscious intention, I fancy the subject of Early Man, his history and remains, was soft-pedaled in institutions that leaned as hard on the Book of Genesis as did all the small colleges of the Middlewest.

Blackburn was Presbyterian, and old Gideon Blackburn had meant it originally to contribute to the continuing supply of Presbyterian ministers, for whom there were still to be had a number of free scholarships. Small and poor as it was, the university pattern was sedulously preserved; it was an admitted center of cultural interest, and for young people like Mary, who knew what they wanted, prepared them in a fairly competent manner to find their way about the world of ideas. To people like Brother Jim, who had no inner leading, I have never been able to make up my mind what it did, besides fixing him at a higher level of reading interest than would otherwise have been the case; I am not sure but its solid contribution to his happiness was in enabling him to join the University Club of Los Angeles among men whom he would have greatly missed had he been excluded. There were scores of just such small colleges throughout the Middlewest, such as have undoubtedly played their part in determining the character of its culture and prescribing the limits of its intellectual assumptions. I can only say that I am sorry to see so many of them absorbed into the vast caravansaries of book learning which now prevail. As for Mary, Blackburn left her, so far as her professional proclivities go, without so much as a thumb-print of predilection; and that I count entirely to the good. I am quite sure she could never have escaped from one of the larger, better regimented institutions with so free an intelligence and so unhampered a use of herself.

At this time, when Mary was going on toward her eighteenth birthday, she was so habituated to think of herself as falling short in so many particulars of desirability as a young lady that it came rather as a shock, looking over for the first time in nearly forty years, old school photographs, and especially class pictures, to discover that she was probably not any more conspicuously lacking in feminine attractiveness than the rest of her classmates. College, in the eighties, wasn't the place to discover pulchritude, and if genuinely pretty girls were occasionally entered there, they were more than likely to get conditioned out by the second year. About any girl who attained to a degree, there was sure to be an aura of seriousness.

Mary was rather under the average height, not well filled out, with the slightly sallow pallor of the malaria country, with a tendency to bluish shadows under the eyes, and made to look older than she was by reason of the mass of tawny hair, brown with coppery glints, thick and springy, falling below her knees when loosed, and difficult to get under any sort of hat suitable to her years. The fashion the winter that Mary was eighteen was for conspicuous bangs, all the front hair cropped to the eyebrows, and in Mary's case curling thickly, while the remainder was somewhat clumsily disposed in braids about the back of the head and neck — a style popularized a few years earlier by the famous Jersey Lily. By the time Mary graduated, the bang had grown out and was tucked and puffed into a high pompadour, the end disappearing under a coil, to the top of which the prevailing wide and much-trimmed hat was securely pinned. The dress of that period was probably the worst ever designed for the immature girlish figure, the plain 'basque' front and the heavily draped skirt, puffed out in the back over huge bustles of wire and buckram, and drawn in about the waist with the popular 'glove-fitting' corset. Under such a dress, one wore six or seven undergarments, mostly wool in winter and cotton in summer, but never on any account diminished or dispensed with. Mary had too little figure to draw in effectively, and as she always constitutionally despised the wire 'dress forms' with which worldly minded young women concealed their lack of womanly endowment, it happened that the only really attractive feature that nobody denied her was a pair of shapely, expressive hands. Her arms, too, were graceful, but that was a matter nobody was allowed to discover. Sleeveless dresses were customary for evening wear, but long white gloves covered all but a few inches of the arm, and were usually held securely in place by ribbons at-

tached to the arm hole. Necks were V-shaped, and the rule was
four inches from the base of the throat. Not that the lady teachers
at Blackburn went about with tape measures as was done in some
schools, at parties, measuring the necks of dresses, but I remember
that there was quite a lot of talk when Mona McClure, who had
the prettiest plump neck imaginable, appeared in a dress with the
neck cut square all around.

I think it extremely likely that Mary had never been so homely
or *gauche* in appearance as she had grown up thinking herself.
There had been the contrast with her sister's beauty for one thing,
and there was the pink-and-white, ringleted wax-doll prettiness
which was the American ideal at the time. And there was the veil
of withdrawal behind which even as a child she had concealed
both her sensitivity and that absorbed, selfless attention which she
gave to the external world, the product of an intensity of interest
which had the unfortunate effect of making her appear uninterested. Young men were a little afraid of it, and older men,
friends of the family who enjoyed the quality of response which
could be occasionally elicited from Miss Mary, complained to her
mother about it. They were, I believe, genuinely piqued at Mary's
failure to keep up with the prevailing notion that the most desirable feminine trait was to 'draw people to you,' which was second
only to the other mannerly obligation that you must not 'antagon-
ize people,' to both of which Mary appeared fairly immune.

That this effect of apartness was owed to her having grown up as
the least important member of the family, I do not doubt; but also
it sprang in part from a deeper detachment of the spirit. 'And
what,' she would say to her mother, who did her best to correct
what seemed to Susie social deficiencies, 'would I do with the
people after I have drawn them to me?'

Naturally such an attitude put Mary a little at a disadvantage in
the social life at college, where her indifference to the ritual of sex
attraction stood in the way of unself-conscious pleasure in the society of boys she had more or less grown up with. Except that
young people were not expected to go away together entirely outside the recognizance of their elders, the custom of chaperonage

could not be said to exist. It was, however, to some extent substituted for by the custom of 'going together.'

Self-elected couples made a practice of being seen in each other's company until the association had almost the sanction of a betrothal. If you were not 'going with' one boy or another, you had to depend for escort on your brother — as far as the girl he happened to be going with allowed it — or on the complaisance of a more attractive girl friend, or, unhappy condition, associate yourself for protection with two or three other girls equally neglected. Against these alternatives, Mary's aloofness was not quite proof. As a measure of self-protection she had to have an assured companion to be 'going with.' Her range of choice was not large; for though Susie knew next to nothing of college society, and like most Middlewestern mothers, seldom appeared at young people's social functions, she was particular about the sort of young men who came to the house. She preferred Divinity students; set herself out to make things pleasant for them as she wouldn't have done for any others. Like many good Christian mothers, next to having a preacher for a son, she rated having a preacher for a son-in-law.

In the spring after returning from normal school, when Mary was, besides her connection with the art department, attending two or three classes, there had been a young man that she had rather liked; but he wore bright neckties and smoked cigars, and Susie did not encourage him. Years after, when Mary accidentally ran across him, when they were both married to someone else, he told her that he hadn't exactly known whether he was in love with her; she had had for him the same sort of attraction, in her admitted oddity and reputation for intellectuality, that a girl touched with the rumor of witchcraft might have had in New England times. But her mother's preference for Divinity students had daunted him.

There was one trait of the young candidates for the ministry, for which they could all be counted on, which was complete seriousness. Toward the end of the sophomore year, one of them had let her know handsomely that she met all his requirements of what a preacher's wife should be, and he thought they might as well be engaged. Confronted with the enormity of telling a serious young man that she'd rather be dead than married to him, Mary was, for once, evasive. She said that she couldn't herself seriously think of being married to a man who believed in Infant Damnation, which as a devout Presbyterian he was bound to believe. Naturally, Mary's young candidate was shocked at such evidence of laxity on her part, coupled by her unwillingness to be reassured that, if he was so happy as to have children, he would see to their baptism instantly. I recall how we trudged slowly up East Main and along College Avenue, all the way to the campus and back to Johnson Street, from the Presbyterian Church, where we had been attending a sacred concert, solemnly discussing this point of doctrine which Mary had trumped up to save herself the unpleasant necessity of refusing the young man on his own account. It was an evening in spring, with a thin moon and the sticky sweet pods of the maples going plop under our feet. We parted sadly, and on the part of the young man with some dudgeon, since within a day or two he had worked around to writing to say, that in view of Mary's obduracy on so vital a doctrine, he would like to withdraw his offer of marriage. And so it was arranged. I have often wondered what the young man thought a few years later, when his Church met in Convocation and rescinded the doctrine of Infant Damnation.

This incident no doubt had its place in breaking down Mary's resistance to the fixed custom of 'going with' a particular young man who exercised a prior claim on the girl's company, but over whom the young woman had only such rights as she could enforce by her natural attractiveness. At the beginning of her junior year, Mary drifted into accepting for a regular escort, the best of the youthful callers at her mother's house; 'worthy' was the word then in use for his type. He had for Mary the special attractiveness of offering no resistance to her accustomed way of thought, and making few demands on his own account. It was Mary's way to expect, on announcing her settled intention toward a literary career, that it would be taken seriously, with all that that implied. Whether her friend did so take it, or, like most Middlewesterners, was so

alien to the creative way of life that it never occurred to him that
there would be anything in it inimical to the business of being a
Presbyterian preacher's wife, or whether, in fact, at that time he
had no intention in that direction, I have very little notion. At any
rate, his steady regard, his natural honesty and sweetness of disposition enabled her to get through the next two years with complete relief from other social complications. That they were able
to accept each other's religious interests with entire simplicity
satisfied Mary's half-realized sense that the true ground of intimacy
between men and women is their common fixation on an unde-
scribed Third — a Way of Life, a child, a common attack upon the
Wilderness; but the certainty that she never afforded him any
other encouragement toward marriage did not make it any easier
for her, a year or two after leaving college, to refuse him. It was a
great relief to learn several years later that he had made a suitable
and happy marriage.

Marriages did so often result from these college companionships
of several years' standing, marriages on the whole so much more
successful than seem to arise from the less restrained associations of
young people of today, that I can only think that a degree of pre-
marital restraint may be one of the conditions of success. In a
shared college life there exists that prototype of the impersonal
Third which seems to me to be implicit in the married relation, and
indispensable to its success.

Other items that I recall, besides the relations of young people
of both sexes, differentiating college of forty years ago from that of
today, was the extent to which the girls with whom I most associated were interested in other matters. We talked constantly of
careers. We, for the most part, quite frankly admitted the expectation of marriage, but were also, for the most part, determined
to 'do something with our educations' as our teachers and monitors
were continually advising us to do. Nine of us, I recall, formed a
secret society, out of which we got no end of important-feeling entertainment, known by the initial letters N.M.S. And since I have
it on the word of fellow members that the significance of these
initials has never been revealed, even to husbands, I shall not be

the one to break their spell. At our first meeting, I remember, we wrote out over our full names the programs we had made for ourselves, which were entrusted to Mary, who holds them still. Mary's was exactly as I have described it, to teach, preferably natural science, and then 'to write novels and other books.'

They were very happy days at Blackburn, happy and important seeming. I could wish they had turned out as important in the event, so that I might have the pleasure of living them over again. As a matter of fact, when Mary did go back forty years later, it was only Clem Lumpkin who remembered the days touched with romance of a pioneer past, and only Ollie Vancil — who married Louis Rinaker — recalled with any vividness the meetings of the N.M.S. I was shocked even to find figures warmly remembered out of that so happy intimacy, putting me apart across the years as Mrs. Austin.

Jim had graduated in '86 and been faced at once with the realization that a college degree didn't in the least provide youth with a means of making a living, let alone for his proper niche in the society a young man would wish to adorn. Only a few days back he had been deeply occupied pronouncing on such problems as 'The Wealth of the Nations,' 'The Influence of Napoleon on European History,' '*Ad Astra per Aspera*,' and suddenly he was a rather bewildered young man with no money in his pocket and nothing to do. There were several things he would have liked to do; he would have liked to own a farm and work it; and he had a fancy for studying medicine; both of which were unrealizable from want of capital. To the notion of studying medicine, which would have been not altogether unhopeful, Susie was deeply opposed. It was true that she had never taken medicine seriously; even for her own children she seldom called a doctor until other people pressed it upon her. It may be, too, that in my brother's case, she shrank from the long strain of keeping him in medical school on borrowed money; perhaps she feared that so alien an interest as medicine might come between them. I know as a fact that two friends of the family offered to advance the necessary funds for my brother's professional studies, and that she did not think sufficiently well of it to let him know.

Perhaps my mother fully realized that Jim's wish was not so much for medicine as for the life of a country doctor. To be close to people, in everybody's confidence, helpful and important, to be out along the country roads, noting the earliest tapping of the flicker in the woodlot, the seldom flash along the creek of the scarlet tanager, farming a few acres, maintaining a favorite team, with an occasional venture into fancy stock, experimenting a little in horticulture as his father had done — that would have suited my brother admirably. I wish with all my heart it could have happened to him; Mary I know would have cheerfully resigned her own chance of college to bring it about. But, in fact, the urge to medicine had not been of sufficient force even to wrest out of his college course such help as it would have given him; he was deficient in Latin and had almost no science. He did what lay closest at hand and taught a country school for his first winter.

The truth was that life in central Illinois for that time had come to a dead level of fulfillment. Any young man would have had difficulty trying to move about in its saturated environment. Other young men in situations similar to my brother's were scattering west. What made Jim think of California was the letters we had from Cousin George Dugger, who, notwithstanding that Cousin Beck had died there, was immensely struck with Southern California's promise of expansion. Added to that was the rumor of public lands still to be had for the taking. Jim left, at the end of his teaching term, for Pasadena, where Cousin George and other Carlinvillians were located. Thereafter, the sharpest item in Mary's personal environment was the rhythm of her mother's missing him, missing him more than it was easy for the rest of us to bear. The anxious inquiry for letters, the waiting, walking the floor, the weeping in the night; the arrival of the letter and the relief of reading it over and over to anybody who would listen, the happy hour of answering it, the waiting again.

I don't know now just when the plan developed of her joining Jim in California as soon as Mary was through college; but there it was. Mary had not been consulted. Not that she greatly cared; she did not see how being in one State or another would affect her own plan to earn a living teaching until such a time as her writing would support her. Of California she knew nothing except what she read in Bret Harte and Helen Hunt Jackson, and that was all of times past. The opposition she raised to her mother's plan did not arise from any preference of her own. Young as she was, she had the sort of knowledge a professional story-teller has for human values and situations, and was profoundly convinced that it would be better for Jim to have a life of his own, better for her mother to keep to the life and society she had grown into, the house she had built, the useful place she had made for herself.

What Mary knew about her mother by this time was that Susie had always wanted another sort of life for herself than Mary remembered so happily in Plum Street, a life of seeing and hearing, of social participation. She used to say when other women commented a little enviously on the time she found to spare for W.C.T.U., for Church and Sunday School: 'I served my time at staying at home when my children were little. Now I mean to enjoy myself.' It was what most women wanted; time and adventure of their own. Perhaps there was back of Susie's impulse toward the West something of the pioneer urge that brought Polly McAdams out of the settled places of Tennessee to the wilds of Illinois. Against all advice our home was dismantled, our goods sold or shipped, tenants found for the house. Within a week or two of Mary's graduation in June, we were on our way.

BOOK THREE
EL CAMINO REAL

BOOK THREE
EL CAMINO REAL

I

THE road for which we had set out was El Camino Real, which is the King's Highway along which the towns of the Spanish foundation were strung from San Diego to San Francisco. The precise location of our journey's end was that district known as Tejon in the extreme southern end of the San Joaquin Valley, where there was still to be had Government land for the taking. But in spite of her anxiety to reach my brother, Mother was not proof against the Middlewestern obligation of visiting. We stopped over five days at Denver to see the Farrells, who were delighted to have us. Beyond the renewal of friendly interest, Mary recalls little of Denver except its impressive back-drop, and her disappointment that the city itself failed to differ markedly from other American cities she had seen.

We traveled 'tourist,' a special provision for the flocks of home-seekers which, in spite of the recent collapse of the California 'boom,' crowded westward with their families and as much of their goods as the passenger traffic allowed. As 'tourist' you were permitted to carry your own food, with arrangements for making tea and warming up the baby's milk, and otherwise full Pullman accommodations minus the green plush and the obsequiousness of porters. Also you had to listen to an intolerable amount of repetitious comment; people reading the railroad guides aloud to each other; men travelers counting the family wash hung out at farmhouses, to guess, from the reduplication of feminine wearing apparel, whether it was or wasn't a polygamous household. When we passed, as we did a number of times, twin farms lying alongside each other with two houses exact replicas of each other, the whole carload of tourists practically hung out of the window with their eyes glued upon the sight. So it wasn't until we were well out of the fertile valley, snaking endlessly across the Great American Desert, that the sight-seer's interest relaxed and allowed Mary to be happily absorbed into its vast space and silence, faintly stirred by the sense of something expected, familiar yet remote in the marching landscape line. All that long stretch between Salt Lake and Sacramento Pass, the realization of presence which the desert was ever after to have for her, grew upon her mind; not the warm tingling presence of wooded hills and winding creeks, but something brooding and aloof, charged with a dire indifference, of which she was never for an instant afraid.

Suddenly we were at San Francisco, and Uncle Charlie Lane was meeting us at the Ferry. We found our aunt and cousins handsomely housed in a part of the city I have tried many times without success to relocate, a district of tall, narrow houses, pale gray like gulls' backs, with heliotrope and geraniums growing up to the second-story windows. Out of respect, however, to one of those temporary reversals to which the profession of mining engineer is liable, the house was filled with 'paying guests' — a euphemism for plain boarders which was just then coming into use. Aunt Mary's boarders not only abounded in suggestions of places we must see, of things we must not on any account miss, but were heartily willing to accompany us to the spot. I recall in particular a young woman — Miss Smiley or Smalley, or something of that sort — who took me to a matinée, the subject of which now escapes me, without disturbing the delighted sense of joining with her afterward the homegoing theater crowd — the Matinée Parade it was called — up Sutter and down Kearny, between Market and Powell, men in top hats, women tall, and high-colored as all San Francisco women seemed to be in their own right, so smartly dressed, with such an unprecedented air of gayety. For years afterward, until the whole pattern of the city's life was changed by the Earthquake-fire, Mary never went there without snatching at least one Matinée Parade, past the showy shop windows, the open flower stands, among the tall full-bosomed women with the beautifully flushed complexions. It was her first, and remains to this day the most cherished, of her experiences of the Pride of Cities.

There was another of Aunt Mary's boarders, a man whom Mary would have supposed quite grown up and mature except for his determined attitude of being still young, connected, in a manner never quite clear to her, with the newspapers, always hinting about trips to strange haunts of artists and writers, which never quite came off, although he did take her to Chinatown, where for the first time in her life she had tea in the middle of the afternoon, and later to the Chinese theater.

At the theater, Mary was completely entranced; like being taken behind the Looking-Glass with Alice. There were other places, the Golden Gate, the Cliff House... places the outlines of which so faded into subsequent visits that Mary made on her own account that the first impression is lost. There were restaurants, where, besides the 'good eating' for which San Francisco was famous, the Illinoians were startled by the casual way in which wine appeared with meals. Mary's newspaper friend took her to one or two of these places, Zincand's, I think, and an Italian place where they were served with red wine and something else... could it have been Pisco Punch? I recall in the Carmel days that this was a drink of Old San Francisco with a reminiscent flavor which you had to seek out in various odd corners. According to her bringing-up, Mary should have made the fine, shocked gesture of 'turning her glass down' — that was out of a popular Temperance recitation — which she shamelessly didn't. She sipped a little courageously, relieved to find that she really didn't like the stuff and needn't fear acquiring an 'appetite.' What she did enjoy was the romantic accompaniment and the red track of the light through the glass on the white cloth. She also distinctly recalls that when she was out with her newspaper friend, their itinerary was supposedly in the trail of places once frequented by one Robert Louis Stevenson, to whom, Mary gathered, she would be introduced if they met him, which they never did, though Mary forgets whether this was mere accident, or because he was no longer to be found there. She quaked between wish and apprehension; she was prepared to believe what she was told, that Mr. Stevenson occasionally took a great deal of wine, that his fingers were stained with nicotine, and

that there was usually dandruff on his collar. In her heart, however, she never believed that his finger nails were half-mooned
with black; people who wrote like R. L. S. didn't go about with
dirty finger nails. Years afterward, when she knew more of the
background from which the author of 'Treasure Island' was derived and more of foreign-born writers in general, she reconsidered
the possibility of this being the case, but in 1888 she simply didn't
believe it.

On the whole, her most lasting impression of San Francisco at
that date came of her wanderings with her Cousin George. George
Lane was in a broker's office, but he had Sundays and occasional
afternoons off, a well-turned-out youth, good-looking, acceptably
mannered. He knew the city well and was especially partial to
the views from Russian and Telegraph Hills, from either of which
you had the whole map of the Peninsula spread out, on clear days
including Berkeley and Tamalpais, with the Bay eating into the
land as far south as Santa Clara; gray and white houses like
huddled sea birds, wet blue strips of woodland, fawn, and silver
streaks of dunes. They would pick out, from the heights, places
to explore, then and on those future visits which Mary faithfully
promised to make... in fact she never saw her cousin again and
does not even know, since her mother's death, if he is living.

And the next thing was that the Hunters were on the Pacific
Ocean, cruising coastwise... stopping off six hours at Santa Barbara where Mary was driven frantic by the numbers of people
reading aloud to each other about the Old Mission... it is incredible always to Mary that people should insist on talking so much
while they are looking; reading a line in a guidebook,... 'Oh, yes,
that's it; see, Aunt Ella, that's where it says' — as if one could not
see at all what one has not first heard about. Which is with most
people probably the case. Mary got away from them as soon as
she could and went to look at the sea birds on the Esteril.

We found my brother Jim in the little foothill half-town of
Monrovia, where he had been working in a drugstore, half lightly
and ornately built and half-outlined with cement curbstones and

feather-duster-shaped palms, exactly like those marvelous structures that children built of broken stones and shells and fading
flower petals. But to be led through one of these outline cities by a
citizen was to be made aware that the superstructures were as
brightly realizable to them as to the children their fairy palaces.
Monrovia was but an hour or two from Los Angeles, where we still
had, before we could set out for my brother's homestead, several
spells of visiting — four or five Carlinville friends, and Cousin
George Dugger.

There were still warm traces at Los Angeles of the old Spanish
settlement. Except for the single street-car track that ran through
it, the plaza of the Church of the Angels was practically unchanged.
One saw Spanish-speaking natives lounging there, and immensely
impressive Chinese merchants in silk, shading their slant eyes with
little fans. I recall the old Verdugo residence, Frémont's house,
with the deep portal screened by century plants, other ample, sedate adobe haciendas, tall agaves, bright pricked blooms of the
pomegranate; later American residences, their nondescript architecture redeemed by deep bowerings of la marque and banksia
roses, West Adams Street made impressive by brown columns of
palm boles with waving feather-duster tops. At Pasadena, where
most people went to stare at the houses of patent-medicine million-
aires, Mary recalls a street lined with lacy shadows of pepper trees,
the spicy smell of the scarlet litter, crisp underfoot. Everywhere
she was enchanted by the eucalyptus trees. At that time it was
plain that the eucalyptus cherished an intention to possess the
land; the way they took the local contours, lent themselves sedately to the direction of the prevailing winds, filled in their ranks,
whispered together, indifferent to their being tolerated chiefly for
their quick growth, and for the notion that they somehow accelerated by their aromatic odors the healing effect of the climate
against the dread White Plague. Also they were supposed to drive
from their neighborhood the pest of fleas. In the small coast towns
and country places, you put eucalyptus leaves between your sheets.
In San Diego, in those days, still, like Santa Barbara, a Spanish
town, if you took a handful of the top soil, half of it hopped out and

the rest of it ran through your fingers. Nevertheless, Mary liked San Diego, the slow sea, the low foreshore, and the endless inner green sea of the chamise. At Los Angeles, she was daunted by the wrack of the lately 'busted' boom: the jerry-built bungalows, the blameless young palms abandoned along with the avenues they had been planted to adorn. The unwatered palms had a hurt but courageous look, as of young wives when they first suspect that their marriages may be turning out badly. One recoiled from the evidences of planlessness, the unimaginative economic greed, the idiot excitation of mere bigness, the strange shapeless ugliness, which, now that they were stripped of the leafage of boasting, was uncovered against the outraged loveliness of the coastal slopes. Mary was frightened; at least she was never more nearly frightened in her life; frightened of the commonplaceness of intention behind the exploded boom, the complete want of distinction in the human aspect of the country; frightened of the factitious effort of every-body to re-create a sense of the past out of sentiment for the Old Missions, out of 'Ramona,' a second-rate romance very popular at the time, out of the miracle-mongering of overgrown vegetation and inflated prices. The few homes that she was admitted to were hodge-podges of cheap makeshift and tasteless newness, not en-tirely extenuated by the temporary character of residence. Mary began to ask herself, What have I come to? What if this thing should catch me? Of the Tejon, which she began to be inordinately anxious to reach, she asked but one question, How far is it from San Francisco? She had an idea, in the event of the homestead enterprise not turning out satisfactorily, she might escape thence to the Bay City.

The Hunters were six or seven days on their hundred-mile journey, Mary on horseback, and the rest of the family by wagon, camping on the way. They went out past Eagle Rock, past low rounded hills on which the wild oats had dried moon-white and standing, patterned singularly with the dark cloudy green of live-oaks. They passed other boom towns, ambitiously laid-out plazas, partially surrounded by empty 'business blocks,' many of them stopped in mid-construction where the collapse of the boom had caught them; past acres of neglected orchard and vineyards being retaken by the wild. At San Fernando they turned out to visit the Mission, half-renovated to be the objective of tourist sight-seeing. Beyond that, old adobe ranch-houses with marks upon them of continuing Spanish occupancy began to appear, strings of chile drying on the outer walls, hides on the staked fences, chicken yards defended by prickly pear, old gnarled vines over the ramadas. We passed Camulus, the traditional home of 'Ramona,' the actual home of the Del Valle family. In San Fracisquito canyon at late afternoon, deer started from the ruddy thickets of manzanita; all along the hillsides tall fruiting stems of the yucca, called Candles of Our Lord, stood up. Between such points of interest, long stretches of the road, long since straightened for automobiles, rambled along the shallow dry beds of seasonal streams, called arroyos, dustily aromatic... rabbits and horned lizards scuttled there, road-runners perked and tilted, quail ran in droves.

There was something else there besides what you find in the books; a lurking, evasive Something, wistful, cruel, ardent; something that rustled and ran, that hung half-remotely, insistent on being noticed, fled from pursuit, and when you turned from it, leaped suddenly and fastened on your vitals. This is no mere figure of speech, but the true movement of experience. Then, and ever afterward, in the wide, dry washes and along the edge of the chaparral, Mary was beset with the need of being alone with this insistent experiential pang for which the wise Greeks had the clearest name concepts... fauns, satyrs, the ultimate Pan. Beauty-in-the-wild, yearning to be made human. Even in the first impact, Mary gave back a kindred yearning; it was in her mind that all she needed was to be alone with it for uninterrupted occasions, in which they might come to terms. And, as in this instance she was carried past the opportunity by the determination of her family to reach the San Joaquin Valley, so, later, the counter-obligations of a husband, a child, the necessity of earning a living, intervened.

The occasion for giving herself up wholly to the mystery of the arroyos never arrived. And meantime, the place of the mystery was eaten up, it was made into building lots, cannery sites;

it receded before the preëmptions of rock crushers and city dumps.

And still, whenever, out of a car window, over the wall of a rich man's garden, about which I am being proudly shown by the proprietor, I get sight of any not utterly ruined corner of it, I am torn in my vitals. This is the way a Naturist is taken with the land, with the spirit trying to be evoked out of it. This is the authentic note of confession for which autobiographies are supposed to be written, for which they are quite certainly read. It is time somebody gave a true report. All the public expects of the experience of practicing Naturists is the appearance, the habits, the incidents of the wild; when the Naturist reports upon himself, it is mistaken for poetizing. I know something of what went on in Muir... for him, quite simply, the spirits of the wild were angels, who bore him on their wings through perilous places. But for Mary, the pietistic characistics of the angels she had heard of prevented such identification. The human experience, which in the general mind could be most easily made to illustrate what she felt in the desert wild, was told her by a man she met years after, of the One Woman. He had met her when he was young and obsessed with the Life adventure. He knew her for what she was to be to him, and refused to know; there were so many other charming women in the world; he didn't want to be taken with the net of permanence so early; he could come back to her when he had tried and preferred. And he was never able to get back. That was a long time ago, he said, and there were still times when he would be seized with the certainty of the One Woman, the dreadful, never-to-be appeased desire of her... That was how it was with Mary. She meant to come back to wrestle with the Spirit of the Arroyos, and she was never able. One quiet year to get a modern return on a persisting type of human experience on which even the intelligent Greeks spent themselves... not obtainable in the wealthiest country in the world!

Sometimes I think the frustration of that incomplete adventure is the source of the deep resentment I feel toward the totality of Southern California. It can't possibly be as inchoate and shallow as on its own showing it appears, all the uses of natural beauty slavered over with the impudicity of a purely material culture. Other times, away from it, I wake in the night convinced that there are still uncorrupted corners from which the Spirit of the Arroyos calls me, wistful with long refusals, and I resolve that next year, or the *next* at farthest... and I am never able to manage it.

That is what began to happen to Mary on the way up from Los Angeles to the Tejon that late summer of 1888. It took shape then as an intention; it seemed not difficult at all to come again, next summer, or the next. So, on the whole, that first trip made a very pleasant passage. At Gorman's, one of the oldest stage stations, we met Three-Fingered Bob, who told us that in Antelope Valley, which we passed through, the wind often blew so hard that it battered up the ends of crowbars. At Castac, under the oaks, a bear came down and frightened the horses, so that Mary and Jim had to take turns lying awake so that Susie might not be alarmed. Susie had taken timorously to sleeping out nights. The next afternoon they looked out from Tejon Pass on the vast dim valley. Mary wrote an account of that journey, a few weeks afterward, for her college journal, in which all the derived and imitative influence of academic training fell away, and she wrote for the first time directly, in her own character, very much as she did in 'The Land of Little Rain.'

Three roads come into the oval curve of the San Joaquin Valley from the south. Toward the west the Temblor Road cut through the inner range to join El Camino Real, along which were strung the San Franciscan Missions; by this the sea and the low-lying coastal plain was reached. To the east the railroad came in, over Tehachapi Pass, touching Mohave where the desert wedged in, and connecting the central valleys with Los Angeles. Between the two, the Tejon road tapped the earliest settled districts and joined the Camino Real near San Fernando. At full length the road connected Los Angeles with San Francisco by way of the San Joaquin Valley towns, strung along the west-fronting slope of the Sierra Nevada, wherever a fruitful stream came down. The road's chief interest for the Tejon homesteaders was that it connected them with Bakersfield, the most southerly town, their source of supplies.

It was down this way Mary came, riding a buckskin horse, and watching as she came the road's white ambling beside the dark line, visible still from the heights, straightly drawn by the long-disused United States Mail Coach Line, and both of them disappearing into the vast dim hollow of the Valley, in the midst of which she could just make out the dark hieroglyphs of the Tulares. Off to the right, between barbed-wire fences, stretched the thirty thousand acres of Rancho El Tejon, and directly below it, outside the lower fence, in a narrow strip of waterless and therefore unprofitable country, the half-dozen cabins of the homesteaders, in one of which she was now to make her home. There were no trees growing there, and no green grass, nor any shrubs taller than the sparse knee-high sagebrush; all tawny pale with summer heat. Pale cusps of treeless hills clipped the homesteaders' strip on either side, and between it and the hollow of the Valley lay a low ridge of whitish, sandy dunes. Far on the eastern horizon, above the heat haze, hung the long, snow-whitened slopes of the Sierra Nevada, from which the rivers came down to feed the vast tule swamps, whose intricate dark blurs were lost to sight as the travelers came down from the Pass.

I have forgotten, if ever I knew, why my brother came to fix upon this site for his homesteading venture, nor by what specious promises he had been led to suppose it even a fair gamble for success. There were not so many places where Government land could still be had under homesteader's filings, and like most of the then population of California, Jim was so newly come that he had as yet only a speaking acquaintance with the miracles of irrigation. Having seen these accomplished, newcomers were the readier prey for all manner of half-formulated and often rankly dishonest schemes for inducing their participation in irrigation canals that never were intended to be built, that never could have been built in the regions for which they were advertised. Perhaps for those who have it in their blood to 'take up land' and expect to make a living out of it, no hazard seems too adventurous. In the case of my

mother, there was the added inducement of having my father's
service time deducted from the time requirement of 'holding down
a claim.' We had a shack on hers and my brother's quarter-section; Mary's holding, being what was called a 'timber claim,' required no building.

There was something quaintly ancestral in our settling in; a one-
room cabin, calico-curtained, bunks against the wall. The very
names of our settler neighbors were familiar, Valentine, Morris,
Stahl, Dunham, Adams, Johnson — tribe of congenital homesteaders. We combined on the necessary excursions to the waterhole, to the canyon for wood, to Bakersfield, thirty miles away
across heavy sand, for mail and supplies.

For an age that counts distance on speedometers, one must
reckon the trip to Bakersfield as between two and three hundred
miles; two days of travel. Our neighbors usually started in the
afternoon, camping on the way, but my mother never could quite
bring herself to that; to camp out in the neighborhood of people
like herself had for her the desolation of poverty. Fortunately, the
Tejon Road had been not too remotely a stage-road, so that there
were still respectable roadhouses at possible intervals. More than
any other of the settlers, the Hunters sought the alleviations of the
company store at Tejon Ranch, though the prices were high and
the stock indifferent. The owner of the combined ranches of Tejon,
La Liebre, and Castac had not lived on the property for years, but
visited it occasionally from his home in Washington. The acting
superintendent was an Englishman bred to the idea of landed
estates, to whom the homesteaders outside the gates were no more
than a slightly superior sort of gypsy. Nevertheless, we were all
treated with reasonable courtesy. When the waters of Grapevine
Creek, which in good seasons spread far below the Tejon fence
upon the plain, failed in the drought, we were allowed to go through
the gates to a perennial waterhole under the cottonwood trees; and
permits to hunt on Tejon property were not withheld. For the rest
we all faithfully went through the motions of 'making improvements' such as certified our intention to establish homes; heaping
stones at the four corners of the land, plowing and planting where

no seed could sprout, and by the prudent use of waste water coaxing a few cottonwood slips to grow.

As it turned out, we had come into the adventure at the worst possible juncture. The season of 1888 had been dry; 1889 was drier; 1890 proved the peak of desolation for an arid country. All that first winter rack-boned cattle tottered in the trails and died with their heads toward the stopped watercourses. The Tejon fences were cut and the cattle roamed where they could on Government land, cropping a few tindery mouthfuls. Since they could by no means keep the starved beasts from the unfenced homesteads, Tejon paid the settlers a nominal price for the non-existent grass, which was the only income any of us ever had from our claims. In February when the settlers went through the perfunctory plowing and planting for the rains that did not come, pocket gophers and kangaroo rats walked in the powder-dry furrows and carried off grain after grain, as it fell, in their cheek pouches. That summer I recall it was necessary for the Tejon management to keep men and horses ready for dragging away the carcasses of the dead and dying cattle from unpleasant proximity to the settlers' water-barrels. It was the dreadful task of Mary and George to keep them from lying down in that vicinity; once down, they seldom got up again. For months the loma was all black with buzzards and the horrid announcing croak of them.

By the time the Hunters had settled in at Tejon, Mary suffered something like a complete collapse. There had been, in addition to the emotional stress of breaking up home, the two years of exhausting college work, in which so much of the other two years had to be made up by extra hours, after which had come the relaxing California climate, and the problem of food. I suppose few people who pioneered on the Pacific Coast between the Gold Rush in '49 and the Real Estate Rush in the eighties ever realized the natural food poverty of that opulent land. By that time the Spanish with the art of irrigation, and the Chinese, wise in food-growing, had mitigated the handicaps of an almost total want of native roots and fruits and nuts on which the Middlewest pioneers had managed mainly to subsist. It was only the few like the Tejon homesteaders, cast away on a waterless strip in a dry year, who realized that it had been the wiping away of the slowly accumulated Indian knowledge of native foods under the Franciscans, and the replacement of the wild herds with privately owned sheep and cattle, that made the tragedy of the forced abandonment of the Missions. For the settlers on the Tejon there was not so much as a mess of greens to be raised or gathered. It had all to be fetched from the town two days away, at prices that forced a cautious balancing between that and the still expensive and not very satisfactory canned fruits and vegetables. Strange now to recall that my mother never did become skillful in the utilization of canned foods, and that there persisted among housewives out of the self-sustaining rural households of the Middlewest an irreducible remainder of prejudice to their use.

During the first six months of homesteading, Mary suffered the genuine distress of malnutrition. There was no butter, and if anyone remembers what canned milk was like at that time, diluted with stale water from a dry-season waterhole — but I hope nobody does! For meat, we had game, plentiful if monotonous; rabbits, quail, and occasionally bear meat and venison bought from the 'mountain men,' grizzled derelicts of an earlier period, hidden away in tiny valleys, subsisting chiefly on the killing of venison and the robbing of bee trees. Mary, however, did not like game, especially rabbits, though she might have done better about it if she had not had to kill them. Mary was a fair shot, and with George to pick them up after they were killed, contrived to keep the family table reasonably supplied. Every little while the men of the neighborhood would go on a community hunt, especially in the winter months when there were ducks by thousands on the sloughs, and so we managed to live. My brothers, in fact, throve; George, who up till then had shown signs of being undersized and pudgy, began to shoot up and ended by being the tallest of the family. But Mary grew thinner and thinner, stooping under her weight of hair, and fell into a kind of torpor, of which undernourishment was probably the chief factor, a condition to which nobody paid any attention.

Appetite, or the loss of it, was a purely personal matter. People guessed you would eat if you wanted it. What finally worried her mother was that Mary was unable to sleep. She would lie in her bunk with fixed, wide-open eyes, hearing the cu-owls on the roof, the nearly noiseless tread of coyotes going by in the dark, the strange ventriloquist noises they kept up with their cousins miles away beyond Rose Station, hearing the slow shuffling tread of the starved cattle, momentarily stopped by the faint smell of the settlers' water-barrels, but too feeble to turn out of their own tracks to come at them.

Nights when she and her mother slept at Susie's cabin, which was in a sandy wash, Mary would sit out among the dunes in the moonlight — Susie would never sleep there at any other times than full moon — watching the frisking forms of field mouse and kangaroo rat, the noiseless passage of the red fox and the flitting of the elf owls at their mating. By day she would follow a bobcat to its lair in the bank of the Wash, and, lying down before its den, the two would contemplate each other wordlessly for long times, in which Mary remained wholly unaware of what might happen to her should the wildcat at any moment make up its mind to resent her presence. There was a band of antelope on the Tejon range, fully protected by law, roving far down the hollow between the hills, passing between the wires of the fence as cleanly as winged things. There was a lone buck — the one who figures in the story of 'The Last Antelope' — who tolerated her — it was not in his lifetime that the antelope had been accustomed to pursuit from men. Once in a storm of wind and rain they took shelter together in a half-ruined settler's shack. That was how Mary spent the first three months on the Tejon, all the time growing apparently more apathetic, until Susie was genuinely worried. 'I can't help but think,' she would say, 'if you'd rouse yourself to take some interest in things...'

But the fact is Mary was consumed with interest as with enchantment. Her trouble was that the country failed to explain itself. If it had a history, nobody could recount it. Its creatures had no known life except such as she could discover by unremitting vigilance of observation; its plants no names that her Middlewestern botany could supply. She did not know yet what were its weather signs, nor what the procession of its days might bring forth. Until these things elucidated themselves factually, Mary was spellbound in an effort not to miss any animal behavior, any bird-marking, any weather signal, any signature of tree or flower. Animals are like that, thrust into strange captivity, caught up into fearful question, refusing food and sleep until they die. But in Mary's case there was no fear but that she might miss the significance of the question, to which as yet she had no answer, the magic words which would unlock as much at least as anybody knew of the meaning of what she saw. For Mary is one of those people plagued with an anxiety to know. Other people, satisfied by the mere delight of seeing, think they pay her a compliment when they speak of her 'intuition' about things of the wild, or that they let her down a deserved notch or two by referring to her fortunate guesses.

The deadlock was broken by the discovery, after the leaves were off, of wild grapes in one of the Tejon canyons, and after a week or two of almost exclusive grape diet, Mary began to pick up amazingly. It was so *like* Mary, her family remarked, to almost starve to death on a proper Christian diet and go and get well on something grubbed out of the woods. But there was more to the incident than that; there was the beginning of a notion in Mary's mind of a poor appetite of any sort being cured by its proper food; that there was something you could do about unsatisfactory conditions besides being heroic or a martyr to them, something more satisfactory than enduring or complaining, and that was getting out to hunt for the remedy. This, for young ladies in the eighteen-eighties, was a revolutionary discovery to have made. So that it appeared in the nature of a happy accident that General Edward Fitzgerald Beale, the owner of Tejon Ranch, came back to it along in January, 1889, and released Mary from the black spell of her wanting to know.

II

THERE is an account of Rancho Tejon in 'The Flock,' and something of the adventures of the *haciendado*, which seems a pity. It would be so delightful to do it all over as it comes fresh in the mind, not detached from the significant personality of the owner, around whom dramatic incidents multiplied. It would have been early in the beginning of rains when he came. The banksia roses over the portal were bursting whitely from their green sheaths, the oleanders making lacy shadows on the warm adobe walls, oranges in the walled garden beginning to glow goldenly, and far down the valley innumerable greens and tender lilacs flushing the chamise and the chaparral. I have no recollection of how we began to know him; I think he came first among the settlers, interested and kindly.

Edward Fitzgerald Beale was that young lieutenant who volunteered for Kearny to hold parley with Pio Pico, last of the Mexican Governors of the West, at San Pasquale. It was Beale who threw away his sword when Pio Pico's ambassador did the same, as well as a pistol he had concealed beneath his clothes, and founded that reputation for complete dependability which was so much to his country's advantage in dealing with the Spanish-speaking peoples taken over with California. He was that Lieutenant Beale who carried to Washington the official evidence of the discovery of gold in California, the Beale who became first Indian Commissioner, gathering into the Tejon the remnants of Central California tribes, where still in Mary's time a handful of them lingered. It was into Beale's hands the California division of the camel herd, which Jefferson Davis designed to be natural transportation for the Great American Desert, was delivered. Beale had known everybody, Kit Carson, Old Bill Skinner; he had been partner with Baker for whom Bakersfield was named, and had had dealings with Bishop, whose town was for two years Mary's home.

I shall come back to that and to the sort of thing that unlocked for Mary the long trail of 'The Flock,' the best of which is in that book. Beale knew Henry Miller. There was nothing General Beale did not know, or had not seen, or had not been a party to, since Pio Pico's time.

I have no recollection of how many times we sat there, Mary looking, as the family always complained, 'as if she weren't all there at all,' as indeed she wasn't. She was always *there*, yonder at San Pasquale, at San Fernando, wherever the story was.

General Beale took her to the Indian village and the site of that medicine-making described in 'The Flock,' probably the only official rain-making in which our Government was ever involved. He had Sebastiano, one of the half-dozen authentic Mission Indians Mary was to know, relate to her the story of how he ferried Frémont across Kern River at flood. He had in Pete Miller, the modest, inarticulate, blue-eyed official bear-killer of El Tejon. Later there was Jerke Johnson, who elucidated the true story of Monarch, the San Francisco 'Examiner' Grizzly, and the prototype of Ernest Seton's bear of Tallac, as Mary has told in her 'One Smoke Stories.' He did better than that by Mary; he put her in the way of getting Government documents, old reports of military explorations, agricultural reports. He secured for her geological and botanical surveys. There was at that time very little available print of the early history of California, and there was nothing of which General Beale had not some personal knowledge, of which Mary, through that contact, was made free.

Immediately Mary was made sib to the Tejon region through explicit knowledge of it, she was able to relax her strained fixity of attention, to take it enjoyingly. Her health improved rapidly. She was out every day and sometimes all day on her horse — noting how the spring came on sparsely that dry season, making contact with sheepherders, Indians, and tall Spanish-speaking vaqueros. She attended round-ups, brandings, shearings, shearing *bailes*... you can read of these in 'The Flock.' She saw other things; how the cattle bedded on the warm, last-lighted slopes, turning around before lying down as a dog does; how the coyotes hunted in relays; how the stallions managed their seraglios of brood mares, guarded and served them. She began to learn how Indians live off a land upon which more sophisticated races would starve, and how the land itself instructed them. As she saw these things, the whole basis of her social philosophy and economy altered beyond the capacity of books to keep pace with it. She was altered herself to an extent and in a direction that nothing she has yet written fully expresses.

In April that year, Mary was released from the long spiritual drought that was coincident with her commitment to organized religion. It was a dry April, but not entirely barren; mirages multiplied on every hand, white borage came out and blue nemophila; where the run-off of the infrequent rains collected in hollows, blue lupine sprang up as though pieces of the sky had fallen. On a morning Mary was walking down one of these, leading her horse, and suddenly she was aware of poppies coming up singly through the tawny, crystal-sanded soil, thin, piercing orange-colored flames. And then the warm pervasive sweetness of ultimate reality, the reality first encountered so long ago under the walnut tree. Never to go away again; never to be completely out of call... 'Nearer than hands or feet'... Only the Christian saints have made the right words for it, and to them it came after long discipline of renunciation. But to Mary it just happened. Ultimate, immaterial reality. You walk into it the way one does into those wisps of warm scented air in hollows after the sun goes down; there you stand motionless, acquiescing, I do not know how long. It has nothing to do with time nor circumstance; no, nor morals nor behaviors. It is the only true and absolute.

The boundary of the Tejon grant came down five or six miles from the mouth of the Cañada de los Uvas, and the fertile strip outside the fence, which comprised the new homesteads seven or eight miles farther on, passed insensibly into a windblown strip of shifting sand dunes. Beyond that lay the Weed Patch. This was another fertile strip where conditions of drainage had made possible a summer growth of tall weeds, such as had already attracted home settlers of its own. Beyond that were patches of saltweed, alkali, and acrid sloughs of wastage, gradually merging into the cultivated lands about Bakersfield. The Weed Patch was not too far from Tejon for fraternization with the later home-steaders, and since there was so little else for them to do, there was a great deal of such fraternizing. It would be difficult to convey to people whose pioneering had been done in the wooded lands east of the Mississippi the complete helplessness of the individual in the arid West. Many of those who came directly from one to the other never did understand it; they were inclined to attribute their difficulties either to the malignity of fate or to their having hap-pened on the wrong section of the country, and made haste to escape into surroundings in which the water company played the part of Providence in making farming possible, and went on adjust-ing themselves just as their ancestors had done where the rain fell equally on the just and the unjust. Many of the people about us in the Southern San Joaquin Valley were in a state of supposing that, wherever there were enough people who wished to farm, an irrigating ditch would simply appear. I suspect that as being the case with my brother and our neighbors. They plowed and planted the requisite acres. Fortunately, many of the homestead-ers were young people, who came and went in the intervals of other employment, and were quite content to make of their en-forced sojourn on the land a perpetual picnic. There were a few school teachers among them, a cowboy or two, several young men from the railroad. I recall one, a favorite among all of us, whose normal occupation was to take the great Mogul engines back and forth over Tehachapi, to haul heavy passenger trains up and down the Pass; it was a great entertainment to us to take him out with a team and wagon, and watch him sit terrified at the motion, clutching the wagon-seat until his knuckles were white with apprehension.

None of the homesteading neighbors were quite the sort that Jim and Mary were accustomed to, but they were all companion-able, wholesome young people, immensely worth knowing. The association which quickly sprung up among them was a little hard on Mary, who was still thoroughly occupied with her business of knowing what she saw. But Mary's training in concealing her private interest had been of long standing; if she were not called upon for a too intensive individual response, she was able to go on uninterruptedly with her observations. I fancy one or two of the young men were a little piqued at their failure to elicit a more personal responsiveness, which did not, however, interfere with their all getting an immense amount of wholesome entertainment out of their situation. They visited every point of interest that could possibly be reached by wagon or on horseback. I recall our coming, four or five of us, on quite the largest puma I shall ever see, asleep above his half-eaten kill on the horizontal bough of a live-oak, all of us being so intrigued by it that we sat there motionless before it occurred to anyone to release a gun, until one of the horses snorting, waked the great cat and sent it loping into the twilight wood. I recall on one of the visits we organized to a neighboring ranch for fruit and green vegetables, where we were always kindly received, meeting an English youth who turned up for Mary many years later as Norman Angell, of the 'Manchester Guardian.' Again, we went with blanket rolls tied behind our saddles to a ruined stage-station said to be haunted. The haunted station had been on the road to some now abandoned point of interest, a mine, I think, and had been the scene of a triple murder of a man coming in on the stage, whom the station-keeper had for his own purpose to kill, and then to dispose of the other two possible witnesses, and finally of the stage itself and the horses, to cover his tracks. He gave out that the stage had never arrived. But the secret was finally revealed by the singular occurrence that whoever stopped the night in the station afterward heard at the recurrent hour the sounds of the stage arriving, the feet of the horses, the click and rattle of harness chains, the passengers disembarking.

Another of our expeditions in which all of the Tejon families participated was down to the Tulares duck shooting. The Tulares were vast swamps of tule rushes, netted with unending,

MABEL AND TONY LUHAN
(See pages 340, 354, and 355)

intricate waterways, filling the whole middle valley as far as the influx of the Sacramento River. You will read of those in 'The Lands of the Sun.' At the time Mary knew them the Tulares were one vast breeding-place of water-loving birds. The time for lovers of the strange significance of natural things to go there was in the breeding season, when the cranes danced and the pelicans of the Pelican Islands, but that was later. On this occasion our objective was ducks and duck feathers, of which we took home a wagonload. Pot-hunting was still a popular practice in California: grouse, sage hen, and quail. Over toward the Temblor, quail blackened the trail to the waterholes in the early morning. The record pot-hunter's shot there was ninety-six. It was at the Temblor, on an occasion when some of us had gone to a ranch — San Emigdio, was it? — for black figs which lay in a thick pasty carpet on the ground, that Mary met the Walking Woman who, in 'Lost Borders,' was the means of Mary meeting H. G. Wells, which was an excess of benefits, seeing that Mrs. Walker — as the country people called her — was so well worth while in herself.

In the summer of 1889 the Hunters moved to Rose Station, which was the old stage-station just below the Pass. It stood on the Tejon Ranch property, and the arrangement had been made by the courtesy of General Beale. There was farming land and water attached to the station, and especially hay which it was thought could be sold to travelers going through; also meals could be furnished. In several ways the arrangement was an improvement; life on the homestead would have been impossible during the two or three summer months. Others of the homesteaders were established, also by General Beale's courtesy, at old Fort Tejon, and the shacks on the homesteads generally abandoned. I don't know that we made much money by the change; travel was at a low ebb in the complete deflation of the boom, but in many ways my mother was happier. The Vancil girls, Effie, who had been Jim's classmate, and Ollie, who was Mary's, visited us and brought a renewal of the sense of home.

That second summer Mother was beginning to suffer terribly

from homesickness. Consider the strangeness of it all, and the fact that, except for the brief time she had been with my father in the Civil War, she had never been for more than a few weeks from the home in which she was born and brought up. Also she was not a little bored. Susie was never one to care much for out-of-doors nor for the unusual; all her interests had been in the familiar life of Church and the W.C.T.U., with which she was now completely out of touch.

It was about this time that the young Divinity student Mary had known in college felt that he could afford an engagement, and he had accordingly written, to Mary's dismayed surprise, since worlds and years seemed to her to lie between the Tejon and anything that had happened in Illinois. But Susie was greatly distressed. Mary found her crying under the China-berry trees at Rose Station, and was aghast. 'But, Mother, you don't really *want* me to marry a preacher, do you?'

'Not if you don't want to.'

'Then why are you crying about it?'

'Well, I've brought you out here where there is nobody of your sort to marry ——' Mary sniffed. Like most young women she thought it would be perfectly easy to pick up a husband when she needed him. 'And, besides,' Susie finished, 'I'd know where you were.' You understood that what your mother couldn't bear in this new life was the dreadful insecurity of it. You didn't know where you were. There was nothing Jim could do about it until he had 'proved up' on his claim. And about that time he began to get himself entangled with one of the homesteader girls. He wasn't seriously interested in her, but he had drifted into one of those dangling, philandering relationships which had occupied so large a part of his youth. Only in this case the girl had no intention of dangling; she wanted to marry, and she had a mother who thought it high time she should. Jim began to get alarmed, and Mary, to whom the helplessness of the male creature in such situations was always a matter of fine contempt, came plop into it with both feet. It is enough to say that Mary's rescue work was prompt and efficacious. But it brought Mary herself around to the serious consideration of the family situation. For more than a year her only contribution to family welfare had been to keep George from getting completely out of touch with school, and learning to cook Spanish. It was already on the cards that George would have to be sent down to Bakersfield to high school, and Mary began to realize that if she needed any money for her own plans she would have to earn it. Jim could do nothing for at least another year, and the next girl might get him. Mary began to think about stepping out in the world, and almost at once an opportunity was offered.

III

ALL this Mary business is a nuisance; having to stop and tell why she did things and what she thought about them. There were then going on in the Southern San Joaquin, affairs of the utmost constructive importance to the commonwealth, to which her status was that of a short person at a circus parade. She edged in, she scrooged and peeked between the elbows. She had to judge many times what was going on from what taller people said. She has had it in mind ever since that she would write a novel sometime, in which the reader would have to guess the main action from the spectators in the third row back, hearing the band playing and the calliope — *cally*-ōpe, I mean — and what is said to be the lion roaring from a closed cage, with glimpses of the Oriental Beauty who rides on the elephant; and the rest is comment from the bystanders.

This was after the struggle of the wheat-growers with the Octopus, which Frank Norris wrote about, and already the rained-on Bay Counties were beginning to feel the competition from the irrigated districts. The railroad through the great valley connecting Los Angeles and San Francisco was hardly ten years old. Henry Miller had built his canal! Haggin and Tevis had bought into the flat lands around Bakersfield and the struggle was on between the old Spanish procedure of water right by appropriation and the English rule of riparian ownership.

At that time, and for nearly twenty years before, Henry Miller had been, in the San Joaquin country, the god from the machine. It was his own machine; he had built and worked it himself, and if his decisions were Jovian in effect, they were actuated by a kind of wisdom to which the Nordic peoples had always more or less paid divine honors, the wisdom of the subjection of the land to the possessorship of man. He possessed at the time Mary began to hear about him, enough land to be able to drive his beef on their own feet all the way from Lake Tulare to San Francisco, and bed them, so it was said, every night on his own land. But his manner of handling it was essentially Nordic. He cherished and enriched rather than despoiled it, but tolerated no interference with its use.

Henry Miller was born in Brockenheim, Germany, and his name was Keisel; Miller he took out of respect for the English-speaking people among whom he had come to live. He had arrived in San Francisco in the early fifties. He was a butcher by trade and understood his calling seriously as a social contribution to the feeding of the West.

Miller had another characteristic which was instinctively recognized by Mary as significant, the capacity to arrive directly without noticeable fumbling at the structural features of any situation, and to maintain within the main structures an immense amount of detail which was inherent in the situation itself; was true for the observer and successful in the outcome because it was related to the main structure as the twig is to the branch and the leaf to the twig. But to people lacking in structural capacity, Miller's handling of large enterprises appeared tricky, and to all those who by temperament are unable to pronounce the word capitalism without a hiss, his acute attention to the minor necessities of success appeared mean and grudging. Actually he practiced a well-thought-out generosity toward his employees, toward even the casual hobo passing by what was known as 'the dirty plate route,' reasonably fed and housed the whole length of Miller's demesne. It was called the 'dirty plate' because the order was that tramps sat at second table and were not allowed to make trouble for the other employees.

With the necessity the writer is under of keeping what happens to Mary the determinant of the story, one must telescope impressions in time as in fact. So far as Mary was personally implicated, Henry Miller simply happened, a local phenomena. Actually, she saw him three times; twice in Bakersfield and once in San Francisco in connection with the Panama Pacific Exposition in which they were each according to their several capacities interested. Henry was, in 1890, well on in middle life, was slow-mannered and quiet of voice, always with a marked German accent, and his favorite and frequent expletive was 'Chesus.' This was the figure that dominated the scene to which Mary had arrived, somewhat prepossessed in his favor by what Beale had told her.

Up to this time the Spanish colonists had employed, for the allocation of waters, a usage by which control of water was made contingent upon 'beneficent use' rather than by ownership of the land through which it flowed. Such control was acquired by 'appropriation'; that is to say, by declaration of the intention to use, made at the point of diversion from the natural channel, and promptly followed by practical provision for use. Diversion might occur at considerable distance from the land upon which the water was to be utilized, but once such diversion of the water had been effected, no subsequent ownership of the land, either along the banks of the original channel or along the route of the division ditch, could affect the appropriator's right to the water in keeping with his original declaration. In California, the hasty Act of Legislature, before the State was admitted, established arbitrarily the English riparian rule. But early in the homesteaders' westward movement, it began to be seen that much food-bearing land was, by the riparian rule, deprived of the necessary irrigation, while vast quantities of water wasted in the control of riparian holders. Still, in 1890, all up the west slope and across the southern end of the San Joaquin Valley, Henry Miller held land in the European proportion of principalities, under such restrictions that the only way water could be obtained by the late-coming small owners, who had smuggled into the nooks and corners of his huge straggling domain, was to buy it from him at his own price, when and where it pleased him to make it available.

Two measures designed by the Federal Government for the accommodation of homeseekers were defeated by those very beneficiaries. One of these measures was known as Government Scrip. Early in the history of Western development, the Government had paid for geographical exploration, for expeditions against Indians and other pioneering work, with scrip which could be laid upon any land afterwards surveyed and discovered to be suitable for settlement. Such scrip was also made negotiable, so that the holders of it had no difficulty in disposing of it for cash to men like Henry Miller, who promptly laid it upon land wanted for purposes which they foresaw. A second provision, made by the State Legislature in 1851, for securing individual holdings on reasonable terms was known as the Swamp Land Reclamation Act. It applied to precisely the lands which Henry Miller more than any man in the State showed marked ability in handling. By this Act large tracts of flooded land could be cheaply purchased by 'reclaiming' it through drainage and diversion of waters. Of this means Miller liberally availed himself, and the purchase of titles to Spanish grants of enormous acreage.

Henry Miller had only to be thoroughly, virtuously Germanic to make his steadfast way against the original owners of Tesquisquito, Buriburri, Orestimba, Bolsa de San Felipe, Salispuedos, and Rancho Sajon de Santa Rita which became Miller's home. All of which is important if the reader is to understand how radicals are finally made on the Pacific Coast. From the time that the transcontinental railroad made Western immigration possible, there began to be antagonisms between small holders and the land barons. By the eighteen-nineties the struggle in the San Joaquin Valley for water, such as would make small holdings possible, had become acute.

It was against this situation that Mary's own small problem of income developed. Almost before she was aware of personal necessity for earning a living, the local demand, among the hordes of incoming homeseekers, for more and better-prepared school teachers had reached out for her. Without quite knowing how it happened, she found herself in the fall of 1889 engaged at Mountain View Dairy, one of a chain of similarly owned company ranches in the very heart of the disputed section, in which long-settled general farmers made cause with the newcomers for water privileges.

I have been so much concerned to miss no item of the thoroughly objectionable qualities of a young woman in the late eighteen-hundreds making her way to intellectual independence and the forefront of a feminist revolt that I have almost forgotten to record that Mary had a few genuinely good points. She was by endowment a naturally good teacher; never at a loss for a word, a cross-reference, a memorable illustration. She could come around at an old subject from such unsuspected and challenging directions that the most obstinate determination not to be interested was shattered before it had time to jell; she could at any moment take off from so many byways and incidental angles that, before you knew where you were, you had come back into the trail a long way past the place where you meant to balk. I know this is so because old pupils go out of their way to come back and tell me. 'Just when we were all set not to go anywhere at all,' they said, 'the fireworks would begin.' Perhaps you haven't noticed that I described her as teaching the infant class in the Methodist Sunday School at seventeen. This meant that for three years she kept twenty to thirty infants regularly attending on the meagerest entertainment ever offered to children; for which she hopes she may be forgiven.

At Mountain View there were three: presently — after she had tried and failed to make a more formal connection with the public school system — it was arranged that she was giving half her time to the Pyle children and the rest traveling about the countryside in a cart to as many private pupils as she had time for: underprivileged or delicate children, young people preparing for admission to higher schools, mothers of young families oppressed with the necessity of 'keeping up,' which is the particular obsession of women in a servantless land. Nothing better could have been devised for Mary's own business of getting to know the West as one must who expects to write about it.

The farmers of the neighborhood were of all sorts, new settlers out of New England and the Middlewest, old settlers from the South of the Reconstruction Era, native sons and daughters of the Gold Rush, many of them pleasant to know and all of them rewarding. As she went she gathered that intensely particularized knowledge of the Western scene which is garnered in her books, phases of the life there that, except where she has recorded it, has vanished from that quarter of the world. Busily as an ant, she laid up inconsiderable items about Henry Miller and the intricate interrelations of land, water, crops, politics, and personal life in the great Valley. There is a book extant now of Miller's life, but so confused in its manner and so little knowledgeable of the land that without this further notation it would hardly be intelligible. It gives you the man, but of his widely diffused effect on the destinies of the people who occupied the country contemporaneously with him, nothing has yet been written that answers my purpose.

From any of the passes that entered the Valley from the south could be made out the dark patches, like cloud-shadows, that, fed by the overflow of Kern, Kings, Merced, Tuolumne Rivers, made all down the middle of it one vast continuous Tulare. When the flow was at its least — and now that the water of contributive rivers was taken out to water the benchlands along the Sierra foothills slope, that was most of the time — the overflow shrank to Kern, Buenavista, and Tulare Lakes, out of the last of which the San Joaquin River took its rise. Henry Miller's land had been originally all north of Tulare Lake. He began with the Spanish Grants nearest to San Francisco, on down past Gilroy, and the San Joaquin and Kings River Canal watered the land between them and the Tulares. There had been no railroad in the valley when he built it in '71, and all the material for it had been hauled from San Francisco by teams — it was at this time that the Fresno scraper was invented — out of vast clouds of choking dust. This had been a branch of a projected ship's canal project of Gargantuan dimensions, such as no man knew better than Miller could never be built and should never be attempted. But he could use the branch canal to spread the water on his grass lands, so that his cattle in the season stood belly-deep in pastures. This was the land he knew as most men do not even know their own dooryards, so that after he had shown the San Francisco promoters where and how to build the canal, he proceeded by way of his extraordinarily intimate knowledge to wangle it out of their possession and into his own, at about one third of what it had cost them. Besides his own land, this canal watered immense tracts of smaller, private holdings and no sooner had Miller come into possession of it than the trouble began.

It began with the Grange, which was the point at which Mary recognized the story as hers, and began to carry it in her mind. The Grange was one of the earliest of those popular movements of the American farm interest, like the Populist and Non-Partisan League movements, to deal with the incubus of organized capital, organized to lift from the agricultural districts all, and a little more, than they could possibly bear. Mary recalled that her father had been a Grange organizer, the first tunes she had learned to play on the melodeon were out of the Grange song-book — all about the ruddy farmer boy and other time-honored sentimentalities. When she heard that the Grange had wrestled with Henry Miller, she clicked in with it, and began to go along with the story as it unfolded in the talk of the countryside. It seemed that, as in the case of the railroad, the people of the San Joaquin Valley had been pleased to have the canal built by private capital, but when they heard that Henry Miller had contrived to buy it from the promoters, there was the usual popular clamor about utilities privately owned.

There is something almost fateful about the way in which, once you are thoroughly interested in a subject, odd bits of information begin to gravitate your way. Mr. Pyle it was who told Mary how the problem of Sunday irrigating had played into Henry Miller's hands. The Pyles had come from Gilroy, not far from Miller's ranch. Farmers who had contracted for so many hours of water running over the gate discovered that when they turned it back for Sunday, there was no place for it to run but on Henry Miller's land, so that one couldn't be virtuous even without working to Miller's advantage. It is long since settled in California that land and water in their conjunction are not subject to Christian ritual. Sunday or not, you stand at the intake and manage your water as it comes from the *zanjero's* hand. Then there was the problem of rates: whether these should be apportioned on the original cost or present value. Jurist and economist still differ on this question. The water company maintained that a water-right, however little it may have originally cost, was always worth its present price, a contention that was lost in the trial court and established by the Supreme Court. And still the demand grew for irrigated land, and still the waters of the Sierras rolled down to inundate the fruitless fields and be carried away through the San Joaquin and wasted in the sea. To obviate such seasonal loss, Miller put in execution a canal to utilize the overflow on land that had no natural riparian rights, as such rights were understood by California law. This new canal was capable of reclaiming from desertness one hundred thousand acres, and brought Henry Miller down the Valley into the vicinity of Bakersfield. Here a new complication of interest was added. As against the immense holdings of Henry Miller, the combined rights of the settlers and small farmers were not negligible, although strategically at a disadvantage. But about this time men of wealth began to acquire median holdings with the idea of parceling them out to small farmers, furnished with accommodation ditches, water-gates, and all the studied means of irrigation.

At Bakersfield the land company of Haggin and Tevis had made a footing just prior to the time of which I write. Haggin was a picturesque figure, of Arabian descent, interested in horses, and, it was said, in women, in a truly Arabian manner. Tevis was from San Francisco, called the Ward McAllister of the Bay City. Haggin, in association with others, was the titulary lord of the chain of ranches of which one was Mountain View where Mary stayed for two years.

It was a time of fierce and strained antagonisms. Farmers aligned themselves, as they thought their interests best served, under the reigning duke, and guarded their ditches with shotguns. Armed employees of the great companies went about cutting dykes and tearing out water-gates; of all of which, as it reacted into the homes of company employees and small farmers alike, Mary was made aware through the talk of the women. One morning she would see white water-birds against the warm colored dykes, performing their wingspread dances, and the next, grim figures sitting with their guns across their knees. When active warfare was about to break out, the courts intervened.

Nothing more dramatic ever happened in the history of Western jurisprudence, nothing ever engaged a more brilliant array of legal talent than this struggle between the English and Spanish traditions of water usage. It spread like one of the summer floods over the region in question, over the whole State, coloring its politics for years. The weight of legal tradition and scholarship was on the side of the English usage, and, against the more immediate necessity of the common good, determined the decision and became nominally the law of the State. When the decision was announced which gave Henry Miller all that he claimed, even the Governor publicly stated it as a calamity. Such it would have proved had not Henry Miller voluntarily nullified his advantage by proposing a compromise between the integrity of legal tradition and a practice thoroughly in harmony with the practical considerations. And so the matter was finally adjudicated. It was Mary's first grown-up encounter with the salient American capacity for loyally upholding the legal formula at the same time that its inutilities are completely evaded. She remembered it years later in London when a friend of hers, a California engineer, was being criticized by an Englishman who had had dealings with him. 'He never,' said the Englishman, 'breaks a law, but when one gets in his way, he knows more ways than I ever thought of for getting past it.'

'Oh, yes,' said Mary, 'we do that in California at least once every morning before breakfast. It keeps us in practice.'

IV

ONE of the thoroughly picturesque incidents of the San Joaquin settlement was the beginning of peripatetic labor, the wave of traveling wage-workers that swept up the State, beginning about Riverside in December with the early orange-picking and moving steadily north by way of apricot, grape, and prune harvests to the hop-picking in August in the Sacramento, and back by way of the raisin and prune packing to the orange orchards again. Mary wrote one of the earliest accounts of it, which in the East nobody would publish until it had long been an old story, seen by a sufficient number of Easterners for an account of it to have credibility in the printed page. That was how it was with a great many things Mary wanted to write about; when they were new and fresh to her, Eastern editors wouldn't believe them, and by the time the East had become aware, Mary had moved on to something wholly new and unauthenticated by New York. Always when she was collecting the items so slightly sketched here, she had a notion of making a novel of them. She still has yearnings in that direction...

There was also a trick she had of catching up impressions and sealing them into sentences that were made more easily rememberable by being rhythmic, occasionally assonanced or rhymed. Mary herself never called them poems, but when these happened to have been made in the interest of the children, they were. I recall when the whole State was caught up into the impending tragedy of the loss of its orchards to what was known as San José scale. The bulk of its vineyards had been recently destroyed by the irreducible plague of phylloxera, and the whole energy of the public mind was now given over to the world-wide search for an enemy of the scale bug who could be made an ally of the fruit-growers. It had always been a knack of Mary's even as a child to reshape the familiar nursery jingles to immediate interest of the play group. It was Elva Pyle who reawakened that habit by inquiring if the newly discovered Australian ladybug who ate scale was in any way related to the ladybug so familiarly adjured —

> Ladybug, ladybug, fly away home.

Which Mary promptly completed with

> The scale bug is down in the orchard alone,
> He is eating his way to the topmost limb,
> Ladybug, ladybug, go and eat him!

How dramatic, how intensely personal and immediate that seemed to the children concerned, can scarcely be guessed. It spread rapidly by those secret channels of communication which children use. Every now and then, when Mary is lecturing in California somebody with graying temples will waylay her reciting 'Ladybug, ladybug' — or the later and more cryptic

> If you *ever* ever *ever* see a *grizzly* bear...

In that fashion we began the work recently published as 'The Children Sing in the Far West,' some of which, besides being immensely popular with the children who helped to make it, is intrinsically good.

Professional writers, once they are recognized as such, are often astounded at the numbers of people who suppose that literature begins with pieces of paper. Mary found that not only was the ancient art of story-telling going on in the Mountain View district, but she could definitely profit by it. Before she left that district she had seized on the folk method of character drawing by myths, the sort of myths that accumulated about a man like Henry Miller in which the narrator tells, not what Henry Miller thought and felt, but what the narrator would have been thinking and feeling had he been in a position to do what Henry Miller did. I shall come back to that later, after Mary was in a position to know, of her own direct observation, how what men think while doing great things differs from what common men assume them to be thinking. There was also a fund of local hero and bad-men tales, the bad man as hero, Joaquin Murieta and Vasques, who 'stole from the rich and gave to the poor,' after the Robin Hood pattern. There were stories of Kit Carson and Frémont which would have astonished those gentlemen very much. Mary herself popularized several of the Beale stories. At Tejon she had already picked up a number of animal stories such as men seldom think of telling to women, not because they were untellable, but because they seem perhaps to belong so exclusively to the male life, such tales as 'The Last Antelope,' which could only have happened in America, and in America only in the Southwest; Pete Miller's bear stories, Jerke Johnson's horse stories, sheepherders' tales, deeply touched with a far derived pagan lore, Basque, Mexican, Old French. These she filed for reference.

It was the children's interest that made the continual thread, perhaps because it was the only intellectual process going on there, corresponding to the intense, inexperienced passion of the parents for the objective conquest of the soil. Children were re-naming what they found, either outright or by transference of names for analogous types in the regions from which they or their parents had come. Those names gained footing and competed with the Old Spanish and Indian and the nomenclature of middle-aged tourist ladies. Thunder-pump, for bittern, meant Scotch ancestry, shitepoke was out of the Mississippi, South; baby-blue-eyes for nemophila was tourist; 'clocks' for seed-pods of alfilaria which caught in your stockings and went around with the sun was as truly child-naming as alfilaria (threaded needle) is Spanish Colonial. Lantern flower for one variety of calochortus would never have happened except to children accustomed to seeing globe-shaped paper lanterns bobbing about at the end of bamboo sticks among the small fruit and truck gardens. This was the sort of thing that kept Mary from taking on the doubtful color of what Thomas Beer has called the Mauve Decade.

All that country about Mountain View had become the favorite training-ground for hunting dogs in preparation for the field trials, sponsored by various hunting clubs of San Francisco. While Mary was at Mountain View, a popular trainer was stationed there with various dogs of notable breed, whose owners visited them from week-end to week-end, so that she saw the pedigreed pointers and setters following the talk in the gunroom, proud, embarrassed, complimented, knowing what talk is for; participating in as much of it as their training-book vocabulary included. What Mary could not help but notice was that the dogs listened most attentively, participating, to the fullest extent, in stories of experienced events, such as a lost scent or elusive game retrieved under difficulties. Words, even the words that made up their common vocabulary, although they elicited occasionally a low whine or a tail rap of recognition, interested them not much, but a whole pattern of signs and sounds arranged around an event made that event live again for them; automatically accompanied by its original automatic reaction. And this was the first time it had occurred to her that the story pattern is older than man; that the story as communication between creature and creature is an older function of story art than the schools had taught her.

Up to this time Mary had had no theory of literature whatever, no notion even that some sort of regularized take-off is indispensable to flights of mind, kept up from incident to incident of a literary career. Nor do I mean to suggest that a literary theory leaped into clearly defined existence out of this primary perception of the story as communication, the communication of experience as patterned, integrated, taken whole, before the separate factors which made it one thing or the other could so much as be named or identified. I am not sure that in the instance recorded Mary got so far as knowing explicitly what she had seen; all that she was sure of was that what she had observed was important. She checked it off as something, when she got back in touch with sheep dogs, to be tried out again in that medium. Difficult to realize that it happened forty years ago. But that is the way creative memory works, blazing out for itself incidents to serve as perpetual markers for rewarding starts and excursions.

I must write these things the way they happened to Mary, swiftly flashing, in a flame spurt. She would be looking at something that all the world could see, had seen, without being stirred by it, and suddenly, from deep down, there would come a fountain jet of recognition. The thing was relevant, indispensable to some other thing not yet encountered, charged with a significance on no account to be neglected. Looked at in retrospect, the thing so announced would be seen to be the beginning of a long train of incidents widening to take in new arcs of Earth Horizon. Always the idea, the event, to which the new angle opened would be unfamiliar to Mary. Often it would be new in the thought of her time. And nothing Mary does has so irritated the critics against her as her habit of writing of these things in all the shining sharpness of her first perception of them. Nobody would have been surprised to have her write of a love seizure, a devastating loss by death, a perception of ultimate reality, with the full pang and incisiveness of the stroke. Writing of that kind about the oncoming of emotional experiences is called by a whole covey of commendatory phrases kept ready to let fly the critic's hand. But ideas, it appears, to be communicative must be toned down almost to the hue of those they are to replace, the quick bright hurry of their wings subdued to the homing flight of the familiar; they must be launched toward the minds meant to receive them as toward their proper cotes. And every little while Mary neglects to do just that. She suspects that the studied brown and drabness in which it is usual to present such new idea is merely another mark of the monastery in which modern learning originated; perhaps out of monasticism comes the notion that the chief use people have for new ideas is to get them accepted by somebody else, the missionary itch to contrive somehow or other that other minds should fall into the monastic shuffle behind yours. Mary has never done any shuffling. Without apparently having any choice about it, progress has meant for her a series of forward flashes, long spells of concentrated observation, patient, even anguished inquiry, and suddenly thunder, lightning, rainbow, and the sound of wings.

I don't see why it should be so much the literary mode just now to pretend that ideas are not intrinsically exciting and that one's own life isn't interesting to one's self.

V

DURING the time — approximately two years — she spent at Mountain View, Mary saw very little of her family. They had finished with the homestead and were trying out various contacts in the vicinity of Bakersfield, without happening upon anything very satisfactory. Nothing was settled yet except that Jim was more than ever determined upon a farming life, and Mother had joined the church at Bakersfield, feeling that she couldn't longer get on without the privileges it afforded of participating in the round of small-town activities in which she had been brought up.

It was quite clear by the summer of 1890, when Mary began to have her own reasons for needing a closer touch with her mother, that the only chance Jim would have of establishing himself in the farming life would be for his mother to realize on her small capital and become his partner in the adventure. To such a decision as she saw it shaping in their minds, Mary was openly and argumentatively opposed. The proposed arrangement, she said, would be for Jim tantamount to his marrying a middle-aged widow with two children. It proved the wrong thing to have said. That was what, in essentials, my mother wanted; that Jim should be married to the situation; involved past all possible intraventions, in the one authentic life pattern that she knew, the pattern by which all the past experience of women was shaped; the family bound by kinship and affection and industry in one place. But when Mary offered the objections to the projected plan that occurred to her as touching both her mother and her brother, she was inhibited from saying anything on her own behalf, since she was planning to be married herself, and so, as her mother put it, 'going out of the family.'

Mary became engaged in the summer of 1890. It was only a few months later that her mother and Jim settled upon a small ranch about three miles from Bakersfield, to none of the details of which was Mary a party. Mary never saw it until early in 1891, when she returned as of right to her mother's home to make preparations for her approaching marriage. That she should have remained so apart from so important an undertaking as the ostensible relocation of the family in a new environment was in part owing to her known objection to the plan, and in part to the general situation of unmarried daughters in the family interest; especially engaged daughters. It was not only unthinkable that the family fortune should be hypothecated to give the daughter 'a start in life,' but her right of inheritance, while conceded in public sentiment, was treated as a concession rather than a right. Mary knew perfectly that all she could expect for her own setting-out was a 'present'; and that in view of the involved expense of reëstablishing the family on the ranch, the present would be small. Mary got her wedding check under her plate at Christmas, marked 'From Mother,' and no more was said about it, which does not mean that no more was felt.

Another characteristic incident followed on a discovery made about that time that, through oversight or misunderstanding, the one item of profit connected with the ranch for the first year must be foregone. The few acres of grapes from the sale of which it was hoped to meet the interest on the mortgage assumed were discovered to be not raisin grapes as the Hunters in their innocence had taken for granted, but wine grapes. It couldn't possibly have been supposed by the original owners that this would prove an objection. In the old days in California, everybody made a few barrels of wine as a matter of course. As I recall it now, though detail of that sort escapes me generally, there wasn't any winery at Bakersfield, and the grapes, if the vines had been allowed to fruit, could probably have been sold for household purposes. It was the idea of raising *wine* grapes that proved intolerable to the disciple of Frances Willard.

One thing that Susie could always count on was the absolute backing of her children for her moralistic enterprises. I can't recall that even Mary suggested a more rationalistic treatment of the situation. Root and branch, out came the grapevines, and nobody thought of counting the cost. It is one of the things I like best to recall about my mother, that, when there was a principle at stake, she never counted it herself. More than any other thing she taught me, I am glad to have learned that swift, unpremeditated rejection of what one has come to recognize as unjustifiable.

I keep picking up these small items of behavior and moving them about, hoping, after all these years, that they will fall into such relation to one another that I may read in them the answer to those curious lapses from the norm of their own destiny to which all humans are more or less liable, one such as was about to overtake us.

Mary was, as I have suggested, more than ordinarily intelligent about everything but other people. At twenty-two she knew more about marriage as a social institution than most young women of her years. She hadn't taken the first man that asked her, nor at the first time of asking. She had engaged herself to a young man of similar social background to her own, and with a university education. She had been entirely frank as to her intention toward a writing career. She had not concealed the fact of her lack of physical robustness, which she hoped to compensate for by teaching, if necessary, until writing began to pay. She had said all that a high-minded young woman could say, and more than most of them dared to say on the subject of children and what she had herself to contribute in the way of inheritance. And she remained totally unaware that her own clear intelligence about herself, her straightforward intention, might be impossible to other people about themselves. She understood that her mother was not entirely at ease about her engagement; that she had expected Mary to do better than that. Susie had not been entirely unaware that the girl had possibilities! she had had, as nearly as Mary could make out, a sort of vision of her in a black silk dress, with lace, reading papers at educational conventions, a corollary to the hope she had once had of sending Mary to Mount Holyoke College, where along with Christian idealism there was a touch of elegance not lacking from the intellectual life. It was clear that she felt something in Mary's marriage which would disappoint her in this direction, but from speaking out so that the girl would have understood her, she was inhibited by her own approach to marriage. In Susie's generation, an engaged girl had 'met her fate'; there was an inviolable quality in love affairs before which even mothers hesitated; and there was always the consideration that a daughter married was a problem settled, a responsibility ridded.

As for Mary's part, the questions she knew should have been asked she took for granted had been; it was not in her yet to realize how far the postulates about marriage and inheritance so ardently espoused by her mother's contemporaries were from being actualities of conduct. From the intimacies that might have led to clear understanding, Mary was withheld by the certainty that they would have to be discussed with her brother as they might properly have been with her father, a condition which she resented. That was how, at the time when it was most important that they should have come together, Mary and her mother missed each other. On every point but one they missed and never found one another.

So it came about, confidence for confidence, that Mary confessed to her mother, what she had never admitted to anyone else, her own bold and unprecedented stroke of revolt. Up to this moment I have been in doubt about admitting it here, doubting my power to give it the quality it had, at the time, of the utterly inadmissible. Now, after the women who smashed windows, poured acid in letter-boxes, women who picketed the White House and heckled the President of the United States, women who in a fury of deliberation shattered the sacred tradition of woman's chastity, unashamed, one is tempted to turn it to an after-dinner anecdote, and does not quite. But telling it to my mother, I was perfectly sure about. My mother, of all the women I have known, was the most innocent of heart. She judged conduct and events by the standards by Church and Society provided, but not persons. Never in my life did I hear her speak of any person with envy or malice or the color of ill nature. If it is true as reported that the American consciousness is divided between a thin flow of premeditated well-meaning and unplumbed depths of instincts soured by repression, hatred, and hypocrisy, it was not true of her. She was too crystal-clear to understand the alternate cloud and lightning of the creative temperament, but there was no chance of her misunderstanding Mary's contribution to militant feminism.

It was after my mother had told me something of the desperation that seizes on women who, with all possible intelligent reasons for not desiring another child, find themselves without possible resort from having another and another; after we had agreed that, before there can be any rational release from the endless chain of bearing, there must have arisen in the public mind a conviction of the rightness of such release, Mary told her how she had slapped Bill Williams — Bill Williams being a generalized name guise in the West.

In the district neighboring the one in which Mary taught, there was a man well enough to do, but not at all well liked on account of a certain violence of temper which included his wife, and particularly her unhappy situation of not being able to avoid presenting him with a baby every year or two. By this perversity, she not only deprived him of much of her own labor, but, since the babies were seldom strong and died easily, was also a source of considerable expense, as he had no scruple about letting everybody know. Mary had heard these things of him; she had had glimpses of the pale cowed creature with the racked body; she had been called in one day in passing by the poor frightened woman, who hoped that she might be taught something about the management of the cabinet organ, that she might in turn communicate it to her girl children. But since she was the sort of farmer's wife who never has any money and Mary could not use any of the exchange commodities she had access to, such as eggs or dried peaches, nothing came of it. And then one day Mary was stopped by a neighbor woman in a state of near hysteria. Mrs. Williams's time had come upon her suddenly and there was no one to go for a doctor or the midwife. The neighbor woman had come over in response to a signal agreed upon. She had put the poor lady to bed, and now, she wrung her hands, 'He's in a terrible tantrum and I can't do a thing with him.'

Mary tied her horse and went in to get explicit directions for finding the midwife; the neighbor woman between tremblings was trying to heat water in the kitchen. Williams himself came in from the stable, where it had been hoped he was hitching up to go for the doctor, white and cursing. Happily Mary couldn't recall all the verbal vileness he visited upon women, his woman in particular ... 'bitches,' he said... 'just bitches, every one of them.' Mary, without premeditation, hauled off and slapped him across his slobbering mouth, once with the right hand, and then once with the left. She could hear the poor 'bitch' upstairs groaning heavily; the neighbor woman put up scared, shaking hands over her own mouth which remained open with astonishment. I remember that she forgot to put down the stove hook, which stood up from one of her hands like an exclamation point. Bill Williams shook, too, white, except for the red mark on his mouth. To Mary's surprise, he seemed about to burst into tears. 'You've no call to treat me like that,' he said. 'You've no call to.'

'I'll do it again, if you don't get right out after the doctor,' Mary told him. She would, too. 'I was just a-hitchin' up,' he said; 'I come in after a piece of harness I was fixin'.' He began to move blubbering, 'You've no call to treat me that-a-way...' As soon as she saw that he was actually putting the horse into the buggy shafts, Mary started on her own errand. 'Better not tell anybody about this,' she cautioned. 'Catch me!' said the neighbor woman. 'If this was to get around, he'd take it out of her' — with a gesture of her head upstairs.

It had happened more than a year before Mary told her mother. Susie was pink with excitement, her eyes were shining. She got up and moved about aimlessly. It was in the code that girls could slap young men for liberties taken, but to slap a married man for vile words about his wife in childbirth — her own girl! She came round after a while to saying, 'You did right, daughter; it was a risk and I wouldn't want you to do it again; but I want you should know I think you did just right.' For a moment you could believe that she had discovered a genuine respect for Mary.

That was how things stood May 19, 1891, when Mary was married at her mother's house to Stafford Wallace Austin.

BOOK FOUR
THE LAND OF LITTLE RAIN

BOOK FOUR

THE LAND OF LITTLE RAIN

I

THAT nothing in Mary's married life turned out as she expected it was due in part to discoveries she made within the year, which it would have been convenient to have made earlier. The first of these was that her husband had no natural qualifications for the calling of vineyardist. It was a discovery that many of their neighbors were making about that time for themselves. Where so many were involved in the event there was no special sense of failure, but general bewilderment.

The thing that had happened to the young couple was happening all around them, and was being met as best could be; those with an authentic feeling for the land recasting their plans and holding on for general farming, others holding on because their means still held or because they did not know what else to do. But Mary had grown up in a farming country, of farming kin; she knew the signs. Once the matter was called sharply to her attention, she was able to save them the prolonged misadventure of despair. She missed the first chance out of the young wife's natural hesitancy to press upon her husband an occupation so obviously not to his taste as teaching the district school when it was offered him, but as winter closed in and there was nothing to live upon but the income from her private pupils, she took the not unnatural course of insisting on a move which would offer the best advantage to her intention. She knew by that time that Panama District was no better suited to her own business of writing than it had proved to vineyarding.

She had liked the year and a half she had spent there, liked the people, liked immensely the swelling sense of significance in the confused activities of subduing the land to human use and occu-

pancy, but once she had settled in her house, she found that to
write she needed people and things that Panama could not afford
her. She needed what all young creative workers need, communication, the firming pressure of shared technical certainties; the
need taken for granted among farmers, bankers, educators, small
business men, but assuming to the American mind, when it occurs
in the Arts, a savor of improbity. At that time it would have been
impossible to overestimate Mary's ignorance of the professional
procedure of writing. And not only was there nobody in Panama
to tell her, but toward her disposition to inquire concerning its details there was a marked disposition of avoidance.

This was an attitude to which Mary was more or less accustomed.
Formerly, she had carried such queries to her mother and been
turned away with 'Oh, Mary, if you want to write, why don't you
just write! Why do you want to talk about it so much?'

By this time Mary was completely committed to the idea that
she was to write of the West. She meant to go back to the Middlewest sometime, but for the moment it had dropped behind her, a
far horizon, and all her interior energies were bent on sorting her
really voluminous notes about strange growths and unfamiliar
creatures, flocks, herders, vaqueros, Henry Miller, pelicans dancing
on Buena Vista, Indians, phylloxera, and a vast dim valley between great swinging ranges. Along with these things, there were
collections of colloquial phrases, Spanish folklore, intensively
pondered adjectives for the color and form of natural things, the
exact word for a mule's cry — 'maimed noises' — the difference
between the sound of ripe figs dropping and the patter of olives
shaken down by the wind; single lines of verse imprisoning these
things, all the sort of thing that her mother, when she found it
about the house, thrust into the waste-basket impatiently — Oh,
Mary, if you would ever finish anything! Well, Mary considered,
Mr. Kipling must have spent a great deal of time over that sort of
thing, but when she tried to discuss it with her young husband, he
was equally polite and uninterested. 'Why talk about it?' he said;
'why not just enjoy it?' And if Mary so much as intimated the need
of *somebody* who would talk — people interested in the same things

that interested her, in the same way — her neighbors appeared miffed; as though they said, I suppose *we* aren't good enough for you.

At that time almost the whole expressive energy of California went into what was beginning to be called 'publicity' literature; highly objective and extravagantly descriptive articles about the region which Charles Dudley Warner had just named 'Our Italy,' and other more particular matter designed to increase the number of real estate investors, prospective orange-growers and vine-yarders. There was an incredible amount of sentimental aftermath following 'Ramona,' and the popular tourist interest in the Old Missions, and out of the south a gush of minor verse. Around San Francisco there was still the tradition of authentic literature of the Bret Harte period, and at least one poet of more than local acclaim, Ina Coolbrith, who had been associated with Harte on the 'Overland Monthly.' It was to San Francisco, then, that Mary's mind turned when it became evident that for the reasons given a change must be made. As it happened, there were also reasons why it offered the best opening for her husband. In those days, the Austins, though they had lost their plantation in the Hawaiian Islands, were still important figures there. They were an old missionary family, and my husband's father was circuit judge. Before that, when Kalakaua was on the throne, they had been figures of distinction, and Frank, the eldest of my husband's brothers, had been sent, on business I have forgotten, as special envoy to the Court of St. James's, in connection with which he had pulled off a deal in sugar, or other Island commodity, with spectacular success, the tradition of which lingered in the family recollection long after there was any occasion for recalling it.

At the time of which I write, Frank was in San Francisco hatching an irrigation scheme for which much was hoped, and it was to him in his own emergency that my husband applied. That was how it happened that my first professional adventure was made in the first literary magazine that had sprung into national prominence in the new world of the West, the 'Overland Monthly,' and, curiously, under the friendly direction of the first woman ever to have attained literary prominence there.

It came in very quietly, this opening movement of an activity that was to mean more to me than anything that was ever to happen to me; quietly as I suppose all growing things begin, under the fallen leafage of my husband's expectation, in the first instance of detached independence I had ever had, after my husband had gone away to San Francisco, and I had been left to find a tenant for our house and make such disposition as I could of the broken ends of that adventure, how disastrously ruined I did not yet realize, being stayed against regret by that inward consciousness of rightness as sure as a bird's homing flight, which, when not dominated by other people's necessities, was so often vouchsafed me. Alone in the half-dismantled house, when my family supposed me entirely occupied with packing, I wrote two short stories, which owed, if nothing else, the occasion of their release to Mr. Kipling.

It had never been any part of my intention to write short stories. If you have access to the popular examples of them in the early nineties, you will not need to be told how little appeal the sentimental personalities of that form would have had for a mind always reaching wider and more deeply into the movement of American society. But the Kipling tales, with their slightly mocking detachment, their air of completely disengaging the author from any responsibility for the moral implications of the scene and the people of whom he wrote, had at least pointed the way for a use of the sort of material of which I found myself possessed. There was then — there still is I suspect — deeply rooted in the American consciousness a disposition to take offense at what is strange, because being strange it implies a criticism of the familiar of which we lack any criterion of authenticity other than that it is ours. Mr. Kipling had, happily, made his tales so completely strange and far away that comparison failed, and one could, as my husband had said, 'just enjoy them.'

I do not know how much of this I was conscious of at the time. There was that stream of knowingness which ever since adolescence I had felt going on in me, supplying deficiencies, affording criterions of judgment, creating certainties for which no warrant was to be found in my ordinary performance, setting up in me the conviction, which as experience I have named I-Mary, that all I know has always been known by me and used as known. At any rate, it was as I-Mary walking a log over the creek, that Mary-by-herself couldn't have managed, that I wrote two slender little sketches, one of which is so completely lost that I recall only that it was about the death of a Mexican lad in Tejon Canyon, and another about what happened to a Chinese truck gardener, which I have included in the 'One Smoke' stories with few alterations, to show that at any rate from the beginning Mary had a true instinct for her own best way.

It was late in the spring of '92 that I joined my husband in San Francisco, and made it my first business to get in touch with Ina Coolbrith. Miss Coolbrith had been associated with Bret Harte on the 'Overland Monthly' since its inception in the year that Mary was born, and, with him and Charles Warren Stoddard, had made a starry cluster of names which no Californian at the time failed to maintain was equal in luster to any literary trinity of the envious East. Miss Coolbrith was not only the first, but for a long time the only, woman poet of the Coast country whose verse found welcome in the Eastern magazines. I found her at the Oakland Free Library, where she was employed, a tall, slow woman, well filled out, a pretty woman, wearing an expression I was to front later in my glass, which I think she must have acquired crossing the plains as a child, the look of one accustomed to uninhabited space and wide horizons. She had a low pleasant voice; now and then a faint smile swam to the surface of her look, and passed without the slightest riffle of a laugh; and she was entirely kind and matter-of-fact with me. She told me how to prepare my manuscripts and advised me to see the editor of the 'Overland.' I regret that I cannot now recall his name. The 'Overland' was then undergoing one of the periodical revivals to which, between California's native indifference to literature and its prideful sense of the magazine as a cultural asset, it was subject. He took both my stories, although he said he did not pay until publication and not what one would expect even then — actually, as I recall, between the publication of the first and second stories, the publication suffered a complete lapse and the second was never paid for.

Of the two months or so that we spent in San Francisco, that is all I recall, except that I saw a play — W. S. Gilbert's 'Pygmalion and Galatea' — my first since Joe Jefferson, and revisited the Chinese theater for one of those serial dramas that last interminable evenings, and preferred it to the Gilbertian comedy, even with a popular actress whose name I have forgotten.

That Mary should have recalled so little of what she had come to the Golden Gate expressly to find was due perhaps to its being pushed out of immediate consideration by the strange, perilous, and yet welcome expectation of a child. That would account, too, for her knowing so little of the business which took her husband so early from the city, into that region which is still largely known by the name she gave it, 'The Land of Little Rain.' It was there that Brother Frank had possessed himself of an irrigation project from which such great things were expected that he had dispatched Mary's husband to be his representative on the ground. That the project was highly speculative, that it was incompetently financed, and that neither of the brothers had any experience whatever of the work in hand, there was no way for her to have discovered. She went happily, secure in the traditional preciousness of the young wife and expectant mother. She was satisfied that, for the time, she had got all that San Francisco had to teach her. She knew that Ina Coolbrith was a minor poet and that the 'Overland' was an unimportant publication. It was much too easy. Knowing now how the trick was done, she would fly higher. As for the place where her husband's new work was, she knew no more of it than its place on the map; she supposed that paper and pencil could be had there as well as anywhere.

II

OWENS VALLEY, the precise point in it to which the Austins were
bound, lies directly east of the southern San Joaquin, as the crow
flies, but between them rose the Sierra Nevada in that notable cluster of peaks amid which the great rivers, Kearn, Kings, and
Tuolumne, take their rise. The way into it from San Francisco
was by way of Reno and a hesitant narrow-gauge railroad mean-
dering down the Nevada, the snowy slope of the Sierra Range, to
a long narrow trough of the earthquake drop that makes the great
Sierra Fault, through which a river burrows to a bitter lake,
cupped round with desertness. The road ends at Keeler on the
shore of the lake, a bare huddle of houses beside the leprous-looking
crusts of a vague business of commercial salts and borax-making,
and an intermittent bottling of the waters from a hypothetical
Castilian Spring of supposedly medicinal properties and unimagin-
able taste. The lake had been larger once, when the seasonal run-
off of the mountain rains had been fuller, and was now so shrunk
within its salty banks that nothing could grow near it but grayish
salt bush and the arsenical green pickleweed. It lay there so thick
with mineral residue that it was said no swimmer could sink in it,
blankly opaque like a vast lidless eye, and gave always a portentous
look to that end of Owens Valley. East and south there were low,
treeless, mottled ranges beyond which was Death Valley, endless
sun and silence. West and northward rose the stark wall of the
Sierra Fault, and behind it thick ranks of peaks blotched dark with
pines and white with snow, between which snow waters leaped and
shouted to the thin line of towns to reach which one left the railroad
and crossed the sunken river to within a mile or two of the canyons
where the waters came through.

There were five of those towns, with several rural communities
between, strung along the foot of the Sierra Wall, and it was to
Lone Pine, the most southerly of these, that the Austins were
bound. The irrigation ditch, the construction of which Wallace
was to manage, had been taken out of the river in that vicinity; an

earlier project which had been dropped for want of funds, which
Frank was now supposed to have found. It was thought to be not
only feasible, but promising immense returns through land opened
up by it to settlement. That was all, absolutely all that Mary ever
knew of the business that had brought her to that country. It
was not expected of a young wife that she should inquire too
closely into her husband's affairs. Mary's business, so far as the
physical distress of her condition allowed, was to sit under the huge
cloudy cottonwoods that hung above the Lone Pine Hotel and
take in the strange wild beauty of the scene, and the quaint, whimsical quality of the life there. Abruptly on the west rose the vast
ghost-gray bulk of Opopago, and behind it Whitney towering to
look down on Death Valley and west away to the rim of the Pacific.
Nothing saved the town from the sense of imminent disaster from
that overhanging bulk but the backs of an ancient line of treeless
hills called Alabama, that ran along from the lake's head a matter
of a dozen miles or so to the north. On the east rose the Opalescent
Range that fenced the valley from pure desertness, called Inyo, the
name of the country, an Indian name of which no one knew the
meaning.

You can read all this and more in 'The Land of Little Rain,' or
you can reach the land itself by motor bus from Los Angeles in
a few hours. But on the life there, the unforgettable life, modern
America has laid a greedy, vulgarizing hand. When Mary was
first there, life stood at the breathing pause between the old ways
and the new. In Death Valley wheel tracks lay undisturbed in the
sand where the unhappy Jayhawkers had passed in '49, and marks
of the tent-pegs where Booth played 'Julius Cæsar' in the great
days of the Comstock, faintly tracked the ground. There were
people who remembered these things. Others recalled when the
Paiutes in their last stand were driven into the bitter waters of the
lake, and dying, sunk there. There were Indians who had stories
to tell of the last great struggle between Paiutes and the Southern
Shoshones and of the gathering-up of the clans when Beale became
Indian Commissioner and removed them to Tejon. Older and
older there was myth and legend, and all up and down that coun-

try the pictoglyphs that marked the passage of ancient migrations, and strange outline ruins of forgotten villages in the black rock country which must have been made when the rains fell plentifully and game roamed over regions where now not so much as a wind stirred.

During the latter days of the Comstock era, mining enterprise had spread all down the inner ranges, as far as Coso and Panamint, and was still going on there feebly. Towns had sprung up in Owens Valley where food could be raised, and men kept their families while they ransacked the waterless hills. With the slow decline of mining, agricultural possibilities in Inyo began to come to the fore, until the sudden enlargement during the past decade of irrigation and fruit-growing in Southern California had drawn off both interest and capital to the more accessible lands, and there, between the old era and the new, the Valley hung, so that if Frank Austin's ditch company had succeeded, something of the same thing that was happening elsewhere might have happened here in the shadow of the Sierras between the highest point of American land and the lowest. But the district about Lone Pine was still full of myth and factual reminder of lucky strikes, stage-coaches, bandits, and Indian uprisings. Mary sat contentedly under the cottonwoods for a few weeks absorbing these things.

Then one day her husband disappeared soon after breakfast, and Mary, coming back from her daily walk, found her trunk out on the sidewalk and her room closed. She sat on her trunk in the sun and looked anxiously up and down the road. She felt that the landlady had taken an unfair advantage to bring matters to this pass while her husband was away. She sat on the trunk for hours, all her energies concentrated on not breaking down. About four o'clock a woman she knew came by and suggested that there was a boarding-house on the far edge of town where she might find accommodation. It proved a longish walk to the farmhouse which was now a place where miners, touched with the lead poisoning common to the local ores, recuperated under a diet of milk and fruit. Mrs. Dodge, the landlady, was having a Kaffee Klatch all by herself. She offered Mary a piece of coffee cake along with the information that her feet hurt, that her cook had left her, and that too many of her boarders were dilatory about paying their board. Mrs. Dodge was an ample, toilworn German woman, speaking English very badly, rough of tongue, but kind of heart. When Mary revealed who she was and what she wanted, Mrs. Dodge did her best to steel herself to remember only that she was a land-lady. She wouldn't be taking any more boarders. The way she was situated she ought to be out in the kitchen this minute making pies, but with her feet hurting the way they did, she didn't see how in hell — besides, everybody was saying that the ditch people weren't paying their bills — but she had revealed too much. 'Oh, well,' said Mary, 'I'll make the pies.'

The pies turned out beautifully, and Mrs. Dodge, appeased, agreed to let Mary stay and help with the cooking for her room and board. At supper Mary had a good look at the other boarders, and on the surface of her mind considered that she might be entertained by the situation. Deep within her there was a place where humiliation and anxiety should have been, which was dull and stonied. About dusk her husband came — he had been to the hotel and someone had told him where to find her — and she realized that he had been all day without food and had no money to buy it. She began automatically to do the things a young wife will do when her man comes home at night and she must feed him. You should have seen the imperturbable ladyhood with which the newly acquired cook at Dodge's overrode the German woman's sense of imposition. Did I say somewhere that Mary was an actress — in the bone? David Belasco, who saw her once when she was at it, said, 'Oh, lady, if you had come to me twenty years ago!' Mary was too polite to tell him that twenty years ago she had not heard of him. You would have thought the case-hardened land-lady would have done herself an injury through suppressed indigna-tion as Mary set out the remains of the supper without so much as leave asked. 'You don't look like you was goin' to be able to earn your board and his'n,' remarked Mrs. Dodge significantly. But fortunately Mary remembered that at a pinch she could sew; she could even cut and fit.

The three months that Mary spent at Dodge's proved even more entertaining than she anticipated. Mrs. Dodge had knocked about the mining country for thirty years and loved talking. Dodge was an old timer whose every word was interlarded with the quaintest blasphemies, between priceless idioms of the camp. By this time Mary had come to realize that blasphemies were a sort of poetizing.

The miners who stayed at Dodge's while Mary was there were courteous, even gentle toward her, but less rewarding than other sorts of Westerners. Their minds ran wholly on lost mines, rich strikes, hold-ups, and sordid killings. The exciting contribution to her stock of folk interest came from Lupe and her husband Bill Withrow, the town's one professional gambler. They had come to stay at Dodge's a week or two after Mary's arrival. Lupe had been left at the age of three months on the doorstep of a childless woman in the Mexican quarter of Lone Pine, with money pinned to her blanket. Thereafter money came at irregular intervals, with which Señora Lopez did her best to bring up the child in agreement with what she guessed of her origin. That she was part Indian proved itself at a glance. According as the money came in, Lupe had private teachers, dancing, lessons on the guitar; at other times she resorted to the public schools; and at one time had taken refuge with her mother's people in the campody (Spanish, *campoda*, Indian camp). Tall, handsome, with all the insolence of the half-white, Lupe in her latter teens had been the more or less flaunting subject of male quarrels and one knifing. A few weeks earlier she had disappeared from the town, and now she had turned up as the common-law wife of Bill Withrow, a Bret Harte type, broad-hatted, frock-coated, and the only man, besides Mary's husband, who habitually wore a boiled shirt. He said that he had been brought up in Michigan to the calling of a minister. He had all the traits of one: the need of public approbation; the need of talking. Times when he had to be away from Lone Pine, collecting the cash capital of neighboring towns, Lupe would sing Spanish songs to Mary and do dances. One of her tricks was to beat down with a leafy branch the bats that come out of the eaves at dark, until we had collected a shoe-box full, and make tiny rolls of cigarettes which we would set alight in the jaws of the bats and let them go twinkling and smoking, taking away with them, so Lupe insisted, ill-luck, sickness and spite. Mr. Dodge never liked us to do this; he was afraid we would set his haystacks afire; but he was afraid to say anything to Lupe. Every week he gambled with Bill for his wife's board and he was afraid she would tell about it. But if I were to tell what Lupe did and what finally became of her, I would tell too much. If I were to tell one tenth of all the engaging incidents in other people's lives to which Mary became a party through her incurable want of a proper sense of social distinction——The last I saw of Lupe was five or six years later. That was at Mojave, where I used to make connections between the stage-coach and the train, going to visit my mother at Bakersfield. Crossing from the railroad to the hotel, where one changed, one was in full sight of the whole inquiringly minded community. A few moments later there burst into my room a tall, handsome, showily dressed young matron followed by a little boy in the popular velvet and lace of the Fauntleroy period — Lupe! Bill was proud of his son, for whose sake he had left off faro-dealing for the solid re-spectability of barkeeping in Mojave's *élite* saloon. Mary went across to supper with them, where it was plain that Lupe rejoiced in everything that the young wife of an old man has a right to expect, including genuine rhinestone earrings and a cabinet organ.

Mary contrived to get back to her mother in September. That night Susie came to her bedside and kissed her... in accordance with Susie's Scotch bringing-up, the Hunters kissed only for the formal occasions of greeting and parting. Mary could have wept over this one voluntary caress she had to remember, except for the necessity she felt for not letting her mother know what other reasons she had for crying. Mary's daughter was born October 30, and called Ruth, as the only name that had not yet been sponsored or opposed by some member of the family. The interest that her brothers took in their new niece was the one spontaneous relief to an occasion the memory of which is like some poor prisoner's of the wheel and the rack.

I know now, of course, that Mary was not physically constituted for child-bearing, and that the medical care accessible was not even the best for the time; the merely acceptable rural practice, not untouched with the superstitions of my mother's generation. The doctor was called away in the midst of it for four hours, to cut off a man's leg, hurt in a well-boring accident. On the ninth day, said her mother, any woman with any pride in herself must get up. Mary did as she was told; the next day the doctor had to be sent for, and months of shattering, debilitating consequences ensued.

There was worse. Mary had come to the end of her own resources for warning or acting. Since the failure of the ditch company, Wallace had earned not more than a few dollars. Mary was not only dependent on her family in every particular, but before she was out of bed with her confinement, there broke around her the realization that everything relating to her marriage had been done, as it was easy to do at that time, on a credit basis, and that there were debts going back of the marriage and involving practically every event of the last two years. Wallace, who had established himself at a mountain camp with one friend he had made in Inyo, on what terms Mary was afraid to ask, could not be easily got at. He wrote to her to do what she thought best about things and let it go at that. The Hunters were not people who went in debt. It was probably the expectation of 'getting it out of the family' that brought her husband's creditors down upon her at this time. Jim was at first disposed to undertake adjudication of the mess, but was put out, naturally, by Wallace's failure to make any contributive admissions or statement of his affairs. If at this time Mary had chosen to put herself entirely in their hands, her family would have taken her back, and against all their moral prejudices have agreed to a divorce. But Mary was not yet prepared for that. She had to face, as the family was still unable to realize, their incomprehensible want of sympathy with her way of life and the total surrender of her right to it that would have been involved in such a concession.

She still believed in the solution of the personal problem by the application of intelligence. The surprises of the past two years had

been disconcerting, and the obligations of her condition had prevented their being forcefully met. But she thought that if she
could only talk things over with her husband —— She knew now
that he knew, that day he left her alone at the hotel, what was to
happen. And Mrs. Dodge had told her that it happened when it
did because the community had offered him the principalship of
the school a few days before and he had refused it. This was difficult to understand, but Mary felt confident that there was an
explanation. She would go to her husband and they would talk
it out and come to an understanding and begin all over again.
There was nothing two intelligent people couldn't do together if
they set about it.

While Mary was still in bed, the first of her stories was published
in the 'Overland.' Susie read it aloud to her, but she could never
be got to express an interest in it. 'I think you could have made
more of it,' Mary finally dragged out of her. Where was now the
triumph and encouragement that should go to one's first professional adventure! The 'Overland' paid, on publication, three
dollars a page if I remember. Mary sent it secretly to her husband
for a Christmas present, and that was that.

Early in the spring, Wallace was elected to fill out the term at
one of the district schools, which the teacher had just abandoned
in order to marry. On that assurance of food and shelter, as soon
as the weather would permit, Mary packed her baby in a market-
basket and set out by rail and stage-coach for Inyo. She was then
something less than twenty-three and had not sat up for the whole
of any day since her confinement.

III

THE third year of Mary's marriage was largely devoted to the discovery that between being born with intelligence and behaving intelligently there is a gulf fixed. Mary had been brought up with traditions of thrift and ingenuity in economic practice. She had been brought up in a university town where people of intelligence and taste contrive, on incomes little better than those of highly skilled labor, to achieve for themselves security and certain of the appurtenances of good living. She was herself well versed in the method which she proposed to apply to her own emergency. What she had to discover was that to her husband these things were unheard of and strange. There were, in his experience, no such traditions, no such approaches to the problem of the good life. Brought up on a huge carelessly kept plantation, in assumptions of social superiority such as accrue to Nordics living among brown peoples, he had at sixteen removed to the mainland where he spent the next twelve or fifteen years living in boarding-houses and going to school on an allowance from home. He had never heard of such things as budgeting the family income, of competence achieved by cumulative small sacrifices and savings. Now that he did hear of it, he thought it all rather cheap and piffling. It was a long time before he got over being indignant at being required to subscribe to what he felt to be totally inadequate measures for reconstituting the family welfare. He was surprised to discover that Mary had arranged with the creditors left after parting with the house and the vineyard, that they were to be paid in installments in the order of their standing. He was surprised that Mary had not understood, when he left everything in her hands, that she was to put him through bankruptcy; entirely overlooking the fact that Mary didn't know that such relief was possible for private individuals, besides the fact that her family wouldn't have permitted it.

All this had to be gone through with; it was much longer for

Mary in the realizing than in the telling. What it came to in the end was that, although he grew into great faith in his wife's personal capacity to 'manage,' Wallace never accepted the factual basis of her success at it. He remained, to the end, unaware of the extent to which the problem of rational living on a small income had been worked out by the professional classes in America; he never subscribed either to the detail or the philosophy which Mary has come to feel, after long experience with the people who have not heard of it, is one of the minor achievements of democracy. It was a painful process finding all this out. To her inquiry as to why he had turned away the principalship of the Lone Pine school, he answered simply that he hated school teaching. It was a long time before she understood that this meant something less discreditable than it sounded. It did not mean that he had measured his dislike of school teaching against his wife's impending crisis, which could neither be lessened nor postponed, and taken the chance in favor of his own predilection. It meant that he simply hadn't thought at all; but had reacted characteristically. Whether by nature or lack of training, Mary's husband lacked the normal exercise of foresight. It was only painfully and after a long time that he learned to lay today's exigency beside tomorrow's necessity; nor did he, naturally, learn from the event. He had never once, Mary gathered, all that long, miserable, impecunious time of pain and peril, said to himself, 'If only I hadn't ——' Asked why he had not let his wife know that she was to be turned out of the hotel, he looked surprised. He said, 'How would that have helped?'

And that was the note on which Mary's faith in the efficacy of an intellectual understanding ended; on the realization that her husband suffered no such need. After years of rasping, disappointed struggle, during which she contrived to pull their practical affairs into some sort of working shape, he never once came toward her; was most silent when there was most need of talking; absent when there was the sharpest demand for his presence. That he suffered occasionally at such times there was evidence, but never enough for suffering to have cut clean through the spell that bound him. So far as I was able to reach with the knowledge available at that time, my husband was so deeply and intimately committed to his own way of life that what he really feared in a crisis was that something would happen to dislodge him from it.

This has to be gone through with because it formed the confused, disorganizing background of my practical life for fifteen years. It did not all unfold itself that first winter at George's Creek, where my husband taught, but prolonged itself distressfully from point to point of decisions forced by the total want of coördination in the most venerable of the fidelities of marriage, the common fronting of man and woman to the wilderness. Once he had given himself to me, my husband never looked at another woman; but also he never looked with me at any single thing. He never, any more than he could help, afforded me a clue as to where he himself might be looking.

The dramatic interest of that winter at George's Creek was Dr. Woodin. He had been originally a successful consulting physician in New York, but had contracted tuberculosis, from which he had recovered in the high, electrified air of Inyo, where he had been drawn while it was in the flush of its mining era by the contagion of gambling in his blood. He was approaching fifty at the time I knew him, a wide-whiskered figure of Santa Claus, ruddy always with the wind of his driving, with bright wintry eyes; still an extraordirary diagnostician, without any absorbing interest in the general practice which was thrust upon him. His office was at Independence, the county seat, and his orbit ran through there and Lone Pine, eighteen miles away, to Keeler, and on into the waterless mountains, Coso, Panamint, Cerro Gordo, to patients who endured the two or three days' wait before he could be summoned rather than submit themselves to any less practiced hand. If you lived in any of the intermediate rural neighborhoods, you tied a rag on a forked stick at the crossing of the ways, and Dr. Woodin followed it, unless he happened to be bound for a confinement still two hours away, or a premature blast at the Lucky Jim, which he would reach sometime tomorrow. Although he had fallen away from the particularities of practice to a degree that would have been thought criminal in other communities, it was believed all up and down the Valley that Dr. Woodin never lost a case once he really gave his mind to it; providing, of course, that he got there in time. He kept excellent horses, and had arrangements for changing at stated points on his round, and there was no team in the Valley he couldn't and wouldn't have commandeered to his use if his own failed him; and his rattling old top buggy, tipped rakishly to one side by the Doctor's immense weight, went like the ark of the covenant between the infrequent fields, with hope and healing. In that treeless country you could see him coming for miles, and patients able to be on their feet often walked out to the country road, flagging him for quick consultation. I recall once waking early in the morning — that was when we were living in Lone Pine in a house close to the road — and looking out to see Dr. Woodin gathering my baby's white dresses from the line where they hung. He was on his way to succor the victims of a mine explosion in the Coso hills, and had been reminded by the sight of the white linen that he had brought nothing for bandaging. I managed to substitute for this occasion a clean sheet and a couple of old pillow-cases, though in truth the Doctor could have had the child's every stitch if he had required it, for I do not know how I should have lived through that first winter without him. Fortunately, he took a fancy to Mary — there were times when he was taken with immense homesickness for the intellectual environment of his early life — and found recompense in talking to her, making excuses often to bring her a magazine or a book and to give a directive word about the child, which at his regular price for a visit the poor distracted mother could not have afforded.

I know now that he must have known from the beginning what was the matter with the child, and had made a shrewd guess at the cause, though he never told me until after I had found out in other ways; and that one counts greatly to his credit, for there was a strange, almost pathologic streak of cruelty in him which came out when he was drinking. You would know when this had begun again by the sly craftiness which came into his eyes, the lancing thrust of gossip and wounding surmise which characterized his talk, mounting, as the influence of secret indulgence grew into open debauch and downright meanness. He told me himself long afterward that the habit of drink was a substitute for drugs which he had begun to take when he felt his own illness increasing upon him and the decision had not yet been made to surrender the place he had made for himself in the professional competition of New York. But that winter he was wholly the friend and physician, and so remained one of the few figures of kinship in that ragged edge of the world at which Mary had so much without her will arrived.

When the Doctor failed, there was always Mrs. Skinner. The Skinners were our nearest neighbors; Old Bill Skinner, as he was called, had come into the country with Kit Carson, serving Frémont. Beale had known him. He was the type of congenital homesteader which the open country calls; neighborly, with a whimsical twist of humor, a mild, wide gaze such as misses the event at hand for the sake of that on the horizon. Everywhere in the early West you met men like that, following the 'something lost beyond the ranges' which Kipling, nearer than anybody, made us understand. And Mrs. Skinner was precisely the type of woman who follows that type of man; gentle, noble, too hopeful always of the event to be daunted by its failure. She had raised a large family in the wilderness, without being ever too busy or troubled to afford Mary the help a graduate mother can give to the novice...

Here I come upon the unfeasible task, the true presentation of a life-story uninformed by the contributory solutions snatched in passing from lives unable to profit by their own instruction. The lives one has no right — and no room — to tell, which serve no other purpose than by their unconscious or virtuously intended deviations from their course, the missing of clues too close for discrimination, the nobly motivated violations of cumulated racial perspicacity, the way in which other people's false gold glitters, other people's chickens come home to roost. I suppose every life that attains any degree of expressiveness is largely lessoned by these things. Mary, who had the incipient novelist's gift for arriving shortly at the constructive elements of life-stories that in a country such as I have described, wide-spaced and socially uncomplicated, lay open to the perceiving mind, was greatly instructed by these things. That her own mind was shaped and sharpened by such perceptions of nobility, of inutility, of false argument and unsound premise, the personal exemplar of which good breeding forbids the use, as well as by those which it is permitted to relate, should never be lost to the reader's consciousness. I do not know but that it is one of the culturally retarding influences of sparse populations that individuals live too nakedly in each other's sight, and that a reasonable privacy may not be one of the constituent factors of social progress. I am sensible of the obligations involved in this possibility as I write. I recognize no right of mine to minute particularity in the lives that did not actually press constructively on mine, and at the same time admit my indebtedness to the truth those lives revealed. I am aware that any autobiography written with due regard to such acknowledgments must seem to present the chief figure in it as moving in the ample space of admitted importance. But during all the years of Inyo, Mary did not so move; she neither escaped nor wished to escape the intimate pressure of neighborliness, nursing the sick, washing the dead, salving the wounds of disgrace and sorrow. Her last remnant of finery, a pink plush evening cape with white satin lining, went to cover the pine box in which a neighbor's child was buried. That winter, when she lay sick in bed day after day with no help but the uncertain visits of Indian women, she grew gradually aware, by the way the child throve, that the *mahala* [15] was nursing it along with her own beady-eyed, brown dumpling. Mary roused herself sufficiently to have the Doctor see the Paiute woman to make sure that they ran no danger, and for the rest, since the *mahala* was shy about her service, accepted it gratefully in silence. Two or three years later, because Mary's child was not talking as early as it should, that *mahala* came all the way to Lone Pine to bring her dried meadowlarks' tongues, which make the speech nimble and quick.

It was in experiences such as this that Mary began genuinely to know Indians. There was a small campody up George's Creek, brown wickiups in the chaparral like wasps' nests. Mary would see the women moving across the mesa on pleasant days, digging wild hyacinth roots, seed-gathering, and, as her strength permitted, would often join them, absorbing women's lore, plants good to be eaten or for medicine, learning to make snares of long, strong hair for the quail, how with one hand to flip trout, heavy with spawn, out from under the soddy banks of summer runnels, how and when to gather willows and cedar roots for basket-making. It was in this fashion that she began to learn that to get at the meaning of work you must make all its motions, both of body and mind. It was one of the activities which has had continuing force throughout her life.

Mary found herself too much hampered with the baby to hunt, but there were trout in the near-by creeks, often quite large ones brought down by the seasonal storms and stranded in the shallows. On one occasion there had been a cloudburst in one of the narrow canyons opening on the neighborhood of George's Creek. It came out of the mountain, tall and shining, with a sound of thunder, advancing on the plain for a space without diminution, and then gradually sloping as it drained away by shallow arroyos, passing within a few rods of her house. Mary went out with the baby on one arm and a hoe on the other to look for what it had left, a very large and lively lake trout thrashing indignantly in a transient pool. Mary laid the baby under a sagebush while she dammed the shallow trickle below it before undertaking to flip the trout out with the hoe. At that instant an eagle hovering, who must have already marked it for his own, swooped and snatched. Mary struck him with the hoe, so that he dropped the trout, which Mary fell upon; the eagle sharply with a resentful scream darted for the sleeping child. Mary sweats still to think what might have happened if she had not laid it so close up under the covering sage. Once more the hoe came into play and the eagle swooped, this time raking the raised arms with a long claw before, screaming, he made off into invisible blueness. I do not even yet recall how Mary got back to the house — with the trout; but it was days before she would so much as take the child outdoors without a preliminary survey of the wide haunt of eagles, and she left out that part when she accounted to Wallace that night for the trout at supper.

At George's Creek, Mary's interest renewed in the wandering
flocks that infested the whole of California during the last quarter
of the century. They passed, spring and autumn, close under the
Sierra Wall, on their way to and from the summer pastures, between the Sierras and the Alabama hills, spreading out on George's
Creek, where they not infrequently lingered on stubble pastures
hired from the farmers. There is in that grassless land always a
signal dust arising from the passing of a flock. Mary would walk
out to meet them sometimes with an armful of garden greens —
fresh garlic they liked, eating it crunchingly as youngsters eat
apples, often without even bread as an accompaniment — to exchange for lumps of fresh mutton. Among the herders she recognized several she had begun to know about Bakersfield, and renewed exchanges of news from the wild pastures which she coveted.
Sheepherders are a lonely folk, responding gladly to the incredible
circumstance of interest in their way of life. Mary's mother, during
those first years in Inyo, used to complain that Mary wrote too
seldom and skimpingly. The truth is that Mary would not write of
those things in her life which she regarded as the fruit of mere
stupid blundering, the misery of poverty and ill health and un-
congeniality, and Susie was not interested, was a little shocked by
the things that gave life and the color of intellectual interest to
Mary.

The next winter Wallace taught at Lone Pine, where the salary
was larger and living conditions somewhat easier. We had a house
on the main street between the hotel and the town's most popular
saloon, the one at which Bill Withrow used to practice his profession. There was a larger place on the next corner, where by moving
the bar and pool tables into the back room, we could hold church
festivals and fashionable wedding festivities. That is the one at
which it was usual, after the church festival was over, to hand the
minister the profits of the occasion in his own hat, after which we
would all file out of the front door and in again at the back to begin
dancing, with no clerical feelings hurt.

At the other saloon there was a wide portal which overlooked

Mary's garden — I do not recall any place where we lived for as much as a single season where Mary did not have some sort of a garden. The proprietor was a friendly soul, and on dull days he would lean over the end of the portal and gossip with Mary working among her beans and cabbages. I recall still how the portal looked, set out with paper garlands, and black crêpe on the chairs where the judges sat for the horse-race we held in the afternoon after Fitz's funeral, in his honor. Fitz was an Irishman with a club-foot and an obsession over Napoleon, in the key of whose character he had set his own behavior, which peculiarity had been augmented by an injury to Fitz's head from a mine cave-in. He had been originally a man of more than ordinary capacity and characteristic Irish instability. He had played a not unimportant part in the mining activities of the region, of which I recall the slight, the picturesque incident, such as his marrying for his first wife an Indian woman, dressing her in silks and forestalling on arrival at hotels any possible intention of proprietors of drawing the customary racial lines against her, by shooting up the place. His mine was somewhere on the top of Panamint, from which he would daily scan with a glass the perilous passage of the Panamint Valley, for unwary prospectors into that damned region where the evaporation from the body was so rapid that a man might drop in his tracks with water in his canteen. Fitz would make bets with himself, if no other takers offered, on how far the prospector might be allowed to go before a rescue was staged. It was said that he was exceedingly annoyed if the victim fell before the selected point was reached, or managed to stagger on farther. Toward the last, Fitzgerald spent a great deal of time in Lone Pine, and had a high opinion of Mary's intelligence, which he demonstrated by reciting to her most of Moore's Irish lyrics and his favorite theories about Napoleon. That was how I came to take such an interest in his funeral besides the fact that the services were read by my husband, wearing *the* hat; this was a high silk topper which had been brought into the Valley by a young Jew, who had bought it for his wedding and afterwards had no use for it. It was always produced for important funerals. The judges of the horse-race — who had been the pallbearers — sat on the portal next to Mary's garden; between heats they would retire to the bar and with the air of ritual, drink and remark, 'Well, Fitz would sure have enjoyed this.' You will find other such reminders of the days that were, in Mary's books; others are too dim now for recounting... even as I write there comes back the tall, black-bearded figure of a lone Mormon, skirt-coated and black-hatted, with a rifle always in the crook of his arm, supposed to have taken part in the Mountain Meadow Massacre, whose house and all its appurtenances, table, cook-stove, and bed, were so arranged that, as he moved about them, he had always his back to a wall. He had a quick, covert manner of glancing continuously at an invisible presence at his shoulder, which gave rise to the conviction that he was haunted. So were they all, those relics of the great mining days, whose trail went up like smoke even as Mary watched them.

Tragically quaint were the once favorites of fortune who had clung a little too long to the curiously inconsequent faith of mining folk that a good strike will inevitably 'come back,' and so were caught in the last of the recessive waves of prosperity in which the great Comstock era passed into tradition. The mingled pathos and whimsy of whose lives has been so perfectly dealt with by Harry Leon Wilson in the story of the house with the silver doorknobs... even in their poverty glamorous with the last traces of the period when the power of spending lavishly had been the prerogative of superior souls. They had their memories... first nights at the Academy of Music; the Easter Parade on Fifth Avenue in the seventies; Paris; spring on the Riviera. In those days when Mary knew them, they wanted everything but food and a certain consideration as arbiters of elegance and the fine art of spending. It is not wise to neglect those whom the gods have once marked for favor.

At Lone Pine there was less opportunity for Mary to keep up her interest in sheepherding, so inexplicable to other people; here the flocks passed behind the Alabamas, going swiftly till they came on the broad mesa pastures at George's Creek. Only at Julien's supply store the *capitans* arrived, the head shepherds, having under them

six or eight herders with their dogs and two to three hundred sheep.
Julien was French, an owner in a small way, made a little wine in
his own way, and had four or five pretty and circumspect daughters
about whom it was his perpetual worry that so few eligible — from
the French point of view — suitors could be found. It was there
that Mary learned how the whole business of sheepherding was
bound together and made one with the Cro-Magnon past of Man
by mutton-cabbage soup... Take the bones of one sheep, what are
left after the herder has satisfied himself with the usual roast and
broiled; one thick slice of salt pork, one carrot, and two onions for
each sharer of the pot... oh, the precise and well-debated allotment of savory herbs and the possible native substitutes for the
same!... one cabbage for four men, and just at the last the crusty
'heels' of the huge round loaves of 'sour dough' bread. If you tasted
that after a day in the open, you would understand why it required
one whole cabbage for four diners. You drink off the broth before
attacking the solid residue. It was on such occasions that Mary
recalled with grave satisfaction that she had had a French ancestor.
It was on the remainders of this delectable dish that the herd dogs
were fed.

About half the population of Lone Pine were true 'Mexicans';
not early Californians (Spanish), but descendants from one of the
refugee groups of the last disturbance before Porfirio Diaz, still
so immensely patriotic that they always made more of the Six-
teenth of September than the Fourth of July. They had settled in
Inyo about the time of Cerro Gordo. There was the remnant of
gentility among them — manners, old silver, and drawn work.
I do not know from what States they hailed, but they seemed to be
largely akin, and the Indian blood most noticeable among them
was Yaqui. Juan Ruiz, who was runner for several mines, used
to make a twenty-to-thirty-mile run with a package of mail and
medicine and such-like on his head, in about the same time as
a good horseman, and for half the money. It was not good form at
Lone Pine to make social equals of the Spanish-speaking families,
except, perhaps, one or two, like the Relles Carascos; but Mary

collected folklore, Spanish idioms, and cooking recipes among them with great gusto. What goes by the name of Spanish cooking in most parts of the United States is a bastard relation devoid of art. Only among the old families of New Mexico is the fine discrimination of *chile* mixtures to be found, especially the *chile moreños*. There are no such *tamales* and *enchilladas* made anywhere now north of the border as were taught to Mary by the Señora Josefa Maria de la Luz Ortiz y Romero. There is the savor in them of the hours of happy concentration that goes to the making of them, which is one of the ways in which the linkage of cookery and culture is proved. Food in which there is no flavoring of brooding attention has no value but as an antidote to hunger. Sometimes still, when the flow of words with meaning is stopped at its source, and the typewriter, as Doña Josefa would say of her *metate* 'does not wish to work to-day,' Mary will go shopping along the side streets and *placitas* of Santa Fé, and come home with just the right kind of pounded corn meal, with a fine fat *pollo* or two, with red beans and chiles, *colorado* (only we say *colora'o*), with a pile of clean white corn husks, with garlic, sesame seed, chocolate, olives, and goat's-milk cheese. Upon these she will brood awhile, and fix and prefer, and afterward work circumspectly for a day and a half before asking anybody in to share the result. After which the typewriter is never so willing. These are the accustomed motions of the self in creation, the better now and then for ancestral exercise.

One singular contribution to the social background of Inyo was made by the presence of peregrinating Britishers, drawn there for their health's sake, or to wear out those curious lapses of income to which it appeared their estates, under hired stewards, were liable. They were, once you overcame the native American reaction against the placid acceptance of a career devoted to peripatetic idleness, often charming, cultivated gentlemen. One such at Lone Pine became the chosen companion of my husband and a frequenter of our house, Alfred de la Cour Carroll, of ancient Irish family. He had a camp in one of the Sierra canyons, and whiled his time with hunting, trout-fishing, mountain-climbing,

and slightly philandering social relations with the people of Lone
Pine. To him accrued, from time to time, others of his kind,
making a pleasant note of cultivated interest in a background
rather lacking in intellectual diversion.

The year that Wallace taught at Lone Pine, we took up a homestead on the mesa between the Alabama hills and the huge,
upflung, naked bulk of Opapago. I should have said that here,
between Owens Lake and the northern end of the Alabamas,
clustered all that enchanted charm of the district which people
who found themselves enmeshed in it sometimes cursed as they
curse the beauty of women. The Alabamas were of exceeding
ancientness, and their fire-stained rocks Time sculptured into
strange shapes of weirdness, between which the filmy flame of
cactus flowers ran red and orange and apricot, with little patches
of a more fiery green and blue pools of lupine wetted by artesian
springs. The rocky core of the hills broke off somewhat abruptly
just above Lone Pine, and behind that our homestead lay, looking
off toward the lake and the cloud-mottled Coso country, all fawn
and red and black with faint tinges of citron. The hot flat sun
always 'drawing water' from the lake, so that toward morning and
evening, it could be seen letting down broad ladders of irised light
on which, said the Indians, the children of the Rainbow came and
went. Behind us in towering blocks of gray and black and white
gathered the peaks of Whitney and Opapago. Down by the rim of
the hills there was an old signal smoke station of the Paiutes,
which Mary used as an altar; there was also an Indian burying-
ground, strewn with blue beads. Our shack was just a little off the
trail to Carroll's camp, and when we were there he often visited us.
I recall perfectly one occasion when, as was possible at the turn of
the seasons, there was a sandstorm. These would come in with a
few days or hours of high electric tension, running lightning along
high rocks, or fine brush like sprays from rocks touched in passing,
followed by a suffusion of pale yellow murk through the upper air,
the murk deepening toward the ground at last in sand-laden,
gusty flaws, now hot, now cold; finally all vision blotted out in the

sand smother and the long steady push of the wind. I have known flocks to be smothered by them: nothing to show but huddled humps of sand where they had been. On this particular evening, Carroll and a visiting friend had lingered on their way back to camp, for supper, and by that time, by a sudden veering of the wind, the trail had been blotted out. All of that night the four of us sat up in the tiny one-room shack, with the sand drifting in triangular heaps through every crevice, drinking hot tea from time to time against the icy cold, clustered around the one small lamp, wrapped in our shared bedclothes, reading aloud by turns Kipling's 'Five Nations,' which Carroll's friend had brought new from the press. I recall that the friend, who had been in India, reading with great gusto, apologized occasionally for the phrases he thought a lady shouldn't hear.

IV

DURING all the years I lived in Inyo, I went every summer to visit my mother, being in a great need of her, and yet somehow always failing to make a vital connection. I had already written a few things, under my own name or another's, about which I could never get my mother to admit the smallest interest. She never pasted them in the family scrapbook, as had been her habit, and, driven into a corner by family friends who assumed her natural pride, she would say, in that Middlewestern manner of humility which concealed a secret self-gratulatory core, 'Well, they are beyond me.' Which was sheer nonsense, since my mother had been all her life a devoted reader of 'Scribner's,' 'Harper's,' and the 'Atlantic Monthly,' to the level of which Mary's maiden efforts by no means attained. If there were any logic in her attitude, it must have been that what came by way of the 'Atlantic' came from recognized centers of authority. Sometimes I think my mother's attitude toward my writing really grew out of her recognizing something in it which she might have admitted had it come as the Tables of the Law should come, from Sinai, which, when she saw it starting from her own side, made her afraid.

On one occasion I had been quoted as favoring some sort of institutional application of the best human experience to the less favored individuals. It was all very much in line with what was in the best minds of the time, which led to various institutionalized expressions in juvenile courts, probation officers, and the final court of domestic relations — which should have been called domestic adjustments. Impossible now to recover the shock of mingled hurt and indignation with which certain elements of our population met a proposal so offensive to the traditional delicacies and exemptions of the personal life. I recall middle-aged gentlemen who were affected to the point of apoplexy by it.

That summer I had not been home more than twenty-four hours when Jim, having taken me aside in the most solemn manner, gave me to understand that, while the family claimed no control over my pronouncements while under my husband's roof, in *their* house, nothing so injurious to domestic propriety could be hinted, on pain of my being refused that shelter ever after. You could see that he had worked himself up to it; that it had formed the subject of family council. If you see Mary's name mentioned rather frequently in defense of people resting under penalty of opinion, you will understand that she has touched in her own person the indignity of exile. How could my mother have held that out against me, without so much as an inquiry? How could my home be less my home or how could my mother be not my mother because of what life had taught me? I could see her looking at me a little apprehensively as I came from that interview, and I knew that if I had stormed at her, had rejected the stricture with tears and indignation, she would have broken down. But the incident touched too nearly on that thing which middle-class America understands less than anything else, intellectual integrity, which does not admit of an emotional corrective. And I was far too young to have realized that nearly all moral disapprobation is really an emotional and egoistic release for the shock of interrupted habit, which quite often expends itself in the expression. Fifteen years later, I sent my brother a clipping with an account of my being a guest of honor at a dinner of the New York Women Lawyers' Association, in which the now well-established court of domestic relations came in for public sanction. I suspect that by that time he had forgotten that he had ever disapproved of it.

There was also the distress growing out of my increasing knowledge of what had happened to my child. I had had several talks with Dr. Woodin, in which he had repeatedly assured me that whatever had happened had happened before she was born, and that I could not be the least to blame for it.

I hadn't told that to my mother, and the need of having her know had so grown on me that I was no longer able to endure it; the need of having her know that I was not to blame; the desperate need of some attitude on the part of my family more consoling and warming. My mother was always writing that she wished she could see more of little Ruth. Some friends of mine being on the point of driving down, I sent the child to her grand-mother. I don't know what I expected: that she would discover the truth; that her instinct and intelligence would penetrate to my suffering; that she would come to me and that we would weep and console one another. Surely this would be a time when she would put away my brother and feel with another woman inno-cently offended in what had always been insisted upon by my mother and her group as a sacred function. What I got was a letter from Jim in his accustomed aura of high moral dudgeon, re-questing me to take the child away. I did not go, but sent the child's father, leaving him to say what he would. I learned later that nothing whatever touching the child passed between them. My mother wrote, 'I don't know what you've done, daughter, to have such a judgment upon you.' It was the last word that passed between us. It was an attitude in which, I should have known, my mother's time would have concurred.

I shall speak again of this in its place, and then no more. That nerve ached out at last, but because it was a grief too long borne in secret for surface recovery, no one ever does speak to me about it. My mother did not live to know the truth, and, though my brothers did, I doubt if they ever gave it space in their minds, too long possessed by an earlier notion of my own culpability, or at least of moral deserving.

The country through which these visits to my mother were made was the strip of almost pure desertness which skirts the Sierras, curving west to meet the Coast Range around the southern end of the San Joaquin. There is a shorter way through the Sierras by Walker's Pass, open only in summer weather, but at all seasons the ancient thoroughbrace stage-coaches rocked steadily by eighteen-mile relays from Keeler, at the head of Owens Lake, to Mojave, on the Southern Pacific, which carried one back on the track to Bakersfield. If one happened not to know enough to engage in advance the seat beside the driver, the trip was rather a horror, crowded into the stuffy interior between 'oldtimers,' liquor salesmen, mining experts, an occasional stray 'girl' from the local bawdy-house, or one of those distressed and distressfully pitiable 'lungers' of whom you had the grace only to hope that he wouldn't die on your shoulder. Outside there was a magnificent panorama and often very good entertainment. Among purveyors of story material, stage-coach drivers bear the palm. Mary was always able to secure the outside seat. No matter how many times she had been over the road, she was always ready to hear the tale again and could give story for story, besides being well provided with baskets of fruit and chocolate layer cake and such-like comestibles as while away the midnight hours, for the trip was always made of one continual stretch of twenty-six hours, with eighteen-mile relays. I have incorporated so many of those tales into 'Lost Borders' and 'One Smoke Stories,' that there is little left but that inconclusive sort of actual incident of which the point is always that of your being there for it to happen to. I recall once setting out for Mojave at such an hour that midnight brought us to Red Rock Canyon, one of the weirdest wind-sculptured defiles of the West, with nobody on board but three or four nondescript male passengers and Mary on the boot beside the driver. Where we slowed down by the drag of the wind-sifted sand in the dark of the canyon, a figure moved mysteriously up on our right... the driver laid his hand warily on his hip and the stranger hastened to make known his quest...

'Ye got anybody on board that can pray out loud?'

The driver halted, gun-hand squared to the stranger's direction. Nothing came out of the interior but the sound of heavy breathing.

'We got a man here's pretty badly hurt,' apologized the interlocutor; 'he'd like to have somebody pray for him.'

After another dead interval, Mary leaned across the driver's knee. 'I could pray,' she said.

The dark stranger peered and hesitated. 'You're a lady, ain't ye? The man's pretty bad ——'

'I got the mail,' the driver explained; 'I could wait fifteen minutes.'

Mary began to clamber down in the dark.

'Here you,' the driver called indignantly into the interior, 'ain't some o' you fellows goin' with the lady?'

Grunting, two male figures took form in the mitigated dark of the stage lantern; we followed the stranger around a coign of the canyon wall. There was a camp there and a low fire; a wagon bulked darkly and beside the fire the hurt man propped on a bedding roll under a blanket. 'Here's a lady come to pray with you, Bill.' Bill was evidently far gone. He tried to speak; tried to push back the blanket, which showed him bandaged about the breast. Another man came up from the wagon, carrying one of his arms awkwardly, muttering something. The guide put the blanket firmly back. 'Don't keep the lady waiting, Bill.' Mary caught the wandering feeble hands of the hurt man in hers... 'Merciful Father...' she began; behind her she could see, or rather hear the standing men taking off their hats. There had been, Mary considered, some sort of a shooting scrap... no time to think of that... 'Repeat after me: Christ Jesus, forgive my sins... Jesus ... forgive,' very faint; 'and receive my spirit...'

When we got down at Keeler the next afternoon, the two men who had stood behind Mary when she prayed came up solemnly and shook her by the hand. Later the driver told me that on his daylight trip back he had stopped long enough to visit the death camp, but besides the cold ashes he found no trace.

Things had a way of happening at Red Rock. It was there Mary came upon an altar once, and a priest saying mass to three herders kneeling among their silly sheep... and there she saw the ghost of Vasquez' horse; Tiburcio Vasquez, the most popular bandit... 'He stole from the rich and he gave to the poor.' And after his death the horse used to go over and over the accustomed route looking for his master, in life, and regularly after it became a ghost.... (That's not the only ghost horse seen in the West.) Vasquez used to keep a lookout on the tall rock above Coyote Holes for the bullion teams out from Indian Wells, and to make a signal smoke. There was a story at Coyote Holes — but I've written that.

Once — but whether it was later or earlier I forget — there was a woman at Coyote Holes that interested Mary greatly. She was a middle-aged school teacher from Vermont, or perhaps Connecticut, who had come out under the protection of a matrimonial bureau to marry the keeper of the stage station. He was middle-aged too, and had been known as the Bad Man from Bodie — Bodie you'll find in Mark Twain's account. Mary used to see that sign — Water, Hell, or China — when she went that way, and always meant to possess it, but a high wind blew it away. The Bad Man was reputed to have nine notches in his gun, but after fifty years he began to yearn for respectability and the peace and pleasantness of his mother's home in New England; hence the resort to the matrimonial bureau. Mrs. Bodie, as we will call her, came on and married him sight unseen at Mojave. She brought braided rugs and a melodeon, and planted hollyhocks in the station yard. Mary used to bring her geranium slips and saved seeds. She said she was perfectly happy, but missed her church privileges. Bodie did what he could to make it up to her. Sundays he shaved and put on a clean shirt, and the two of them sat on the porch rocking and singing Gospel Hymns. She never knew that he had been called the Bad Man from Bodie.

Mary saw more than a few matrimonial agency marriages in the old West; they turned out on the whole as well as other people's; where no deception had been practiced, often more satisfactorily. There were instances, of course, that were ludicrously pitiful... meager, defeated souls tricked out for the dance of ecstasy recaptured, looking out aghast, from their wigs and paint, at what they saw of themselves in the other.

Several adventures of the Mojave stage-coach couldn't have happened to anyone else. Mary always took it going south or to the San Joaquin Valley, 'over beyond' as the phrase was. For getting 'down below,' which meant anywhere about the Golden Gate, one took the narrow-gauge on one of its three weekly trips, connecting with the transcontinental lines at Reno. There were peaks in Inyo from which it was solemnly averred by people who had climbed them that ships could be seen going in and out of the Bay. The narrow-gauge was slow enough, as railroads were esti-

SANCTUARIO

The old Spanish chapel bought by Mrs. Austin and presented to New Mexico
(*See page* 359)

mated, and once they stopped on the Divide for Mary to make a snow man, and at Walker Lake, when there were no ladies aboard, for the train men to take a swim; but you couldn't hop on and off to pick strange flowers, nor hold up the train while the station keeper at Black Rock finished a long-drawn gruesome tale of a traveler going out with his 'pile,' who was killed there and fed out to the passengers as pork, so that his ghost, in the form of a large black pig, took to haunting the place about meal time. And of course you couldn't have taken the train in, as you did the stage once, when, with nobody in it but an English mining expert going to Indian Wells and Mary with her baby, the driver tried to turn round about halfway between Mojave and the eighteen-mile house. He said he was sick because the water of Mojave hadn't agreed with him, and passed out. Mary and the Englishman contrived to double him up and project him in that condition onto the front seat, and the mining expert, who professed to know nothing of horses, held the baby while Mary strapped herself to the boot and took the stage in to the eighteen-mile house. We were late, of course, and it was several days before Mary got the stiffness out of her arms, but it was great fun. A dozen years later, dining at that place in London where they do you so marvelously with hot and cold joints trundled about on a gigantic tea-wagon — Simpson's, wasn't it? and it would have been the Hoovers who took me there — the mining man recognized me and recalled the incident to memory.

There were still a few mines going far out, toward what a few years later became the Johannesburg-Rhyolite district, who got their mail at the Mojave-to-Keeler stage stations, some of them doing assessment work merely, and, in rare intervals of uncovering rich leads, piling up double and triple shifts. This would have been about 1900 — exact dates for that period are impossible for me to recover — and by this time Mary was a well-known and somewhat dramatic figure whose passing made a stir. Lonely men in remote stations, men who had not seen their own womenkind in months, when they heard of it, would get into the stations just for the sake of the half-hour's chat with her while meals were eaten and horses changed. On one of these occasions she found waiting for her a pleasant-looking man, superintendent from let us call it the Lost Burro Mine — there was one of these in every district — who said openly, before everybody, that his old mother was out at the mine with him, hungering for women's company; would Mary go out and spend a day with her? The plea was valid for the time and country; Mary had always wanted to see the Lost Burro, and, as it happened this was one of the few times when she did not have her daughter with her, the stage-coach could pick her up at the same place the day after. It wasn't until they were four hours on the road that Mr. Burro, so we will 'call him — he did make something of an ass of himself — began to exhibit great uneasiness. His mother, he confessed, was safe in her home in Philadelphia; he had cooked up that yarn to save my face with the station people. The boys, he said, meaning his staff, assayer, foreman, and accountant, had been taken with the idea of having a visit from Mary, and he had been appointed to arrange it. Could she possibly forgive him and go on with it? That was where he showed himself most asinine, since simply to have driven out in the desert and to have returned in the middle of the night would have been incredible. The adventure had to be gone through with.

'Who else knows that I am expected?'

'By this time, probably everybody.'

'And you know what they will do to you if I tell them I have been insulted?'

He knew well enough; the mining gesture of chivalry is high, wide, and handsome.

'Well, I *will* tell them that,' said Mary, 'unless you do exactly as I tell you from now on.'

The 'boys' were all out to welcome the lady — they could have seen us coming for an hour up the grade — including the four China-boy cooks, all stiffly starched and with new green and cerise tassels on their pigtails. They had made in her honor all six of the American desserts they knew, three of which proved to be bread pudding. After dinner, all three of the shifts — the grave-yard shift for that occasion had been omitted — all shaved and clean-shirted, came up to have a look at The Lady. They found her with the staff on the long platform that ran the length of the mess-house, in full sight of the camp and each other, with all the implications of constituting themselves a guard of honor. The miners were mostly Cornishmen, with short backs, legs wide apart and lithe but bulging muscles. Two or three had their wives with them, childless women who made a footing in these predominantly male communities by doing laundry and mending. At the very last, two or three other women edged in a little cluster by themselves, to whom everybody pointedly paid no attention. The evening entertainment included cowboy songs, Spanish *canciones* with guitar accompaniment, frontier ballads, such as 'Sam Bass,' and about the 'dirty coward who shot Mr. Howard and laid Jesse James in his grave.' Two men danced what was probably once a sword dance. The foreman and accountant did the quarrel of Brutus and Cassius, which was much appreciated. Somebody else did card tricks. Then The Lady recited poetry, something of her own, after which there were sentimental songs with choruses. The Lady made, about eleven o'clock, a dramatic withdrawal that would, I am sure, have done credit to Mrs. Siddons, after which most of the songs were sung over as a serenade. The next morning she was shown ceremoniously over the mine and driven back to meet the stage by a relieved and humble superintendent. It wasn't, however, an adventure that Mary talked much about.

All told, I have had little travel in my life which has yielded so much profit on the exertion as the old Mojave stage. I understand that the road is well furnished now with gas stations and hot-dog stands, and the trip can be made in a few hours without incident. Which seems on the whole a pity.

V

IN THE autumn of '95, Mary took Ruth and settled in Bishop, the most northerly of the Valley towns, of about one thousand inhabitants, with a large farming contingent. The ostensible reason for her going was to be easily accessible to medical attention, for herself as well as for the child. There was also the need of reorganizing her life in view of contingencies which she could never persuade her husband to make explicit items in their joint future. Incredible today that a life should be planned in which the wife's capabilities, her health and fitness for the part assigned to her to play, should be negligible properties, but the strange thing would have been that it could have been otherwise. Men made their own plans and endured the wife's unsuitability to them with magnanimity or impatience according to their natures. Mary's husband was uncomplaining and kind, but it simply did not enter into his calculation that his own adjustments should take into account her want of physical endowment for the life of pioneer housekeeping on a small income and the combined care of a permanently ailing child. It was a situation which Mary by this time fully realized she must meet herself, and for that she wanted a little space of detachment. At Bishop a plan for reviving a so-called Academy offered her a teaching possibility. She was to teach English, literature, and art.

The educational episode proved of no particular moment, owing in part to inexpert management and in part to its being undertaken under the least propitious circumstances. Those who live through them will recall Coxey's Army and the panic of the two preceding years, and in Inyo the gradual draining away of the mining interests which left the farmers with no market for their produce. This was how it came about that the most dramatic incident of Mary's first year at Bishop was the Free Silver Movement. The most intellectually intriguing incidents of her stay in Bishop clustered around the sheep interests and the Indian school. There

were a number of wool-growers about Bishop — named for an old
partner of Beale's — of whom Waterson, who figures in 'The
Flock' as the Manxman, was the largest. Two of the Waterson
young people were pupils of Mary's and the acquaintance so
formed led on to her completing at the Waterson Ranch the experiments begun several years earlier with hunting-dogs at Mountain View. It had been for a long time in Mary's mind that the
story — that knot of related and inter-consequential incidents
which make up the pattern called experience — must have come
down to man by more intimate ancestral inheritance than the
poem even. What she needed for uncovering the line of descent
was a vocabulary expressive of experience — that is, things done
leading to appreciable consequences, by which stories could be
conveyed. She was finally to discover that vocabulary in the
language of signs — arm signs chiefly and two or three vocables —
invented by herders for communication with their dogs. This is
much more than the vocabulary of verbal commands such as are
used in the hunting-fields; a vocabulary of sentences expressive of
the whole phase of an experience such as *Sheep missing on the left,
go and find them; Round the flock and hold; Round and bed the flock.*
What Mary discovered that winter was that, by piecing these
sentences and signs together in the pattern of an incident which
had happened often enough to come easily to mind, and by nar-
rating the incident in this fashion on occasions on which it was
plain to the dogs that it could not refer to a *present* circumstance,
she could afford them pleasure, such as they learned to invite in
the same way a young child invites the re-telling of a favorite tale.
Of course there were dogs who remained always uneasily in doubt
as to the relevance of such a narrative to the momentary reality,
and dogs, who, convinced that it did not refer to anything actually
going on at the time among their charges, were always a little
suspicious of your intention, so to speak, of 'pulling their leg.'
Curiously, although the certainty so arrived at, that given the
proper vocabulary there can be transmissions of *experience* between
man and dog is probably the most important contribution to the
story-teller's art that Mary will ever make, I have found no story-

teller in America in the least interested. Indirectly it opens up the whole question of the communication of experience among animals, and alters the comparative values of instinct and training in animal behavior. It led on, for Mary, to a renewed curiosity about Indian sign languages and their experience-carrying possibilities, which made for many years a stimulating minor intellectual interest.

There was a large campody at Bishop and the largest Indian school in the valley. It was from the teacher, a more than ordinarily competent and intelligent woman, that Mary began to learn the sort of thing that made of her a fierce and untiring opponent of the colossal stupidities, the mean and cruel injustices, of our Indian Bureau. I have thought this over and intend not to say too much in detail of that long and not yet entirely triumphant struggle. It is a story in itself which will yet have to be written as those other stories of labor, of suffrage, of religious and intellectual freedom, all the deeply felt and determined effort to realize in our communal relations the constitutional guarantees of democracy. There are other Indian episodes that are so intimately connected with my life as an artist, with what ultimately I came to understand, and stand for, in the structure and meaning of human society, that they cannot be omitted. But the whole business of affecting the governmental policy toward Indians, as the Government itself is now willing to admit it has been affected, might just as well have been any other of those half-unconscious starts of my generation toward the realization and rescue of the underdog, which has been its characteristic concern. At the same time that my contemporaries were joining labor organizations and aligning themselves with wage-strikes, I took to the defense of Indians because they were the most conspicuously defeated and offended against group at hand. I should have done as much even without what I afterward discovered among them of illumination and reformation of my own way of thought. I am consoled by the certainty, which nobody denies me, not even the Government which I fought, of having been of use to them. I got out of the actual activities involved precisely what my contemporaries in cities got, a knowledge of the persisting strain of bruteness, of emotional savagery, of greed and hypocrisy which taints the best of our Western civilization; precisely what my contemporaries learned by seeing strikers beaten up by policemen; citizens deprived by violence of their constitutional liberties; the lowly and underprivileged stripped of their economic opportunities. As for the other things that came to me by way of my Indian acquaintances, they are the gifts of a special grace which has been mine from the beginning, the persistence in me, perhaps, of an uncorrupted strain of ancestral primitivism, a single isolated gene of that far-off and slightly mythical Indian ancestor of whose reality I am more convinced by what happened to me among Indians than by any objective evidence.

What set me off on that trail was dreadful enough, a flagrant instance of a local pastime, known as *mahala* chasing. Many of the younger Indian women were employed in the town as household help, and it was no uncommon experience for them, on their way home unattended, to be waylaid by white men — in this instance two young girls, who had lingered behind to sweep the schoolhouse, and were afterward captured and detained for the greater part of the night by a gang of youths, of whom the only extenuating thing that can be said is that they were still very young, and instigated by an older man not a native of the community. The Indian girls closed their part of the episode by eating wild parsnip root — the convulsions induced by that bane being mercifully shorter than the sufferings already endured — and though the community did actually take measures to prevent the recurrence of such incidents, nothing was done to the offenders, who were sons, some of them, of the 'best families.' And not only at Bishop — I recall at Lone Pine a young wife kicked to death by a white man in a drunken fury at her resistance, and the Indian husband weeping in the broken measures of remediless despair. 'My wife ... all the same one dog.' And the Ghost Dance... and Warner's Ranch... plenty of incident to set off less sensitive natures than Mary's against Christian pretense and democratic inadequacy.

These things had their part in the discovery Mary made that

winter of '96–'97 that she was not only not a Methodist, but that she couldn't, in the orthodox sense of the word, go on calling herself a Christian. I had actually had no opportunities for discovering that since leaving Carlinville; and had renewed my membership in the church at Bishop as a matter of course, after six years of practical severance. In the meantime the experience called the Practice of the Presence of God had come back to me, and a profound movement of spiritual growth *away from* the orthodox Protestant expression of it. It had begun, the movement of growth, in the default of all possible human help in situations in which I had always been convinced that they were not intrinsically helpless. As a matter of fact, I can't recall that Mary ever had surrendered to that blind acceptance of irremediable evil known as resignation. Always she had been deeply aware that there was something that could be done about everything; if not at once, then later, when you had learned this or that, mastered one or another intervening technique. It was at the root of all her religious conviction of every sort that life is essentially remediable, undefeatable; the thing was to discover the how of it. In her own fashion, in her private emergency, she had already set about the business.

The thing that Mary suffered from in the middle nineties was loneness; by which I mean to indicate a state of lacking human resort, rather than any emotional state which involved feeling sorry for herself. There was the trouble about the child, which Dr. Woodin had told her was humanly speaking incurable, and for which she was in no way to blame. This she had accepted intellectually, without being entirely rid of the need of reassurance. She tried things; putting Ruth in the care of other people to see if haply they could do any better about her; employing one doctor and another. (At Bishop she had found a woman doctor, Dr. Helen McKnight, so newly come to practice that Mary might not have resorted to her had it not been for the tearful postulate of a young man who had gone to school with Dr. Nellie, as she was called. He confided to Mary that his hope was that she would 'fall in the ditch,' metaphorically speaking, so as to afford him the

occasion to demonstrate his opinion of her lapse from true woman-
liness by the study of medicine, by 'leaving her lay.' A hope
which she disappointed by succeeding in her practice and marrying the handsomest and most eligible young man in the community.) But except for the doctors, Mary's grief about her child
had to be suffered apart even from her husband, who maintained
about it that curious inarticulateness which characterized all his
intimate thought.

Then there was that very real and heartrending anguish of the
creative worker before the medium and method of individual
expression has been mastered, which is, I suppose, always ludi-
crous to the onlooker not himself tormented by it. As it turned
out, no help from the outside ever did arrive for that, although in
the first onset of the struggle, after Mary had discovered that the
teaching she had had in painting was not only inadequate but an
interference to direct expressiveness, and before the use of literary
forms had become easily available, she had cried out once to her
mother — who else? — and Susie had not understood it.

And finally there was the problem, more bewildering at this
stage than anguished, of adjusting herself to a marriage which had
failed in almost every particular from the pattern to which her
girlish expectation had been educated. It was an axiom of marriage as it was practiced in the Middlewest that the husband's
business or professional interest should constitute the main line of
organization, which it was the wife's business to supplement and
serve. With all her revolt against the accepted pattern of wifely
subservience, Mary had never rejected this necessity to conform to
her husband's way of making a living. She was accused of it; she
endured not only from her family but from his, and from such
individuals as in small towns make it their business to pass judgment on their neighbors' lives, the usual imputation of unwomanly
seeking of her own way of life, but the appalling truth was that
her husband had no well-defined way of life to which she could
tender a confirming devotion. He not only had no business or
profession; he appeared to have no leading in any direction which
could have marked out such a way of life for him. He had allowed

himself while in college to be diverted from the study of law, on the tradition of which his family had provided him with that opportunity, and had never resumed it. He was successful in his teaching, but liked it so little that he would make no sort of use of that success to enhance his advantage. On one occasion, being asked for a photograph of himself to be published in a series of successful principals, and having nothing of his own at hand, he substituted one of his brother's; and his replies to questionnaires and other occasions for making himself known barely escaped ribaldry. At that time, such was the demand for school heads, he could have had almost anything of the kind in the State that he had a mind to apply for; he did receive invitations to larger and more profitable situations, to which he returned a slightly puzzled refusal. He was possessed of no alternative plan for improving the condition of his family, but he had a dream of prosperous and satisfactory employment, between which and present reality there was a nebulous region within which he was to 'get into something' by which such sums were to be earned as would ensure the accomplishment of the dream. And this was so much the approach of men we knew to their own futures that it had all the entrenched impregnability of popular sanction.

To Mary the confounding element in this general view was that the holders of it were all equally convinced that the miracle of something to 'get into' was to happen at its irreducible best there in Inyo. I have little hope of being understood on this point which must nevertheless be gone into because of the searing knowledge of the ways of the land with men, which is burned into my mind because of it. There was a spell of the land over all the men who had in any degree given themselves to it, a spell of its lofty and intricate charm, which worked on men like the beauty of women. It was proof against all prior claims, and required no justification. It is the way Beauty works to set up in men the desire to master and make it fruitful. But it is the restraining condition of Beauty in the arid West that man cannot simply appropriate individual holdings of it; he cannot, in a country where there is an average rainfall of an inch a year and eleven cloudy days, make any quarter-section of it bear. To bring such a land to fruitage requires an available water supply, organizing capacity, and that commodity known as capital. What was lacking in Inyo was the last, and to a lesser degree the next to the last item. Men talking together would invariably express the deeply felt conviction of the inevitability of these two indispensables... 'Well, this country is bound to go ahead sometime; just look at it.' Which seldom failed to elicit the antiphonal response, 'Sure, it's got to, why — look.' Women hearing it would look at one another with sharp — or weary — implications of exasperated resignation.

Resignation was a character never written in Mary's book. She meant by hook or crook to get her husband away from Inyo into any other region in which something 'to get into' was more likely to happen in her lifetime. She had it in mind to take one of the teaching opportunities that her husband refused and establish the family in a more advantageous situation under such circumstances that he could not but follow. It will appear incredible to the modern young couple that considerations of welfare, of suitability, of the wife's natural preference and endowment, would not promptly have prevailed over the spell of locality, but that will be because the young have no recollection of the weight of traditional pattern on the structure of married life; the pattern of male dominance and feminine subservience. I recall that there were instances when it penetrated to my husband that Mary was not 'just talking'; that her feeling for the utter unsuitability of the environment for anything that they could conceivably make of their joint life was the source of acute distress; that she incredibly meant that she should do something about it. She could see the dim perception of such a possibility working in him, bewilderedly, and resolving itself into the relieving conviction, 'Well, but I'm the one who has to decide that, where we live and everything... I'll get into something...'

The only things that naturally could have happened to Inyo were a revival of the mining interest and the investment of outside capital in water development. For the time, the recent panic of '94–'95 had made it unlikely that any such investment would be

made shortly, and the mining interest which had been slowly
dwindling out was now writhing in the last coil of the Sixteen to
One crisis.

It happened picturesquely at Bishop, developing an additional
convolution from the wool interests, between which and the silver
mines the prosperity of the farming districts hung suspended. For
weeks the flocks were gathering on the long Sierra slope, in the
stubble pastures; always about the country lanes a blether and a
roll of bells, the smell of sheep and claret in the streets; trust a wool-
grower not to miss his vote or the votes of his hirelings when
there is a question of wool tariff to the fore. At the hotels the silver
interests were represented by men who carried their liquor well,
and their political enthusiasms by no means so steadily. On election day, the tension reached almost the explosive point. In one
of the saloons knives such as the French and Basque herders wear,
and six-guns, to which their lonely way of life was sanction enough,
were piled high by a cautious barkeeper who would sell them no
liquor until he had secured himself against brawling.... As they
went out toward the dawn-blue, with the wool-growers' candidate
well in the lead, I heard the Basques singing a wild high chant of
triumph... Balzar, the Basque, was a friend of mine; there was
a Balzar on the Seven States Commission of the Colorado River —
I wondered. You can tell a Basque by the way he carries himself,
the focus of his motion being a little higher than with other modern
peoples, almost as high as the Greeks on ancient vases.... The next
morning the herders were well on their way, the remaining
Capitans too happily drunk to keep up with them; at the strongholds
of the Sixteen to Oners, there was a feeling as of the body being
still in the house. The following Sunday the minister — a visiting
incumbent — broke down and wept as he pictured what would
happen to all of us as a result of the Bryan failure. And in a day or
two, everything was going on just about the same. I recall wondering if women were really suited to politics.

I've been putting off the overwhelmingly personal event which
actually happened in the summer of '96. Wallace had joined me

then and we were planning some sort of camping trip. Mother had written for Mary not to come home that year, as her ill health, the worst of which had until then been withheld from me, and had now passed the obligation of delicacy to conceal, had reached the stage when she felt it indispensable to go to Los Angeles for hospital treatment. And within a week Jim had wired that an emergency operation had become necessary. The wire came too late for Mary to avail herself of the tri-weekly connection with the Mojave stage, and Mary put in the day preparing to take the return train around by way of Reno. About dusk, exhausted by labor and anxiety, Wallace sent her out to sit on the high stoop of the house while he fed Ruth and put her to bed. There in the clear obsidian twilight her mother came, all in white as Mary recalled her when Father was still a young man, with a rose in her hair, pink and sweetly smiling... She said there was no need for Mary to take the train now, since everything was well with her, and Mary believed her. She told Wallace to leave off the packing, Mother was quite all right now... and dropped almost instantly into sleep. But in the morning waking in her bed, Mary knew; she was crying and her husband trying to comfort her with last night's assurance, when the telegram came. The operation had been more serious than had been anticipated, and Susie had not rallied from it. She had stirred a little at the surface of consciousness... 'Take care of Mary,' she said, and then no more. That would have been about the hour that Mary saw her. There is no use trying to explain these things. They happen. Something in Mary that kept the unfading impress of her mother at her happiest chose that picture as the sign of what that deep something knew... or else...

There is an element of incalculable ravening in the loss of your mother; deep under the shock of broken habit and the ache of present grief, there is the psychic wound, the severed root of being; such loss as makes itself felt as the companion of immortality. For how should the branch suffer, torn from the dead tree? It is only when the tree is green that the cut bough bleeds.

VI

IN THE song of Earth Horizon man wanders in search of the Sacred Middle from which all horizons are equidistant, and his soul happily at rest. Once the Middle is attained, all the skyey rings that encircle earth's six quarters dissolve into the true zone of reality, and his spirit, no longer deflected by the influences of false horizons, swings freely to its proper arc. In the three years of which my mother's death was the determining event, orthodox Christianity was not the only circle of dark cloud that disappeared from around me into the wide horizon of the sun. It was largely my own unwillingness to cause her unnecessary distress that kept it there so long. It is difficult now to recover the realizing sense of the consternation with which millions of adults saw the circle of the dark cloud of the Hebrew Tribal God lift and dissolve, never again to close upon the thought horizon of the world.

For Mary there is no more contemptible attitude than wishing your own spiritual old clothes onto other people; but it was probably the spiritual vitality that enabled her to abandon orthodoxy with intention that was responsible for her setting out to find — the only one of the family who did so — a new Middle where the inquiring soul could be at rest.

Mary at twenty-six was far too desperately displaced from the true center of her being not to feel obliged to go somewhere. For a long time it had been the fashion to speak of the women who led the feminist revolt as though they had been actuated by malice prepense against the existing order, but the truth is that hordes of them were animated by the bitter disillusion of being pushed out of the sacred quarter for which they were bred and brought up. Nobody had wanted children more than Mary did; few intellectuals of her generation have clung more obstinately to the idea of a home, a house, a garden, the familiar use of hospitality; few have sacrificed more to the fulfillment of the pattern of man and woman working together for a converging point on the Earth Horizon. And from all these, at twenty-six, though it was a much longer time before she would publicly admit it, Mary found herself displaced. Her husband could not be served by her capabilities, wished nothing so little as the concerted attack on the adventure of practical success, in the anticipation of which his wife had been brought up; required of her, out of all the notable range of achievement such as was the normal inheritance of Middlewestern women, only the maternal leniency which rejoiced in what pleased him and refrained from chiding his failures too much. There were special considerations which made Mary's situation more distressful than the average, but I am far from insisting that it was in any large aspect unusual. That was what the swift acceleration of material prosperity had wrought upon the daughters and granddaughters of pioneers; their occupations reduced to quiddities, their valiancy, to gestures merely. As for Mary there was the perpetual torment of a creative talent not yet accommodated to its proper medium... the harassment of the led horse, held too precious to be allowed to pull in harness, and not free to seek its proper pastures.

I can see now how a world of men and unaffected women, looking on, might have read into such situations the nervous quality of unjustified 'revolt'; the 'restlessness' which for two decades constituted the term of utmost reprobation which could be applied to respectable women. Although the old covenant of man and woman against the wilderness had been violated, the old loyalties still held. Even yet I am aware of skimping the evidence of what justified my own distressful search for a new center of personal direction. It was not until this record was actually begun that I realized how completely — and deliberately — outside the factuality of my life my family remained. At this distance, I doubt whether my mother realized at all how desperately driven was the one significant conversation I had with her, of which only the last phase is worth recording.

She said, 'Well, when I had difficulties I couldn't get over any other way, I prayed about it.'

'And did you get what you prayed for?'

'I got what it was God's will for me to have.'

'But did you get what you prayed for?'

'I got an answer.'

'But how, what kind?'

After much pointed insistence it developed that she got a sense of having touched something out beyond herself; she was 'reconciled.'

'But do you ever get what you pray for?'

It turned out that she couldn't put her finger on an explicit instance; things improved, the desperate need passed away, she found strength to bear what couldn't be remedied. And this, in short, was very much the sort of answer that was dragged out of orthodox Protestant Christianity whenever, as she often did in the next two or three years, Mary interrogated it. Prayer was an emotional petition which you went through with as though you believed it effectual even when you knew it wasn't. And the next person Mary asked was the Medicine-Man — 'Do you truly *get* what you pray for?' 'Surely, if you pray right.' But the answer to what was 'right' in the Paiute practice involved an immense amount of explanation. Prayer, to the Medicine-Man, had nothing to do with emotion; it was an act; an outgoing act of the inner self toward something, not a god, toward a responsive activity in the world about you, designated as The-Friend-of-the-Soul-of-Man; Wakonda, to use a term adopted by ethnologists — the effective principle of the created universe. This inner act was to be outwardly expressed in bodily acts, in words, in music, rhythm, color, whatever medium served the immediate purpose, or all of them. Prayer so understood and instigated acted with the sureness of a chemical combination. It was in the nature of Wakonda so worked upon not to be able to do otherwise than to act reciprocally.

It is impossible to convey the freshness of conviction with which the experience of prayer so initiated broke upon the intelligence. This was something you had long known must be so; it was the root of that conviction which Mary had entertained that there is always something to be done about everything. Man is not alone nor helpless in the universe; he has toward it and it toward him an affective relation. This, precisely, Mary was intelligent enough to realize, was probably what Jesus meant with his figure of the branch and the vine, the Son and the Father. The illuminating point, the thing that Protestant Christianity had utterly failed to teach her, was the practice of prayer as an act, a motion of the mind, a reality, which, though it might be set going by an emotion, had nothing to do with emotion as such. Once grasped and sincerely practiced, this new realization of prayer as experience clicked in with much that had gone on as unrelated instances; I-Mary moving with the augmented power of the Wakonda of personality; the God of the walnut tree as the Wakonda of the universe moving toward Mary of its own volition.

It was not all at once that these alterations in Mary's spiritual orientation took place. As experience, it had its origin in intellectual curiosity made personal by desperate need; in that singular actor's gift which Mary so seldom turned to any other purpose than that of initiating new experiences; putting on the character of an Indian woman; making, without in the least realizing that that was what she was doing, man's immemorial gesture of getting inside the universe by imitating it. It began as adventure and became illumination. It went on, by many minor incidents, for years, and gradually embraced all the religious gestures accessible. It will be necessary in the course of this narrative to refer to high points of attainment in the technique of such adventure. It is in my mind to leave a complete and particularized account of these, on some other occasion. It is enough to say that the existence of a practice of prayer as a studious motion of consciousness had already begun by the time I returned to Lone Pine to teach with my husband in the autumn of 1897. It is described here because it proved, though in the beginning I had no notion that this would be the case, the answer to the problem of creative activity.

Another circle of influences that went entirely out of my life, after my mother was no longer there to bring them to my mind, was the one of which Frances Willard had been the generating center. It had begun to dissolve with our removal from the Middle-western scene out of which it sprang, and by the time of her death had begun to melt into the emergent figure of George Babbitt, so that today, for Mary, the identification is complete, the veritable offspring of that horizon. Except, of course, one had to concede to Miss Willard the advantage of proportion. She took in, with the sweep of her ambition, the whole skyey arc, but Zenith City was the prototype of her materialized aspiration. It is as much as anybody achieves of a projected ideal, more than most people arrive at in a lifetime, the evidence at once of the prophetic scope of Miss Willard's genius and the organizing capacity with which she contrived to bring it to pass. It is the method of that genius which has become her monument. In her autobiography she admits Babbittian necessity to tell other people about herself, to feel others palpitating and responsive to her own event. 'To be widely known, to be widely helpful and beloved, was my ideal.... Every life has its master passion, and this — to be one on whom the multitude would lean and love and believe in — is mine.' This is the authentic accent of Rotary Clubs, of radio announcers, and conventions of small-town mayors. It is only recently that economists are beginning to realize, as a charge on the purchasing power of the community, this 'master passion' to be known, the more widely the better, on behalf of three-dollar shoes or porcelain bathtubs, the master passion of democracy, the ungratified passion for distinction which we traded off for the illusory advantage of social equality. What Frances Willard traded for it was the integrity of personal behavior for which Mary's generation sacrificed so much that was to Miss Willard indispensable; she rejected marriage, because to have attempted to follow marriage and her star would have involved precisely the disapprobation that Mary's generation braved. She loathed long hair and the swathing stiffness of voluminous starched skirts, but suffered them rather than make herself singular by tainting her opportunity with revolt against convention, because, at long last, she could not bear 'not to react upon the world about me to the last ounce of my power.' And what Mary knew by the time of Frances Willard's death was that what her own generation must bear was the renunciation of just that power to please (to be loved and leaned upon) which still sicklies with its sticky sweetness the constructive purpose of America.

Past any question, the orientation of significant personalities in their generation is determined for them by the time they are born. For the purpose of this book, I have to treat Mary as having at least the significance of a road mark, a pointer on the trail which generations after her were more or less to take. Otherwise, I could not get my consent, nor hers, to spend so much time upon her. By no process that can be recalled or reasoned out, Mary found the pointers on her own trail going in the direction of women who desired the liberation of women for its own sake; not for its symbolic values nor for any subsidiary propagandist advantage; women touched with the same profound solicitude for the spiritual communion of mankind that moved Frances Willard, but manifesting it by achieved freedoms of their own. They dressed and wore their hair as it pleased them; declined to admit marriage as a bar to public careers; refused on every side to admit the pertinence of personal behavior to public appeal. There were such women beginning to appear on Mary's horizon: Susan B. Anthony, whom once she had heard; Dr. Anna Howard Shaw; Charlotte Perkins Stetson; Jane Addams. It was in the direction of these women that Mary felt herself invisibly drawn. Without previous contact she counted herself in on their claims on the reasonable conclusions of mankind. Without preamble or collusion, she found herself adopting their characteristic renunciation of charm as a means of establishing a personal advantage, the charm which they freely exercised on behalf of an audience. They could charm an audience, these women — well, Mary could in her own measure do that also; but the mark that they set between self-aggrandizement through the quality of that charm was clearly and deliberately thought. Mother Jones, when she came along in her turn, was, in that particular, precisely of their stripe; she could beguile the judge and the jury, or a hall full of the more or less contentious friends of labor; gray-haired and of ample girth, she would diddle newspaper reporters out of their most hard-boiled convictions, or abase her jailers to the condition of adolescent embarrassment; and she would have clouted any one of them on the head for hinting that he could win such concessions of entertainment from her on behalf of his being a male.

It was at this point that Frances Willard, great woman as she was, lost continuity with the purpose and intent of the woman's revolt. What she envisaged, what she almost achieved, was the remaking of society from the Hearth as the Sacred Middle; what those others hazarded was a remaking of the pattern in which the Hearth itself should be reformed, should itself be made to revolve about a Middle whose true name was as yet undiscerned, but as the lodestone of their compass deeply felt.

There was no reason why I should have been surprised to find objection to my securing the assistant teacher's position under my husband at Lone Pine. Married women were at that time barred from holding such positions in the larger towns elsewhere in the State. Twelve or fifteen years were yet to elapse before I was to take part in the struggle in New York City to prevent the ranking of marriage as a misdemeanor of women teachers, calling for summary dismissal. Carroll, my husband's friend, took me aside, I recall, to impress upon me the extraordinary liberality of my husband's mind in allowing me to earn money, and in the process became exceedingly miffed at my rejection of the term 'allow' as pertinent to the case. Carroll, of course, didn't know about the debts. We were ten years paying them off, and lost in the process all the margin of release for our early married life. It is the one thing in my life, seeing that I had never been a party to them, of which I doubt the wisdom; especially as it never had the anticipated effect upon my husband of reorganizing his own attitude toward family finance. When I recall the total irresponsibility of California finance in general at that time, and the extreme probability that few people did concern themselves about the settlement of their accounts, I wonder. Nevertheless, the fact that we did pay them brought me in later years a measure of my own reliability to myself and to society, which remains the unassailable root of whatever social philosophy I have been uncompromisingly able to assert. One way and another, the thing I have liked least in my country has been the mushiness which I suspect arises out of a secretly unadmitted incapacity to pay, on the nail, for what we want.

By this time my husband was also County Superintendent of Schools, and that with our two salaries got us out of the worst of our obligations. Also Mary made progress, more than at the time she realized, in writing. She began where she had left off in Panama District and made up with the help of the children the necessary memorabilia in the form of verse, which caught as nearly as she could manage it the young way of seeing, the young rhythm of feeling, the local terms, the tropes and figures that the thing seen evoked in the young mind. I don't know how much better any other person could have done with the same material; no other in her time attempted it.[16]   And if no better purpose was served by it, it at least gained for the author, especially after it was welded to the Indian contribution, years of the indispensable process of rootage in the West.

At the end of that so profitable and unanticipated adventure, two very upsetting things occurred. Mary, who was a much longer time learning to balance her accounts between intellectual appetite and physical capacity, had to go to the hospital again; and Wallace, leaving his unfinished term as County Superintendent in his wife's hands, resigned his teaching permanently to take office as the Registrar of the Desert Land Office. It was an office no more remunerative, involving residence in a smaller town, with, from Mary's point of view, no single alleviating circumstance. Wallace had worked it up secretly, possibly to forestall objection, but quite certainly because his pleasures were all solitary, because of his notion of the, for him, acceptable way of life was utterly untouched by any consideration of its suitability, its possibility even, of proving acceptable to his wife. Sometimes he would say. 'Well, of course, if I had known you were not going to like it...' There were women of Mary's generation who never outgrew the paralyzing impuissance of this singular obliviousness to their claim on consideration; they went down under it as under a drug; Charlotte Perkins Gilman, I think, went round and round at last under the effect of a trauma too many times endured. Mary happily never lost the capacity to do something about it. On this occasion she went off to San Francisco to the hospital, and met William James.

How much she had read of him previously I do not now recall. The immediate object of his visit to the Coast was an important educational meet, and the title of his public lecture, 'Relaxation,' left his audience, even after they had heard it, almost wholly in the dark, unless they had first read a book of the hour, 'Power Through Repose,' [17] which probably no other philosopher of James's standing would have had the courage so publicly to laud. What he recommended to all intellectuals was the relaxation of the rather strained surface tensions which was the preferred intellectual mode of the time, in order that the whole personality might be flooded by the deep life that welled up from below the threshold of selfness, to make the augmented unity of I-Mary. It is impossible to convey, to a generation schooled in the complexities of modern psycho-analysis, the adventurousness of the undertaking to convey so much to an audience who unless they had read Meyer's 'Human Personality' and the first confused postulates of the 'Psychic Researches,' would be hearing for the first time terms such as subliminal and subconscious, audiences for whom vocabularies salvaged from the writings of the Christian Mystics would first have to be disinfected of the faintest odor of Roman Catholic sanctity which clung to them, before they could be accepted. For Mary, this first hearing of her intimate experience stated as normal and explicit, even recommended, carried her in a kind of daze of illumination in and about several Oakland blocks, to bring up at last at the hotel where, according to the newspapers, Professor James was to be found, and where, incredibly, he received her. Years after, when I tried to recount to people who had studied under James what passed between us at that interview, they were disposed to reject it. That is to say, they rejected his quick interest in what I tried to tell him about the Paiute technique of prayer, how, by making the precise motions of my mind which the Medicine-Man described to me, I got past that cloture of the Way which my Methodist friends described as 'getting an answer' without being at all sure what that answer might be. I have read practically everything that James has written, without finding anything to alter my conviction that he was actually as interested as he seemed to be, and that he did confirm my own experience that prayer is not merely an emotional reaction but a creative motion. Also, in spite of all contradiction, I am firm in my conviction that he validated my own experience of the swinging door, the door that opens out of consciousness with the same effect of a shudder of consciousness and an icy shiver as when an actual door behind you shudders on the latch and lets in a draught of coolness. When you are sitting with the elders of the tribe, when the sayings of the Ancient Men are passing, and suddenly at a word dropped, an incident related, whole areas of human evolution let blow upon you, a wind out of your own past. I told Professor James about that, and I asked him if it could be possible that ancestral experience could rise up *through* you, and be repossessed in that fashion. And though I will not swear to the words he used, I am firm in my contention that William James did say to me that this was possibly the way in which the significance of social evolution could be recovered. Not the facts of social history; not the events, but significance... the ancestral motions of consciousness on its way to wider horizons. If he did not say something of the kind, how was it that I went away from William James that summer dusk, with the lights coming out all about the Bay, through the deeply luminous blue of the Bay shot by the riffling trail of the ferries, assured for the first time in my life that the true Middle of my search was in myself. Afterward he wrote me two letters, mostly concerned with the names of books I was to read, one of which was the text of his lecture, 'Power Through Repose.' I always meant to send him a book I have never written, recounting the best of my Indian adventures, probably not written because there is no living philosopher whose horizon, like that of William James, is wide enough to receive it. What I got out of William James and the Medicine-Man was a continuing experience of wholeness, a power to expand the least premonitory shiver along the edge of primitive apprehension to the full diapason of spiritual sophistication, which I have never lost; a power the record of which, haltingly set down as it happened, makes the full significance of these pages.

VII

KEARSARGE stands out from the Sierra Wall like a tent, pyramidal-sided, and Independence lies open on the lowest slope, taking the eastern sun; a small town and unguarded. From Independence Creek a trail of farms reaches down, and above that a campody and the Indian school. A small town coming abruptly to an end in the strewing of tin cans and dusty windbreaks and unsightly houses; a town of not more than two or three hundred inhabitants at most, for all the seven years that we lived there scattered on two or three streets and bracing itself against desolation with the County Courthouse, two saloons, three stores, and the hotel. And yet, as I recall it, a friendly little town, a town with a feeling of goingness, of affairs, a town in which there was that mysterious something about to happen, on which the population hung, and which never did happen. Precisely the town in which Mary's married adventure was to come to an end, and in knowing at last that her husband could not be served, that he was to be accepted and extenuated; that he had no especial way of life, no bias of talent, no directive ambition. He had no plan either for himself or their common way of life. He had a dream of himself pleasantly and remuneratively employed, but between that dream and the present inadequately paid and not very rewarding situation there was a hiatus always about to be bridged by his 'getting into something.' This was an attitude prevailing among men of Inyo; one on which they constantly reassured one another. *Something* was due to happen soon. There was the promise of the land; its rich and alluring possibility; there was the residue of the romantic mining experience; also something must be allowed to the allure of the desertness. Men of my husband's type of mentality, once they had exposed themselves to it, spent their lives going around and around in it, always keyed to the expected, the releasing discovery. They felt themselves enchanted by its longer eye-reach, its rainbow horizons; but in fact it was the timeless space that held them. With the women it was not so; they felt, as they hung there suspended between hopes that refused to eventuate, life slipping away from them. For women have 'times'; the short recurrent rhythm of well-being, the not-to-be-evaded times of birth, the climaxes of their racial function, the effacing hand of Time across their charm, which points inescapably the periods within which experience is available. Herein I am persuaded is rooted their special gift of foresight; times anticipated to account for their primary contribution to society of organization, times unfulfilled to reckon for their restlessness.

Mary's husband was more than ordinarily lacking in the sense of the passing of time, as it turned out. He never seemed to suspect that it might be too late for things to happen. His wife's acute sense of the goingness of time struck him as surprising, but not necessarily to be taken into account in their married program. He expected to 'get into something good'; there were always things going about, mining projects, oil prospects. They came and went and to Mary exhibited no distinctions of better or worse. Every year or two one of the thin ghosts of mining booms would firm itself to outlines of reality. It would swell and gibber and get itself accepted for brief intervals, in which the head of the family felt it his duty to take advantage.

There was more than the kindness of the common illusion of haunting fortune in those little towns of Inyo, a kindness that forbore and extenuated and sustained the gratulatory gesture, a kindness of a kind not possible in communities of closer growth. There were all the distinctions and none that were absolute. When I think of the women who were my nearest neighbors, Mrs. Webb and Mrs. Gunn, I realize that they were so by reason of qualities that would keep us neighboring still except that we have drifted so far out of touch; that they had standards, behaviors, things done and not done. Now and again I brush wings with old neighbors, still realized; and old distinctions still sharp. I recall that in all the little towns there were women who came into the category of neighbors through renunciations; women who had married out of houses of ill fame, out of the streets of offense, as happens in mining communities, and held on to the skirts of respectability and were made sure of redemption, or were not sure, but were not rejected. I remember women whose children went to school to me, who came into that category, and the extenuations that were conceded them. We were brushed on every side by these, and by the women who came and went. I recall the jest of one of those, the jest that brought a grin to the faces of the men who had not consorted with them, and a sheepish look to those who had. I remember the men standing in line once at a mining settlement where we went occasionally to take off for a favorite excursion into the hills. There was nothing that went on there not seen or noted. All so much in the air and genre of the place; all so matter-of-factly.

We missed at Independence the warm adobe walls of Lone Pine, the guitars strumming, the color of Mexican life. But there was a Chinese plaza there, a resort of the Chinese cooks and house boys of the surrounding mines, where, as the Chinese year came round each season, there would be Geisha girls dancing and juggling. I recall how Mary got herself misappreciated there once, through Sing Lee, her wash boy, who every year presented her with a box of Chinese candy and a lily bulb and a silk handkerchief, so that Mary felt herself obliged to him and returned the favor with a layer cake. I recall the pleased concern with which Sing Lee went off with the back of his neck wreathed in smiles of appreciation, and the next day going down to the plaza to see the noble table set out to the ancestors with my cake on top, plentifully bedecked with punk-sticks and firecrackers and amazement. And a committee of ladies calling that afternoon, all in their best bedizenment, to ask what I had meant by giving a cake to the Chinaman. And the embarrassment of making it plain what I had meant exactly. They used to call on me occasionally to ask what I meant by taking part in Indian dances; there was a suspicion that my interest in these things was touched by failure to apprehend the proper social distinctions. And at the same time there was no lack of appreciation for the things I did *in propria persona*. There was the time I got myself read out of the Methodist Church. I hadn't brought a letter from Bishop, where I was still nominally a member, and I had got myself in difficulties by subscribing to a Sunday School, in which

I taught a Bible class of adults, and taught them the Higher Criticism, which came to the ears of the presiding minister and the elder, of which they made the ritualistic most of reading me out of the office. I shouldn't have let them do it if I had realized how much they would have made of it, and how seriously the community would take it. The worst of it was that I had just organized a community theater, which gave to the church a footing in opposition to what mightn't otherwise have been noted. I had begun community theater work at Lone Pine and had carried it on in Independence with Shakespearian plays and a community swing that carried it on sweepingly. I go back to those Shakespearian plays with tenderness and passion; there was no question that, when it came to the matter of entertainment, I carried the community with me. When we advertised a play, the mining community arranged to be present. We held them in the hall that had once been the scene of the county fair; with the seats from the Methodist Church as reserves; with boards laid on soap boxes, and the wool sacks piled at the back for galleries, where the Indians and natives sat. There was a difficulty at first about the between-acts drinks, until John Gunn undertook to manage that, standing up with his back to the door when the last had been served, so that I always waited for him before giving the signal for the curtain to go up; and there was always time for a comment or two on the comedy parts, Shylock and Falstaff, which were played by Wallace. Several years later, after Tonopah and Bullfrog became popular camps, one Constance Crawley, who had come from England playing Everywoman, tried a Shakespeare experiment at Tonopah on the night after the Gans-Nelson affair, with both the champions sitting in boxes, that failed of the *réclame* of our productions at Independence, failed and dwindled and shrank to the dimensions of musty professionalism, lacking the lusty amateur zest of the community enterprise. It was a zest that the two Austins knew how to give to whatever they undertook, although they missed it occasionally for themselves. There was Mary's effort to interest Wallace in botany, always a consuming interest for her, which he was never able to carry to more than a collector's accent, the mere

naming and classifying of kinds and orders, avoiding her concern
with adaptations and local variations. He liked having her ask
him for names of species she named in her writings, such as she
could very well have named for herself, but he escaped her inquiries as to the strange adjustments of desertness and drought
and *redivivamentes*. There was always a more or less secret antagonism in their excursions to the wild, which made up the bulk of
their entertainment, which grew out of his native unwillingness
toward coöperative activity, a deeply cherished instinct for selfness.
He was not only happier to plan a trail for himself, but to break it
at his own instigation, even at the cost of mutual distress and
aggravation. He never learned to take into account his wife's
physical disabilities as a source of necessity in planning their routes
and resting-places; and never learned to do without her; so that
the memory of the places we went together is troubled always with
the distress of too much pain and too little alikeness of interest.
We did better when we read together, after we had learned to
correct the discrepancies of reading time which were owed to my
husband's slowness of coördination. He saw badly and read
slowly, so that I suffered the interruption of my own coördination,
until I discovered that there were things I could read at the same
time that bridged the gap for me, things like the Reports of the
Bureau of Ethnology, or the Dictionary, things that went on for
me while he was occupied with the latest magazine or popular
novel; he reading aloud, and I silently, and keeping pace with him.
So evening after evening; and evenings when people came in and
talked aimlessly, he would get away with the evening paper, and
I would entertain them endlessly.

There were always people with whom Mary could talk. The
Valley narrowed here at Independence, so that the sheepherders
came down nearly to the town and reported on the flocks and the
trail. Little Pete came often; he was interested in Mary's book
and had acquired an anxiety of his own, which was the source of
his death finally. Pete was a Frenchman and of an important
sheep-keeping family who looked to him to make money and the
means for a creditable return; so that his being involved with

a woman there in California had come as a blow to him and them. She was part Indian, the daughter of another herder and a woman of Olancha, whose mother was about to give her to a dissolute herder from whom the girl revolted, seeking refuge with little Pete; perilous refuge and complete. There was a child, whom Pete loved; and a claim from the family at home, and drunken sorrow, and a pistol shot in the dark. There were other concerns; the withdrawal of forest lands, grazing claims; struggles between the sheepmen and the cowmen. In all of these for Mary there was a part. After 'The Flock' was published, Roosevelt sent a forestry expert to interview her. There was a part for her in the Indian life. She had begun the study of Indian verse, strange and meaningful; of Indian wisdom, of Indian art. The Paiutes were basket-makers; the finest of their sort. What Mary drew from them was their naked craft, the subtle sympathies of twig and root and bark; she consorted with them; she laid herself open to the influences of the wild, the thing done, accomplished. She entered into their lives, the life of the campody, the strange secret life of the tribe, the struggle of Whiteness with Darkness, the struggle of the individual soul with the Friend-of-the-Soul-of-Man. She learned what it meant; how to prevail; how to measure her strength against it. Learning that, she learned to write.

There is a thing called the Friend-of-the-Soul-of-Man, a reality, an influence which you can call up around you. You wrap yourself in it. You are effective through it. You make use of it through rhythm; the beating of the medicine drum; the pound of feet in the medicine dance. You give way to it through rhythmic utterance. You find it expressing itself in rhythmic movement, the running of quail, the creaking of the twenty-mule team, the sweep of motion in a life-history, in a dance, a chant. You perceived that these patterns made writing; you struggled for them; won, caught, and ensnared them.

What Mary continued to feel the need of was the reality of writing experience; getting it onto paper, into print, the reality of the job. There had come into existence in Los Angeles a magazine called 'The Land of Sunshine,' edited by Charles Lummis, drawing to itself writers, names, effects, orientations. Mary had come in touch with it a year or so earlier in one of her too frequent health excursions. She had made a contact with a former wife of the editor, Dorothea Moore, a woman who drew her with strange hooks of steel, who bound her to Lummis by interests that repelled her equally. She knew that there was another wife; that Dorothea had given way to her; that she had yielded place without giving preference and without losing a hold on his life; and the bond constrained her. What Mary knew was that, as there grew upon her the need for writers' society, the other woman would enter into her life, would play a part in it, would become another to the bond. What she would think of Lummis she did not know, but of Mrs. Lummis she knew that she must have been an exceptional woman to have entered into the contract with Dorothea, a woman Mary would need to know. So when it came to Mary that there was a need for her to go to Los Angeles and make herself part of the writing group around Charles Lummis, she counted on knowing Eve and making a place beside her. This was in the late summer of 1899. There was no reason to expect anything to happen in Inyo of a revealing character. Her husband's income from the land office was too slender to hold out promise; the child's health was too uncertain; her own health too frail. She meant to go, to succeed somehow in laying hold of a means of subsistence which would warrant her husband in joining her; in making good a maintenance in a more promising *milieu*. She found herself a place in the neighborhood of the Lummises, on Forty-Second Street to be exact, and laid her plans deeply and well.

Besides the Lummises, she had touch with the Pierces at the normal school, cousins of Dr. Woodin. Dr. Pierce was the head of the normal school, and his wife one of his assistants, kindly people and pleasant to know; people in whom one might rest one's consciousness of being a teacher. They knew one as a contributor to educational journals on an advanced basis. It was not long before Mary made a connection. She had been raking over the model school and had found a teacher snared on one of the 'westerns' — the coyote, snared by ignorance, by a total lack of knowledge of coyotes or their kind; embarrassed, strained, reaching out in vain to the model for help; said Mary, 'If you will let me take the class, I know something of coyotes.' She took it as she had handled her own classes at Lone Pine... going from coyotes to carrion crows and other features of the trail. She noted the model teacher coming and going, bringing in extras, keeping the class moving... getting her address at last. The next day a letter proposing that she keep the work up to her standard, a course laid out and sustained; the thing that California teaching lacked, knowledge of its realities and a concise way of putting them. She taught at the normal school for the rest of the year. There was still in the neighborhood where Mary had settled a way of getting to know these things more explicitly; the spring coming on, the way of wild bloom and small furry things and bird and bush.

But with the literary guild she did not get on so readily. Mr. Lummis did not take to her, nor she to him. She had no genius, he said; talent and industry and a certain kind of knowledge, but little gift. There was a group of local writers circulating about Lummis, who had more or less made a place for themselves in the Eastern magazines: Gwendolyn Overton; Margaret Collier Graham; Sharlott Hall, whom he extolled and introduced. There were artists and poets — Dixon, Keith, and the new man, Edwin Markham, and Dr. Jordan — whom he flaunted. There was the man Mary wanted most to meet, Dr. Frederick Webb Hodge, the Indian specialist, who told her the thing she wanted most to know, the way of collecting and recording Indian affairs, the thing she wouldn't have thought of questioning. 'Let be,' he said, 'the strange and unusual; fix on the usual, the thing that is always done, the way of the tribe; the way of the average; the way and the why of it.' Mary was young enough to accept what she was told, and Dr. Hodge was authority enough to be accepted as telling. The way and the why; it remained with her and colored the whole of her interest in tribal affairs. The thing that is always done. It was the beginning of an influence that lasted out Mary's life, a way

of reference, a contingent. Of Dr. Jordan, Mary accepted less, although it was evident that Lummis accepted more. Too much.
It was a way Lummis had to defer too much, to stress the weight
of authority. Mary shrank from him a little; thought him romantic; felt that he rested too much on the lesser achievement; on
working too many hours a day; on sleeping too little; on drinking
too much; on his wife's translations of Spanish manuscripts. Of
Eve, Mary's opinion grew; of her kindness, her poise, her suffi-
ciency; and of Dorothea too. Of the absurd and embroidered tale
of Charles and the two women, she heard too much to be willing to
let it stand. Dorothea had met him at Cambridge, where she
had been studying medicine. Young and promising, he had
got himself embroiled with a young woman with whom he swore
he was guiltless, and about to be more deeply entangled, except
that Dorothea came to his rescue and married him. This brought
her family into the matter, and he was provided with a job of news-
papering which carried him to the West. Here a physical disability
sent him into New Mexico, where he met Eve and involved himself with her. Dorothea, seeing how matters stood, had waived her
claim and let him go to the younger woman, without loss of dignity. There was no more to it than that, although common report
made fantasy of the wife's renunciation. It was but the beginning
of dignity and divorce, such as was new in American practice, a
dignity that Charles himself renounced a few years later when he
admitted his parenthood of the child by the woman he had renounced to marry Dorothea. There was always the possibility of
such a *contretemps* between Charles and myself; the feeling on his
part for a possible hardness on mine as between the two women
whom I admired; a feeling of his having accepted too much from
both of them for harmony. But there was another case on hand at
the time which called for high partisanship; the case of Charlotte
Perkins Stetson. The Stetsons' had been an unhappy marriage,
unhappy in every particular; the marriage of an artist to the woman least calculated to bear it; made to seem more unwise by the
existence of a friend to both the contracting parties, Grace Ellery
Channing, willing to assume the broken bond; who did assume it

finally, and with it part of the responsibility of the child. I don't know what else either of them could have done about the little girl. Charlotte had no way of making a living except by lecturing, to which she could not drag the girl about; and the father had no way of caring for the child in the interim except by trusting it to his newly married wife, still the friend of the child's mother. Charlotte had returned to Southern California after her lecture trip, only to find that she had affronted public opinion hopelessly by this 'unnatural motherhood,' to the rescue of which Charles Lummis had sprung valiantly. I had been invited to meet her, and been struck by her beauty, the fine lines of her head and the clear look of her eyes, the carriage of her shoulders so erect and precise. I was for her, and for the freedom from convention that left her the right to care for her child in what seemed the best way to her. I recalled what Madam Severance had said — Madam Severance was the leading figure in Los Angeles society; she was of the Severances with whom my husband's family was identified; the mother of women's clubs, who had started the first club in the United States the year that I was born; at whose house I had met Kate Douglas Wiggin; and when I had asked her what she thought about Charlotte Perkins Stetson, she had replied by telling me that Mrs. Perkins, Charlotte's mother, had started the fashion of using English ivy as an indoor decoration in American houses, which she somehow charged up against Charlotte. I never lost the association, but continued to see Charlotte with a decoration of ivy leaves, a flat wreath of them about her head and over her breast. And I always charged up against Pasadena the reproach of unnatural motherhood which we were met that day to clear her from. It was always more or less like that at the Lummises'; people brought to be met; to be challenged or to challenge; to be identified and remembered. Another day, Grace Ellery Channing came, whom I did not see again until years later in Rome with her husband Stetson, of whom I was to hear so much from Charlotte and so unfriendlily.

Eve was expecting a child that spring. There were two already, Turbese and Amado. Turbese was her father's own child, with

his insistence on herself. Amado was one of those children of
whom women say, 'he is not long for this world,' with the knowledge of the grown-up reaction that wrings the heart. He and my
little Ruth were fond of each other; they were touched with tenderness each for each, with extenuations.

Mary came and went, writing, writing. Toward spring she
made the 'Atlantic Monthly'; she sold things to the 'Youth's
Companion' and 'St. Nicholas.' She had an offer from one of the
Northern normal schools. The thing she had counted on had occurred; she had an opportunity to create for herself a regular income under circumstances that afforded a more reasonable living,
an opportunity for her husband to 'get into something.' She wrote
to her husband would he come, would he take the chance with her.
She had to know; the normal school opportunity wouldn't stay
open indefinitely. But strangely he did not see it that way; he had
not been all this time seeing it that way. He was astounded; he
withdrew. The year that his wife had been away meant nothing;
he had not moved toward her; he had given himself the more
completely to Inyo; he could not take himself away. Mary went to
him. When he saw her distress, he was concerned for it. He said
let her go again, let her try another year, and he would try. But
Mary could not do that; the one year that was gone had taken too
much out of her; she knew that if she went again, it would be
permanently; if he came now... and in the end she stayed.

There was a reason that had come into her life; a strange com-
pelling reason that hung like a weight about her knees. She knew
now what ailed her child. Carmen, Frank's wife, had left a mes-
sage for her before she went away. Too late; too late; a tainted
inheritance — recessive traits on both sides of the house. Mary
had it out with her husband, with reluctance. That winter at
Bishop, Father Austin having died, her husband's mother and
sister had come to stay with her; had witnessed her distress and
anxiety lest she had been to blame, and withheld their testimony.
His brothers had known; he himself, and had refrained. 'We never
talk of those things,' he said. It was the way of Christian families.
Mary never got over it; never was able to accept the family con-

sideration, the unwilling admission. It was not long after that she
put Ruth in a private institution at Santa Clara where the difference between herself and other children, which was beginning to
trouble her, would not be felt, where it would not be known. Here
the inability of other people to bear her cross would not be taxed;
where one could say if questioned, 'We have lost her'; where her
brothers would not be called upon to make unwelcome admissions;
where the pain could be borne alone, as it was for another twenty
years. It is a relief to speak of it now, of the cruelty, the weight,
the oppression of its reality, the loss of tenderness, of consideration,
the needless blight and pain.

VIII

THE first thing that Mary did after settling back into Inyo was to build a house there, the brown house under the willow tree by the creek that came down from Kearsarge. There was a reason for it besides the need of a house to live and write in. People were beginning to make their way into Inyo; people from the Sierra Club, mountain-climbers and explorers, botanists, hunting and fishing people; collectors of Indian baskets; people who knew about Mary. The establishing of the Forest Reserve brought writing people; Charles Howard Shinn; Stewart Edward White. Mary went back to the normal school to give a lecture and met Jane Addams there, out of whose attention she has never been so unhappy as to fall. She met Mrs. Otis at the Lummises', and Harrison Gray Otis at his wife's house — the Otises were leading the Intellectual Life in Los Angeles; she met there Harris Newmark who had introduced finger bowls into Los Angeles in 1868. She met the Coronals at the Lummises'; they sang Spanish *canciones* with Charles; Ida Strobridge, who had settled into the neighborhood. She met George Wharton James, of whom Charles did not think very well, suspected him of faking his Indian material.

Mary went back to Inyo and finished writing 'The Land of Little Rain.' She had been trying to hit upon the key for it for a year or more, and found it at last in the rhythm of the twenty-mule teams that creaked in and out of the borax works, the rhythm of the lonely lives blown across the trails. She had great pleasure in writing it. She sold it to the 'Atlantic Monthly,' and began 'The Basket-Maker.' Already she had begun 'The Flock,' shaping it to the movement of herders and their sheep, going back to Bakersfield and the Tejon for renewal, to the shearing at Agua Caliente and the games of handball at Noriegas. Her brother Jim had married there, a good wife and a lovely woman; she brought him back to a reasonable frame of mind and reality. There she met Ernest Seton, who was lecturing. They were taken forth to see the town and succeeded in seeing each other, exchanging way-farers' news of the trail. Part of Mary's excursion to Bakersfield had been to pick up again at Tejon the thread of the story of 'Isidro,' which she recalled from General Beale's reminiscences. She went the following summer to old Monterey to connect it with San Carlos. Already she had been drawn by Eve Lummis to the house of the Hittells — Theodor Hittell, the historian of California, and Kitty, his daughter, and Carlos and Frank, his sons. It was a house of distinction, the center of an intimate circle of writers and painters of San Francisco: Ina Coolbrith; Charles Warren Stoddard; John Muir; William Keith; Carlos Troyer; Edwin Markham. Mary was drawn to it, became a friend of the family — the old historian whose reminiscences trailed back to the eighteen-fifties; Kitty, whose interest took in the whole history of the Golden Gate; its intimacies; its undertakings.

Mary went straightway from San Francisco to Monterey, pick-ing up pleasant companions on the way, with whom the trip was made to San Carlos on foot; wandering about there; touching the old orchards, the Mission buildings, the strange wild beach at Carmel, the matted plots of cedar, the dunes all white and silvery, the glittering chaparral.

I have to go back now to Coppas, where I met George Sterling and Laffler, James Hopper, Xavier Martinez, and the two New-berrys. Sterling had written me and called. One dined so very well at Coppas: such platefuls of fresh shrimps; such sand dabs and crisp salads; such almond tartlets and dago red. Then there were the intriguing decorations; I recall the black cats and the large gentleman with the motto, 'Paste makes waist.' I made an en-gagement to go with George the next day to fill the Stevenson galleon with violets, and after that to take tea and kumquats in the Chinese restaurant, and to sit for a while in the room that had formerly been Stevenson's in the Clay Street hotel. I was stopping there and Eve Lummis was at Hittell's. Eve's little son Amado had died in the interim, and we went there to talk. Sterling was now at Carmel. He had surrendered his first choice of the peninsula near Harry Leon Wilson's house, as being too far from the town, and had built on a hilltop closer in. The center of his house was a large oblong room, with a large fireplace, a wide porch, and back of the house a ring of trees surrounded by skulls, and having in the midst a fireplace in the form of an altar. Jimmy Hopper owned the place after Sterling was finished with it. My house was the next to go up. I was still at work on 'Isidro,' and I spent a great deal of time on the lot of the Mission San Carlos Borromeo. George walked over with me evening after evening, reconstructing the scene.

There was no town at Carmel then; nothing but a farm or two, one or two graceless buildings, and the wild beach and the sunny dunes. In the meantime, 'The Land of Little Rain' was published and had a great success. Mary was at the Hittells' for that, and got to know the elect: Miss Coolbrith, Charles Warren Stoddard, who was living then at Monterey, John Muir, William Keith, and Markham. Of all these I recall John Muir the most distinctly, a tall lean man with the habit of talking much, the habit of soliloquizing. He told stories of his life in the wild, and of angels; angels that saved him; that lifted and carried him; that showed him where to put his feet; he believed them. I told him one of mine; except that I didn't see mine. I had been lifted and carried; I had been carried out of the way of danger; and he believed me. I remember them still. Sterling didn't believe in angels, but he believed in aliveness; sensitivities of stick and stone, of communications of animals, and I believed both of them.

George and I were very much alone in that first year. It was the simplest occupations that gave us the most pleasure and yielded the richest harvest of impressions, observations and feeling responses. Sterling's greatest pleasures were those that whetted his incessant appetite for sensations — the sting of the surf against his body, the pull of the undertow off Carmel beaches, gathering sea food among the 'undulant apple-green hollows' of the Mission Cove. He also delighted to go striding, axe on shoulder, over Monterey hills looking for pitch pine or bee trees or whatever arduous and practical simplicities restored him to the human touch from which it was his weakness to fall away, or perhaps never quite to attain in any other relation. Of all our walks, he loved best the one to Point Lobos; no poet's stroll, but a stout climb, dramatic, danger-tipped, in the face of bursting spray heads torn up from primordial deeps of sea gardens, resolving into whorls and whorls of lambent color. Interrupting or terminating such excursions there would be tea beside driftwood fires, or mussel roasts by moonlight, or the lot of us would pound abalone for chowder around the open-air grill at Sterling's cabin, and talk, ambrosial, unquotable talk.

It was not only Sterling and I and Jack London who initiated the group at Carmel; Laffler and Jimmy Hopper spent much time there, and Harry Leon Wilson and Charles Warren Stoddard and Ambrose Bierce. From the beginning I had heard much about George and Bierce. Bierce had directed his reading. If, as the poet admitted, Bierce also formed his taste, it was a taste that never faltered to either side of a narrowly classic line. Never having met Bierce but once, and that in Sterling's house, I had formed an opinion of him as a man secretly embittered by a failure to achieve direct creative power, a man of immense provocative capacity, always secretly, perhaps even to himself, seeking to make good in some other's gift that he himself had missed; always able to forgive any shortcoming of his protégés more easily than a failure to turn out according to his prescription. Sterling seemed to feel always a sense of guilt in falling short of anything that Bierce expected of him. On the one occasion on which Bierce visited him at Carmel, Sterling shied a little at introducing me on the ground that Bierce might not like my type. So I went quietly along the evening trail between town and Sterling's house only to discover that what Sterling dreaded was that I would uncover to Bierce the extent to which Sterling was implicated with Jack London. Even then I thought Bierce something of a *poseur*, tending to overweight a slender inspiration with apocalyptic gestures. I am sure that he left as many aspirants sticking in the bog of unrealized aspirations as he drew out on firm ground. But Sterling, who carried loyalty to excess, never faced precisely the values of his association with

Bierce. In the end they drifted into a slightly veiled antagonism over George's acceptance of Jack London's version of Socialism.

It was Sterling's humanitarianism which led him in that direction, for he was not really informed on the subject. He was a little touched, too, or perhaps it was only his admiration for Jack that made it seem so, by a feeling of deference for Jack. Only a day or two before, George had wanted to borrow money from me to lend to one of his friends. 'But, George,' I protested, 'that man can never find anything bad enough to say of me; it would be poison to him to take my money.' 'That's why,' he explained ingenuously, 'if you lend it to me and I lend it to him, he'll never know.' George expected generosities like that of his friends, and achieved them too. Jack and I had to shake down a bit before we could get on together. There was the difference of type for one thing, and the constantly dissolving and re-forming ring of his admirers, inclined to resent my being unimpressed by Jack's recent discovery of Darwinian Evolution. We were not, at Carmel, inclined to the intellectual outlook, except that there was a general disposition to take Jack seriously in respect to the Social Revolution. But in time, chiefly by way of Jack's new wife, Charmian, we arrived at Platonic exchanges. They were to me, those two, Jack and George, the first professional men I had known, a source of endless intellectual curiosity. They were, for instance, the first men I had known who could get drunk joyously in the presence of women whom they respected. For in the outlying desert regions where I had lived, this was not done. So I gave myself to discovering what the others got out of it. George was always ridden by restless impotencies of energy which only by sharp exaggeration of sensation would find their natural outlet in creative expression. He could not give himself either to composition or to intellectual exposition of an idea, or even sit comfortably and lounge, until by one of three ways his genius had eased itself into its appropriate path. That was before the terminology now on everybody's tongue had got into the current speech; but we approached it well enough as the handicap of genius, along with another idea that more or less possessed everybody in the group. Within the next two or three years, especially after the fire made San Francisco uninhabitable to professional workers, we settled into a habit of morning work which it was anathema to interrupt. But by early afternoon, one and another of the painter and writer folk could be seen sauntering by piny trails which had not then suffered the metamorphosis of asphalt, concrete, and carbon monoxide, which go in the world of realtors by the name of improvements, to sun themselves along one partially cleared passage to the sea, and to make delightful impromptu disposals of the rest of the day.

George and Jack were not the only ones who established the literary tradition of Carmel. The house that Robert Louis Stevenson had lived in at Monterey, the walks he took, had not yet been improved out of existence. There was a figure of tossed-back hair and long fingers forever busy with a cigarette, Charles Warren Stoddard, bridging the Bret Harte period to ours, and Charles Rollo Peters, the 'other one' of Whistler painters of nocturnes, had his studio on the hill overlooking the scimitar sweep of the Monterey Bay. Harry Leon Wilson made his home first at Carmel, later five or six miles down the coast, and after the fire came Michael Williams, incomparable talker, Irish and fey, and destined, though none of us suspected it then, to become the editor of the most intellectual Catholic journal in America. Professor-folk came from the two universities, contributing a pleasant note of scholarship, though Vernon Kellogg was the only one who was ever completely accepted in the Sterling circle. After the fire came Ray Stannard Baker, Jesse Lynch Williams, the two Irwins and Lincoln Steffens. Henry Laffler came frequently, and Nora May French.

Mary did not stay there the whole of the first summer. She sold the completed serial of 'Isidro' to the 'Atlantic Monthly,' and that fall began to work on an Indian play, a collaborator for which had been foisted on her by her friends, but who turned out to have too little talent and not enough taste for the work in hand. Much that got into the press about Carmel had no more fidelity to the fact than an item reported in a recent visitors' book to the effect that my house at Carmel had a cow's tail for a bell-pull. The truth is that my bell-pull was a strand of ancient Spanish hair rope, at the other end of which had hung a bell that the rope had once supported around the neck of the bell camel that had come with the herd imported by Jefferson Davis for domestication in the American Desert. The bell was hand-made, of bronze, and bore an inscription in Arabic to keep off the evil eye. It had been given to me by the majordomo of the man who had carried the news of the discovery of gold to Washington in 1849. This reduction of an authentic article of use and beauty to an absurdity is symbolic of the major misapprehension of America in general to the true inwardness of the artist life. There were a good many 'cows' tails' hung upon the names that made of Carmel-by-the-Sea an unforgettable experience.

The next spring I was under obligation to go up to San Francisco and see my publisher's agent about the book publication of 'Isidro.' I was to meet him at the Palace Hotel, where I arrived in due time, only to find myself oppressed with an impending sense of disaster. I called up my brother George, who was an interne at the City and County Hospital, and told him that I would have to leave the hotel, which threatened to fall upon me. I called up Kitty Hittell and told her and half a dozen others. My brother said I was suffering from the bad air in the hotel; Kitty thought that I had overworked, but she took me in for the night. I woke in the morning to the obsession of the falling roof, the crash of furniture, of falling chimneys, the pitching of the tall old bureaus, the noise and confusion of the Earthquake.

I stayed at the Hittells' for a week helping out. And I found that what had happened to George Sterling in the meantime was that he was caught up again in one of those entanglements to which he was subject. We all of us did know that George required the stimulus of sex to have a releasing effect on him. We knew, and lived in a kind of terror of what it might bring on Carrie, his wife, for whom we all had the tenderest affection, and combined to shield. Jack London thought — and Jack had material enough, God wot, on which to base a conclusion — that the assault that men of genius yielded to, or withstood according to their capacity, was the biological necessity of women to mate up, ascendingly, preferring, he thought, the tenth share in a man of distinction to the whole of an average man. Women flung themselves at Jack, lay in wait for him. Knowing primitive women as I did, I thought there might be something in this; but also I found an element less excusing in the assiduity of women to come into what they themselves call inspirational relations with men of creative capacity. I thought this disposition of women due in part to psychic indolence, perhaps the fruit of their long parasitism and their failure to produce creative gifts of their own, which they tried to compensate for by the illusion of being an inspiration. I say illusion, because I couldn't help seeing that what was at work was chiefly the accelerated vibration of an affair, raising the poet's plane until he volplaned off into creative achievement.

Striding through the woods at a long-legged gait that few could follow, as one saw him often with Jimmy Hopper, Sterling's long figure always a little in advance, had the same effect on him that Jack, who was, when I came to know him, sagging a little with the surfeit of success, obtained through idleness, making him prefer the lounging pitch-wood fire or the blazing hearth. And so we talked along with another idea of which it now seems appropriate to speak, of the liability of men of genius to find their subjective activities on their way to fruition so largely at the mercy of the effect on them of women. I never needed a love affair to release the sub-conscious in me, nor did Nora May French, who was the only other woman of our circle whose gifts approached Sterling's or London's.

The Sterlings were an old Sag Harbor family. George had played pirate about the Harbor, robbed orchards, hunted Captain Kidd's treasure. At the age of seventeen he had been converted, along with his father, to the Roman Catholic faith. As a result he was transferred to Saint Mary's College, Maryland, where he had an idea of putting his already pronounced literary taste to the use of the priesthood, for which it proved he had no vocation. Priest he was to beauty, and altogether logical to his mystical, rum-drinking, humanitarian, Catholic one-hundred per cent American line. Nothing else so explains a poet of Sterling's austere exoticism. The story of his youth is as meagre as Hawthorne's or Whittier's. While still a youth he went adventuring to California, but no further than a desk in his uncle's office. In his twenties he married Caroline Rand, a stenographer in the office where he clerked. The high points in his own rating were his meeting with Bierce and his friendship with Bierce. He was caught up in London's feeling for Socialism and in London's sense of the importance of the Nordic in the scheme of things. But his true devotion was to beauty. If he took his sociology from Jack, it was not without recompense. At the time, one found him reading manuscript and proof for London with a meticulous interest that never flagged; his diction was irreproachable, and his feeling for the fall of a sentence and the turn of a figure peculiarly sensitive. The two of them used to talk over their literary projects with even exchange. If Jack developed themes of George's originating — for Jack had that pliability of genius which made him able to work freely in anybody's material — he stinted neither credit nor kudos. I have always suspected that Jack's buying of plots for short stories from any writer with more plots than places to bestow them was chiefly a generous camouflage for help that could not be asked or given otherwise.

BOOK FIVE
THE LAND OF JOURNEY'S ENDING

BOOK FIVE

THE LAND OF JOURNEY'S ENDING

I

About this time there began to be an interregnum in Mary's life. She had finished 'The Flock,' but had made no sale of it. She had completed 'Lost Borders,' and made a fair sale to Harpers. She had begun a novel called 'Santa Lucia,' but was not getting on well with it. Strange things had happened in Inyo. In July, 1903, investigation was begun for the reclamation of arid lands there under the National Reclamation Bureau. All reports and estimates of costs demonstrated that the Owens Valley project promised greater results than any other for the cost. Individual owners made transfers of rights and privileges. And all this time the supervising officer of the Owens Valley project and Mullholland, chief engineer, had been working to secure a new water supply for Los Angeles. Suddenly it burst upon the people of Inyo that they were trying to secure the waters of Inyo. Everything had been done. The Reclamation Service had been won over. The field papers had changed hands. Transfers had been made. Sales had been effected. A Los Angeles man, Eaton, had been in the Valley all this time spying and buying; he and his fellows had represented themselves as representing the Government, when they had in fact been representing the city. There were lies and misrepresentations. There was nothing any of us could do about it, except my husband, who made a protest to the Reclamation Bureau. But the city stood solid behind Eaton as one man. Nobody raised a protest except Sam Clover. Clover was a newspaper man and an honest one; he was planning a new journal on his own initiative, and he was made to pay for the protest he made. No citizen protested, no clergyman, no State official. Prominent citizens from Los Angeles came up into the Valley and added their voice to the general consternation. Mary did what she could. And that was too little. The year before she had built a house — the brown house under the willow tree. She walked in the fields and considered what could be done. She called upon the Voice, and the Voice answered her — Nothing. She was told to go away. And suddenly there was an answer; a terrifying answer, pushed off, deferred, delayed; an answer impossible to be repeated; an answer still impending; which I might not live to see confirmed, but hangs suspended over the Southern country.

Mary went away; her husband had to go; he was now out of a job. Mary went back to Carmel. She was stricken; she was completely shaken out of her place. She knew that the land of Inyo would be desolated, and the cruelty and deception smote her beyond belief. There was nothing more for her in Southern California. She began to be ill; she was taken with a pain of which the doctors prophesied dubious things. They gave her nine months and the risk of an operation. She was at work on a novel; but when the framework of the novel was done, and there were still some months left, she began to cast about for what she would do. She had put her daughter in a private institution, being too ill herself to take any care of her. She sold her house in Inyo; she meant not to go there again. She decided to go to Italy. Friends of hers were going; Charlotte and Vernon Kellogg were going to be married there. Mary had wanted to see Rome; she thought it a place to die in; she counted her money and decided that she had enough to die on; she understood that there were places in Italy where one in great pain could die quietly. She did not wish to die with the Sterlings. What she was afraid of was the inevitable spring of recurrent beguilement, the spirit's impregnated flight carrying with it, as the queen bee trails the entrails of her mate, too often the pride and peace of the Muses under study. She did not wish to see that. Nor did she wish to see the death of Nora May French. Nora May was ill and troubled. She was in debt and unable to make a living. She talked of suicide. As a matter of fact she contrived it the next night after Mary left Carmel. She could not afford to live. George scattered her ashes on Point Lobos.

Mary left from Los Angeles, where her brother Jim lived. His wife had died, leaving him with a little girl whom it was a cross to me to leave behind me; but Jim was already engaged to marry another wife. There was no reason why I should linger. I went out early in December, by way of the Azores, Gibraltar, and Genoa. I was to meet the Kelloggs at Florence. After their marriage, I was to go on to Rome to meet the Cardinal Merry del Val. I had met his secretary, Prince Cagiati, on the way over; I was to meet him again at Rome, and Mother Veronica of the Blue Nuns. If you know how I knew these things, you know more than I did. There were people to be met at Florence; a Dr. Harris; Voynich, husband of the author of 'Gadfly'; an English woman, known to Mary's agent, who offered to introduce her to Gordon Craig. The Gayleys turned up; he that was the author of 'Classic Myths.' One day in the Palazzo Vecchio, Mary had a glimpse of a slender woman walking; a slender woman with suave motions incredibly beautiful. Mary followed and lost her; found her again and followed her into the Via Tornabuoni, a familiar address. I thought I would go up to Gordon Craig's apartment and secure the address of a typist, and the beautiful lady came to the door. Mary backed out and went to Dr. Harris, described the woman and learned that she was Isadora Duncan; got herself invited to meet her. A few days later, I met her again on the Lung' Arno and talked with her. She had the effect of being in distress of mind, and showed great willingness to talk; talking of love and its checks and losses. I met her again with Craig at one of the better-known *ristorantes*, and then no more. I talked with him of her grace and beauty and quality; talked with him of her woman traits, of her meaning and significance. Craig had always a score of young women hanging on his words; giving, scrouging, shoving each other. I called them his prairie dogs — those yearning ladies leaning on their wrists with their fingers drooping and their mouths slightly open to receive wisdom. I talked with him of art and the theater; found him gentle, modest, willing, and beautiful; the way his mother was.

The Kelloggs were married in May, at Fiesole, and a change in our plans was made. Charlotte was traveling with a Berkeley girl, Edna McDuffie, a charming and interesting young woman. It was arranged that she was to go with me to Rome and the Southern towns. At Rome, we met Grace Ellery Channing, her that married Charlotte Stetson's ex-husband. We met Elihu Vedder there, and the Prince Cagiati. Cagiati introduced the Cardinal Merry del Val, who met my plea for instruction in early Christian prayer with generosity. The Cardinal had heard of me, knew of my connection with the Mission San Carlos Borromeo. He lent me books out of his private library, and introduced me to Mother Veronica of the Blue Nuns. Mother Veronica was an Irish woman of family, who carried Mary farther in her search for the secret of early Roman prayer. Took her in fact to a priest so advanced in that art that the then Pope leaned upon him. He took me into the crypt of the Vatican and taught me much that except for him I should never have known. It was Mother Veronica who taught me what to do about my pain; how to escape from it into prayer; how to leave it behind me. By the time we reached the Cathedral of Siena, it had receded. At Venice and Ronceno it disappeared. So we came up through Italy and lost it altogether. At Lake Como we met friends who noticed that I was not wearing the sling in which I had carried my left arm for months, and for the first time I observed it. There is no doubt that I had pronounced symptoms of cancer of the breast and that I had evaded it. To understand how this happened, you would have to read 'Christ in Italy' and realize how much like prayer is the attempt to get inside art and understand it, and how healing is the power of beauty; for by prayer I do not mean the practice of petition, but the studied attitude of the spirit in transaction with the creative attitude working from within.

Edna and Jean went into a school at Paris; I went into a *pension* in the rue d'Assas. There I met James Wilkinson, a young man part French, part English, who proved companionable. Isadora Duncan turned up dancing: Gluck, Iphigenia. She danced three hours. And the next night we saw her in a Grecian warrior dance. Said my young companion, 'She looks like a cook.' Everybody was laughing about her and a remark she was reported to have made to Georgette Le Blanc about Maeterlinck. The Americans were very much annoyed; but she was beautiful of body. I went about a good deal with my young man; we were rehearsing parts of 'Macbeth' for a student benefit; I recall that we rehearsed it on the roof of Notre-Dame. We went to exhibitions and plays and dances, and I recall how the first Cézanne I saw, sang to me. Twenty years later, we renewed the friendship in New York. Later that spring I went to London.

I knew well enough that the Hoovers were in London. Mrs. Hoover's father was the cashier of the First National Bank in Monterey. I knew that Anne Martin was with them; they had known Anne at Stanford; they knew that I was on the way. They were living in the Red House in Hornton Street. It was Sunday when I arrived; Herbert's brother Theodore and his family were with them; it was late afternoon and I had an engagement to go call on the Wellses. I had a new book with me, 'Lost Borders,' a collection of short stories; one of them was 'The Walking Woman' which I was anxious that Wells should read. He did read it, and it was the praise excited by that reading which has been, perhaps, too extensively quoted on my behalf for the significance which Mr. Wells himself attached to it. The Wellses asked me to come to dinner later in the week. Duffield, his American publisher, was also to be there. He had also published a book for me and I was interested to meet him. Later, Mr. Wells took me for a walk on Hampstead Heath and we had some discussion concerning a recent novel of his, for which he was being criticized in a manner which gave me a rather shocked perception of the cruelty and injustice which still lurked behind English judgments. The Hoovers, who had heard some talk of the matter, were somewhat worried that I might have to choose between Mr. Wells and my other friends, but it turned out not to be so drastic as that. Mr. Wells discussed the matter in a manner which was extremely pleasing to me because of the impression I received of having at last found someone to whom the actualities of conduct were more important than opinion about it, and at the same time he did not tell me anything that caused me to feel censorious. I also learned to like Mrs. Wells very much. I found that everybody did. She had great charm and gentleness.

The dinner was a great success, although I required a little adjusting to the English custom of not introducing guests to each other. I went down with a Labor Secretary who talked politics. Across from me were the Chestertons. I recall that Chesterton recited the whole of William Morris's poem 'Democracy,' which was new to me. The Bernard Shaws, who were expected, did not come, and oddly I forget most of the other guests, although, as at my first literary dinner in New York, I supposed that I would have recalled every detail.

Herbert Hoover was never quite reconciled to my admiration for Mr. Wells. He has the usual American man's prejudices against variation in conduct from the absolute norm of middle-class life. The Hoovers had very little acquaintance among literary folk in London. One met at their house people from the ends of the earth — from China, Australia, and South Africa, from Russia and the Balkans, mining and engineering people. Their house was always open to these stray visitors and there was an immense amount of interesting and informative talk going on about their table, thoroughly American talk, and a great deal also that was rather boring. Mrs. Hoover's kindness was such that she was always remembering in the midst of her entertaining some poor soul who would have 'so enjoyed' meeting interesting people that the interesting ones were usually sandwiched in between social dubs to the loss of the general character of her entertainment.

I went about a great deal with the Hoovers; week-ends and excursions; we went to Stonehenge by night to see the comet; to Dover and Stratford-on-Avon, to Bath and the Cathedral towns. Mr. Hoover was always in a hurry; many times, Lou and I would gladly have lingered, but sight-seeing bored him; he wanted to get on.

A little later I went down to Capel House to see the Joseph Conrads. Herbert drove me. It was a lovely summer morning; the roses were coming into bloom and the bees bumbled in them. The house was small, an old-fashioned farmhouse with a loft. Mrs. Conrad was lame, and Joseph was ill and not very happy. I gathered that the publishers' returns were scarcely satisfactory. I was one of the few who had written him from the United States. He said, 'I stand on the shore and make my cry into the dark, and only now and then a cry comes back to me.' But he was kind and gentle and appreciative of my interest. He plucked me a rose and kissed it when I came away.

About that time I began to see Bernard Shaw at the Fabian Society. Shaw was one of the leading members; talked there often, and I occasionally fell afoul of him, getting angry when he wittily evaded the point as he so often did. Wells was not showing up so often among the Fabians. He was quarreling with the Webbs, Sidney and Beatrice, both of whom I rather admired. I gathered that the quarrel was chiefly in relation to the incidents I have described, to which their objection was acrimonious. I went down again to the Conrads'.

I met the less-known writers, Hilaire Belloc, who was a guest with me at the Woman's Lyceum Club, William Butler Yeats. I asked Yeats what he thought of American poets. 'American poets?' he said, 'I never read them.' I lunched with Mrs. Humphry Ward. She asked me for my impressions of England. I said that the standard of working-class home was not so high as in America. 'Home!' she said; 'Americans have no homes; they are all divorced.' Also, she talked of Henry James. She regretted that he had not come to her. 'I could have told him how to be successful.' I met Mr. James at a private performance of a play in which Mrs. Pat Campbell played the leading part. Mr. James was unfortunately so deaf that I doubt if he understood to whom he was being introduced, but he understood that I esteemed it a privilege; his intention toward me was appreciative. There were but a few minutes for exchanges, and I am not sure he heard me. It was characteristic of all the English people I met that they seemed uninterested; at least they were not interested and curious about me as I was about them; with the exception of Mrs. Green, the widow of the historian. She declared that she detected Irish traits in me, and at that time I did not realize that I really had them. I had forgotten that one of my great-grandmothers was Irish.

In midsummer I went down to Bramley with Anne Martin. Anne was trying to write and not doing very well at it. She had very little capacity for work, but was getting involved with the Women's Franchise interests. We walked in the processions and Anne got herself mixed with them on various occasions, when Herbert had to rescue her. Herbert was annoyed because he thought American women ought to keep out of England's racket. On one occasion Anne succeeded in getting arrested. She had tried beating up a policeman who had told her that she would have to hit harder than that if she wanted attention. He took her by the arm and twisted it in the iron railing over Westminster Bridge. 'Hang on to that long enough,' he said, 'and I'll arrest you for obstructing the traffic.' So she hung on and finally was arrested. Herbert went down and bailed her out. Not long after that she went home and mixed with the pickets there, to his great relief.

I had my own turn with the London police. I had been to the Hoovers' to dinner, and as it rained I borrowed a raincoat from one of the maids and put it on over my evening dress. At the tube station a group of policemen were coming off duty in high spirits, and one of them caught my arm and said, 'Come on, my girl, and give us a kiss.' I let the raincoat fall open and disclosed my evening dress. The poor man was terribly disconcerted. All of them became profuse in apology. They were in uniform and it meant bad times if I chose to complain. I said, 'I'll forgive you, if you'll tell me just what was in your mind.' 'Well,' he said, 'I thought you really were a girl; we'd been having a scrimmage with the suffragists and my blood was up.' I lost all taste for suffragist scrimmages after that.

About this time there appeared in one of the London literary reviews a notice of my book, 'Lost Borders,' with a complimentary comment on one of the stories. It was signed Francis Grierson, who was one of the Illinoians whom I had known as a child, and had known my father. He had been a musical *improvisatore*, who had played before most of the crowned heads of Europe. He had just written his most important book, 'The Valley of the Shadow' (the shadow of the Civil War). I wrote to him and learned that he was living at Twickenham Ferry, meagerly eking out a living with books. He was no longer improvising, although he was eager to return to the United States and take it up again. I introduced him to the Hoovers, and they made it possible for him to begin again all over. I found him at it when I returned myself, as I did in the middle of the next summer. I had had a cable from William Archer, asking me to return to New York and produce my Indian play, 'The Arrow-Maker,' at the New Theater. Archer had already seen the play. I spent a month with him going over it in detail. It was a folk play, written in the poetic rhythms of Indian verse; formalistic, and climbing up and up to ritual. Archer took me to Edmund Gosse; a kind man, with sudden darts of sharpness touched with humor. He lived in a nest of books saturated with dust. The New Theater was the producing organ of the so-called National Theater, under Winthrop Ames and George Foster Platt. What I did not know about it was that I was twenty years in advance of its time, and the New Theater was twenty years behind its time. Mr. Platt knew nothing of Indian plays or of folk plays either. He wanted 'The Arrow-Maker' more sentimental; more melodramatic. But I was watching the New Theater and felt that they were missing their public. I said so. I protested his idea, stood out for my own. My idea of the New Theater was that it should undertake to do my play newly. I pulled and hauled; insisted on the ritualistic presentation for nearly a year. Anybody who recalls how it came up at the last — even the very last night — will remember that I made a play of it. But I was worn out; exhausted. I wanted no more to do with plays. I was too much worn out to take the trouble to correct the manuscript, which was partly in the key in which I had originally written it, and partly in the broken-down measures in which Mr. Platt had left it. Actually, it was the first play written in 'free' verse, but the agent who placed it for me advised my having it copied to 'look like prose'; and Mr. Platt never found out.   I saw many of the actors puzzling over the rhythms, but they didn't know either.

I went away West and began to work on a novel, 'The Lovely Lady,' and on a group of Indian stories called 'The Trail Book.' They were meant to be prehistoric trail stories, each one illustrating one of the pre-Columbian cultures.   I meant them to be factual, such as 'The Medicine of the Arrows' and 'Young Man Who Never Turns Back.'   My publishers missed the point of them completely.

In the interim before settling down to Carmel again, Mary went to San Diego to lecture.   At the hotel, a Mrs. Snyder called upon her; a tall woman with the remains of beauty.   'You don't know me,' she said; 'would it help if I told you I am Mary Patchen?'

'You were a friend of my father?'

'Ah, I was much more than a friend.'

'There were books of my father's that had your name in them,' said Mary.   They talked of these; and of what Mary's father might have thought of Mary's writing, and of what Mary's mother might have thought.   'She was not much interested,' Mary confessed.   'I am not surprised,' said Mary Patchen.   'I didn't know your mother,' she said, 'but I know she didn't want you.'   She told me how she had called on the Hunters in the summer before Mary was born, and seeing my mother's condition, it came over her that the child was not welcome.   She was grieved, because she wanted nothing so much as a child herself; and George Hunter's child; she felt a warm flooding of emotion going out toward him and his unwanted child.   It came over her as though he had said, 'This should be your child, Mary,' and she felt the stir of the child in her body; 'if it could be,' she said, 'if it could be.'   She felt the stir in him, the comfort of acknowledgment.   She sat there and experienced communication with my father about the child.   Always she had felt the loss in him of the gifts which she had surmised as native to his capacity.   She thought he could have written.   It came over her that this child would redeem the promise; this unwanted and unwelcome one; there was a going out of her interest and understanding to the child.   'I never got over it,' she said.

'When I heard that the child was a girl and it was called Mary, I took it for a sign.' She had never lost interest, she had kept account of the child. She showed me newspaper clippings of the child's first performances. She had clippings of the college paper, of whatever she could collect. She was touched by those things which seemed to her to derive directly from my father; especially the things of outdoors and the literary criticism. She referred to passages in the books of my father; things that were marked in her mind. We talked long and lovingly of these things. She showed herself familiar with the most intimate of my writing. She was moved by the passages which expressed the feeling I had for the West; she had thought they were the things he would have appreciated. She showed me a little spray of grass and flowers she had gathered from his grave. He moved beside us there in the room like a living presence, a loved and reciprocal presence. She made him to live again for me; I saw him, felt him, breathed him in.

When the time came for her to go, I said, 'Is there anything I can do to make you happier?'

'No,' she said; she was happy; she had a good husband; one who understood how she felt; who knew what she felt about me; she had no wish to intrude upon my life. If I would make a point of sending her any little thing of mine which I thought she might otherwise miss, she would be grateful. And if I would think of her as being interested in me; if I would think more intimately of him through her; if I would feel more warmly; if I would never forget the reality of her experience... I felt I never would. I never have. It was the most real and moving contact I have ever known. I did not fail to send her clippings; and sometimes a flower, a personal reminder. I never saw her again, but I never forgot her; there were times when I flew to her, felt comfort and warmth, sustained myself on her interest and affection. I believed in it. It was the most real experience I had, a healing and reassuring experience. I don't know how real it was factually; whether my father had loved her or not. Years after, Lucy Mathews told me that the trouble between her father and mine had been because he felt that my father had been unfaithful to the one great love of his life, but I do not know. There was a great love there, a profound and lasting devotion, from which I am thankful not to have been excluded.

II

ALONG in the middle of my writing career, when I was still struggling with the New Theater, I had more than a little trouble with
editors and publishers. There was a far-reaching idea in most
editorial offices that writers were dancers, posturing at the editorial
dictation. There were more than a few magazines that had no
other idea than to wave their writers back and forth; one, two,
three, turn; four, five, six, turn. I have a notion that more than
a little of it came of the indisposition of women writers to be so
directed; the unwillingness of men editors to step out of their way.
There was a growing interest in the experiences of women, as
women, and a marked disposition of men to determine what
should and should not be written. When I was working on 'The
Arrow-Maker,' there came to me an idea of writing a series of
articles dealing with the amorous experiences of a woman writer in
the midst of a writing career. I knew an editor who would, I
thought, be interested in what I had to say. I made an outline of
my articles and showed it to him. He asked to have it left for a
time, and I forgot it until suddenly I found myself called on the
telephone. 'This,' said a young woman, 'is So-and-So. I am
working on that series of articles of yours, and I want to know ——'
What she wanted was something which had, in fact, nothing to do
with my articles. I said I would see the editor. And when I saw
him, I discovered that he had made another writing of my text,
saying what he thought I ought to say, and turned it over to one of
his favorites to make into articles. I protested. So did he. 'There's
nothing,' he said finally, 'that you can do about it.' I had a friend
on the 'Evening Telegram.' I went to her and showed her the
originals of my articles. She copyrighted and published them,
and I sent them to the editor. And there was nothing he could do
about them. Later I wrote them in the original vein and sold them
to Norman Hapgood in 'Harper's Weekly.' I sold them cheaply
on the understanding that eventually I was to be remunerated

when 'Harper's Weekly' got into a paying vein, which it never did.

I wrote a series of articles on the life of Jesus, and I carefully put every quotation into a modern version. But when it was published, every one had been put back into the original New Testament phraseology. I wrote a story for 'The Century' in which a woman tells what she suffered in finding that she was not attractive-looking. The paragraph in which she described herself was deleted. 'I couldn't bear,' said the editor, 'to have a woman with such beautiful thoughts, looking like that.' Then I wrote 'A Woman of Genius,' in which I had her behave like one; and after setting out on what promised to be a successful career, I found after four months that the publishers had dropped the book and sold the remainders. I was told later that the wife of one of the publishers had decided that the conduct of the woman was immoral. I sold the book to Houghton Mifflin Company and it has been selling ever since, but it has never caught up. This sort of thing was discouraging. Finally there was the advance publicity which frequently contradicted all my notions of how and why the book came to be written. And there was the unwillingness of certain of the more intellectual journals to give my books due notice.

There was, of course, the difficulty that my books were always of the West, which was little known; and always a little in advance of the current notion of it. They were never what is known as 'Westerns'; and they never followed along, one after another. I recall that people used to fret at me because I would not do another 'Land of Little Rain.' I couldn't, of course, I had used up all I had in the first one. I should have had to find another country like that, and pay out ten thousand dollars to live in it ten or twelve years. I wrote what I lived, what I had observed and understood. Then I stopped. The only thing I might have written a second time was 'The Arrow-Maker.' I had an impulse to write another Indian play. I may yet do so; but I wouldn't go through another production. I did, as a matter of fact, write another Indian play soon after I got back from New York. It was called 'Fire,' and was written, as the first had been, in broken verse and

MARY AUSTIN
1910

with a folk rhythm. We did it that year I came back, at the Forest Theater. We all took part in it; George and the Kelloggs, and the Herons and most of the college people. It was an immense success. I recall it particularly because of an incident of George and myself. I hadn't yet put across the fact that I could act. And one day during the production, it occurred to me to do so. I was taking the part of Laela, calling her husband into the door of her hut — 'Come, come into the hut and in my arms forget that any ever loved you but Laela.' I made my point. 'Oh, Mary,' said George, 'you'd have a tentful.' He hung about for several days amorously; he wrote me verses that later turned up dedicated to another woman.

We had a wonderful time that summer. There was Gertrude Boyle's husband's Japanese play, with the flute and the ghost dance. There was Sidney Howard's Indian play; and the next summer we did 'The Arrow-Maker,' with Harry Leon Wilson's wife playing the Chisera. By this time George had made a kind of philosophy of his dependence on women for his fruitful contacts with that terrible and August Lady whose names are Truth and Beauty and Poesy, but without ever realizing, I suspect, his chief incapacity, the failure of ability as a man to enter participatingly into the psychic life of women, not even of the lovely and gracious lady who bore his name, whose pride and happiness were swept from under her by the backwash of one of his own outlived and least profitable adventures.

There was beauty and strangeness to the life at Carmel; beauty of a Greek quality, but not too Greek; 'green fires and billows tremulous with light'; not wanting the indispensable touch of grief; strangeness of bearded men from Tassagara with bear meat and wild honey to sell; great teams from Sur, going by on the highroads with a sound of bells, and shadowy recesses within the wood, white with the droppings of night-haunting birds. But I think that the memorable and now vanished charm of Carmel lay in the reality of the simplicity achieved, a simplicity factually disposed to the quest of food and fuel and housing, as it can never be in any quarter of city life. And very much more than we at that

time realized, it derived from George Sterling between whom and
the environment there was a perfection of suitability that mediated
even for the clumsiest the coveted levels of simplicity.

I had brought home from London a book called 'Outland,'
published by John Murray, under the pseudonym of Gordon
Stairs. It was a romantic story of outdoors; a story of romantic
Outlanders and Far-folk, struggle and treasure. George Sterling
and I were the authors of it; and the rest of the people were pale
simulacra of ourselves, and there was a little of everybody's
favorite story in it. George made the treasure and I made the
story. George liked it. He walked about in the woods reading it;
'a treasury of beauty' he called it. It was streaked with beauty;
the beauty of the sea and the shore and the things of the neighborhood. It was more engaging than anything I had ever
written.

And immediately after that the war occurred. At the time we
were deep in the Panama-Pacific Exposition, and I had been
asked — after two men had been tried out and failed — to take a
turn at the publicity. New York was not giving us the space we
demanded. I went to the city and visited editors, asking them
what they wanted, and reporting back to the office at San Francisco. Practically every one of them expressed a willingness to take
something, but as a matter of fact the local office failed to produce
all that was tentatively accepted. I think there was but one
magazine that made an effective gesture of refusal. That was one
of William Randolph Hearst's many organs, one that soon afterward became extinct. Said the editor before whom I made my
plea for space, 'Now you know, Mrs. Austin, we don't want any
of that stuff. All we are interested in is sex and slush.' 'Well,' said
Mary, 'we are going to have a lot of nude statuary.' They took six
pages.

The next thing that happened after the war was Herbert Hoover.
He had fallen into a way of crossing over, and wirelessing me to
have breakfast with him, and talk. Sometimes I went down to
Washington with him and listened to him talk. He was trying then

to get into something over here. He had ideas: a newspaper, a promoting school for mines, something that would interest and keep him occupied. That was what we talked about. But he didn't know what he wanted; ideas kept rising around him and falling away again. 'But,' he would say, 'I don't want to be just a rich man.' Or he would say, 'I haven't enough money for that. To do that I'd have to take it away from somebody.' Things came up in his mind and turned over, showing white bellies like fish in a net. He had the conception of great ideas, but he could never bring them to birth. The nearest he came to anything was when I talked mysticism to him. Almost he laid hold on it, and then he shied off; he was afraid. But more and more there came into his head the idea of himself as head of the Belgian Food Administration. He saw the way to do that. Then there came the question of a Food Administration here at home and he thought he saw the way to that. He had no notion of what publicity means. It meant to him whatever he thought it meant; advertising, formulas, inchoate talks. He had a great many university people about him; he thought it meant whatever they meant; he had no idea of the pull of organized thought, the solid drawing power of it. It meant a vast amount of talk about food; talk that agreed with him; talk that was pleasant to him to have going on about him. He had devoted followers about him who made an impregnable wall between him and the sort of people I had in mind. He had no feeling for the actualities of the intellectual approach. I had a list made for him of organized women, on a basis of the radius of concentric circles that took them in according to their organization. Said he, 'Are you sure you haven't made this all up out of your own head?' I tried to have him get together a group of women, leaders of their groups; what he got was leaders of 'society.' Because he had been kind to me, I wanted to help him, but he had no idea of what I meant. After a time I got him to realize that there was some sort of reality behind what I was trying to tell him, but never what it was. Never that it was publicity. He had no notion of the constitution of society, the plasticity of it. I saw him fall into the errors that have been the source of much misunderstanding between him and his public, but there was nothing I could do about it.

When it came at last to the point of trying to work out an amateur publicity campaign for his nomination, I had to go to him directly. I had to tell him and have other people tell him that there was a plan to use against him a matter that would work to his disadvantage, the sort of thing that would have directly the opposite effect from what he imagined. And he could not face it. He said, 'Why is it the people of the United States won't stand up against things like this; won't defend their candidates?' And I said, 'Because they don't want to; they want to work it out for themselves, through their own knowledge.' It was almost the last talk we had together on the subject. I tried to talk to him again a year or two later on the Indian matter, but I couldn't get to him. There was no way in which I could reach him with the idea that there was a solid block of opinion between him and the Indians, a block of hard-headed conviction. He was sure again that I had made it all up out of my own head.

I had a standard of behavior in this respect, because at the time I was rather good friends with Theodore Roosevelt. I had come into touch with him through persuading him to intervene in the Indian Bureau's effort to inhibit the use of Indian Music in the schools. He read my books and took an interest in them; he discussed my articles. As the war drew closer, he let me know more of what was in his mind. He had a solid and plangent relation to the public mind; he knew what was going on in it. When we were actually engaged, it happened that I spent an afternoon at his house. He was rather seriously disturbed because he had made application to President Wilson for the privilege of raising volunteer troops, and Wilson showed no disposition to accept him in that capacity. 'But it is so exactly what I could do,' he said. 'There is nothing else I could do so well, and nobody who could do it better.' I agreed with him on that. His sons were trying to enlist, and that afternoon two of them were accepted. He rumpled his hair with vexation. 'Everybody works but father,' he said.

There was a stream of people arriving at the house demanding to be seen. 'Let us walk to the station,' he said. He thought if we were met walking he would not be stopped so often. But he was; every few yards. People came to ask him what was the latest news from Washington, and he was embarrassed with the necessity of saying nothing reflecting on the President. People came bringing boughs of dogwood and blossoming trees. He tried to stick to conversation with me. He said, 'I wish you would write another Indian book; a book I could read aloud to my grandchildren.' I told him I had such a book in hand. He kept making valiant efforts to discuss it. But by the time we had reached the station, nothing had happened; nothing whatever happened. It was the last talk I had with him; I wish it hadn't occurred. I saw him go away with the stress of disappointment; I saw people falling off from question, accepting for him the fact that nothing was going to happen.

The next thing was that I began to know women. I began with Suffrage women; and these I knew better in the English version than the American. Women in England had reached a point of revolt against maternity which was much deeper than the impulse which led to the Birth Control Movement. A feminine refinement, which was only silliness disguised as affectation, disappeared. The masculine vigor, that was only boorishness, slovenliness, and neglect of person, fled before feminine criticism. By totally discarding good sense and delicacy, Freudian psychology had made some interesting discoveries. The natural woman could not afford to be as fastidious as man. She wasn't really, except where she was older, and had grown out of the habit of being, or where she had given herself to propaganda with its imposed inhibitions. There were women like Anna Howard Shaw who kept to the old restrictions, and younger women who let them go. I found myself going with the younger women. The one whose pace I kept most faithfully was Charlotte Perkins Gilman. She had, after being divorced from Stetson about 1896, married George Gilman, and in 1898 had written a notable book called 'Women and Economics.' Her thesis was that women were too much involved in economics; that what we needed was a revision of all our economic arrangements that would enable us to get out of it through coöperative kitchens and nurseries. She was almost fanatic on the subject. About 1908 she began to publish a magazine on the subject, called 'The Forerunner.' The worst of it was that she wrote it all herself — articles, stories, reviews, poems — and she couldn't write. Nor could she be successfully interviewed. Everything she wrote was in the same key. She lectured interestingly, but invariably. She talked well, but without illumination. We all liked her; she was friendly and cheerful and hospitable. She lived on Riverside Drive not far from where I lived and I saw a great deal of her. But we could not keep together; we did not read alike, and we could not write alike. I had to drop her magazine with its terrible sameness, its narrow scope. I could not get her interested in writing. After a time I lost touch with her; so did her other friends. Time went on and left her standing at the old corner, crying the same wares. She had become a Socialist of the narrowest mould. The people I met at her house folded in; they read Lester Ward; Westermarck's 'History of Marriage'; Karl Marx.

Charlotte introduced me to Emma Goldman. Emma was a hairdresser, I believe, and a Marxian Socialist. About this time she was living in Greenwich Village with a group of anarchists. I liked Emma. She was a peasant, but she was perfectly sound; she knew where she was going and who was going with her. I couldn't go along with her; for Emma, modern history began with Marx; modern literature began with the revolt of Labor; archæology had not begun at all, and she thought that I just didn't know; but nevertheless, I liked her. After a while she began to understand me; she listened and took me in. And then there was Henrietta Rodman. Henrietta was a school teacher who lived on the lunatic fringe; she had taken in all the new ideas, accepted them. She read widely and not too well; she had adopted a style of dress, like a mediæval page. She was sure of herself and of her premises. We became great friends. We were all suffragettes, and it was Henrietta who drew me into the struggle to make a place for married

school teachers. Henrietta had got herself in wrong with the
school board and was suspended for a year, but she won out in the
end. There were conflicts of that dimension going on all the time
in that corner of Greenwich Village which was devoted to the
Civic Club. It was there I met Elizabeth Gurley Flynn, although
I believe I saw her first at the Twilight Club, one of those dinner
clubs so popular in New York at the time. Elizabeth was active in
Labor; she was connected with the silk mills at Paterson; a flaming
torch; pretty and serious in an Irish way. She had been stopped of
speaking in Paterson, and a lot of us went over with her and told
the police what we thought of them. It was my first appearance as
an advocate of Labor, but I had been much taken by Miss Flynn
and grew to admire her. Later, when I heard that she had been
arrested and condemned to Leavenworth, I wrote to her lawyer
and offered to do something for her children, which proved not
necessary. The next woman who interested me was Margaret
Sanger, a woman of great strength and power, who grew into
place.

All this time I was giving interviews on Suffrage and related
subjects. I did not talk a great deal; talking on Suffrage bored me.
There were always women who made a point of pulling me back,
of correcting me and setting me right. I was weary of being
pulled into standardized arguments, although I knew well enough
that there was a great deal of reason for keeping the public on the
beaten track, for going over and over it, for rubbing it in. Anne
Martin had joined the Women's Political Union, under Alice Paul.
with whom I worked for a while, but could not keep it up. I took
Anne on two or three speaking tours and gave her instruction.
Occasionally, I spoke too, on the same platform with Anna Shaw
and others. I'd met Ida Tarbell, and Mary Shaw and Minnie
Maddern Fiske and Rachel Crothers at the Stage Women's
Division of Suffrage. Also I had met Alla Nazimova at a meeting
in Washington, although I had met her before that with Miss
Tarbell. She had come up to me and stroked my cheek with her
hand. Also about that time I met Pavlowa. This had been at a
tea-party, where she had come in a little late, and had rushed up

to me and knelt and taken my hands in hers and kissed them, and
sat at my feet and talked with enthusiasm and fervor, as she did
every time after that when she met me. She asked me about
Indian dancing and other matters, and spoke with great affection,
so that I answered her in the same strain, and that was how it was
with us. But it was not so with Isadora Duncan. There were times
when Isadora high-hatted me; when she forgot who I was and what
occasions she had of meeting me before. There were times when
she had been drinking, and other times when she was simply silly.
She had a way of approaching all of us as though she had much to
ask, and then of going off at a tangent and evading the point and
forgetting what she wanted. All that time when we were struggling
to raise money for war matters, I used to raise mine by telling
fortunes with cards. I had a knack at it; I could tell people things
they never dreamed of, and set them on another track. I did that
to Isadora once, to her very great surprise, and asked her things
she never meant to answer, so that she came around to me later
and demanded to know how I knew. And I refused to tell her;
but the truth was that I remembered all the things I had learned
in Florence. This time she had come over to dance in a new manner; more seriously. She had grown heavier and slightly clumsy —
I recall Irvin Cobb saying that she went 'galumphing around the
stage like Grant's tomb in love.' I liked her best when she danced
music rather than pictures or postures. Nevertheless, I liked
meeting these women, taking their measure. But the one I liked
best was Irene Lewisohn, of the Neighborhood Playhouse. She
also knew where she was going. I thought she went after the
Oriental things too much, was too Semitic; but she got where she
was going.

I did not care so much where the women were going who went
after war honors... women walking on their hind legs. We saw a
great deal of them, and gave them what they wanted. Sometimes
I was asked to go along — with the Peace Ship. I wired to Mr.
Ford that I did not feel that I knew enough of the necessary conditions of peace to include myself. But I wouldn't have gone in

any case. I knew too much of many of the people who were going. About this time, it must be remembered, there was beginning to be a great deal of sexual freedom. One heard about it on all sides. One heard about it in connection with prominent suffragettes; but not directly. There was a disposition to keep such matters to one's self. There were young women who were suspect, but so valuable to the cause that nobody wanted it known; nobody would admit it. There was an attitude of the young women that swept clear of condonement; an attitude of a larger outlook; of breaking the usufruct as Roman matrons used; of making love cheap; of making it plentiful; of making it, except for the personal reaction, of little account. This is not an easy attitude to hold; one must be beautiful, provocative, desirable. There was a handsome young suffragist who managed to hold it. Everybody guessed at it, and nobody told. Nobody could tell because it was a thing nobody absolutely knew. She walked with head erect. What she said was of the best; what she did unapproachable. And then she died. I was asked to write something about her, to account for her, explain her. And I wanted the explanation to be true; and nobody would tell me. The Suffragists would not; they hadn't the courage; her people would not. They were all afraid; they knew, but they were unsure; they did not mean to give her over to public condemnation. And so I never knew. If she had been living, I would have asked her. I am sure that she had the courage to tell the truth. She may have wanted it. I think her people knew, and understood her attitude, but nobody was willing to take the first step, and I could not. Everybody would have hated me; nobody would have believed me. And, besides, there was the fact that she was approved; that women in general understood; that chastity was no longer at the head of the list of desirable behaviors for women; that love was to be made cheap; that it was to be taken where found. It was part of the price of war; it was to come with the purchase price of political freedom. She had the strength to take it that way, and it was not for me to contradict her.

III

THE thing I suffered from worst in New York was boredom. The people I met were seldom interested in the things that interested me. I had met Brander Matthews, for example, and found nothing to talk to him about. I met William Dean Howells and discussed with him my problem of isolation, my need to get closer to the people of my time; and he advised me against it; said he had suffered from that very thing; that he had kept too close, narrowed his scope. I asked him about the women in his books; how it happened that they were shallow and slight, that they did not bite down on life. 'That's the way it strikes you?' he said. 'One has to write what one knows.' I met the 'Century' people and did not come within speaking distance of them, except Mr. Ellsworth. I met and liked Jeannette Gilder, but she was a rabid anti-suffragist, and did not like me. I met the editors of the intellectual magazines, 'The Nation' and 'The New Republic,' and found them lashed to their publications, able to talk of what was written, of what was going on under their noses, and not able to talk of what might be going on elsewhere; not willing to accept the idea that there might be anything elsewhere going on. I was bothered by the rage for success; the idea that an immediate success was the sign of capacity; that the little whorls of success that kept appearing on the surface of affairs were final and invincible. I was never very well and unable to go about a great deal; and I was distressed to discover that most people were unable to realize the possibility that where I fell short of the current interest, I might have genuine reasons for it; that I might see farther, might have caught the trailing wing of an ascendent idea.

There was, for instance, my interest in the theater, the Folk Theater. I found, in fact, that nobody knew what I meant. When I first came to New York I had still clinging to my skirts the reputation I had made in Community Theater, the little Country Theater in which I had been more or less involved with Arnold

Arvold. There was a beginning of a movement in that direction, and I was invited to join it, through the Washington Square Players. But that proved not a folk movement; it was really the beginning of the Little Theater. I liked what they did, especially I liked what Helen Westley and Philip Moeller did; I like it still, and go to see their work whenever it is accessible. But I did not see anything in it for me. I joined the MacDougall Street Theater, but I found nothing to take hold of, nothing that was of the folk. I went and worked with the Dramatic Department at Greenwich House. They were mostly Irish and took readily to folk plays, the Irish plays. In order to be neighborly, I settled down into No. 10 Barrow Street. There I found Hendrik Willem Van Loon, two stories above me, and found him immensely rewarding. Sinclair Lewis came there often, and the talk was very good. It came nearer being folk talk than anything else I found in New York; it had substance and plasticity. Sometimes we went over to the Mad Hatter and talked there, always with interest and amusement.

The only other time that I recall folk talk was when I was a guest at the seventy-fifth birthday dinner that was tendered William Dean Howells. I sat between Paxton Hibben and William Allen White, and I talked to White of the folk of the Middlewest. I asked him if he remembered this and that, the police constable who was a member of the G.A.R., the woman who used to sing 'Where is my Wandering Boy Tonight,' Sunday evenings; of the man who delivered the Fourth of July Oration. Mr. Hibben thought we were old acquaintances, and we were from that occasion; but I did not see Mr. White very often. I wanted to talk Indian with him, but he knew very little of Indians. I had a little relief when I began writing 'The Trail Book,' and talked with the staff of the American Museum of Natural History. They let me go into the Museum at night and take things out of the cases, and wear them and be told things about them. But it did not last long enough; it was only now and then I could talk Indian; lecturing and discussing the early stages of human society. I lectured at Mabel Dodge's house and at the Civic Club. I had a little pleasure with Vachel Lindsay; he was interested. He went up to the Museum with me one morning and read me 'The Golden Whales of California,' 'Eagle Forgotten,' 'General William Booth Enters Heaven,' and 'The Congo.' He was the most genuine folk poet we had.

And then I had an argument with Frank Harris at the Arts Club. Harris had been invited to discuss the artistic temperament with the then editor of the 'Literary Digest,' who did not know anything about it. I was sitting next to Harris and got into a discussion with him about David Graham Phillips. Harris thought him the most promising of our younger novelists, and I disagreed with him; I thought Phillips hard and tight. Harris was vexed with me; said I had no right to question his judgment. Harris had had a drink or two, so when he was called upon to answer the speaker, he replied with considerable dudgeon. He said we had no right to ask him to reply to a man who knew nothing of his subject, kicked his chair and sat down, and the chairman for the evening called on me to talk. Well, I didn't agree with the speaker; but then I didn't agree with Frank Harris, and I knew he was talking at me, but it was my club, and I did not see my way to refuse. I talked and said everything I could think of that would be pacifying. Harris talked back to me, protesting that if you had anything the matter with your eye, you called in an oculist; if you had anything the matter with your literary judgment, you called a professional *littérateur*. He told us about his own short stories and their surpassing quality. Gradually he talked himself into a good humor; kicked his chair again two or three times and sat down. Harris never quite got over it; he started in on me again about my Small-Town Man. He said that I had said that Jesus was a commanding personality, and he wasn't. And that I had too high an opinion of Bernard Shaw. I had met David Graham Phillips at Jack Cosgrave's. After dinner, he began reading people's hands. I said, I can do that, and he held out his hand to me. 'I could tell you a great deal,' I said, 'but you wouldn't live long enough to appreciate it.' And in a few weeks he was dead.

I was always getting into trouble like that. I never learned to agree with the other speaker. I disagreed with Walter Lippmann over Bill Heywood's talk about the I.W.W. And I disagreed with Henry Holt about his psychic books. Holt had asked me to read a series he was publishing and tell him what I honestly thought. And I thought they were questionable. He wanted me to go over the work of Mrs. Curran; and I thought that there was nothing in it except what any writer might discover. He was more or less disconcerted, but honest enough to take what I said. I did not find anything convincing in his psychic research except a kind of personal honesty, a direct and straightforward reaching for the truth. Holt was extraordinarily kind to me about my own work. He was a man of great generosity. He said of 'A Woman of Genius' that it looked to him like the beginning of a *Comédie Américaine*; he wanted me to come with him and go on with it. But he was getting old and I felt it would be a mistake; especially as he did not agree with me about the behavior of the people in my books. He objected to sexual irregularities; said Shakespeare didn't use them, and was disconcerted when I referred to Antony and Cleopatra and Troilus and Cressida.

And I did not agree with either the 'Atlantic Monthly' or 'The Century' about my Indian poetry. The 'Atlantic' said they couldn't see any excuse for it, and 'The Century' said that if I would admit that I had made them up myself, they would publish them as poetry, but never on the assumption that they were Indian. And I couldn't accept that. Finally S. S. McClure took them.

Amy Lowell also wanted to doubt that they were Indian. She had written a poem on one of the Pueblo Indian dances, which was in fact a fertility rite, and not a love poem as she presented it. She was a long time getting over it. Margaret Widdemer resented my calling Indian poetry imagistic, suggesting that imagistic poetry was written by people of sophistication. But she got over that. Amy got over it too. I was asked to go to the meeting of the Association for the Advancement of Science at Boston and talk there, and to a dinner afterward; only to discover that I was the only woman invited. I thought that would be embarrassing and asked the secretary if he could provide someone else, and finally suggested Amy. She came to the dinner and proved not very directly interested in science. Finally, when it was time to go home, I took her to the cloakroom. Said she, 'I can see how I happened to be invited; it was your doing. I suppose,' said she, 'you are getting even with me.' 'No,' I said, 'but I think I would be justified.' 'Well, you would,' said Amy. 'What do you want me to do about it?' I said, 'Come out to New Mexico and stay with me awhile and collect some poetry yourself.' And after we had talked a little she said that she would. But she didn't live to accomplish it. I always think that if she had thought of doing that earlier, she would have found what she was looking for.

I remember a talk I had with Robert Frost soon after that. I thought he would catch what I was driving at in the rhythm of the local speech. And after we had finished, he went away, and Madame Bianchi asked me what I thought of him, and I told her that he came nearer getting the local rhythm than anybody else. She was quite vexed with me. She said nobody in his own country thought much of him; they thought him merely a clod-hopper. Madame Bianchi was thinking of Emily Dickinson; she had no consenting for any other New England poet. Not even for Edwin Arlington Robinson.

One day Tony and Mabel Luhan were in town and I took Tony to a Keith show where there was a particularly excellent tap dance; so good, that I made a point of talking it over with Bill Robinson, the dancer, and succeeded in getting a more than ordinarily interesting interview with him; one that fitted in with all the knowledge I had of primitive dancing. It was published by 'The Nation,' and extensively copied. And the next time I went to New York, there was Bill Robinson managing The Blackbirds, and leading in the dancing, to crowds of people.

It was not very long after that the P.E.N. was searching for a benefit performance to show the international meeting, and looking for a genuine American performance. I was on the committee and volunteered to find them one, if they would agree to sponsor it. The play they wanted was Reinhardt's 'Miracle,' but the play

I had in mind was 'Abie's Irish Rose,' which in my opinion was a true folk drama, worthy of attention. There was some objection; the city critics had damned it right and left. Especially, the Jews wouldn't go to it.

But I saw Miss Nichols and asked her what she thought of it. 'I think it is a good play.'

'So that you are willing to stand up to it?'

'I think it's as good a play as anybody has done,' she stoutly countered; so that I asked her for a benefit performance.

I had to do a bit of publicizing, explaining that I thought it a first-class folk play; and had to play up the attendance of the P.E.N.; provide a number of speeches; work up the audience. And they liked it; they found it what I had said, a dramatic version of the Comic Strip. The public was pleased; the critics surrendered. Later, 'What Price Glory' came along, and I wrote about it for 'The New Republic,' describing it as a folk play, gathering up its indecencies and laying them alongside the public practice. And after that was 'Porgy,' which was not so difficult to handle; and then 'The Green Pastures'; but everybody recognized that for a folk play. It had many of the traits my 'Arrow-Maker' had had; those that had been cut out by the management.

I lectured more than a little on the Folk Theater, at the University of California, both northern and southern branches. Three years ago I lectured at the Yale Department of Drama, under George Pierce Baker. But I found that the difficulty lay in the lack of knowledge of folk plays, especially the lack of knowledge of the folk play in the United States. Mr. Baker's pupils had not read far enough back to pick up the American versions of the folk drama, nor far enough forward to grasp what was going on in the Indian drama, the Spanish drama. I had it in mind to go back to Mr. Baker and propose that I should write a brochure on the subject, with a list of the authentically folk plays of the past and a survey of those that will eventually come into the list. But I have never been well enough to undertake it. I have begun to collect the Spanish plays; there are a score or more available. I have translated some of them, and mean to do more if I last out the term. They are washing in from Mexico, and we will need to make the connection.

I wrote folk stories also, such as were published in book form in 'Lost Borders' by Harper and Brothers, most of which were published in 'Harper's Magazine.' But it was years before I could get any of them published elsewhere. After John Farrar took over 'The Bookman,' he published two or three of them, with good results; but chiefly because my folk tales were Western, Indian, and Mexican, there was no demand for them until five or six years ago when Mr. Mencken published half a dozen of them so successfully that other Westerners took heart of grace, and the folk tale found a more general acceptance.

All this time I alternated my living between Carmel and New York. I lived first on Riverside Drive, at the Washington Irving house, for two or three years at the National Arts Club, and at No. 10 Barrow Street. I made frequent visits to the West, to Carmel where I had a house, and later to New Mexico.

I had been deep in the Spanish culture of California, and two or three times, crossing the continent, I had stopped off at Albuquerque and explored the little Spanish-speaking towns of Rio Abajo, looking for folk plays and folk customs. On one of these occasions I had an appointment to meet agents of the Mexican Revolution. I had written several articles for 'The Nation' and attracted the attention of the revolutionists. I don't know who the people were that I met; I am sure they gave me false names. But since that time I have learned that there were men of some distinction taking refuge in Albuquerque, and I have supposed that it might have been they. What they wanted of me was a personal commitment to private phases of revolt, and unlimited publicity. These things, taken with my survey, roused me to realizations of the immense cultural activities going on up and down the great central plateau, and the importance of these matters to the whole Southwest. What I felt in New Mexico was the possibility of the reinstatement of the hand-craft culture and of the folk drama, following the revival of those things in Mexico. I began definitely to plan to locate at Santa Fe and to work explicitly in that field.

IV

THE intervening years, spent largely in New York, had not been barren of experience. I wrote steadily: 'The Ford,' which had a reasonable success; 'The Trail Book,' which owing to inapposite publicity was slow to take hold on the public, but gains with the years, and '26 Jayne Street.' This was my best novel to date, but proved not a popular subject, since it aimed to uncover the sleazy quality of current radicalism, the ways in which the personal expression of radicals contradicted and reversed the political expression. Even my publishers failed to gather the point that I was laying the personal expression of radicalism alongside the political expression, and finding them one and the same stuff. What everybody knows now about the quality of pre-war radicalism proved ten or fifteen years ahead of the times, and, where it was not completely missed by the reviewers, elicited a certain peevishness.

The financial failure of '26 Jayne Street' led to my temporary abandonment of the novel form, and a reversion to books of an earlier type. I republished in America a book written for A. and C. Black, of London, 'Lands of the Sun,' in which I had recorded the final impact of the California scene, the California which I had known and felt before it succumbed to the tourist assault. I began the work of revamping 'The American Rhythm,' adding to it a more extended survey of aboriginal poetry, and copious notes. Also I began to prepare a new volume on the Southwest, 'The Land of Journey's Ending.' For this I returned to Santa Fe, and in company with my friends, the Cassidys, made a circuit of the country between the Colorado and the Rio Grande, binding together in one prolonged survey what had been made known to me in many shorter excursions. A friendship with D. T. MacDougal, director of the Carnegie Botanical Laboratory at Tucson, had drawn me into the study of cactus, and the knowledge of the Papago and Pima Indians, and these had led on to the territory of the Colorado. But before these things happened, I went back to Carmel for the last time.

In June of 1918, it came to me that the war was about to end, and being very tired of it, I yearned for California. I had suffered a shock the year before. My brother Jim had died; my brother George had gone to a base hospital at Tours, and the sisters-in-law were behaving very badly to me. All the family heirlooms had been left, at my mother's death, with Brother Jim, with the under-standing that they should come to me next in order. But the two sisters-in-law had quarreled, and wished to bind me to a condition of not conceding anything to the other. I, hoping for a more reasonable frame of mind, failed to take the papers and family likenesses, which they united later in refusing me. George's wife had appropriated the war correspondence of my father and mother, and refused even to allow me to have copies made, and had taken possession of the daguerreotypes, and even attempted to cut me out of my niece's life. In this she was seconded by Mary's stepmother, who had, in the fear of my contaminating the child with my ideas, forbidden her to visit me. That old family prejudice had bitten deep into my sisters-in-law; neither of whom was in a frame of life capable of accepting a correction. Finding that the child needed me, I went home and carried her off, willy-nilly, to Carmel.

Things were not as they had been at Carmel. George and Carrie Sterling were divorced; the thing we had all feared had come upon them. George was entangled with a young woman, and everybody got to know about it. The young woman talked too much, and people who had kept silent all these years also talked. Carrie got to know things that were better for her not to have known. They should never have separated; but there was nobody to have held them together. I did what I could by letter, but it was not enough. Charmian London did what she could, but the breach was made. By this time, Carrie was beginning to understand what she had done; that her marriage was not only broken, but her home, her circle of interest. She was at work in a bookshop, but lonely and profoundly depressed. I wrote her to come down and spend a few weeks with me at Carmel, but she wrote that she could not. She said that she had hoped that she and George would get together again, but that she had given up hoping. George was away in New York, and she was living on the outskirts of her sisters' lives. And inside of a week, she had committed suicide. George came back from New York; he was greatly distressed; he spoke always of her with tenderness. If he had come a little earlier, a reconciliation might have been managed. But Death was always for him the Dark Mother, the soothsayer. As a matter of fact he was never without the means for accomplishing it for himself. He dreaded nothing so much as that he should lose the power of accomplishing it; he dreaded pain and feared illness, although he had none that I knew of. From that time on he lived on the edge of drunkenness; he suffered the recurrent pangs of dissolution. I never saw him again, except once, although we exchanged letters occasionally. Once I went back to the house, to the altar ring of stones and skulls, but I was too much distressed. I shall never go there again; I shall keep the recollection that I have, the beauty and preciousness.

At the time I was planning to go to Mexico and do some magazine articles. Always I could feel the pull of Mexico. I had it in mind to go there and stay for a year. I had asked for my passport to be sent to me at Santa Fe. But by the time it was due, an epidemic of influenza broke out. I was told by my friends in Mexico not to come; that any moment I might be quarantined and die there unknown and unidentified. The Armistice occurred before I could come to any conclusion. Suddenly one day we heard the whistles shrieking and saw the town band running with its sleeves half in, half out; the band began to play 'Lupita'; we danced in the street. Afterward I went up to Taos to visit with Mabel Sterne — she had divorced Mr. Dodge and married Maurice Sterne. Mabel I had met in New York, where she maintained a sort of radical salon, where I had been entertained. It was there I had met Walter Lippmann and Bill Heywood, who came to tell us what I.W.W. was about. Mabel had heard that I was at Santa Fe and wrote me to come to see her. It was the beginning of the

Penitente season, and I was anxious to see what it was like. Mabel was living with Tony Luhan, a Taos Indian, and was deeply involved with his tribe. Tony had a wife from whom he was not divorced, and Mabel had a husband. The Pueblo and the town were cut up about it. It was the beginning of Lent and the *Penitentes* were out. They had a *morada* on Indian land not far from Mabel's house, and Tony took me out night after night to see the procession. My knowledge of Catholic ritual helped me to get in touch with the *Penitentes*, and I began to get an inkling of how the community felt. There was more than a little small-town opposition to Mabel and Tony's affair, and the beginning of a cabal against them. I advised Mabel to return temporarily to New York, to make a beginning toward a divorce, and to make an allowance to Tony's wife. Then I took pains to explain just what it would mean to Taos financially, to drive her to abandon it. Things began to move forward and to settle down.

I went back to Santa Fe and met there a man from the Carnegie Americanization Foundation, who asked me to make a survey of the Spanish population of Taos County, which is exactly the size of the State of Maryland. Tony and Mabel went with me; and Gus Baumann. We went by wagon over the winter roads, and I began to get a notion of what the Spanish culture of New Mexico meant. When I had finished my survey, I went with the Cassidys to gather up 'The Land of Journey's Ending.' We had gone down the Rio, past Socorro and Belen and San Marcial; and then out by way of Tombstone and St. Davids into the cactus country, to San Xavier del Bac and Tucson, where we would pick up Mac-Dougal at the Botanical Laboratory, and then out by way of Suhuaro and Ocotillo, and then on into the Papago Reservation, Comobai and Santa Rita and down almost to Ajo and into the stag-horn cactus and the argemon and *palo verde*, and so to Prescott and the Casa de los Muertos and Casa Grande. Then we came back by way of St. John and Ramah to Zuñi, and from Zuñi past Inscription Rock and the Encierro, thence to Acoma and back to the Rio by way of Luna, and so to Albuquerque again and home. And on the way we picked up and dropped the Three Wind Rivers and the creosote bush and the little cairns of del Bac. I had begun to be ill before we finished, and went on to New York, where I had a little attention from a doctor. My illness I had picked up in the Indian country; it was endemic intestinal disorder which became virulent. I completed my book and sold it to 'The Century' and put in weeks of anguish on the proof, especially the Spanish part of it, which had been corrected out of all semblance to the original.

When I was too ill to work on 'The Land of Journey's Ending,' I worked on 'The American Rhythm,' which included all my Indian poems to date. And in 1922 I went to England. I let myself be drawn into that by a young newspaper woman, who had it in mind to do a number of newspaper articles about the celebrities we were to meet. But unhappily before we met them, she had let herself out of it.

I had it in mind to see a great deal of May Sinclair, and the Fabians and Bernard Shaw. I saw Miss Sinclair at Stow-on-Wold, where she made me very comfortable, driving me about the country, and especially to Stratford-on-Avon, where we were picked up by a small, plump, blonde woman in a bright blue car, who turned out to be Marie Corelli. Afterward, we went to London, where I met Mrs. Dawson Scott and Rebecca West, a number of young men, Mrs. Belloc Lowndes, and Miriam Ryan, and Sir John Adcock, editor of the clever 'Bookman,' whom I liked immensely. We had a great deal of good talk, especially about the things Miss Sinclair knew about prayer and the spiritual technique. We did not agree so well about books; Miss Sinclair was opposed to the idea that novels should be written about social problems; she thought that they should all be about personal matters; but she talked freely about her own processes and the way she picked up her incredible knowledge of sex, out of the air, so to speak, especially her knowledge of men, of middle-class men. She brushed against one on the top of the bus, or passed one going or coming, and instantly she knew. But she was not in the least middle-class herself. The only middle-class weakness she had was for black cats.

She told me a great deal about her youth, about her struggle with her mother, who was jealous of her sons, and put May to torment about them, so that I wondered how the English put up with one another. Through Miss Sinclair I met Evelyn Underhill, whose works on mysticism interested me greatly. I wrote something about it when I came home, but her publishers failed to take an interest in it, which I thought a pity.

I had no trouble finding the Fabians, except that Joseph Conrad, with whom I renewed acquaintance, kept telling me that the Fabians were no longer the intellectual leaders, and that I was wasting my time on them. But I found them very worth while; especially Bernard Shaw, who spent two weeks with them while I was a guest of the summer school of the society, as a lecturer. He talked and let himself go with me in a way that was extremely gratifying. The two Webbs were there, Beatrice and Sidney, and I had good talks with them, except that they had the weakness that most English people have in talking with Americans, that of assuming to know everything there is to know about America, and that anything that is not English is negligible. Marie Stopes was there, and I had no difficulty in stopping her when I wanted to. It was not possible to agree with her *in toto* on the subject of Married Love.

When the school was over, I went down to Canterbury to see the Conrads again, and to see Bernard Shaw. He was stopping at Hindshead Bay. It happened that just as I was coming out of the Cathedral close, I heard somebody calling me, 'He*ll*o, Mary, what in hell are you doing here!' and I was slapped on the back and embraced by Sinclair Lewis, whom I had known fairly well in New York. His publisher, Brace, was with him, and they began to tell me at once about the new book and how well it was going. So that, not to be completely outdone, I had to ask him if he didn't want to come along with me and have tea with Bernard Shaw. He did, and we did. There were two or three other people who had to be included; Ratcliffe, young Joad, youngsters with D.S.O.'s on the front of their jackets and an air of being free of the place, of being warmly admissible. As they came in, there was an air about them of being liked, of belonging, like the feeling we had once for the group at Carmel, a feeling of kind, of alikeness. There was a feeling for the color and the reality of the evening light and the strange intensity of it, so that we were all caught up in it together and felt it as something belonging to us all. That was how we came out of it at last in the twilight, possessed of it, and rode back to Canterbury in it, and were friendlier than we had been, and shook hands and called each other by our first names; remembered and thought of each other in that fashion.

Mr. Wells was out of town while I was in London, so I saw him but once. He was just coming out of his 'Outline of History,' and appearing a little bit fagged by it. Something, the humor and *élan* that had characterized his earlier novels, was gone out of him. He wished for an American secretary. 'You really have them, professionally trained secretaries in America,' he said, 'but here the relationship is too personal and objective. What one wishes for is greater detachment.' And I wondered how much that had to do with social distinctions general in England and the lack of them in America. I had it in mind to ask Conrad if I might write something about him for one of my editors. I had already asked him if he had got what he wanted out of his work, and found that he had not. He had not, he said, what he wanted Mrs. Conrad to have if he left her; and he was not at all certain that he might not have to leave before long. I told him that I thought I might manage to sell one of his novels as a serial to a popular magazine, if he would furnish me with the material. I told him what I wanted, something very personal and intimate; the material for an article to sell to Arthur Vance of 'Pictorial Review,' on the women of Conrad's novels. Later I discussed the matter with Vance and he laughed. 'You can't sell that to "Pictorial Review."' 'What'll you bet?' I said. 'A thousand dollars,' he came back. And I did sell it to him. And Conrad sold one of his novels to the 'Pictorial Review' for a generous sum. He was immensely pleased.

I came near selling another essay about Rider Haggard, but had not time enough. He came to a luncheon at the Women's Lyceum, and, after looking the guests all over and picking out Mr. Haggard, I said, 'Could you tell me which is Rider Haggard?'

'Well, I am.' And I said, 'Could you tell me something about "She."' What I wanted to know was whether he hadn't figured 'She' as the matriarch, the high priestess of the flame; and when we had talked a little, he admitted that he had. He wanted to know how I knew, and I told him what I knew of matriarchs; but there wasn't time to tell him everything. And I had a talk with Lord Dunsany about some of his tribal folk. There were a great many interesting men who came to the Lyceum luncheons, and if there was time I could get them. I could always get them when it came to a subject I knew. But I couldn't always get them to the subject. And there wasn't always time. They talked to me about America. Graham Wallis told me what was the matter with it and what to do about it, but they never asked me anything, with the sole exception of Lord Charnwood. Charnwood was the only one who didn't know everything, unless it was Lord Northcliffe. Northcliffe asked me questions. He wanted to know, for instance, why he couldn't start a woman's magazine in London which would sell the way our women's magazines in America did. I told him because in London people were half women and half ladies, but in the United States they were, whether ladies or not, always women. He appeared much struck with the idea. I had no difficulty getting in touch with men, but I was constantly thrown out of touch by being asked what I thought 'as a member of our oldest colony.' The chairman was always saying to me, 'Won't you, as a member of our oldest colony, say a few words?'

No sooner had I returned home than I found myself launched on another book, 'The American Rhythm.' At the Fabian School I had lectured on the subject, and Bernard Shaw had spoken of it the day Sinclair Lewis and Mr. Brace were present. He asked me why I didn't publish it, and I had said that I thought it unlikely that an American book publisher would undertake it, whereupon he spoke so interestedly about it, calling it the most interesting thing out of America that he had heard, that Mr. Brace at once asked for it. Now I really thought that it was unlikely that anybody would care for it, but I couldn't resist the invitation. I began upon it

almost as soon as I reached New York. Mr. Brace kept interested
in it for a time, but by the time it got to the publicity agent's hands,
the interest began to decline, and no sooner was it published than
it went out altogether. I should say that there was a general withdrawal of interest in the subject of Indian poetry, an unwillingness
to give it attention. There was an indisposition to admit it to
discussion, especially on the basis on which I had introduced it.
Most of the reviewers took it for granted that I had said that
American poetry was derived from Indian, and scoffed at the idea.
However, the book hung on, and in the course of a few years began
to be inquired for, so that I had Houghton Mifflin Company
bring it out in a complete edition, with additions and footnotes,
by which time the interest had grown and reviewers began to read
it. Now there is no American anthology that does not quote it, and
few Western poets who do not filch from it. Even Amy Lowell did
that, but she had the grace to blush when I referred to it.

The same winter my friends gave me a dinner at the National
Arts Club, the friendliest possible dinner, with everybody there
who should have been there except Herbert Croly, with speeches
and recognition and a speech from me. Herbert Croly had a
scunner against me; I don't know why. He refused to give me space
in 'The New Republic,' or, if he did, used it unkindly, and forgot
to come to my dinner. Whereupon, Bob Halliday, who was his
circulation manager, protested that people were writing in from
the Pacific Coast and complaining of the lack of attention to my
work, and Bob insisted that I should be asked to write something
for 'The New Republic'; whatever I wished, which should be
published exactly as I wrote it. Well, I did, and the result was
that the paper sold out for that number; but Mr. Croly didn't do
anything about it. He grew in time slightly more friendly; took
several of my articles, and once at Mabel's — Mabel used to get
into Croton for the winter occasionally — went so far as to ask
me to look in the crystal for him. Mabel used always to be asking
me to do that for her friends, and on this occasion there was a
singular result. While I was looking, Tony came into the room,
and I said, 'Tony, somebody at the Pueblo has died, somebody

important; not to you, not your mother, but somebody important to the Pueblo.' And Tony said, 'Yes, I've been thinking about that.' And the next morning before I got down to breakfast, there was a telegram from the Pueblo saying that the cacique had died the night before. Mr. Croly was much impressed.

I kept it up, the foreknowledge, the clairvoyant seeing, for a long time. It came to me four hours before my brother died; before we went into the war. There was a Frenchman whom I knew; he was teaching at Columbia, who used to consult me frequently, he was so harried and ridden by presentiments; and when the French Commissioners were laying siege to Washington, and could get no answer, he persuaded me to try if I could get anything. I never could unless the asker was in emotional distress of some sort; which was the case this time. The Commissioner was weeping and wringing his hands; 'I can't go back,' he said, 'I must have something to take to my people.' So I tried four times, and the fourth time I got an answer. 'About the middle of April,' I said; and he was comforted. And when the middle of April came, I got a cable from my French friend, congratulating me. That was the way it worked. Sometimes I did not have to try; the thing came spontaneously. Just as it did in June when I knew the war would end in November.

That was the way it happened about the Negroes. The first time it came, I was following a plan I had for getting to know New York; going up one street and down another, walking and staring. I was living on Riverside Drive then, and had started down from Seventy-Second Street until I came into a district that puzzled me, sloping down toward the river, rather shabby houses with a singular effect of darkness, coming out of the doorways and windows, a light of darkness; so strange that I stopped on a street corner to look. And suddenly I saw three black men crossing the street toward me, black, and walking with the jungle stride. They were so black and so freely walking that I was frightened. I looked about, and saw first one and then another black man, and then black women, going up and down the street, walking and disappearing, coming out black as they came toward me, and losing the blackness. I looked for a street car and discovered that I was walking in a Negro neighborhood; I was, so far as I could discover, in the region of San Juan Hill, and the black folk kept coming and going until I had got clear of that region. I did not forget about it; but it was not long after that, I was at Henrietta Rodman's for dinner, and two Negroes came in and were introduced. When they went to put away their wraps, Henrietta said, 'I suppose I ought to have asked you, but it is such a comfort to me to know that you are the one person I know who won't be disconcerted.' And I said, 'Oh, no, not in the least.' But after a while I began to notice them; they were not entirely black. As a matter of fact, I think it was James Weldon Johnson and his wife; I noticed how pretty she was, and that he was partly white. Somewhat later, we were at the table and Mr. Johnson passed me the bread; then I noticed that his hand was black against the white plate, and I said to myself, 'Why I'm eating dinner with a black man!' I thought I ought to be more astonished at it. And then I heard the Voice; the inward voice which had not spoken to me since the time of the water conflict at Inyo. It was high and amused; it said: 'Well, I don't see it.'

'Oh, yes,' I said, 'that's a black man.'

'Oh, no,' said the Voice, 'I don't see it' — and when I looked again, I didn't see it either. I asked Henrietta about it afterward; if she had noticed anything in me, but she had not. After that I kept watching, and occasionally I would see that he was black, and then I wouldn't. And the Voice kept chuckling.

It would have been months after that; summer time, and I was staying at the Arts Club, and Mr. and Mrs. Speed asked me to go riding with them in their car. They were going up toward Harlem, and I said I would like to go because I had never been to Harlem. We went along and I kept looking out, expecting to see black folk; but there were none in sight. So after a while I asked where they were, and my friends said, 'Look along the sidewalk'; and there they were, black folk walking. But I had to watch them; they walked out of their blackness, and I heard the Voice again, high and amused and jeering at me, 'I don't see them.'

Then it was two or three years after that; and a dinner was being given to Du Bois, who had just come home from Liberia. Ernest

Gruening was managing it; there were three hundred blacks and about the same number of whites. I sat at the speakers' table between Walter Hampden and Countee Cullen, and picked out the white people I knew, and a few blacks, John Farrar, Walter White, half a dozen others; nobody was put out except the waiters. There was a long string of newspaper people, and we were all wondering a little what the papers would say; there were so many of us. And I said to Hampden, 'They will not say a word; there are too many of us.' And Hampden said, 'Do you notice what a pleasant feeling there is, a feeling of warmth and willingness?' I said, 'It makes you forget they are black.' 'Oh, I do,' he said. And that was the way I felt. I would look up and I would see that they were wearing their blackness, and then I would look again and they had laid it aside, the way people lay masks aside; so I knew at last what had happened to me, I was not seeing their blackness, and the Voice said, 'I told you so.' And I didn't see it again; I never did see it. I remember meeting Paul Robeson, and noticing that he was black and forgetting it. And I was right about the newspapers. They reported the dinner, and said not a word about there being black and white sitting down together. If you had read the report, you wouldn't have known. Evidently I wasn't the only one who couldn't see blackness. A year ago I was in Florida and Alabama, and I noticed that there weren't any Negroes. I spoke about it, and people said to me, 'Oh, you don't go where they are!' But I have been wondering. I wonder how much the black is in our eyes.

I never went back to Harlem, popular as it became to do so. I did not wish to see them black, and I feared that with much looking, it might come upon me. I did not mean to go against the Voice.

V

THE journey I took before writing 'The Land of Journey's Ending' did more for me than simply to gather up the detailed present-ment of the Southwest. It gathered all the years of my life, all my experience; my intentions; it determined the years that were left. California had slipped away from me. Sterling's death and other changes at Carmel had made of it a faded leaf, pressed for remembrance. New York had failed to engage the exigent interests of my time. It was not simple nor direct enough; bemused by its own complexity, it missed the open order of the country west of the Alleghenies. It was too much intrigued with its own reactions, took, in the general scene, too narrow a sweep. It lacked freshness, air and light. More than anything else it lacked pattern, and I had a pattern-hungry mind. I liked the feel of roots, of ordered growth and progression, continuity, all of which I found in the Southwest. Although I knew that I was probably putting much of my audience behind me, I knew that in electing to live there I was releasing myself to a larger scope. I knew that my work, which was essentially of the West, like 'The Land of Little Rain,' 'The Flock,' and 'The Land of Journey's Ending,' had a permanent hold on the future. It could not be overwritten nor left to one side. After I came back from that journey, I began explicitly to put New York behind me.

I had already put my marriage aside, though I have put off telling about it because it is still a painful recollection. When I came home from Europe the first time, I knew that I could never take it up again. I had said to my husband when I left, when you can make a place for me, a background in which I can live with reasonable comfort and rationality, I will join you again. But that he never contrived. After a year of somewhat aimless clawing, he reverted to the desert, even deeper into its desolation, at Death Valley, and, although he had actually a competent income, he never managed it competently so as to make a frame of life secure for me and comfortably patterned. We would begin a plan as before, and suddenly it would be disrupted by alterations to which I was never a party. He was never able to make of our marriage a Thing, a planned, progressive arrangement. In the midst of an agreed-upon activity, suddenly I would be thrown upon my own resources, scrabbling for means, dislocated in my professional career. I was driven, in order to meet the uncertainties of professional life and my too easily shaken constitution, to live where I could live best, apart from him. And in that apartness, I was subject to the solicitation of other men, to the exigencies of being neither wife nor widow. Hopeless at last of effecting a more satisfactory arrangement, the proposal for a divorce came from me. I was grieved to find how grieved he was, but I thought there was still a chance that if he were free he might make a more satisfactory marriage. That expectation was never fulfilled.

I laid myself open to every possibility of an effective reconciliation, possibilities which he failed completely to realize; he had no capacity for concerted action, for coöperation. We remained friends, but we were neither of us very happy; I am stricken still to recall the impulses which held us together and the lack of coordination which drove us apart. It grew upon me finally that there is a male incapacity for re-patterning the personal life which is insuperable. It cropped up in other men whom I might possibly have married. Twice I was near it, but felt the happy arrangement inhibited by the incapacity of the men involved for making the adjustment. They could not come even halfway, as men of a younger generation have done. As was to have been expected, the men who might have married me were of the intellectual class, often involved in creative careers, and not financially secure. One or the other of us would have to make sacrifices; and it was always sufficiently plain that I should have to be the one. Once when I was younger, before I had thought of dissolving my marriage, I had talked with a woman who was bitter with the sense of being cheated of her own career to fatten her husband's. 'But,' said I, 'when a man is really great like your husband...' Said she, 'That does not count. You want your own, even if it is small.' It never came to me to make a decision on that basis. There was no man who wished to marry me who carried the sanction of greatness in his hand.

I have had it in mind to give a more explicit account of my love life, but I am inhibited by considerations of fairness. A personal experience of that dimension is not exclusive to one member, but is the property of both partakers of the experience. If I tell all my truth, I know of no way in which the equation can be squared. I recall that a man who had lied about his relation to me excused himself on the ground that 'You can tell this story so much more effectively.' Men, I am convinced, do not volunteer information on their intimate experiences except when they are conscious of the necessity of exculpating themselves. I have never heard a man explain his love affairs without becoming aware that he is explaining himself away. I said something like that to Frank Harris before he had written 'My Life and Loves,' finding him disposed to agree with me. But I had no opportunity to talk with him after that book.

I came too late into the social scheme to have cared for love without responsibility. And of the men who so early accepted love without obligation, too many had rejected other things along with it, truth, integrity, intention, the shared sacrifice. Sometimes I think if I had had the wit to look for a Jew for a partner, I might have found both love and opportunity. Only the Jews are warm enough to tolerate art as a shareholder. But I didn't know that at the time. On the whole, what I regret is not the lack of a satisfying marriage, but the loss out of my life of the traditional protection, the certification of ladyhood. I have never been taken care of; and considering what that has meant to women in general, I feel a loss in the quality of charm and graciousness which I am unable to rationalize. The experience of being competent to myself has been immensely worth while to me. It gives clarity and poise. But without having had the experience of being taken care of, I am unable to realize the significance of that measure. I feel always a little at a loss.

There was a curious light thrown upon this problem of the es-

sential relationships of men and women by a set of experiences
initiated soon after my arrival in New York, and continued at
intervals throughout my stay there. It began with an effort to
know New York, the face of it, what went on in its streets and
neighborhoods, its hours and occasions. As soon as my day's stint
of writing was done, I would be out, going up one street and down
another, observing, inquiring, and checking, and, where I found
special quarters of interest, arranging to stay in them for days,
even for weeks, in whatever character would get me closest to the
quality of the life there. Sometimes I simply rented rooms in the
character of a typist; other times I sought employment and made
myself part of the working community. What I was looking for
was the web of city life, the cross-ties and interweavings which
brought all classes into coalition, made the city unit. It was one of
the complaints of my life there that it was too limited, kept within
a narrowly circumscribed social round, so that with the immense
mass of city dwellers I had no manner of contact. I had it in mind,
of course, that I would make fiction of my findings, fiction which
would do what nobody was doing in fiction for New York, presenting a closely woven section of the life of the city. As a matter
of fact, I never found it. There were cities; whorls of social contact
and activity which went on within themselves apart and aside from
all other manifestations, except as they were deliberately sought
out as I was seeking them. I went down into the Cherry Street
district and plied my typewriting trade, completely alienated from
every other contact. I stopped in the neighborhood south and east
of Washington Square and worked at artificial flowers. I went
'partners' with a peddler of shoelaces and pencils. Over on the
west side below Forty-Second Street, I boarded at a place which
catered to railroad employees, and picked up a 'steady' of the
Brotherhood of Railway Engineers. I sublet two rooms in the
Chelsea district, from a woman who told me her husband was
'in the law business; at the City Hall, you know.' It turned out
that he was a hanger-on of the city courts, an 'alibi' man, who,
when an alibi or a witness was wanted, engaged to produce him.
He was a friendly soul. I was ill with flu while there, and he used

to bring me a comforting brown bottle and sit by my bed and tell me incidents of his practice. In the same house was a couple who had three sons in the police, who came home once or twice a week to play a game of pinochle with their old man and have a taste of mother's cooking, to which I was occasionally invited. In another place I made the acquaintance of a stranger from Chicago, an expert in cement foundations for skyscrapers, who taught me more about the city that is under the city than I could have imagined, the trend of the rocks, the underground waters. He was a clean and sober Irish-American, one who had fathered his widowed mother's brood and brought them to successful issues, and was now at forty-two alone and at loose ends. We went to the pictures together, and to a 'show,' which was all he knew of the drama, and to concerts in the social hall of Saint Patrick's Parish. And finally he began to tell me how cheaply one could live in Chicago, and about the butchers' picnic and the Sunday lakeside excursions, so that it became necessary for me to behave like a gentleman and — having on that occasion represented myself as a newspaper woman — get sent out of town, leaving no address behind. I worked under the Elevated at a hairshop, which specialized in dressmakers' show window dummies. The keeper of the shop was a middle-aged German Jewish woman, plain and harsh to everyone but her husband, younger than herself, a hunchback, and an artist in his trade. He used to go to the Opera House and to the streets of fashionable weddings to observe the hairdressing of the fine ladies, which he repeated in his dummies, working at them with an artist's concentration. He chose to make me the confidante of his raptures, so that his wife became aware of it, and I lost my job. For that was the one single item which held throughout the whole range of these experiences, that the men accepted me at face value, they never found me out, never so much as suspected me of a life of my own apart from what I showed. Sometimes the women were suspicious; the mother of my policemen friends, the wife of my alibi man. But no man ever discovered in me anything but the attraction of strangeness, the flattery of interested attention. My cement foundation worker never so much as inquired which paper I worked upon, nor did my Brotherhood engineer question my complete satisfaction with the scope and outlook of what he had to offer; so that it comes over me, when I think of the men who with more reason might have expected to mate successfully with me, that the failures grew out of an essentially male incapacity to realize what other factors than reciprocal passion entered into such mating. There were none of them able to make room for me, as a person, however much as a woman I might be desired; and on my part, love was not enough.

It was with the realization, however, of the limitations of experience that I settled in my mind that I would write the closing years of my life into the history of Santa Fe. I could be useful here; and I felt I could get back a consideration from the public that would in a measure make up for the loss of certified ladyhood. I do, in a measure, get taken care of here; I call on the community for help and coöperation — from the doctor, the lawyer, the banker, the artist, the business man — and the response is prompt and sure. It was an intuitive feeling for the reality of such response that led me, shortly after my return from the long journey, to purchase a plot of ground at the foot of Cinco Pintores Hill and later to build upon it.

Once having determined upon Santa Fe as my future home, I never quite let go of it. I returned from time to time; especially I visited Mabel and Tony Luhan at Taos. By this time they had brought their several affairs to the conclusion of marriage and a satisfactory social adjustment. Mabel had built a spacious house on the edge of the Pueblo allotment, and half a dozen guest-houses on the adjoining field, where one met people of interest and distinction. One meets there people like Robert Edmond Jones, a great favorite of mine, and Robinson Jeffers, D. H. Lawrence, Georgia O'Keefe, Agnes Pelton, Carlos Chavez. I went there often, for while there is practically no likeness between Mabel and me, very little consenting approval, there is the groundwork of an intelligent approach to problems of reality, and a genuine affection. There is about Tony a warm stability of temperament which makes him an acceptable third to all our intercourse, so that I count among the unforgettable experiences of New Mexico the journeys we have taken, journeys of exploration and recollection, laying ourselves open to the beauty, the mystery, and charm of New Mexico. Tony is an exceptionally good driver, not like the average American driver who constitutes himself merely the master of the car's mechanisms, the exhibitionist, but making it the extension of his personality. Tony puts the car on, and when he begins, as he does usually, to sing the accentless melodies of his people which fit so perfectly to the unaccented rhythms of the machine, one has the sensation of sailing on the magic carpet along the floor of space. Time brings us all closer in these things, so that my life here is extended, practically and emotionally, by the inclusion of Mabel and Tony and the house at Taos.

When I finally withdrew from the East, and determined upon a house at Santa Fe, all the circumstances were favorably arrayed. I had a novel half-done, several good magazine commissions, and money on hand to accomplish the house as I had planned it. I rented a place at the top of the hill and engaged a builder. I had at the time one unresolved difficulty, which was the education of my niece Mary Hunter, my brother Jim's daughter. Mary's mother had died at her birth, and my brother had married again, and was now dead, so that the child had nobody capable of taking a genuine interest in her. From the first she had shown marked artistic and creative ability, toward the development of which I had worked as persistently and as wisely as I could, considering the opposition which the rest of the family imposed to me. It was not only that my family had never realized the quality of my artistic success, but that they had never forgiven me for succeeding against their advice. They still thought of me as failing of normal achievement, of being odd and queer, if not downright abnormal. Like most middle-class families, they resisted the idea of an artistic career for the child, and the stepmother in particular resented any movement on my part to further it. 'I'll give her,' she said, 'a good practical education first.'

Now, one knows that when the average middle-class person

says that, he means exactly the opposite; not a practical training, but a dull one. Mary was not to be examined for salient traits, for speed and quality, fitness, but she was to be held down to the lowest and slowest levels, to the utterly commonplace and the absolutely standardized. And that had already happened to Mary; all interest and *verve* had been taken out of her schooling; she had been slowed down and inhibited. And no 'practical' instruction had taken the place of what I had wanted to give her. The step-mother was not even an ordinarily educated person, but she was utterly unshaken in the conviction of the superior rightness of her decisions. Mary's father, before his death, had selected Wellesley College for her, and Mary was not doing well there. I had kept as close to her as possible and knew what the trouble was, and had done what I could to remedy it. What she needed was, not only to be released into creative work, but to have practical training, work with her hands; the business of spending her money wisely, the use of personal decision.

Mary came to me at Santa Fe, and there it seemed wisest to dis-continue her college work and put her to the business of reality. The rest of the family was roundly opposed to it, and her Uncle George, who had acted as her guardian, took great umbrage. I don't know just what we should have done about it, except that I fell ill and needed her. I had let the contract for my house and was in the worst possible situation to endure a serious illness such as, on consultation, mine proved to be, and the decision that I must have an operation. The circumstances were such that it was im-practicable for me to undergo anything of the sort unless someone could come forward and shoulder the situation. The doctor wrote to my brother George, himself a practicing physician, telling him what was necessary for him to know, and asking him to come. We waited a week, the doctor preparing to meet him at the train. Finally came a letter saying that he should not come, but that if I would come to him and put myself absolutely in his hands, he would do what he could for me. But that was, of course what I could not do. I could not leave my house, my literary commit-ments, nor this business of Mary. For Mary was beginning to develop a rather serious disability which derived from the years during which she had been under my brother's care. For myself, I could do nothing but suffer. I lay in bed in great pain for eight months, and in great anxiety about Mary, about whom my brother would take no steps. He was frightened and fell back on the family attitude. He did not believe my physician; he would not even consent to a physical examination of Mary; it was all my queerness. If Mary would abandon me and put herself absolutely in his hands, he might do something for her, but otherwise, not. In the end he sent me a few hundred dollars, and when my house was completed so that I could leave it, I took Mary to a hospital, went myself to another, and had an operation from which I was a year in recovering. What I discovered was that not only had I been obliged to give up my commissions, but the manuscript of the novel which I had half-completed was missing. In the confusion of my illness and moving, it had been lost.

I do not know how I should have survived all this illness and disaster had it not been for that kindness and care which I had intuitively anticipated among my friends at Santa Fe. Particularly the Applegates. They were an Illinois family of old kin and kindness, and my nearest neighbors. Frank was an artist, and equally interested with me in the Spanish colonial arts and crafts. Alta reminded me of my sister Jennie, in appearance and in the quality of lovableness. She played a sister's part to me. By means of these things I began to regain my health, and Mary hers. She completed her education at Chicago University and is competently launched on a career.

After a time I began another novel, called 'Starry Adventure,' in which I gathered up the knowledge I had gained of the various levels of native life in New Mexico. About that time Frank Applegate and I had gone so far with the Spanish colonial arts that it seemed worth while to attempt their revival. I did not know that I should live to see the enterprise through, but I thought that if I had to leave it, somebody would be raised up to carry it on. Also I knew that if I could make a tolerable beginning, I should increase my own chances of living. I knew by this time that what had seen me thus far was the persistent character of my progressive activity. If something in me went on, I would go on with it. I got up from my bed and set the revival of the Spanish colonial arts in motion.

New Mexico is a bilingual country; the courts, the legislature, most public worship, is conducted in two languages. And in two languages everything made is expressed. The colonists who came here originally came direct from Spain; they had not much tarrying in Mexico. They brought with them what they remembered, and as soon as they began to create, they made things in the likeness of the things of old Spain, modified by what they found here among the Indians. For the first hundred years they made very little; they were simply being conditioned by what they found. They accepted the Indian house, but added a fireplace; they brought chests, but added tables and chairs in the Spanish pattern. They made *santos* and *bultos* in the pattern of the holy images of of sixteenth-century Spain. When they began to weave, it was in the pattern of Southern stuffs with a little suggestion from Mexico. They mixed with the Indians, the peon class, and brought into their blood an Indian strain, Indian capacity for making things, for design and color. These things had been beautiful, but the hundred years of American influence had broken them down and they had not learned to make much else. It takes more than a hundred years to destroy patterns in the blood.

Frank began to collect the old things, to sort them and put values on them. He bought an old house and began to restore it; he collected *santos* and old furniture and tin work. By this time I had begun to collect the folk literature, the plays, the legends and songs. We began our work of revival by starting a Spanish market, and an exhibition with prizes. It grew and grew. There was an annual *fiesta* at Santa Fe which was attended by the natives, but not very successfully. There was a tendency to divert it to tourist uses. This grew to be an offense to the artists, so that Witter Bynner, John Sloan, Gus Baumann, Will Shuster, and a dozen other artists set out to create a *fiesta* that should be Spanish; they persuaded the natives and finally the rest of the community. It has grown to be notable, and thoroughly, alively native. We began a permanent collection of native arts; I collected scores of native plays and *corridos* and songs. There was, a little north of Santa Fe, an excellent example of an old private chapel, with painted reredos and altar and decorations. The family who owned it was dwindling and finally decided to sell it, made terms with a curio dealer. I was away from home when this happened, at Yale. Frank wired me, and I managed to raise the money to buy it in, to keep it for a religious memorial.

That was after Willa Cather came to write 'Death Comes for the Archbishop,' and I had to go to the hospital. Miss Cather used my house to write in, but she did not tell me what she was doing. When it was finished, I was very much distressed to find that she had given her allegiance to the French blood of the Archbishop; she had sympathized with his desire to build a French cathedral in a Spanish town. It was a calamity to the local culture. We have never got over it. It dropped the local mystery plays almost out of use, and many other far-derived Spanish customs. It was in the rebuilding of that shattered culture that the Society for the Revival of the Spanish Arts was concerned. It goes on; it broadens and extends itself; it penetrates the educational system. It gathers up sustenance for itself and supporters who will carry it on when I am no longer here. It has reached across the border and made liaison with kindred movements in Mexico. It touches the kindred arts of music, dancing, and poesy. And it has kept me going with it. I live largely by the living stream of creative artistry which it pours into New Mexico.

VI

WHEN I came back to Santa Fe in 1918, I had an idea of writing another book about Indian art. I had been thirty years collecting material on that subject, and there did not seem to be anyone else capable of writing the sort of book I had in mind to do. I had been creeping up on it for a long time, by way of the Paiute, Shoshone, Mojave, Washoe, Ute, Pomo, Pima, Yuma, Cohuelia, Apache, Yaqui, Papago, Navajo, and then out to the Plains tribes and Rocky Mountain groups. And now I had come to the most notable, the Pueblo, the tribes among whom ardor and beauty were passing, had already passed. In the early reports of the *adelantados* of New Mexico, it was said that the decorated pottery art of the Pueblos was more beautiful than anything in Mexico, and the early textiles as lovely as anything south of the border; their houses were more attractive, the charm of their dances exceeding those of the Aztecs. But when I came into the Rio Grande country, there was but one woman making pottery which had the remotest claim to beauty of form, of proportion, of color and design. There was a little cotton-weaving, a little jewelry, and there were dances of surpassing interest. This one woman was Maria of San Ildefonso, who had been persuaded to make the old designs, and kept at it by offers of prices far in excess of the 'tourist' pieces. There were a few good old pieces treasured in the lower rooms of Pueblo houses, which now and then could be purchased; but Maria was the only one making them fresh and fresh.

There were already American artists living about Santa Fe who appreciated the choice examples, and bought them when they were available. They went to the dances and ceremonials; they wrote and made them known and praised. When I had been there a little while, Alice Corbin Henderson brought me water-color paintings of the dance figures, cleanly drawn and faithfully colored. They had been done by Indians who posed for her husband, who had during their rest hours made use of the materials at hand. Alice said she couldn't go on with the work, but suggested that I might; and I did. The School of American Research began about that time to buy examples of the dance paintings, and after a little while we had an exhibition which excited general interest and created a demand. The demand grew and the quality of the paintings increased. They were in no way related to white men's work; they remained thoroughly Indian, exquisitely done and colored in accordance with the Indian philosophy of color. They extend the whole range of pictorial art in America.

About the same time the artists were collecting the best obtainable examples of the old pottery, and the idea grew up in their minds that there should be a collection of them; that they should not be carried away by tourists and random collectors. Everybody had one or two such examples, and there were still others in the hands of the Indians. The artists drew into an organization called The Indian Art Fund, and began to interest the visitors. We added jewelry and blankets and embroideries and paintings; we began to accumulate a collection. At first it was supported by the people who came to Santa Fe; there were people of taste and intelligence coming and going, who contributed. We put it to them that what we wanted was an Indian museum for Indians; where they could refresh themselves in the notable examples. By this time several other Indian women had begun to make good pottery. Pueblos in which the making of pottery had completely failed began to feel about for old designs. Our collection grew so rapidly that we began to realize the need of a museum. I had some land and offered it to them; we began to discuss plans for raising money to build it. At that time the Indian Bureau initiated a scheme for putting an end to the Indian dances. It was the dances we depended on chiefly for calling attention to the work we were doing, and the Bureau, possessed of the idea that we were corrupting the tribesmen, issued an order that they should be stopped. There was a protest on the part of the artists, opposed by the missionaries, and supported by the visitors. In the end we won; the order was withdrawn and a new Commissioner was appointed. This brought the artists and the Indians closer together and

strengthened our position. And about that time John D. Rockefeller passed through the town and was shown our collection. He
became so interested that he had inquiries made, and proposed
that he join with us in the erection of the museum. Our answer
was that we were interested in a living museum, for the benefit of
Indians and the pouring of their capacity into the stream of
American culture. Mr. Rockefeller replied that he had been
looking for something of the kind for a long time. He agreed to
our terms, and was taken in; he added many items of interest and
value; he made terms for us to add to the scope and usefulness of
the museum.

By this time we had come to a general understanding of the
meaning and value of Indian art; that it concerned itself entirely
with the principle of the conscious unity in all things, the gesture
of a rhythmic beauty to interpret the significance of common
things, the ploughing and watering and planting of the corn, the
fine moralities of nature. The Indian has sought incessantly for
the precise values in his body and soul of what is presaged to him
in the sun and the cloud and the rain. He is an artist because he is
sensitive to the spirit of existence. Living things came to symbolize
this sense of existence. Art for him is a logical necessity, and there
is no art without the inclusion of the body. We have made him
understand that we realized his nakedness as a part of his expression, and his symbolism as the speech of his soul. So we worked
together, and we had little difficulty in persuading the rest of the
community to work with us. Even the traders, most of them, were
persuaded. We included not only the Pueblo peoples, but the
Navajo; we made a beginning with the Apache. The pictorial art
increased amazingly, and extended to outlying tribes.

All this time I kept my interest in Boulder Dam and the local
problems. My Governor appointed me a delegate to the Seven
States Conference. I said what I had to say, being profoundly
convinced against it; but I discovered there is little one can say
against an enterprise that will not come to the proof for perhaps
fifty years. The other New Mexican delegates were for it, and the

Conference was so heavily weighted by Los Angeles that there seemed nothing to say, in any case. None of us will live to see that *débâcle*. I withdrew from the Conference, although not from foresight and opposition. If I am mistaken in what is to eventuate, it will be the first time my prophetic gift has failed me. I never went back to Inyo. The city of Los Angeles bought the towns there, the house I built. The place is given over to desolation.

People began to crowd into the Rio Grande country. D. H. Lawrence came. That was when I was very ill, and I never saw him but once, walking down the street. He stayed at Mabel's house, and alternated between quarreling with her and being more than kind, and fretting at her for being too kind. Spud Johnson came and began to issue the 'Laughing Horse,' an amused and amusing journal with illustrations. Lynn Riggs came; he used to spend evenings with young Mary, sitting out on the *placita*, playing the *guitarra*, and singing Oklahoma folk songs. Marie Garland came with her young husband, and made a warm and appealing circle under the cottonwood trees at her ranch. Sinclair Lewis came, and refused to behave like a celebrity. John Galsworthy came at the same time, and made good talk. He wanted to know what I felt about democracy, and I told him that I did not find it a success, but that I was glad to have been in it, as an experiment. Will White and Sally came: the last time it was their wedding aniversary; they came because they had spent the first days of their married life there. I was always glad to see Will; he had things to tell always that were worth hearing, Washington news and politics. The Misses White arrived. The Lewisohn sisters came and made contributions to our enterprises. Mary Wheelwright bought the Ortiz house, near San Gabriel, and furnished it with old Spanish colonial things. She began almost at once to be interested in the Navajos, collecting folklore and copies of sand paintings. She had a flair for that sort of thing, and was generous; nobody gave us so many things for our Spanish collection. Mrs. Meredith Hare built herself a house on the Acequia. Grant Overton came and spent a year. Arthur Ficke spent two years. There was a constant stir of interesting people. Witter

Bynner had always somebody at his house, and a perpetual flow of teas and dinners. Fola La Follette and George Middleton came; I was immensely glad to see them; I hadn't had a visit with them since Suffrage times. Henry Goddard Leach spent two days in town. I had a Spanish supper for him with the Governor. Hosts of people came. I was often too ill to see them. Nobody gave me more pleasure than Bronson Cutting. He had an extensive and intimate acquaintance with the native people; I could always talk to him; he took me into his plans, and discussed affairs in Washington freely. He gave me a feeling of belonging. It is a matter of keen regret to me that his political experience is scarcely long enough to warrant his being commandeered for Presidential possibilities.

After a year or two, I began to recover. People were generous with their automobiles; I was always invited to ride and made to take the easiest seat. Everybody drove slowly and carefully; still that is the case. I am still unable to travel much, but nobody is put out if I am sick when I go about, not even the young men. If there is a party anywhere, I am taken along. It is expected that I will talk about whatever is in my mind. If Phelps Putnam or Lynn Riggs wish to talk about what they are doing, it is taken for granted that I will let them know, and that Mary Wheelwright will keep me informed about what is going on among the Navajos. If René d'Harnoncourt is getting out a new book, or Witter Bynner is, we shall all know about it and nothing will go amiss. The country is too large, too unified, too much on a single plan to be missed. Frank Applegate was more than kind. We had begun to discuss the possibility of doing a book about the Spanish arts; we collected material and made notes interminably; we exchanged items of information. Frank wrote two books; one of 'Indian Tales from the Pueblos,' and another, 'New Mexican Tales.' We handed these about, taking what we liked best. But we are all more or less of an equality about our material. We began to include Mexico in our interests. Many of our people went there and began to talk and write about it. We all took the greatest interest in Dwight Morrow's exhibition of *Artes Populares de Mexico*.

A year ago I went down to lecture at the Seminar. I wanted to know what was going on there. I have been in the Yaqui country, at Compostella and San Miguel de Horcasitis. But this time I wanted to see Diego Rivera and his murals.

I went with Paul Kellogg. There had been an interesting program at the Ministry of Education, especially a dance based upon an old Aztec performance in honor of the dead. When it was over, we began at the beginning of Diego's work and traced it foot by foot, seeing how the artist had worked his way into it, how it had grown upon him, filled him out until it ballooned about him like a cloud. We began to arrive at patterns of communality; the patterns of the people; patterns of braided hair and little bare feet sticking out below benches, and figures drawn into ovals of *rebosas*; patterns of activity; the slow ripe movement of women's bodies; patterns of color and emotion, of compassion, of gratitude, of relief; beautiful, more than beautiful. I saw the patterns of machinery; machines made into elements of design, and the patterns that came out in the people responsively. I began to fill and overflow with tears. These were patterns I had long known, the patterns of the American Rhythm. I let Paul Kellogg go; I went about alone, weeping. I was down in touch with what I had known so long, where I had so long wanted to be, next to reality; the things I had long missed from American life; the thing every woman misses from American life; tenderness, the strength of tenderness, compassion, surrender. I wrote to Diego Rivera and told him what I had seen. Afterward I talked with him and found that he was not unaware of what he had done. 'That,' he said, 'is what I was trying to do.' I told him what it made me feel about my own work; that I, too, had done what I tried to do; that my work on the American Rhythm was good; that it was sound; that I was not disappointed in it.

A few days later, I went down to Cuernevaca and watched him painting on the murals in the Hall of Justice, with a quiet fury, with justice and understanding. He drew it out of himself, as Indians paint, out of the thing absorbed, reworked, made new and whole. It came forth with charm such as is missed by Nordics.

It was a relief to me to discover that there was no Nordic taint in Diego Rivera. There was Moorish blood, a little Jewish, perhaps, Spanish and Indian. Especially the Indian; poised, centered, at home with his work. A great painter; a great man.

The year before, I had brought to a conclusion a matter which I had much on my mind, which was to persuade the Department of the Interior to make public declaration of its interest in Indian art and its approval. What I knew most about Indian art was its derivation from the Indian ceremonial, its binding-up of the body and the self with its expressiveness. I have already described the struggle we had had with the officials of the Indian Bureau to preserve the dance drama; and, although we had been practically successful for the time being, we were by no means secure. The missionaries were against us; opposing the dances on the ground that they were pagan, that they interfered with the Christianization of the tribesmen. I worked upon Secretary Ray Lyman Wilbur. Everything was propitious; the opposition was temporarily at rest, public attention had been gained, public approval of the arts; the financial standing of the Indian artists. Here at Santa Fe a plan was begun for an Intertribal Exhibition of Native Arts. The collection of the Indian Arts Fund was handsomely shown in the new Rockefeller Museum. Secretary Wilbur gave himself freely to my suggestion, consented to the widest publicity. But I had another reason for clinching the matter. What was going on in Mexico reawakened the desire in me to write a book on the subject; the need of such a book. But to do the book I had in mind would require strength and money, and I had not much of either. There were people coming into the work, approaching it from all sides. I began to wonder if it were necessary for me to write it. I thought I might leave it to Diego Rivera and to the widely awakened interest. At least I owed it to Diego that I was assured that I was on the trail, that I had not erred in the idea of the use of aboriginal art to express the immediate impulse. What other people were writing about Indian art was really of art work, the thing done, handled. I could not suppose that they would fail

THE AUTHOR WITH DIEGO RIVERA AT CUERNAVACA

wholly of understanding. I began to feel reconciled to the possibility that I might not have either the strength or the money to write that book.

I felt still the need to write the book of Spanish colonial arts. I urged Frank on with it; I arranged for publication and illustrations. We laid it out and shaped it into a design. And then, the spring after I came home from Mexico, Frank died, suddenly, without warning. I did not know how much he had meant to me until he was gone. Now I miss him more than ever, since I have become involved in a plan to build a chapel contiguous to Bishop Lamy's Cathedral, for the housing of the rare and beautiful stone reredos out of the old chapel of the Castrense, and some of the other historic remainders of the really creative period of Spanish Colonial Art. I gathered up our notes and laid them aside. I shall go on with the work when I have finished with what I have on hand. Life has gone somewhat heavily with me since, but I know that when I am at the work at last I shall be reassured. I shall have his coöperation. But first I had to write a book called 'Experiences Facing Death'; I had to face it.

In admitting so much, I realize that practically all my books have been done in this fashion; they come out of the arc of the Earth Horizon from which, for me, 'all its people and its thoughts' come to me. That is why my books have no sequence other than the continuity of the search for the norm of moral and spiritual adjustments which I have tried herein to describe. They take their rise in the deep blue ring of the encompassing horizon. They originate in an inherent sensitivity to the spirit of existence which has been set in motion by the activities of my horison, the zone in which sky and earth meet and commingle. I have written religious books, and realize that all I have said is that religion, to be a factor in experience, must be pleasurable. I wrote a book on genius, and got no further with it than the discovery that it arises in the natural, aboriginal concern for the conscious unity of all phenomena. I have written about the business of re-creating our daily life in the veracities of soul, which is the perfection of the adjustments of wholeness, I have written about the earth performance, the multitude of bright and shining things that contribute to the sense of beauty and fitness, and find that the aboriginal has anticipated them. All this has come upon me practically unawares; I have had no set scheme nor any arrangement of ideation. A few years ago I called upon the editor of a notable reviewing magazine, to inquire why Indian books were not reviewed, and was told that there was nobody to do it. I offered to undertake it, expecting no reward, and discovered that I had drawn after me a host of reviewers and commentators; set a mark for them, an interpretive mark; made for myself companions in appreciative æsthetics of aboriginal splendor; increased our collective power to visualize what has been observed and imagined. That is the manner in which it has come about that I have seen America emerging; the America which is the expression of the life activities of the environment, æsthetics as a natural mode of expression.

I have not been entirely happy in my adjustments. I have suffered in my life, in my means, in my reciprocal relations; but I have this pride and congratulation, that I have not missed the significance of the spectacle I have been privileged to witness. I have not only had the pleasure of associating with those who have known what it means, but I have had glimpses of its meaning. I have known, to some extent, what the Earth Horizon has been thinking about. Measurably, its people and its thoughts have come to me. I have seen that the American achievement is made up of two splendors: the splendor of individual relationships of power, the power to make and do rather than merely to possess, the aristocracy of creativeness; and that other splendor of realizing that in the deepest layers of ourselves we are incurably collective. At the core of our Amerindian life we are consummated in the dash and color of collectivity. It is not that we work upon the Cosmos, but it works in us. I suffer because I achieve so little in this relation, and rejoice that I have felt so much. As much as I am able, I celebrate the Earth Horizon.

THE END

NOTES

1. The buffalo left the east bank of the river in 1780, following a severe winter, and were never seen there again.

2. Illiniwek, changed by the French to Illinois, a confederacy of broken Algonquin tribes, Cahokias, Kaskaskias, Peorias, and others, occupying lower Wisconsin, Illinois, and sections of Iowa and Missouri. The French established a military post at Kaskaskia about 1700. Ceded to the United States by Virginia as part of the Northwest Territory by the Ordinance of 1787. Created Territory of Illinois, 1809. Admitted as State, 1818.

3. Ninian Edwards was Territorial Governor.

4. After Thomas Carlin, Governor.

5. *The Valley of the Shadow*, Francis Grierson (Shepherd), The Bodley Head, London, 1909. General Grierson, his mother's brother, instituted his famous raid in April, 1863, from the town of La Grange, Tennessee, and ended it at Baton Rouge in May of the same year.

6. Milo was the son of Jared Graham, of Scotland, and Theda Case, of Ireland. He was born at Canton, Connecticut, June 17, 1817. Four years later his parents removed with him to Portage County, Ohio. In 1839 he came to Carlinville, and on June 14, 1841, married Hannah, fourth daughter of Jarrot and Polly Dugger, who died January 4, 1853. On April 11, 1854, he married Eliza Boring, daughter of Ichabod and Delilah Eccles Valentine, widow of Hiram Boring. She died September 10, 1867, and on October 15, 1868, he married Sophia Applegate. At his death, August, 1884, she survived him, with his five children, Susan, William, and Mary Graham, Effie and Otis Licander Graham.

7. The tracing of the original Daguerres proved not so much an impossibility as laborious and expensive to an unjustifiable degree. The chief difficulty appears to be disentangling them from Duggers of other stocks throughout Virginia, Kentucky, and Tennessee. In Illinois, the sense of kin was augmented by the families of John and Wesley, scattered throughout southern Illinois, and the feeling for clan by the general longevity of their stock. The family records supply the following:

Jarrot, son of Pierre D.; b. 1792; d. 1850.

Mary (Polly), daughter of Wm. McAdams; b. 1792; d. 1871.

Their children (those that died in infancy omitted):

Elizabeth..............1812–1846 — m. Nicholas Deck, 1832
Joseph Castlebury.......1814–1866 — m. Phœbe Ann Barton, 1834
Leonard Wesley.........1815–1882 — m. Sarah Penn, 1837

William Ferguson........1817–1847 — m. Mortacai Womac, 1839
Rhoda Ann.............1819–1865 — m. Alexander Lewis, 1836
Hannah................1821–1853 — m. Milo Graham, 1841
Susannah..............1824–1894 — m. Abraham Woods, 1847
Jefferson Lewis.........1826–1863 — m. Mary E. Gill, 1854
John Hogan............1831–1907 — m. Sarah M. Neil, 1854
Samuel Bastion.........1834–1903 — m. Catherine M. Odell, 1853

8. The dates for Louis Jacques Mandé Daguerre are 1787–1851.

9. Sarah Childress was born near Murfreesboro, Rutherford County, Tennessee, September 4, 1803, daughter of Joel and Elizabeth Childress. Her father was a farmer in good circumstances. She was educated at the Moravian Institute, Salem, North Carolina, and married James K. Polk in 1822. The Childresses had formerly lived in North Carolina, and in 1807 they were living in Sumner County, Tennessee. Thus her acquaintance with Polly McAdams must have begun there, after the McAdamses had returned from their first venture in Illinois, and Polly would have been eleven years her elder.

10. Black Hawk was a subordinate chief of the Sauk and Fox tribes who became their war leader, about 1790. An Algonquin people, the original seat of the Fox Clan had been about Fox River, and about Lake Winnebago, while the Sauks came into Wisconsin from the Michigan Peninsula. By a treaty of 1804, they resigned their rights on the east bank of the Mississippi, but were left undisturbed until the country was thrown open to settlement. In the War of 1812, under Black Hawk, the Fox and Sauks fought on the side of the British. All the serious Indian troubles the early settlers in Illinois had were with these tribes, and the Potawatamies and Kickapoos they persuaded to join them. Claiming he had been deceived as to the terms of the treaty, Black Hawk made a last stand against the tide of white settlement, in 1831–32, known as the Black Hawk War. Early in the Indian troubles, the two Dugger brothers, who had come to Illinois in 1818, were commissioned: John, Eighth Regiment, Militia, Ensign, 1822; Wesley, Eighth Regiment, Militia, Lieutenant, 1825.

In 1812, the brothers enlisted as follows: Jarrot Dugger, Sumner County Tennessee Cavalry, 1812; Wesley Dugger, Sumner County Tennessee Cavalry, 1812; John Dugger, Sumner County Tennessee Militia, 1813.

11. William McAdams was the son of Joseph McAdams, who was born at Ayre, Scotland, and moved to York County, Pennsylvania, previous to 1760, at which time his son William was born.

William McAdams, having previously served as surgeon's mate for some months, volunteered at Hawsfield, Orange County, North Carolina, in the spring of 1779, as a private under Captain John Carrington and Colonel Armstrong, for three months. He reënlisted at the same place under Captains Douglas and Christmas and Colonel O'Neale; was in the battle of Haw River and many skirmishes; and had more than two years of actual service. He applied for and was allowed pension while living in Madison County, Illinois, in 1832; died, 1843.

About 1790 he had married Mary Hendricks, daughter of Samuel Hendricks, of whom in 1792, his daughter Mary (Polly) McAdams was born. Removed to Tennessee and finally Illinois with his family.

Mary Hendricks McAdams died at the age of ninety-four years, having produced eighty-seven children, grandchildren, great- and great-great-grandchildren, all but five of whom were living at her death.

12. It seems, in view of the importance attached now to these things, interesting to record that the descendants of Jarrot and Polly were under rather than over the average height, and that with few exceptions they were stocky of figure and tended to overweight, a tendency which seems to have come from the Hendricks strain. The McAdamses were long-lived; one nephew having lived to ninety-four. In her old age Polly and her two sisters were weighed together and found to average 245 pounds each. The direct descendants of Jarrot and Polly tended to blue eyes and dark hair; their most notable feature being rather full eyes with a tendency to drooping upper lids.

13. 'It must be understood that to me God *is* the experienceable quality in the universe...

' I must have been between five and six when this experience happened to me. It was a summer morning and the child that I was had walked down through the orchard alone and come out on the brow of a sloping hill where there was grass and a wind blowing and one tall tree reaching into infinite immensities of blueness. Quite suddenly, after a moment of quietness there, earth and sky and tree and wind-blown grass and the child in the midst of them came alive together with a pulsing light of consciousness. There was a wild foxglove at the child's feet and a bee dozing about it, and to this day I can recall the swift, inclusive awareness of each for the whole — I in them and they in me, and all of us enclosed in a warm lucent bubble of livingness. I remember the child looking everywhere for the source of this happy wonder, and at last she questioned — "God?" — because it was the only awesome word she knew. Deep inside, like the murmurous swinging of a bell, she heard the answer, "God, God..."

' How long this ineffable moment lasted I never knew. It broke like a bubble at the sudden singing of a bird, and the wind blew and the world was the same again — only never *quite* the same.' From *Experiences Facing Death*. Bobbs-Merrill Company.

14. Charles Roberston, Instructor in Botany and Greek, Blackburn, 1880–86; Lecturer, 1888; Professor of Biology, 1897–1909; author of numerous pamphlets on Mutual Relations of Insects and Flowers. (American Men of Science.)

15. Mahala; Indian Woman, corrupted from the Spanish *mujere*.

16. *Everyman's Genius*. Bobbs-Merrill Company.

17. *Power Through Repose*. Annie Payson Call. Little, Brown & Co.

INDEX

Lightning Source UK Ltd.
Milton Keynes UK
UKHW041858010622
403847UK00001B/26